# Posing Questions for a Scientific Archaeology

# Posing Questions for a Scientific Archaeology

Edited by Terry L. Hunt, Carl P. Lipo, and
Sarah L. Sterling

Scientific Archaeology for the Third Millennium

**BERGIN & GARVEY**
Westport, Connecticut • London

**Library of Congress Cataloging-in-Publication Data**

Posing questions for a scientific archaeology / edited by Terry L. Hunt, Carl P. Lipo, and Sarah L. Sterling.
     p. cm. — (Scientific archaeology for the Third Millennium, ISSN 1529-4439)
     Includes bibliographical references and index.
     ISBN 0-89789-753-6 (alk. paper)
     1. Social archaeology—Philosophy. 2. Ethnoarchaeology—Philosophy. 3. Social archaeology—Methodology. 4. Ethnoarchaeology—Methodology. 5. Social evolution. I. Hunt, Terry L. II. Lipo, Carl P. III. Sterling, Sarah L. IV. Series.

CC72.4 .P67 2001
930.1'01—dc21

00-037834

British Library Cataloguing-in-Publication Data is available.

Library of Congress Catalog Card Number: 00–037834
ISBN: 0-89789-753-6
ISSN: 1529-4439

First published in 2001

Bergin & Garvey, 88 Post Road West, Westport, CT 06881
An imprint of Greenwood Publishing Group, Inc.
www.greenwood.com

Printed in the United States of America

The paper used in this book complies with the
Permanent Paper Standard issued by the National
Information Standards Organization (Z39.48-1984).

10 9 8 7 6 5 4 3 2 1

*We dedicate this book to Robert C. Dunnell,
mentor, colleague, and friend.*

# Contents

Contents

# Series Foreword

Few would deny that archaeology has seen a number of theoretical and methodological changes in recent years. These developments have brought archaeology
into new relationships with several sciences—biology, geology, physics, chemistry, and computer science—and has modified archaeology's earlier relationships with other disciplines—history, ethnography, and anthropology. Regardless
of when we got our degrees, none of us can deny that archaeology today very is
different from the archaeology we studied as graduate students.

To confront, to incorporate, and to advance beyond the recent theoretical
upheavals are challenges that archaeology will face early in the new millennium.
Maintaining scientific rigor in the midst of vaporous theoretical debates may be
the biggest challenge of all. This is the reason we are launching the series
"Scientific Archaeology for the Third Millennium," which we hope will be a
medium of academic and scientific discussion in contemporary archaeology. The
series' general goal is to promote new scientific perspectives in archaeology by
drawing on new theories, methods, and techniques that archaeologists are developing in different parts of the world.

Archaeology's current challenges involve all professional archaeologists
regardless of nationality and/or theoretical orientation. As a young science, we
have gone through a process of searching and experimenting that has given us the
theoretical-methodological diversity that we see today. Now we must begin to
evaluate the contributions of the various perspectives by putting them to work in
building a scientific understanding of the past.

We thank Greenwood Publishing Group and especially our editor Jane Garry
for the opportunity to disseminate studies that promote archaeological science. We
also thank the members of our advisory board for their helpful and frank advice
about which manuscripts might be appropriate as initial issues in our series.

We invite colleagues who view archaeology as a science to join us in meeting the challenges that face us during the first decades of the third millennium.

Jose Luis Lanata
Department of Anthropology
University of Buenos Aires

Mark Aldenderfer
Department of Anthropology
University of California, Santa Barbara

Hector Neff
Missouri University Research Reactor
University of Missouri

# Preface

So, in short, the real equipment of an archaeologist is a scientific mind.
—C. Wissler (1917:101)

*Posing Questions for a Scientific Archaeology* is a series of essays documenting the process of asking questions of the archaeological record to obtain empirically and theoretically defensible answers. While *Posing Questions* is a book
rich in archaeological method and theory, it is a decidedly different sort of volume than most books of its kind in archaeology. *Posing Questions* explicitly
focuses on the interplay between theory, methods, and the generation of data
from the archaeological record. Our primary reason for creating this volume was
to address a growing need in the discipline—despite advances in building an
archaeology founded in evolutionary theory, little progress has been made in
exploring and detailing the process of linking theory with the empirical world.
While documenting the process of how to describe the world is typically unnec-
essary in normal science (Kuhn 1962, e.g., physics, chemistry), such explication
is now critical in archaeology as we converge on describing the archaeological
record in terms allowing us to produce a falsifiable answer. As Richard Lewontin
(1974:8) wrote for building theory for historical science, "we cannot go out and
describe the world in any old way we please and then sit back and demand that
an explanatory and predictive theory be built on that description." For some evolutionary archaeologists, this quote has become a tired platitude of a programmatic literature. However, we believe this volume takes Lewontin's admonition
beyond a programmatic call. This book is *precisely* about the process of going
out and describing the world so that we can build theory for archaeology as historical science. Such an ambitious project will go at least some of the way toward
resolving the methodological quandaries raised for evolutionary archaeology.

We anticipate this book will provoke a number of reactions. Some may argue that the book is "too evolutionary." But we make no apologies, for it has become clear that evolutionary theory, in at least some form, is the foundation for a scientific archaeology. As a careful read of the chapters will show, the use of evolutionary theory is a consequence of pursuing scientific explanations for historical change and not an a priori position. Others might complain that the chapters lack substantive results that leave the reader "hanging" without knowing whether the research design "worked" or not. But we do not promise results, only ways to ask questions in the context of theory and the empirical strictures of science. We believe the source of such criticism is our tradition of blind empiricism in archaeological training and research. Although many *believe* that archaeological knowledge consists simply of empirical "findings," this notion is false: data are generated with the guidance of theory, or some sense-making system acting in its place whether researchers recognize this or not. Failure to understand the relationship between theory and the empirical world has led to the many debates and frustrations of contemporary archaeology. Despite years of trying, the atheoretical, empiricist foundations of archaeology have left us little but a history of story-telling and unsatisfying generalizations about historical change and human diversity. Thus, *Posing Questions* offers promising directions for building theoretically defensible, empirical results by providing well-designed case studies that can be used as guides or *exemplars* as Bettinger and Richerson (1996:223) have recently called for in evolutionary archaeology. As the chapters illustrate, the application of the research design is, for the most part, a trivial matter that determines whether one or another theoretically specified, empirical condition is true. The *real work* (or our archaeological "product") is in devising research questions to assess correctness—the basis of any scientific endeavor. Herein lies the unique value of this book.

## REFERENCES CITED

Bettinger, R., and P. Richerson
  1996  The State of Evolutionary Archaeology: Evolutionary Correctness, or the Search for Common Ground. In *Darwinian Archaeologies,* edited by H. Maschner, pp. 223–231. Plenum, New York.
Kuhn, T. S.
  1962  *The Structure of Scientific Revolutions.* Chicago University Press, Chicago.
Lewontin, R. C.
  1974  *The Genetic Basis of Evolutionary Change.* Columbia University Press, New York.
Wissler, C.
  1917  The New Archaeology. *American Museum Journal* 17:100–101.

# 1

# Posing Questions for a Scientific Archaeology

*Terry L. Hunt, Carl P. Lipo, and Sarah L. Sterling*

Supporters assume that the greatness and importance of a work correlates directly with its stated breadth of achievement: minor papers solve local issues, while great works claim to fathom the general and universal nature of things. But all practicing scientists know in their bones that successful studies require strict limitations. One must specify a particular problem with an accessible solution, and then find a sufficiently simple situation where attainable facts might point to a clear conclusion. Potential greatness then arises from cascading implications toward testable generalities. You don't reach the generality by direct assault without proper tools. One might as well dream about climbing Mount Everest wearing a T-shirt and tennis shoes and carrying a backpack containing only an apple and a bottle of water. (S.J. Gould 1998: 19)

Many archaeologists share the goal of developing a scientific archaeology that has the ability to assess the correctness of its conclusions. To realize this goal, we face two related challenges. First, archaeologists must develop a systematic body of theory to bring explanatory meaning to the archaeological record and the history it reflects. Second, we must be able to generate data that are consistent with that body of theory and its explanatory structure. Archaeologists need theoretically informed "rulers" and "yardsticks" with which to measure relevant aspects of the empirical world. While others have considered the first challenge in the outlines of an evolutionary archaeology (e.g., Boone and Smith 1998; Dunnell 1992a; Lyman and O'Brien 1998; Maschner 1996; O'Brien and Holland 1990; Ramenofsky and Steffen 1998b; Schiffer 1996; Teltser 1995a), it is the second

with which we concern ourselves here. As Stephen J. Gould (1998:19) points out
in the quotation above, one of the greatest challenges that faces a scientist is how
to specify a problem, build questions, and generate a data set in such a way that
answers can be reasonably—and defensibly—produced. This book, therefore,
presents a set of research designs that exemplify the process of posing archaeological questions with the goal of building an historical science. Our goal is to
initiate a discussion about the actual process of constructing research method-
ologies within which testable hypotheses may be formulated. The reader should
be aware, however, that this is not a book about answers or results. Rather, this
volume presents a number of carefully constructed research designs generated
within the framework of evolutionary theory. While the chapters address a range
of specific archaeological questions and concerns, each of the research designs
can be used as a guide to the process of formulating questions about the past
within a scientific framework. We hope the contributions of this volume will
serve as exemplars for building a scientific archaeology.

## WHY SCIENTIFIC ARCHAEOLOGY?

For more than a century, archaeologists have sought to build a scientific discipline. This goal was expressed by early Culture Historians (e.g., Holmes 1892;
Wissler 1917; see Dunnell 1992b; Lyman et al. 1997a, 1997b; O'Brien and
Lyman 1998), and later advocated more strongly by proponents of New
Archaeology (e.g., Watson et al. 1971, 1984). Some archaeologists have recognized the enormity of building a scientific archaeology, but maintain the results
will be worth the effort (e.g., Dunnell 1992a, 1992b). As many have conceived,
a scientific archaeology would address processes of cultural change and the origins of human cultural diversity (Boas 1896, 1902; Wissler 1917; Binford 1962;
Dunnell 1980), fitting comfortably within the larger disciplinary goals of anthropology. And importantly, science would bring to archaeology more certain conclusions, and as a result, the growth of a cumulative body of knowledge about the
past. Science is a reasonable goal for archaeology because we study a physical
record of human history. Our subject matter—the archaeological record—is
empirical. In short, our goal of understanding historical change based on an
empirical record forms the logical foundations for a scientific archaeology.

Science, however, is widely misunderstood. At least two major sources of confusion contribute to misunderstanding. First, perhaps given our social science
heritage, archaeologists have often conflated science and systematic empiricism
(Dunnell 1982:14–18; see Willer and Willer 1973). Systematic empiricism operates by making generalizations from observations, but without the deductive role
of theory. As Dunnell (1982:16) points out, "as summaries of observations, they
are contingency-bound, phenomenological statements which can never, by virtue
of their empirical foundations, be true in any absolute or universal sense." And
"without theory in the scientific sense of the term, this strategy is unable to

specify meaning apart from the commonsense element that enters into the initial observations" (Dunnell 1982:15). For the systematic empiricists, theory is the product of research, not its intellectual foundation (Dunnell 1982:16). Yet systematic empiricism's empirical content and assertions of rigorous methodology and objectivity contribute to its mistaken reputation as science. The confusion over theoretical laws and empirical generalizations provides ample evidence of such conflation (e.g., Binford 1981, 1983; cf. Binford 1968). Second, some archaeologists, in their rush to adopt science for New Archaeology, borrowed aspects of the physical science methodology as a template for their own research pursuits (e.g., Watson et al. 1971). As Dunnell (1980, 1982, 1986b, 1989b) and others (e.g., Lyman et al. 1997b) have discussed, the ahistorical sciences would prove to be particularly inappropriate models for archaeology. A related hindrance was the New Archaeology's focus on the philosophy of science as a prescription for proper conduct in performing science, resulting in a formulaic or ritualistic application (Dunnell 1989b). A science of archaeology could not be built simply by applying aspects of the methodology of physics or chemistry. Science was neither the simple systematic gathering of facts, nor was it a formal or ritualistic pursuit prescribed by philosophical accounts. The development of a scientific archaeology would require much more.

Science is a logical system in which theory is used to explain a general class of phenomena and as such, it is a way of knowing (Moore 1993). It employs an empirical standard of truth to assess correctness of conclusions. Science requires *theory* as a deductive tool for explanation and observation of relevant aspects (units) of the empirical world (Lyman et al. 1997b:3). Its empirical standard of truth makes science a continually self-correcting system (Hull 1988a; Ruse 1999). Certainty of conclusions means that science produces *knowledge*. Contrary to some postmodernist rhetoric (e.g., Andreski 1972; Aronowitz 1988), science is not a guise for the imposition of Western values (Gross and Levitt 1994:42–70; Ruse 1999). Science is a ubiquitous system for acquiring specific kinds of knowledge (Wilson 1998:45–65). It is, in the words of E. O. Wilson (1998:53), "the organized systematic enterprise that gathers knowledge about the world and condenses the knowledge into testable laws and principles." The naive postmodernist view denies the complex practical knowledge and achievements of many non-Western and ancient populations (e.g., celestial navigation and the colonization of the remote Pacific Islands; see Finney 1994). As philosophers of science illustrate, science is better understood by its practice and products rather than by any succinct or formal definition (Hull 1988a). Rather than being a monolithic entity with a single overriding process or dogma, science is "accretionary, built from blocks of evidence joined artfully by the blueprints and mortar of theory" (Wilson 1998:59). Archaeologists, for the most part, are no strangers to science: archaeology has seen the seeds of science throughout its growth as a discipline. Understanding why archaeology *is* and *isn't* a science requires examining the history of the discipline.

## CULTURE HISTORICAL FOUNDATIONS

Culture history emerged as the dominant paradigm in archaeology by the 1930s (see Lyman et al. 1997b). For the most part, it quickly became the predominant framework for archaeological investigation when archaeologists began to converge upon methods for using distributions of particular kinds of artifact attributes (i.e., "stylistic") to order artifact assemblages in time. Using independent lines of evidence of artifact similarity gained from stratigraphic excavations and surface collections, culture historians began to produce chronological sequences. This was a revolution in how time could be measured using artifacts (Lyman et al. 1997a:4). This methodological accomplishment brought with it testability—archaeologists could be wrong and know it on the certainty of empirical standards. If a chronology was produced, for example, it could easily be falsified by further excavations or by additional collections. This breakthrough was decidedly scientific, and yet its impact, not surprisingly, was seen as substantive (Lyman et al. 1997b). Until this time, archaeology had been closely aligned to interests in natural history (Dunnell 1984). But with the development of a chronological method, seriation, archaeologists built a tremendous substantive record that forms the present foundations of prehistory worldwide.

The methodological core of culture history is based upon two empirical generalizations: the occurrence law and the frequency law (Dunnell 1970, 1984; Lyman et al. 1997b). These generalizations account for temporal distributions of artifact forms described in particular ways (i.e., by stylistic attributes) and used to define units such as types, phases, and foci. The generalizations ensured that units had contiguous distributions in time and space. For the culture historians, similarity denoted relatedness. Thus, similarities invoked explanations of homologous processes (i.e., various forms of cultural transmission) such as diffusion, trade, persistence, and migration. Invoking these processes in explanations was wholly consistent with the way the archaeological record had been described for analytic purposes (Dunnell 1984). Based on formal similarities, culture historical explanations could, through the occurrence and frequency laws, be assessed for their correctness. Consequently, an empirical standard was firmly established as a cornerstone of the culture history paradigm (Lyman et al. 1997b). In addition, archaeologists began to develop a relative uniformity of archaeological pursuits. There was only one way to do archaeology and it was dictated by the synthesis that emerged with the culture history paradigm (Lyman et al. 1997b). However, because this synthesis developed largely through consensus among practicing archaeologists, there was little discussion given to the theoretical underpinnings of the method. This in part would lead to its demise.

## NEW ARCHAEOLOGY AND NEW QUESTIONS

Culture history ran into trouble as archaeologists became increasingly interested in aspects of the archaeological record not related to chronologies and historical relationships. Influenced by British social anthropology, archaeologists after World War II began to envision archaeological research in terms of systemic relations, behavior, and cultures (e.g., Taylor 1948). Research focused on topics of interest in contemporary ethnographic practice. Archaeology was to become anthropological and in so doing, address questions of similarities among human systems. But the methods and incipient theory developed by the culture historians failed to account for analogous traits. In these matters, the empirically falsifiable strength of culture history was lost. Instead the reconstructionist efforts of the New Archaeology would use ethnographic analogy, often uncritically, to create accounts of behavior that would eventually prove unsatisfying (e.g., Allen and Richardson 1971; Binford 1967, 1978; Hill 1970). No empirical warrant or performance criteria were available to evaluate these reconstructions, a problem that became the focus of some discussion (e.g., Ascher 1961; Gould 1980; Gould and Watson 1982). The only means to evaluate a reconstruction was by reference to the professional competence of the researcher or the general plausibility of the reconstruction judged in terms of common sense and knowledge of the ethnographic record (e.g., Sabloff and Willey 1967; Thompson 1956).

The New Archaeology, and culture reconstruction in particular, developed as a response to this predicament. A critical view for the new archaeologists was that the archaeological record was the product of human interaction—both among people, and between people and their environment. The goal would become scientifically rigorous reconstruction of behavior reflected in the record (Binford 1962, 1964, 1965, 1967, 1968). New Archaeology sought the same degree of certainty for behavior that the culture historians had enjoyed for matters of archaeological distributions in time and space. Consequently, strategies to create meaningful units, construct relevant analogies, and assess the correctness of conclusions, emerged to meet the goals the New Archaeology had set for itself.

## Unit Creation

In 1953, Albert Spaulding proposed a statistical method (chi-square) for discovering units (types). His method produced types Spaulding claimed were *real* as unambiguous reflections of ideas held in the minds of the ancient artisans. This new concept of unit creation (i.e., "discovery") epitomized the changing goals promulgated by the reconstructionist efforts of the New Archaeology. Culture historians quickly recognized that these units were incompatible with culture historical types, which had proven their utility as chronological tools (Ford 1954). Spaulding's method is inductive, yet relies on commonsensical input to provide meaning for the units that it generates. Because Culture Historians had entered a productive period of normal science (sensu Kuhn 1962), and rarely discussed the methodological underpinnings of their units, their deductive approach to the archaeological record was mistaken as inductive. The theoretical deductions, although often implicit, played an integral part in the methodology of culture history. In sum, the units of culture history were tied to an empirically sufficient (i.e., testable) research program. The "discovery" of units of meaning proposed by Spaulding remains untestable, reflecting the *faith* necessary for accepting culture reconstructions.

### Analogy

The culture reconstructionists of the New Archaeology were quick to recognize the sloppy and intuitive uses of analogy in culture historical accounts. Culture historians used analogy in a post hoc fashion—it gave meaning to stories and characterizations of "culture" once they had reduced their analysis of change to phases, periods, and so on. Analogy gained greater significance for culture reconstruction. It provided a strategy for deriving the missing content (behavior) for archaeological reconstructions. Consequently, some of the first efforts of the New Archaeologists were to develop an explicit, deductive, and rigorous use of analogy (e.g., Binford 1967; Gould 1980).

In terms of assessing correctness of conclusions, however, the use of analogic reasoning remains problematic. The logical structure of analogy does not provide a means by which conclusions can be falsified or tested (cf. Munson 1969; Sabloff et al. 1973). Using analogies raises problems of equifinality—where different processes can produce the same apparent outcome. Thus, the only criterion available for evaluating conclusions drawn from analogy must be the plausibility and the concordance with common sense, or other well-established accounts. There are no empirical standards for assessing correctness. Therefore, conclusions are mere arguments about the plausibility of particular reconstructions.

### PHILOSOPHY OF SCIENCE

In efforts to become scientific, New Archaeologists turned to the philosophy of science (e.g., Binford 1968; Watson et al. 1971, 1984). In retrospect, the New Archaeologists were hoping to find a prescription for success. Philosophy of science, they reasoned, provided accounts of successful scientific fields, and archaeology could follow its lead and attain the same status. From the contemporary literature of the philosophy of science, Binford (1968, 1972) drew upon a particular version of logical positivism espoused by Hempel (1965). This version of positivism focused on the structure of scientific explanations and their verification in the empirical world. Using logical positivism as a foundation, Binford (1968) argued that the veracity of archaeological explanations is a function of degree to which modern observation can be linked to laws of cultural functioning and to the past, material record. In his view, accurate knowledge of the past is tested by the standard and traditional procedures embodied in scientific practice. In short, this approach led many archaeologists to perform *ritualized* applications of "the scientific method." Not surprisingly, attempts to assess the correctness of untestable archaeological conclusions made no progress.

Ritualized attempts to evaluate correctness shifted the emphasis from empirical testing to the formal properties of the argument used to produce inferences (Dunnell 1978). Thus, the scientific character of archaeology came to be measured by the degree to which the form of argument conformed to the Hempelian model (Dunnell 1989a; e.g., Watson et al. 1971). However, some quickly recognized that the Hempel-Oppenheim model was not the only model of science constructed by philosophers (e.g., Levin 1973; Morgan 1973, 1978; Salmon 1976, 1982; Salmon and Salmon 1979). As it turned out, the Hempel-Oppenheim model was a particularly inappropriate choice for archaeology, since it was developed as an account for physics, not historical science. Yet archaeologists ritualistically applied the model as a guide for assessing correctness and searched in vain for *laws* of cultural behavior. Their search would lead to the conflation of theoretical laws (as established in the physical sciences) and the empirical generalizations so at home in the systematic empiricism of the social sciences (Fritz and Plog 1970; Carneiro 1970; cf. Binford 1968; Dunnell 1982, 1989a; Willer and Willer 1973).

## REACTIONS

By the 1980s, a climate of frustration developed over the goals of the New Archaeology. A movement dubbed "post-processual" provided the lead in rejecting any scientific goals for archaeology. In many ways, a rejection of science is the only unifying theme of the movement. Fueled by the rather spectacular failures of the New Archaeology to provide an empirical means by which to evaluate conclusions, post-processualists argued against the notion of any independent means of evaluating conclusions. Instead, by adopting the position that knowledge is subjective, they could only rely on critique, plausibility, and logical consistency to evaluate conclusions (e.g., Hodder 1984, 1986, 1989; Hodder et al. 1995; Shanks and Hodder 1995; Shanks and Tilley 1987). In various rejections of objective knowledge, the post-processualists proposed narratives to explore the *reading* of the archaeological record as a text. Within the post-processual paradigm, therefore, "explanation" is a matter of positioning oneself within the "text" of the archaeological record to illuminate meaning.

A variety of critics have pointed out the *cul-de-sac* of the post-processualists' argument (e.g., Binford 1988; Earle and Preucel 1987; Kohl 1993; R. Watson 1987, 1991). The movement rejects all notions of science rather than critically examining the potential for archaeology as a historical science. This position leaves the post-processualists with no means of evaluation, just endless arguments in which, by their own logic, no approach is better than any other. This perpetual relativism holds the seeds for its own irrelevance. Why should the archaeological record be squandered to serve as props in such narratives? Why should archaeologists be paid to tell stories that say more about who they are than what happened in the past? If anything, the post-processualists' sometimes-perceptive critique warns of the urgency of resolving archaeology's current methodological dilemma.

The perspective shared by the authors of this book is that a science of archaeology, integrating the theoretical and empirical aspects of scientific inquiry, is not only feasible, but necessary if we are to build a cumulative body of knowledge about the past. But a scientific archaeology demands more of archaeological research—telling stories is a creative effort that requires nothing more than a comfortable chair and a good cup of tea. Building scientific knowledge, on the other hand, takes not only tremendous creativity but also a good deal of *hard work:* time, effort, attention to rigor, perseverance, daring, knowledge, and obsession. For some, what is gained in certainty of conclusions will detract from pondering diverse or "interesting" questions about the past (e.g., Wylie 1995:208–9). However, without a scientific archaeology as a system to build knowledge about the past, the product of archaeology will be reduced to "just-so stories" (Gould and Lewontin 1979).

Science *is* the means to gather information about the way the world works. Rejecting science as a goal for archaeology dooms the discipline to a quagmire of relativistic, individualistic, and noncumulative stories about the past (see Fox 1996). However, if archaeology is to become a science, then we must consider what gives science its particular character and how this might be accomplished within the field.

## BUILDING A SCIENTIFIC ARCHAEOLOGY

As apparent from our review, we have not yet succeeded in building a scientific study of the human past. Why is this the case? What are the major impediments? Binford (1977), Dunnell (1982), and others (e.g., Bettinger 1991) have argued, as we argue here, that a scientific approach to explaining culture change requires theory. Scientific theory provides the essential component of all scientific explanations because it is a coherent system of propositions that stipulates construction of meaningful units, and specifies the nature of the relations between those units (Dunnell 1971). Theory articulates ideas with the empirical world. E. O. Wilson (1998:52) writes:

Nothing in science—nothing in life, for that matter, makes sense without theory. It is our nature to put all knowledge into context in order to tell a story, and to re-create the world by this means. So let us visit the topic of theory for a moment. We are enchanted by the beauty of the natural world. Our eye is caught by the dazzling visual patterns of polar star trails, for example, and the choreography of chromosomes in dividing root tip cells of a plant. Both disclose processes that are also vital to our lives. In unprocessed form, however, without theoretical frameworks of heliocentric astronomy and Mendelian heredity, they are no more than beautiful patterns of light.

Although the word carries with it a certain amount of weight, any statement about the world can be a theory in the colloquial sense; there are no special logical requirements for statements identified as theories.[1] *Scientific* theories, on the other hand, do hold a special status. Scientific theories are constructed in such a way so that they can be proven wrong. Lewontin (1974a:6–12; also Dunnell 1982:7) has outlined three critical parameters by which theory (or an explanation generated by it) can be evaluated:

1. *Dynamic sufficiency* addresses the completeness of theory. Does the theory have the requisite number of pieces of the right kind to generate scientifically acceptable explanations of the phenomena of interest?
2. *Empirical sufficiency* demands that the units are observable and measurable in the phenomenological world, making empirical testing feasible.
3. *Tolerance limits* address the question of how close is close enough? The question concerns standards of accuracy in a match between an account or theoretical description and the phenomena of the real world.

As Lewontin (1974a:8) describes, the process is iterative:

It is not always appreciated that the problem of theory building is a constant interaction between constructing laws and finding an appropriate set of descriptive state variables such that laws can be constructed. We cannot go out and describe the world in any old way we please and then sit back and demand that an explanatory and predictive theory be built on that description. The description may be dynamically insufficient. . . . That is not to say there is an insoluble contradiction. Rather there is a process of trial and synthesis going on. . . . in which both state descriptions and laws are being fitted together.

It is the iterative process that lies at the heart of the scientific process. Since scientific theories are characterized by the logical requirement that they can be proven wrong empirically, it is the practice of scientists to make their "mistakes" as quickly as possible and begin again. In light of the iterative process of theory construction, theories are the product of *informed* imagination stocked with information from previous attempts. The best theories are those which generate the most fruitful hypotheses that can be "translated cleanly into questions that can be answered by observation and experiment" (Wilson 1998:53). Theories or their hypotheses compete with one another to explain the available data; the survivors become placed in the current set of "accepted wisdom" until replaced by new theories that better explain the data. Lewontin's (1974a) account, and Dunnell's (1982) analysis for archaeology, emphasize the inventive aspects of constructing theory in concert with building the appropriate units. This effort stands in marked contrast to systematic empiricism (Willer and Willer 1973) and "business as usual" in archaeology.

In this way, building a scientific archaeology requires formally initiating this iterative process, that is, building a theory that articulates principles of historical change with the phenomenological record of archaeology. Such a theory will link dynamic sufficiency with empirical sufficiency and tolerance limits. And, because evolution is the only scientific theory that accounts for historical change and organic diversity, such a theory will be evolutionary (Dunnell 1980, 1992a).

The chapters in this volume begin from a theoretical framework in evolution, build the appropriate units, and show their fit to actual cases.

## CONSTRUCTING UNITS

Building a scientific archaeology requires a means to evaluate our explanatory accounts against an empirical standard of truth. This goal, as we have outlined, requires theoretical and empirical units to link mechanisms (such as natural selection) with our subject matter (the archaeological record). The archaeological record at various scales provides the empirical foundation (Dunnell 1989a, 1995). That physical record, not behavior, is archaeology's true subject matter (cf., Schiffer 1995). Our theoretical and explanatory goals are historical, thus, evolutionary. From the cornerstone of evolutionary theory, the *methodological* goal for the discipline becomes building explanations (*theoretical units*) and observations (*empirical units*) for relevant aspects of the empirical world. As some have described, this involves an expansion of evolutionary theory as formalized in biology to cultural and archaeological phenomena (e.g., Boyd and Richerson 1985; Cavalli-Sforza and Feldman 1981; Dunnell 1980; Leonard and Jones 1987; Madsen this volume; Teltser 1995a). As Teltser (1995a:1–2) points out, such an expansion has critical methodological implications for creating different units of measurement with enormous, but fairly specific, data requirements.

Despite the significance of the empirical basis for archaeology, many debates have surrounded the methods and meanings of the units constructed (Dunnell 1986a; Ramenofsky and Steffen 1998b). As Lyman et al. (1997b) show, the Culture Historians had achieved a significant degree of empirical sufficiency in matters of chronology. With little explicit theoretical justification, their discussions of how and why to construct units for chronology building were deductive, problem-oriented, and conceived in a materialist (population thinking) ontology (e.g., Brew 1946; Ford 1954; Krieger 1944; Rouse 1939; see Dunnell 1986a, 1986b). Units at more inclusive scales, such as phases, proved more problematic in empirical and conceptual terms (e.g., Rouse 1955, 1965; Willey and Phillips 1958; see Dunnell 1971). Beyond Culture Historians' strength in chronology building, their description of the record largely as homologous relations limited the explanations they would offer for cultural change (Dunnell 1984, 1986a). In contrast to the Culture Historians, few contemporary archaeologists pay attention to how and why they construct units of measurement. They may cite the antithetic views of Adams and Adams (1991) who acknowledge units are arbitrary structures informed by purpose, but then describe the process of unit construction (classification) as merely procedural (Ramenofsky and Steffen 1998b:4). Dunnell's (1982) analysis of common sense and systematic empiricism permeating archaeological practice explains much of the current apathy and confusion. Theory and method constructed in concert will necessarily sharpen our focus on how and why we do what we do.

## GENERATING HYPOTHESES

The theoretical rationale for an evolutionary archaeology meeting the strictures of historical science has been discussed in some detail (e.g., Dunnell 1978, 1980, 1992a, 1992b, 1995; Leonard and Jones 1987; Lyman and O'Brien 1998; O'Brien and Holland 1990, 1995; Rindos 1989), as well as the integral role of unit construction (e.g., Dunnell 1995; Hull 1988b; Lipo and Madsen n.d.; Ramenofsky and Steffen 1998b; see also Lynch 1998; Pocklington and Best 1997). Ignoring the unit issues, some have jumped on a bandwagon, taking Darwinian theory as just another interpretive algorithm for archaeology (e.g., Kirch and Green 1987; Maschner and Mithen 1996). Lipo and Madsen (n.d.) outline the liabilities of developing such *interpretive* models where units derived from common sense are used in intuitively satisfying accounts that are nonetheless simply "just-so stories" (Gould and Lewontin 1979). Commonsense-based units and interpretive models may seem to provide "explanations" of empirical cases, but in reality, they are incomplete and untestable (see Dunnell 1982, 1987, 1995; Hull 1980, 1988a). We might think of these as "processual reconstructions." They may be informed by theory, but they are actually untestable assertions about what happened in the past.

As philosophers of biology have suggested, Darwin's greatest contribution was to develop a methodology for historical science (Gould 1986; Lewontin 1974b). This kind of methodological challenge for archaeology has recently gained some attention (e.g., Dunnell 1995; Jones et al. 1995; Lipo and Madsen n.d.; Lipo et al. 1997; Neff 1993, 1998; Neiman 1995; Pierce 1998; Ramenofsky and Steffen 1998a; Teltser 1995a, 1995b). As Lipo and Madsen (n.d.) have described, "theory building is an iterative process, proceeding from descriptions of process with ad hoc variables to the creation of units with which to examine the model's performance in explaining particular empirical problems." They suggest "the current situation in anthropological attempts to apply Darwinian models to cultural phenomena reflects only the youth of our efforts, not fundamental problems with existing theories" (Lipo and Madsen, n.d.).

Bettinger and Richerson (1996:223) have viewed the methodological issues in similar terms, emphasizing the importance of attempts to explain real world cases. Evolutionary archaeology, they argue, surely has the requisite general theory and instrumentation, but still lacks proven research routines that show how one might reasonably address real data within this larger conceptual structure. They suggest that what is needed might be called "paradigmatic case studies, or *exemplars* . . . closely specified research designs, the principles of which, if carefully followed, can be successfully applied almost endlessly" (Bettinger and Richerson 1996:223).

## CONTRIBUTIONS

We believe the contributions of this volume provide exemplars for building a scientific archaeology. Thus, the chapters do not provide answers to the questions they pose. Rather, their purpose is to demonstrate how the *process* of building these "paradigmatic case studies" can be conducted within a scientific framework of evolutionary theory. As such, these chapters are united theoretically and methodologically by the goal of explaining evolutionary change in the archaeological record. The cases represent significant temporal and geographic diversity in archaeological research, ranging from Old Kingdom Egypt, North and South America, to Hawaii. The kinds of materials and artifacts examined include flaked and groundstone tools, ceramics, bone and shell fishhooks, faunal assemblages, and human bone. The chapters also range in the scale of research from the form and function of discrete objects, regional spatial-temporal patterns, settlement-subsistence change, to population structure and cultural elaboration.

We are not the first to note the importance of formal research designs that link explanation to the empirical world (i.e., Taylor 1948; Watson et al. 1971, 1984). It has been the case historically, however, that the interface between theory and phenomena has not met Lewontin's (1974a) three criteria of empirical sufficiency, dynamic sufficiency, and tolerance limits. The chapters that follow are case studies that also outline problems with previous attempts to explain particular archaeological phenomena. These chapters then demonstrate how the application of evolutionary theory avoids the logical problems entailed in more traditional approaches to explaining the archaeological record. Thus, the diverse contributions of this book illustrate the process of developing theory and method within the history of archaeological practice, for a variety of archaeological problems.

One major theme of the works in this volume concerns identifying the nature of artifact variation and building evolutionary explanations for the causes of that variation. In Chapter 2, for example, Kornbacher examines various groundstone wedge tools (termed "axes") from northern South America. Applying engineering and use-wear analysis, controlled experiments, and distributional data, she investigates traditional assumptions about wedge tool function and morphology and shows how analogous and homologous features of these tools can be distinguished. In Chapter 3, Pfeffer describes the use of finite element analysis and performance tests to evaluate the degree to which the structure and design of prehistoric Hawaiian fishhooks are determined by functional properties. In this innovative study, Pfeffer questions a priori assumptions about homologous similarity in descriptions of fishhooks used to infer cultural affinity and shows that the use of engineering analyses and distribution studies can be used to sort style, function, and pleiotropic attributes. Similarly, in Chapter 4, Wilhelmsen uses engineering studies of formal properties of projectile points from the central Mississippi River valley to determine how these properties determine the performance of flight, cutting, hafting, and other functional aspects of piercing artifact classes. Wilhelmsen shows that descriptions of projectile points that consider attributes not governed by performance make it possible to construct detailed relative chronologies for this important class of artifacts.

In addition to examining variability in artifacts, chapters by Broughton, Greenlee, and Madsen address questions about the interaction between phenotypic variation within human populations and environmental structure. In Chapter 7, for example, Greenlee notes that settlement changes may occur for many reasons and that they may be determined by examination of settlement, subsistence, dietary, and environmental data. She uses dietary data to question traditional assumptions about the appearance of maize farming in the Ohio Valley and its role in settlement nucleation. In Chapter 8, Broughton shows how changes in faunal richness in the shell middens of San Francisco Bay in California can be used to assess a model for resource abundance and composition with changing human population sizes. Broughton's model demonstrates how ecological models are compatible with a scientific archaeology. While Broughtons's research is not particularly historical, it uses theory derived from ecology with assumptions about the nature of historical change as a way of examining the archaeological record. In Chapter 9, Madsen models how selection favors "bet-hedging" life history strategies in unpredictable environments. Madsen's research focuses on the emergence of the elaborate mortuary complex of the Hopewell in the eastern United States. Traditionally, the long distance trade, mound constructions, and burials have been explained as evidence of cultural elaboration made possible by surplus agricultural resources. Madsen, however, argues that increased investment in apparently "wasteful" activities might be explicable as behavior that reduces the variance in reproductive success, leading to an overall increase in fitness in unpredictable environments. Madsen's work offers a glimpse of how archaeologists might begin to incorporate ecological models derived from life history with historical contingencies to build fully evolutionary explanations for archaeological phenomena such as mounds, elaborate burials, and monumental architecture (see also Madsen et al. 1999).

Finally, two contributions in this volume demonstrate how the concepts "style" and "function" are useful in explaining variability in the distribution of artifacts reflecting the temporal and spatial structure of human populations. In Chapter 5, Sterling examines stylistic variation in the morphology and distribution of Meidum ceramic bowls from Egypt's Nile River Valley during the Old Kingdom. Sterling presents explicit criteria for evaluating the scale of craft specialization as part of a larger study of functional integration at this time. In a similar study, Lipo (Chapter 6) uses frequencies of decorative elements on late prehistoric ceramics to construct seriations for the central Mississippi River Valley. In his research, Lipo shows how seriation can be used to study the prehistoric interaction and structure of communities. Identification of prehistoric communities provides a basis for mapping the configurations of complex and functionally integrated entities. Lipo's work details the complex factors contributing to estimates of stylistic similarity. He demonstrates how one can generate error terms for each component of measurement, and evaluate results against tolerance limits derived from theoretically derived hypotheses about cultural transmission.

The chapters in this volume extend recent theoretical and methodological discussions (e.g., Boone and Smith 1998; Dunnell 1992; Lyman and O'Brien 1998; Maschner 1996; O'Brien and Holland 1990; Ramenofsky and Steffen 1998a;

Teltser 1995b) by providing case studies that outline the methodology for implementing a scientifically based evolutionary archaeology. The authors identify or reanalyze problems, construct the appropriate theoretical and empirical units, and outline the means to evaluate the problem through the acquisition and analysis of data. They *do not* offer substantive answers about the past. The contributions in this volume are instead concerned with constructing research strategies that bridge dynamic and empirical sufficiency. Our goal is to build the "exemplars" advocated by Bettinger and Richerson (1996:223) and demonstrate how evolutionary theory, unit construction, and empirical measurement can be used in concert to build a scientific archaeology and a cumulative body of knowledge about the past.

## NOTE

1. As E. O. Wilson (1998:52) points out, it is probably this character of theories that has mislead the empiricists, post-processualists, and postmodernists. Since everyone's theory has some validity, all theories must be equally interesting. This misunderstanding would explain, we think, postmodernist "theories" such as Jaques Lacan's identification of the erect penis with the square root of minus one and Luce Irigaray's diagnosis that male physicists, fatally lacking precious bodily fluids and hampered by rigid protuberances, have difficulties understanding fluid dynamics (from Sokal and Bricmont 1998). Archaeologists are certainly no strangers to this sort of "everything is valid theory" thinking. Recent examples include Hegmon and Trevathon's (1996) explanation of odd-looking birthing events painted on pots as indications of male painters and Mobley-Tanaka's (1997:437) argument that subterranean features found among the Anasazi represent female-biased "gender-specific ritual power."

## REFERENCES CITED

Adams, W. and E. Adams
   1991   *Archaeological Typology and Practical Reality: A Dialectical Approach to Artifact Classification and Sorting.* Cambridge University Press, Cambridge.
Allen, W. L. and J. Richerson
   1971   The Reconstruction of Kinship from Archaeological Data: The Concepts, the Methods, and the Feasibility. *American Antiquity* 36:41–53.
Andreski, S.
   1972   *Social Sciences as Sorcery.* St. Martin's Press, New York.
Ascher, R.
   1961   Analogy in Archaeological Interpretation. *Southwestern Journal of Anthropology* 17:317–25.
Aronowitz, S.
   1988   *Science as Power: Discourse and Ideology in Modern Society.* University of Minnesota Press, Minneapolis.
Bettinger, R. L.
   1991   *Hunter-Gatherers: Archaeological and Evolutionary Theory.* Plenum Press, New York.

Bettinger, R. and P. Richerson
   1996   The State of Evolutionary Archaeology: Evolutionary Correctness, or the Search for Common Ground. In *Darwinian Archaeologies*, edited by H. Maschner, pp. 223–231. Plenum Press, New York.

Binford, L.
   1962   Archaeology as Anthropology. *American Antiquity* 28:217–25.
   1964   A Consideration of Archaeological Research Design. *American Antiquity* 29:425–41.
   1965   Archaeological Systematics and the Study of Culture Process. *American Antiquity* 31:203–10.
   1967   Smudge Pits and Hide Smoking: The Use of Analogy in Archaeological Reasoning. *American Antiquity* 32:1–12.
   1968   Archaeological Perspectives. In *New Perspectives in Archaeology*, edited by S. Binford and L. Binford, pp. 5–32. Aldine, Chicago.
   1972   *An Archaeological Perspective*. Seminar Press, New York.
   1977   General Introduction. In *For Theory Building in Archaeology*, edited by L. Binford, pp. 1–10. Academic Press, New York.
   1978   *Nunamiut Ethnoarchaeology*. Academic Press, New York.
   1981   *Bones: Ancient Men and Modern Myths*. Academic Press, New York.
   1983   *In Pursuit of the Past: Decoding the Archaeological Record*. Thames and Hudson, New York.
   1988   Data, Relativism, and Archaeological Science. *Man* 22:391–404.

Boas, F.
   1896   The Limitations of the Comparative Method in Anthropology. *Science* 4(102):901–907.
   1902   Some Problems in North American Archaeology. *American Journal of Archaeology* 6 (1):1–6.

Boone, J. L. and E. A. Smith
   1998   Is it Evolution Yet? Critique of Evolutionary Archaeology. *Current Anthropology* 39(Supplement):141–173.

Boyd, R. and P. J. Richerson
   1985   *Culture and the Evolutionary Process*. University of Chicago Press, Chicago.

Brew, J.
   1946   The Archaeology of Alkali Ridge, Southwestern Utah. *Papers of the Peabody Museum of Archaeology and Ethnology* 21.

Carneiro, R.
   1970   A Quantitative Law in Anthropology. *American Antiquity* 35:492–94.

Cavalli-Sforza, L. and M. Feldman.
   1981   *Cultural Transmission and Evolution: A Quantitative Approach*. Princeton University Press, Princeton.

Dunnell, R. C.
   1970   Seriation Method and Its Evaluation. *American Antiquity* 35:305–19.
   1971   *Systematics in Prehistory*. Free Press, New York.
   1978   Style and Function: A Fundamental Dichotomy. *American Antiquity* 43:192–202.
   1980   Evolutionary Theory and Archaeology. *Advances in Archaeological Method and Theory* 3:35–99.
   1982   Science, Social Science, and Common Sense: The Agonizing Dilemma of Modern Archaeology. *Journal of Anthropological Research* 38:1–25.

1984   Methodological Issues in Contemporary Americanist Archaeology. *Philosophy of Science Association* 2:717–44.

1986a Methodological Issues in Americanist Artifact Classification. *Advances in Archaeological Method and Theory* 9:149–207.

1986b Five Decades of American Archaeology. In *American Archaeology Past and Future*, edited by D. Meltzer, D. Fowler, and J. Sabloff, pp. 23–49. Smithsonian Institution, Washington, D.C.

1987   Comment on "History, Phylogeny, and Evolution in Polynesia" (by P. V. Kirch and R. C. Green). *Current Anthropology* 28:444–45.

1989a Aspects of the Application of Evolutionary Theory in Archaeology. In *Archaeological Thought in America*, edited by C. Lamberg-Karlovsky, pp. 35–49. Cambridge University Press, Cambridge.

1989b Philosophy of Science and Archaeology. In *Critical Traditions in Contemporary Archaeology*, edited by V. Pinsky and A. Wylie, pp. 5–9. Cambridge University Press, Cambridge.

1992a Archaeology and Evolutionary Science. In *Quandaries and Quests: Visions of Archaeology's Future*, edited by L. Wandsnider, pp. 209–24. Center for Archaeological Investigations, Occasional Paper No. 20.

1992b Is a Scientific Archaeology Possible? In *Metaarchaeology*, edited by L. Embree, pp. 75–97. Kluwer Academic Publishers, The Hague.

1995   What Is It That Actually Evolves? In *Evolutionary Archaeology: Methodological Issues*, edited by P. Teltser, pp. 33–50. University of Arizona Press, Tucson.

Earle, T. K. and R. W. Preucel
   1987   Processual Archaeology and the Radical Critique. *Current Anthropology* 28:501–38.

Finney, B.
   1994   *Voyage of Rediscovery*. University of California Press, Berkeley.

Ford, J.
   1954   The Type Concept Revisited. *American Anthropologist* 56:42–54.

Fox, R.
   1996   Art/Science in Anthropology. In *The Flight from Science and Reason*, edited by P. Gross, N. Levitt, and M. Lewis, pp. 327–345. New York Academy of Science, New York.

Fritz, J. and Plog, F.
   1970   The Nature of Archaeological Explanation. *American Antiquity* 35:405–12.

Gould, R.
   1980   *Living Archaeology*. Cambridge University Press, Cambridge.

Gould, R. and P. Watson
   1982   A Dialogue on the Meaning and Use of Analogy in Ethnoarchaeological Reasoning. *Journal of Anthropological Archaeology* 1:355–81.

Gould, S. J.
   1986   Evolution and the Triumph of Homology, or Why History Matters. *American Scientist* 74:60–69.

   1998   Writing in the Margins. *Natural History* 107(9):16–20.

Gould, S. and R. Lewontin
   1979   The Spandrels of San Marco and the Panglossian Paradigm: A Critique of the Adaptationist Programme. *Proceedings of the Royal Society of London, series B* 205:581–98.

Gross, P. R. and N. Levitt
  1994  *Higher Superstition: The Academic Left and Its Quarrels with Science*. John Hopkins University Press, Baltimore.
Hegmon, M. and W. R. Trevathan
  1996  Gender, Anatomical Knowledge, and Pottery Production: Implications of an Anatomically Unusual Birth Depicted on Mimbres Pottery from Southwestern New Mexico. *American Antiquity* 61(4):747–754.
Hempel, C.
  1965  *Aspects of Scientific Explanation, and Other Essays in the Philosophy of Science*. Free Press, New York.
Hill, J. N.
  1970  *Broken K Pueblo: Prehistoric Social Organization in the American Southwest*. Anthropological Papers of the University of Arizona, Tucson.
Hodder, I.
  1984  Burials, Houses, Women, and Men in European Neolithic. In *Ideology, Power, and Prehistory*, edited by D. Miller, C. Tilley, pp. 51–68. Cambridge University Press, Cambridge.
  1986  *Reading the Past*. Cambridge University Press, Cambridge.
  1989  *The Meanings of Things*. Unwin Hyman, London.
Hodder, I., M. Shanks, A. Alexandri, V. Buchli, J. Carman, J. Last, and G. Lucas
  1995  *Interpreting Archaeology. Finding Meaning in the Past*. Routledge, New York.
Holmes, W.
  1892  Modern Quarry Refuse and the Paleolithic Theory. *Science* 20:295–97.
Hull, D. L.
  1980  Individuality and Selection. *Annual Review of Ecology and Systematics* 11:311–32.
  1988a  *Science as a Process: An Evolutionary Account of the Social and Conceptual Development of Science*. University of Chicago Press, Chicago.
  1988b  Interactors versus Vehicles. In *The Role of Behavior in Evolution*, edited by H. Plotkin, pp. 19–50. MIT Press, Cambridge, Massachusetts.
Jones, G., R. Leonard, and A. Abbott.
  1995  The Structure of Selectionist Explanations in Archaeology. In *Evolutionary Archaeology: Methodological Issues*, edited by P. Teltser, pp. 13–32. University of Arizona Press, Tucson.
Kirch, P. and R. Green
  1987  History, Phylogeny, and Evolution in Polynesia. *Current Anthropology* 28:431–56.
Kohl, P. L.
  1993  Limits to a Post-Processual Archaeology (or the Dangers of New Scholasticism). In *Archaeological Theory—Who Sets the Agenda*, edited by N. Yoffee, A. Sherrott, pp. 13–19. Cambridge University Press, Cambridge.
Krieger, A.
  1944  The Typological Concept. *American Antiquity* 9:271–88.
Kuhn, T.
  1962  *The Structure of Scientific Revolutions*. University of Chicago Press, Chicago.
Leonard, R. and G. Jones
  1987  Elements of an Inclusive Evolutionary Model for Archaeology. *Journal of Anthropological Archaeology* 6:199–219.

Levin, M.
   1973   On Explanation in Archaeology: A Rebuttal to Fritz and Plog. *American Antiquity* 38:387–95.
Lewontin, R.
   1974a *The Genetic Basis of Evolutionary Change.* Columbia University Press, New York.
   1974b Darwin and Mendel: The Materialist Revolution. In *The Heritage of Copernicus: Theories Pleasing to the Mind*, edited by J. Neyman, pp. 166–83. MIT Press, Cambridge, Massachusetts.
Lipo, C. and M. Madsen
   n.d.   The Evolutionary Biology of Ourselves: Unit Requirements and Organizational Change in United States History. Manuscript.
Lipo, C., M. Madsen, R. Dunnell, and T. Hunt
   1997   Population Structure, Cultural Transmission, and Frequency Seriation. *Journal of Anthropological Archaeology* 16:301–33.
Lyman, R. and M. O'Brien
   1998   The Goals of Evolutionary Archaeology: History and Explanation. *Current Anthropology* 38:615–652.
Lyman, R., M. O'Brien, and R. Dunnell
   1997a Introduction. In *Americanist Culture History: Fundamentals of Time, Space, and Form*, edited by R. Lyman, M. O'Brien, and R. Dunnell, pp. 1–16. Plenum Press, New York.
   1997b *The Rise and Fall of Culture History.* Plenum Press, New York.
Lynch, A.
   1998   Units, Events, and Dynamics in Memetic Evolution. *Journal of Memetics— Evolutionary Models of Information Transmission*, 2: 34–65
         http://www.cpm.mmu.ac.uk/jom-emit/1998/vol2/lynch_a.html
Madsen, M., C. Lipo, and M. Cannon
   1999   Fitness and Reproductive Trade-offs in Uncertain Environments: Explaining the Evolution of Cultural Elaboration. *Journal of Anthropological Archaeology* 18:251–281.
Maschner, H. (Editor)
   1996   *Darwinian Archaeologies.* Plenum Press, New York.
Maschner, H. and S. Mithen
   1996   Darwinian Archaeologies: An Introductory Essay. In *Darwinian Archaeologies*, edited by H. Maschner, pp. 3–14. Plenum Press, New York.
Mobley-Tanaka, J. L.
   1997   Gender and Ritual Space During the Pithouse to Pueblo Transition: Subterranean Mealing Rooms in the North American Southwest. *American Antiquity* 62(3):437–448.
Moore, J.
   1993   *Science as a Way of Knowing: The Foundations of Modern Biology.* Harvard University Press, Cambridge, Massachusetts.
Morgan, C.
   1973   Archaeology and Explanation. *World Archaeology* 4:259–76.
   1978   Comment on "Descriptive Statements, Covering Laws, and Theory." *Current Anthropology* 19:325–26.

Munson, P.
  1969   Comment on Binford's "Smudge Pits and Hide Smoking." *American Antiquity*
    34:83–89.
Neff, H.
  1993   Theory, Sampling, and Analytical Techniques in the Study of Prehistoric
    Ceramics. *American Antiquity* 58:23–44.
  1998   Units in Chemistry-based Ceramic Provenance Investigations. In *Unit Issues in
    Archaeology*, edited by A. Ramenofsky, A. Steffen, pp. 115–127. University of Utah
    Press, Salt Lake City.
Neiman, F.
  1995   Stylistic Variation in Evolutionary Perspective: Inferences from Decorative
    Diversity and Interassemblage Distance in Illinois Woodland Ceramic Assemblages.
    *American Antiquity* 60:7–36.
O'Brien, M. and R. Lyman
  1998   *James A. Ford and the Growth of Americanist Archaeology.* University of
    Missouri Press, Columbia.
O'Brien, M. and T. Holland
  1998   Variation, Selection, and the Archaeological Record. *Archaeological Method
    and Theory* 2:31–79.
  1995   The Nature and Premise of a Selection-based Archaeology. In *Evolutionary
    Archaeology: Methodological Issues*, edited by P. A. Teltser, pp. 175–200. University
    of Arizona Press, Tucson.
Pierce, C.
  1998   Theory, Measurement, and Explanation: Variable Shapes in Poverty Point
    Objects. In *Unit Issues in Archaeology*, edited by A. Ramenofsky, A. Steffen, pp.
    163–189. University of Utah Press, Salt Lake City.
Pocklington, R. and M. Best.
  1997   Cultural Evolution and Units of Selection in Replicating Text. *Journal of
    Theoretical Biology* 188:79–87.
Ramenofsky, A. and A. Steffen (Editors)
  1998a  *Unit Issues in Archaeology: Measuring Time, Space and Material.* University of
    Utah Press, Salt Lake City.
Ramenofsky, A. and A. Steffen
  1998b  Units as Tools of Measurement. In *Unit Issues in Archaeology*, edited by A.
    Ramenofsky and A. Steffen, pp. 3–17. University of Utah Press, Salt Lake City.
Rindos, D.
  1989   Undirected Variation and the Darwinian Explanation of Cultural Change.
    *Archaeological Method and Theory* 1:1–45.
Ruse, M.
  1999   *Mystery of Mysteries: Is Evolution a Social Construct?* Harvard University
    Press, Cambridge, Massachusetts.
Rouse, I.
  1939   *Prehistory in Haiti: A Study in Method.* Yale University Publications in
    Anthropology, No. 21, New Haven.
  1955   On the Correlation of Phases of Culture. *American Anthropologist* 57:713–22.
  1965   The Place of "Peoples" in Prehistoric Archaeology. *The Journal of the Royal
    Anthropological Institute of Great Britain and Ireland* 95:1–15.

Sabloff, J., A. Beale, and A. Kurland
   1973   Recent Developments in Archaeology. *The Annals of the American Academy of Political and Social Science* 408:103–18.
Sabloff, J. and G. Willey
   1967   The Collapse of Maya Civilization in the Southern Lowlands: A Consideration of History and Process. *Southwestern Journal of Anthropology* 23:311–36.
Salmon, M.
   1976   "Deductive" versus "Inductive" Archaeology. *American Antiquity* 41:376–81.
   1982   *Philosophy and Archaeology.* Academic Press, New York.
Salmon, M. and W. Salmon
   1979   Alternative Models of Scientific Explanation. *American Anthropologist* 81:61–74.
Schiffer, M.
   1995   *Behavioral Archaeology: First Principles.* University of Utah Press, Salt Lake City.
   1996   Some Relationships Between Behavioral and Evolutionary Archaeologies. *American Antiquity* 61(4):643–662.
Shanks, M. and I. Hodder
   1995   Interpretative Archaeologies: Some Themes and Questions. In *Interpreting Archaeology*, edited by I. Hodder, M. Shanks, A. Alexandri, V. Buchli, J. Carman, J. Last, and G. Lucas, pp. 30–33. Routledge, London.
Shanks, M. and C. Tilley
   1987   *Reconstructing Archaeology: Theory and Practice.* Cambridge University Press, Cambridge.
Sokal, A. and J. Bricmont
   1998   *Fashionable Nonsense: Postmodern Intellectuals' Abuse of Science.* Picador USA, New York.
Spaulding, A.
   1953   Statistical Techniques for the Discovery of Artifact Types. *American Antiquity* 18:305–13.
Taylor, W.
   1948   A Study of Archaeology. American Anthropological Association.
Teltser, P.
   1995a The Methodological Challenge of Evolutionary Theory in Archaeology. In *Evolutionary Archaeology: Methodological Issues*, edited by P. Teltser, pp. 1–11. University of Arizona Press, Tucson.
   1995b Culture History, Evolutionary Theory, and Frequency Seriation. In *Evolutionary Archaeology: Methodological Issues*, edited. P. Teltser, pp. 51–68. University of Arizona Press, Tucson.
Thompson, R.
   1956   The Subjective Element in Archaeological Inference. *Southwestern Journal of Anthropology* 12:327–32.
Watson, R. A.
   1987   Make Me Reflexive—But Not Yet: Strategies for Managing Essential Reflexivity in Ethnographic Discourse. *Journal of Anthropological Research* 43:29–41.
   1991   What the New Archaeology Has Accomplished. *Current Anthropology* 32:275–291.

Watson, P., S. LeBlanc, and C. Redman
1971　*Explanation in Archeology: An Explicitly Scientific Approach.* Columbia University Press, New York.
1984　*Archaeological Explanation: The Scientific Method in Archaeology.* Columbia University Press, New York.
Willer, D. and J. Willer
1973　*Systematic Empiricism: Critique of a Pseudoscience.* Prentice Hall, Englewood Cliffs.
Willey, G. and P. Phillips
1958　*Method and Theory in American Archaeology.* University of Chicago Press, Chicago.
Wilson, E. O.
1998　*Consilience: The Unity of Knowledge.* Alfred Knopf, New York.
Wissler, C.
1917　The New Archaeology. *American Museum Journal* 17:100–101.
Wylie, A.
1995　An Expanded Behavioral Archaeology: Transformation and Redefinition. In *Expanding Archaeology*, edited by J. Skibo, W. Walker, A. Nielsen, pp. 198–209. University of Utah Press, Salt Lake City.

# 2

# Building Components of Evolutionary Explanation: A Study of Wedge Tools from Northern South America

*Kimberly D. Kornbacher*

## INTRODUCTION

Stone tools commonly referred to as "axes" are widely distributed across diverse environmental regions of northern South America and occur in a variety of T-shaped, trapezoidal, and other forms. Despite the diversity and ubiquity of these artifacts, many researchers (e.g., Burger 1992; Cole 1977, 1983; Denevan 1993; Lathrap 1962, 1970; Tello 1960; Villalba 1988; Zalles Flossbach 1989) endorse a traditional notion of the role played by stone axes in agricultural subsistence systems as expressed by Lathrap (1970:62–63, my emphasis): "It is *certain* that the [archaeological] stone axes were used mainly for clearing agricultural land, and that the presence of a reasonable number of axe fragments in a site is a good indication that agriculture was economically significant." The argument is that since stone axes were used to clear land in lowland tropical forest environments ethnographically (Carneiro 1961, 1974, 1979a, 1979b; Denevan 1974; Lathrap 1962; Schmidt 1974; Up de Graff 1974), similar objects derived from the archaeological record constitute evidence of prehistoric agriculture.

It has never been demonstrated, however, that the archaeological tools are the functional equivalent of those observed in use by ethnographers. Wear studies or other physical analyses that bear directly upon artifact use and constitute the necessary warrant for functional inferences are lacking. The practice of assigning functional labels to prehistoric artifacts by analogy with modern forms has limited our understanding of the diversity of tools subsumed under a single name, and has thus impaired our ability to detect and explain change.

A particular tool form, the "T-shaped axe" (Figure 2.1), is also used as evidence of interregional interaction between highland and lowland South American populations (Cole 1977, 1983; Lathrap 1970, 1973; Stothert 1985; Villalba 1988). The foundation of this assumption is that the tools found in the lowlands are reportedly manufactured from volcanic materials collected in the highlands. Following the same line of reasoning, it has been suggested that the use of axes originated in the Amazon Basin (Carneiro 1979a, 1979b; Denevan 1993; Lathrap 1962, 1970; Lathrap et al. 1975; Richardson 1969), implying that interaction between populations of the highlands and the lowlands has been in place as long as the lowland occurrence of axes. Proponents of this idea have acknowledged, however, that there is little information about the raw materials from which the tools are manufactured. Data have not been generated pertaining to how the tools are distributed in time and space. Consequently, inferences about interregional interaction and cultural origins based on the lowland occurrence of a particular tool form are premature at best.

**Figure 2.1. T-shaped tool from La Tolita, Ecuador.**

If archaeologists are ever to be in a position to use groundstone artifact form as an indicator of a particular activity or as a stylistic marker that provides information about prehistoric interaction, we must develop an understanding of the historical relations between variants and generate data about how different forms were used in diverse environments. Evolutionary theory integrates these two objectives into a coherent program of research focusing on the study of collections of objects termed "axes" from northern South America.

To construct a foundation for an evolutionary explanation, temporal and spatial variation must be documented in terms of analogous and homologous features. As a first step in this process, engineering and distributional analyses are employed to isolate functional features—those that affect fitness and can be explained in terms of selective processes—from those stylistic features that reflect drift and other transmission processes. Use-wear and design analyses form the foundation of the engineering analysis, since they are crucial for understanding the nature of the tool-environment interaction and whether variants are functional alternatives. To use the physical traces of interaction (wear) as a means of studying artifact function, researchers must generate experimental data that clarify the relations between particular motions and materials and particular traces. These data are virtually nonexistent for groundstone. Thus, part of this research involves conducting experimental work necessary to begin to build an experimental data base for groundstone. Once the use-context of the artifacts has been determined, experiments are also used in the engineering analysis as a basis for formulating hypotheses that distinguish stylistic and functional attributes. To the extent possible, distributional data are used to test hypotheses about which aspects of variation are functional and which are stylistic. Hypotheses for the explanation of changes in frequencies of functional variants are derived from documented changes in the archaeological and paleoenvironmental records, and regional ecology. These are tested in a preliminary fashion with the distributional data generated in the initial analyses of museum collections from Ecuador and Peru, and may be tested further as more data become available. Changes in frequencies of stylistic attributes, once documented, are a potential source of information about the developmental history of tool form and also provide a basis for constructing testable hypotheses about the extent and frequency of information transmission. This study is undertaken with the goal of constructing a foundation for such work and for increasing our understanding of the archaeological record of northern South America.

## THEORETICAL FRAMEWORK

Understanding functional and historical relations between artifact variants and the role they may have played in the history of the people who produced and used them requires that research be conducted within the framework of evolutionary theory. This is simply because evolution is the only scientific theory that encompasses both unique historical processes and functional description in a single explanatory system (Dunnell 1980; Lipo and Madsen 1998; Lyman and O'Brien 1998; O'Brien 1996; Feathers 1990; Pierce 1998). Archaeology conducted within such a framework is an historical science, and "first and foremost . . . explains why frequencies change and why particular variants expand at the expense of others" (Dunnell 1992:218; also see Sober 1984). As applied to the archaeological record, the basic structure of such an explanation involves two steps. The first is *the identification and quantification of variation*, and the second is *inference of the history of selection of those variants* (O'Brien and Holland 1995:185, emphasis added). These steps parallel Lewontin's (1970) requirements of evolutionary change: establishing that phenotypic variation exists, describing that variation, and then determining the selective history of variants.

As these programmatic statements imply, variation is the substance of evolutionary explanation. As such, descriptions of artifacts and other aspects of archaeological and biological phenomena cannot be essentialist constructions that emphasize modal aspects or central tendencies; rather they must be built in materialist terms that can accommodate variation (Dunnell 1980, 1992; Hull 1965, 1978; Mayr 1959, 1988; O'Brien 1996; Sober 1980, 1993). Three critical components of the materialist metaphysic are identified by Dunnell (1980:84): 1. empirical variability is the subject of investigation; 2. such variability must be regarded as continuous; and 3. change must be conceived of as a selective rather than transformational process.

Constructing evolutionary explanations requires that archaeologists not only embrace a materialist metaphysic and conceive of the record as continuous, but use a different kind of descriptive language as well. The appropriate descriptive language is founded in the essentialist sciences (Dunnell 1978a, 1980, 1992). While it may at first seem paradoxical that an essentialist data language is required for a materialist science, the apparent paradox is resolved if one considers why *any* particular descriptive language is important. Empirical sufficiency is one of the three components for building an evolutionary theory, and for applying scientific theory to the problem of explaining archaeological phenomena. Empirical sufficiency addresses the measurability of variables: the units and parameters specified by the theory must be identifiable empirically and measurable in the phenomenological world (in our case, the archaeological record). It follows that the language we use to describe archaeological phenomena must be derived from physics and chemistry since they are the only sciences that describe the world in terms of units and laws that are just as applicable to past and future phenomena as they are to the present.

. . . . physical and chemical laws necessarily *determine the data language*, or how we describe the archaeological record. If we persist in treating function, for example, with terms like *chopping*, then the only way to falsify such statements is to transport the observer . . . back in time. If, on the other hand, we deal with the same problem in terms of friction, fracture mechanics, and other physical forces, we can say how an object interacted with its environment with exactly the same certainty as if it were moving in front of us (Dunnell 1992:217; emphasis in original).

Thus, empirical sufficiency—a necessary component for building a scientific archaeology—cannot be achieved unless archaeologists employ a descriptive language founded in the essentialist sciences. It is important to note that this is not simply a semantic issue. Restructuring or reconceptualization cannot be incorporated into a research program sometime after data have been generated, but is basic to the entire effort. This study is a case in point. For example, in developing a protocol for the collections work, it was necessary to determine which objects to study. Should all artifacts catalogued as axes and adzes be included? What about celts, hoes, hatchets, or chisels? What about objects called axes with wear indicative of uses other than chopping? One might say a simple solution is that all "woodworking" tools should be included; yet how can we determine what tools were used to work wood prior to undertaking functional analyses? All identifying labels we are accustomed to using (axe, chisel, wood-working, chopping, etc.) are derived from ethnographic analogy and common sense. Each has direct behavioral implications and usually only implicit or poorly defined criteria for identification (Dunnell 1978b; Hayden 1977; Mills 1993). Thus, application of these terms to guide my selection of objects included in the study would be incompatible with the research objectives, since discrete entities that reflect empirical variability *could not* result. Given these considerations, at this scale of analysis, the units become *all objects exhibiting a wedge-shaped working end, or bit*. These objects are henceforth referred to as "wedge" tools. This term is derived from mechanical engineering and is used in the sense of one of five classical machine elements identified by the Alexandrian Greek, Heron (Drachmann 1963:21, cited in Cotterell and Kamminga 1992:75). Development of this aspect of the data language and the resulting formal criteria ensures objects exhibiting a range of variation are included in the study, rather than simply the modal or "ideal" axe or adze.

Aside from developing essentialist data language, another aspect of the material-ist reconceptualization concerns the role of artifacts such as wedge tools in understanding human evolution. An important consequence of evolutionary biol-ogists' shift from the study of museum specimens to field studies of living organ-isms (Mayr 1982) was the recognition that the phenotype is not simply bounded by the skin of an organism and that manufactured objects are part of the human phenotype (Dawkins 1990; Dunnell 1989; Leonard and Jones 1987; Sober 1984). It follows that selection can determine the differential persistence of artifacts, and artifacts affect the reproductive success of the larger selective unit of which they are a part (Jones et al. 1995; Pierce 1993). In terms of wedge tools specifically, these objects are a part of the phenotype that may be considered technical arti-facts. Technical artifacts are broadly defined by Feathers (1990:109) as physical attributes that are transmitted culturally or cultural extensions of the genetic body that allow an expansion of physical capabilities. Mechanical technology may thus be regarded as a supplement to the muscular system.

This understanding—and the more general recognition that artifacts are part of the human phenotype (Dunnell 1980)—provides the link between evolutionary theory and artifact analysis and is the key to constructing evolutionary explanations using material remains (O'Brien and Holland 1995).

The work of constructing descriptions of phenotypic variation that form the basis of evolutionary explanation involves separating those elements that are affected by natural selection from those that are not (Dunnell 1978a, 1978b, 1980, 1989, 1992; Neiman 1995; O'Brien and Holland 1990, 1995; O'Brien 1996). Phenotypic variation is *functional* when variants have effectively different fitness values, i.e., when the reproductive success they confer on their bearers varies. Functional variation is explicable in terms of a deterministic process, specifically natural selection. One of the major changes in biology in the past three decades has been the recognition that not all variants are under selection. In fact, a great deal of variation is neutral and structured by stochastic processes, such as drift, rather than selection (Mayr 1988; Kimura 1983; King and Jukes 1969; Sober 1984). Archaeologists have termed these selectively neutral aspects of phenotypic variation *style* and regard them as potential markers of homologous relations (Dunnell 1978b, 1983, 1989; Lipo et al. 1997; Neiman 1995). Stylistic and functional aspects of variation have the potential to provide entirely different kinds of information. Both are necessary for addressing my research objectives, as well as the traditional objectives of anthropological archaeology.

Distinguishing features that owe their differential persistence and spatial distribution to different evolutionary mechanisms necessarily form a major portion of this research. Two kinds of analyses may be used to differentiate those aspects of phenotypic variation explicable in terms of natural selection from those sorted by transmission processes alone: engineering and distributional analyses (Dunnell 1980; Dunnell and Feathers 1991; Feathers 1990; Meltzer 1981; O'Brien et al. 1994; Pierce 1993, 1995). Given the nature of the artifactual data currently available, this study emphasizes engineering analyses. As more data become available, distributional analyses can be employed to a greater extent. Engineering analyses inform on differences in relative engineering fitness of variants, and are constructed in terms of *cost* and *performance* within a specific context. Fitness differences (evaluated as variation in cost and performance parameters) give one variant a selective advantage over another under a specific set of conditions. If an engineering analysis demonstrates that potential differences in fitness exist between variants, the feature is hypothesized to be functional. If no or negligible differences in engineering fitness are documented, the feature in question is hypothesized to be stylistic or selectively neutral. Distributional analyses document differential persistence of traits or replicative success (Leonard and Jones 1987) and also provide a means of testing the functional and stylistic hypotheses. Evolutionary archaeologists and biologists have formulated expectations about the spatial and temporal distributions of traits that are derived from evolutionary theory, empirical observation, and formal modeling (Dunnell 1989; Dunnell and Feathers 1991; Feathers 1990; Kimura 1983; Neiman 1995; O'Brien and Holland 1990; Sober 1980), and hypotheses derived from the engineering analysis can be evaluated with respect to these models.

Important exceptions to the distributional generalizations are pleiotropic traits, a kind of neutral trait that mirrors the distribution of a selectively advantageous trait to which it is linked. If architectural constraints link traits together, a particular trait may become prevalent because selection is acting on another part of the architectural package and it simply "rides" along (Mayr 1988; Sober 1984, 1993). Sober (1984:99–100) illustrates pleiotropy clearly with his "selection toy" example in which balls of different sizes are shaken through levels with successively smaller-sized holes. Balls are selected for their smallness; those that make it to the bottom are favored by selection. The balls of different sizes are also different colors, and the smallest are green. The pleiotropic trait then (the color green in this example), may be regarded as a "free rider" since its increase in frequency is not due to its conferring any advantage but to its link with a functional trait, which in this example is smallness.

While the engineering analysis and distributional descriptions are essential for distinguishing among functional, stylistic, and pleiotropic phenotypic features, they do not explain the existence of the features or their evolutionary history. They do not address the question of *why* the frequencies of different variants may have changed over time, or the nature of the relationship, if any, between the replicative success of variants and the differential persistence of populations possessing them. To understand the evolutionary relations between variants, one must link the functional data to other aspects of the archaeological and paleoenvironmental records. Thus, it is crucial to collect data that identify changes in subsistence, settlement patterns, climatic warming and/or cooling, vegetation regime, and other relatively large-scale, persistent alterations that are likely to have had a major impact on prehistoric populations (Jones et al. 1995). As these data are compiled from extant archaeological and paleoenvironmental literature, hypotheses can be developed that link these selective agents to changes documented in the frequencies of functional traits (e.g., Dunnell and Feathers 1991; Feathers 1990; O'Brien et al. 1994; Pierce 1993; Rindos 1984). Once stylistic aspects of variation are identified and distinguished from functional elements, distributional data can provide information about community structure, population organization, and the extent and intensity of interaction within and between these units (Dunnell 1983; Hunt et al. 1995; Lipo et al. 1997; Lyman and O'Brien 1998; Neiman 1995). Only at this point can we begin to generate testable explanations about *why* frequencies change.

## THE ARCHAEOLOGICAL COLLECTIONS

This research uses existing archaeological collections from Ecuador and Peru (Figure 2.2). Some data are generated from published sources, while others are derived from collections to which I have had direct access. Each of the seven collections is associated with materials from which chronological information has been or can be derived, although the scope and quality of contextual information varies. Table 2.1 summarizes the sample information. For each collection, the

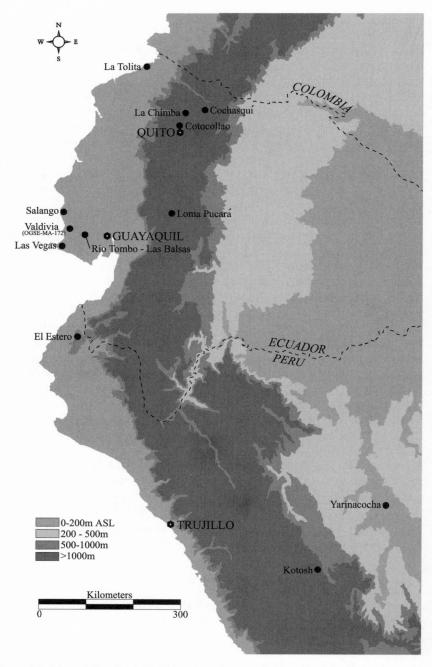

**Figure 2.2. Map of Northwestern Ecuador and Peru showing locations of sites discussed in text.**

**Table 2.1**
**Archaeological Collections**

| Collection | Environment/Location | Culture Historical Unit | Chronological Range (B.P.) | Context | Artifact Freq |
|---|---|---|---|---|---|
| La Tolita | north coast | Tolita 2 | 2000-1000* | mound | 13 |
| Cotocollao | northern highlands | Late Valdivia-Early Machalilla | 3500-2200* | structures/various | (8 flakes/frags) 11 |
| La Chimba | northern highlands | La Chimba (Early, Middle, Late) | 2650-1700* | midden | (232 flakes/frags) |
| Cochasqui | northern highlands | Cochasqui I, II (Integracion) | 1300-500* | mound | 15 |
| Salango | north coast | Bahia-Salango II | 2200-1400 | structure/surface | 5 |
| Las Vegas | north coast | Late Las Vegas | 8250-6600* | midden/burial | 3 |
| OGSE-MA-172 | north coast | Early Guangala | 2500-2000* | midden | 2 |
| Rio Tambo-Las Balsas | western foothills | Guangala | 2500-1500 | stratified deposit | (8 flakes/frags) 7 |
| Loma Pucara | central highlands | Cerro Narrio | 2600-750* | stratified deposit | 2 |
| El Estero | north coast uplands | Early-Middle Preceramic | 9000-7000 | surface/midden | 7 |
| Kotosh+ | central highlands | Chavin-Higuera | 3000-2000* | structures/various | 23 |
| Yarinacocha+ | Upper Amazon | Tutishcainyo-Pacacocha | 3500-1500 | stratified deposit | 9 |

*Absolute dates available and fall within time range specified by culture historical unit

+Direct access to collections not obtained: information derived from published sources (Izumi and Sono 1963; Izumi and Terada 1971; Lathrap 1962)

name, source or location, available chronological information, and number of objects is listed. Some fragmentary materials were obtained for elemental (XRF) analysis. For these collections, the number of fragments is indicated in parentheses after the number of complete objects studied in Ecuador. Collections are derived from highland, tropical coast, semi-arid coast, and tropical forest environments (Figure 2.2), although these areas are not equally represented. Many of the objects analyzed are associated with temporally diagnostic ceramics; the cultural historical units listed in Table 2.1 are based on those associations. In several cases, the age ranges provided for the Cultural Historical units are supplemented by radiocarbon dates, as indicated. The majority of the collections are associated with materials that range from approximately 500 to 3500 B.P. The remainder of the collections are much older, associated with materials ranging from 6600 to 9000 B.P.

The primary substantive concern of this research is to provide an empirical basis for evaluating traditional assumptions about the function and relatedness of objects termed axes. The protocol was therefore designed to generate descriptive data on use-wear, morphology, and raw material properties. Most of the complete artifacts cannot be removed from the museums in which they are housed. Thus, the protocol for analyzing museum collections involves the production of scale drawings and photographs, in addition to physical measurements and descriptions of artifact shape, raw material properties, and macroscopic traces of use. The physical analysis of the objects also involves microscopic analysis of wear traces using a microprobe and image analysis system. Portions of the artifacts were replicated in Ecuador for later microscopic analysis. Replication was accomplished using the peel technique with cellulose acetate sheets, a high-resolution, efficient, low-cost, and highly portable means of replicating surfaces (Kornbacher 1994; Young and Symms 1980).

Some of the data generated from the analyses of museum collections (Table 2.1; Kornbacher 1995) were used initially to specify the parameters that structure the experimental analyses. For example, Figures 2.3 and 2.4 display data that were used to guide the selection of raw material and a range of tool sizes and edge angles for the experiments. Ultimately, all of the results of the artifact analyses will be evaluated with respect to the experimental data. The findings will be used to investigate the veracity of traditional assumptions about the function and relatedness of tools termed "axes" and add to our understanding of the role of these tools in South American prehistory.

## EXPERIMENTAL DESIGN

### Previous Experiments

The experimental archaeology literature involving wedge tools emphasizes questions of feasibility, time, and energy (e.g., Carneiro 1974, 1979a; Coles 1979; Denevan 1974, 1993; Harding and Young 1979; Hayden 1979b; Iversen

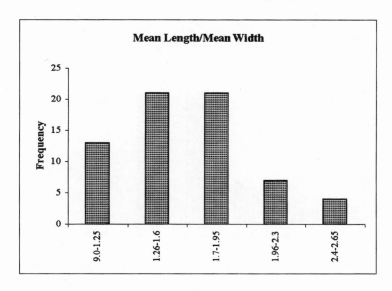

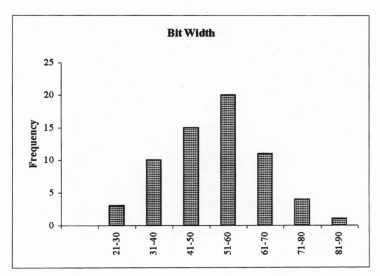

**Figure 2.3. Artifact Data: Bit-Width and Length-Width Ratio.**

1956; Jørgensen 1953; Keller 1966; Leechman 1950; Mathieu and Meyer 1997; Phillipson and Phillipson 1970; Pond 1930; Saraydar and Shimada 1971). Scholars have been primarily concerned with determining whether a given task can be accomplished with a stone tool, determining how much time and energy

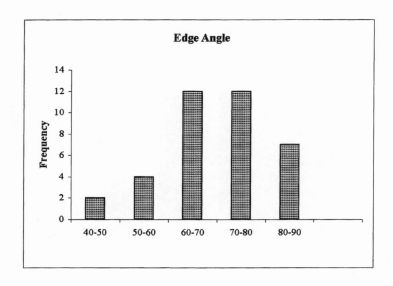

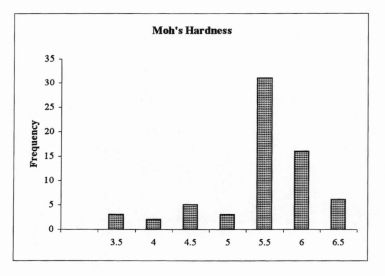

**Figure 2.4. Edge Angle and Moh's Hardness.**

is required to chop down a tree or clear a plot of land with a stone axe, and documenting the relative time and energy required for tasks using stone versus metal tools. While these studies are interesting from a technological standpoint, they provide little information that can actually be used to increase our understanding of the archaeological record.

A handful of scholars (Dickson 1972, 1981; Hayden 1979; Kamminga 1978, 1982; Mills 1987, 1993; Olausson 1983a, 1983b; Semenov 1964; Sonnenfeld 1962) have attempted to use experiments to distinguish functional and stylistic attributes or document the formation and character of wear on groundstone tools. From these efforts we have begun to learn about the kind of wear produced when specific tasks are undertaken for a specified amount of time, and we have been able to identify some potentially functional features. However, no experiments have been performed under conditions that control the number and range of variables necessary to significantly increase our understanding of the nature of the tool-environment interaction that produces physical traces on wedge tools. Kamminga (1978, 1982), for example, controls for variation due to raw material property differences (of both the tool and the contact material), but does not examine the possible effects of variations in tool geometry, tool technology, applied load, or angle of impact. Mills (1987, 1993) controls for raw material variability to some extent and for variation in tool morphology, but variation in the amount and angle of applied force could not be recorded. Sonnenfeld's (1962) pioneering experiments with hoes resulted in interesting observations about the formation of a certain kind of wear ("scour-grooves"), but properties of the contact material, aspects of tool geometry, raw material of the tools, and conditions of the experiments (e.g., amount of force, angle of impact, duration of work, etc.) were not documented.

To isolate and investigate the myriad variables that may affect wear formation on groundstone tools and to provide a data base from which we can develop an understanding of prehistoric tool function from artifact analysis, experiments must be highly controlled. Such control cannot be achieved by a human agent but requires the use of a mechanical device. Some researchers argue against the use of a machine in wear studies because they believe it creates conditions that are "too artificial" (e.g., Dickson 1981:123–124). Inasmuch as wear is formed by physical processes of motion, however, it may be produced in a rigorous and replicable manner using a simple mechanical device. Such experiments have the potential to contribute much to our understanding of wear formation on groundstone. Thus, the majority of the experimental work of this study must be conducted with a mechanical device that applies dynamic load to contact material in a consistent and measurable fashion and allows precise replication of experimental values (such as amount and angle of applied force). This is necessary if the nature of the conditions under which wear is formed and the effects of different attributes and attribute values on cost and performance are to be understood.

### Mechanical Testing Device

The machine with which the experiments are performed is a compaction device used in civil engineering materials testing. A simple series of parts was designed and machined to accommodate my specific testing program (e.g., a specimen holder, contact material holder, etc.). During each test, a motor-driven cable system with a mechanical hand lifts a central rod holding the specimen until it trips a switch that releases the rod and allows the specimen to free-fall to impact with a work piece or contact material. The distance the specimen falls and the amount of time from release of the rod to impact are recorded throughout the experiments and converted to meters per second to provide a measure of velocity. Tool mass is also easily measured and may be varied using lead weights that are added or removed from the central rod that holds the experimental tool. Kinetic energy is a measure of force impacting the workpiece that can be calculated (since mass and velocity are known) from the following equation

$$T = mv^2/2 \hspace{4cm} \text{(Equation 1)}$$

where $T$ is kinetic energy, $m$ is mass, and $v$ velocity. The part of the device that holds the work piece in place can accommodate materials of different dimensions and properties and can also be set to alter the direction of force (the angle at which the tool contacts the workpiece), allowing a range of motions.

### Experimental Tool Production

Data used to guide the selection of raw material used for the experiments are from three sources. Physical properties of artifact raw materials were recorded during the collections work using a paradigmatic classification that includes dimensions of texture and structure. A standard measure of hardness (Moh's scale) was used to measure hardness of the artifacts. These data, derived from the collections analyses, are one source of information. Results of the analyses of fragmentary artifacts brought from Ecuador also guided the selection of raw material. Petrographic and XRF analyses (Table 2.2) identified the majority of artifact fragments as andesite and metamorphosed basalt ("greenstone"). Although the analysis of fragmentary materials is not yet complete, initial results combined with visual comparison with other analyzed objects suggest that these materials typify the collections. Finally, the small amount of data in the published and unpublished literature in which raw materials were identified was compiled as the third source of information. Of the materials studied, nearly 70% are identified as andesite (Lathrap 1962; Richardson 1969), diorite, or metamorphosed basalt (Izumi and Terada 1971).

The main consideration in selecting raw material for the experimental specimens, then, was to find a source compatible with the artifactual materials as indicated by information from the raw materials characterization of the collection materials, the initial elemental analysis of fragmentary artifacts, and the results of raw material analyses presented in the literature. A single source of material was required for the bulk of the experimental work; a source large enough and homogeneous enough in texture, structure, and mineral composition to enable me to hold raw material constant during most of the experiments. Consultations with geologists (Irving pers. comm.; Swanson pers. comm.) working in western Washington identified an outcrop at the base of Mt. Rainier that is a fairly young (ca. 14,000 B.P.) flow of columnar andesite, similar in mineralogy, structure and

**Table 2.2**
**Results of XRF Analysis of Fragmentary Tools**

| Major | CO-4* | CO-3 | CO-1 | CO-5 | CO-6 | CO-2 | CO-7 | RT-2* | RT-1 | LC74-181* | LC 89-211 | LC89-193 | LC74-88 |
|---|---|---|---|---|---|---|---|---|---|---|---|---|---|
| $TiO_2$ | 49.13 | 52.19 | 50.71 | 55.46 | 61.35 | 50.75 | 60.61 | 56.35 | 67.23 | 58.25 | 56.95 | 60.40 | 59.74 |
| $Al_2O_3$ | 15.56 | 14.10 | 17.25 | 16.49 | 14.70 | 18.33 | 17.44 | 15.48 | 14.16 | 14.74 | 14.72 | 15.36 | 15.65 |
| $TiO_2$ | 0.947 | 1.205 | 1.046 | .845 | .653 | .749 | 1.062 | .326 | .231 | 2.31 | 2.604 | 1.739 | 1.669 |
| $FeO$ | 10.03 | 10.90 | 9.67 | 9.27 | 5.61 | 10.23 | 6.25 | 9.17 | 5.94 | 8.89 | 9.61 | 7.57 | 7.59 |
| $MnO$ | .219 | .230 | 0.198 | .195 | .232 | .209 | .097 | 0.166 | .098 | .132 | .0212 | 0.168 | 0.126 |
| $CaO$ | 11.26 | 9.22 | 10.13 | 6.88 | 10.86 | 11.22 | 5.00 | 10.45 | 6.28 | 4.88 | 3.34 | 2.92 | 4.36 |
| $MgO$ | 10.98 | 8.32 | 6.87 | 4.18 | 2.68 | 5.23 | 1.50 | 6.25 | 3.63 | 2.96 | 3.93 | 2.42 | 2.31 |
| $K_2O$ | .08 | 0.12 | 1.54 | 0.38 | .19 | .09 | 3.02 | .10 | .20 | 2.78 | 3.65 | 3.38 | 3.12 |
| $Na_2O$ | 1.72 | 3.61 | 2.14 | 6.09 | 3.56 | 3.09 | 4.52 | 1.67 | 2.12 | 4.41 | 4.27 | 5.47 | 4.99 |
| $P_2O_5$ | 0.081 | 0.100 | .0442 | .198 | .155 | .110 | .502 | 0.045 | .095 | .64 | 0.7 | .572 | .458 |
| **Trace** | | | | | | | | | | | | | |
| Ni | 207 | 77 | 80 | 6 | 11 | 9 | 13 | 49 | 50 | 5 | 7 | 4 | 3 |
| Cr | 648 | 227 | 233 | 21 | 44 | 42 | 10 | 90 | 176 | 12 | 18 | 3 | 11 |
| SC | 46 | 41 | 32 | 27 | 27 | 41 | 19 | 37 | 22 | 23 | 18 | 14 | 16 |
| V | 289 | 285 | 210 | 288 | 174 | 333 | 118 | 230 | 136 | 215 | 296 | 136 | 136 |
| Ba | 20 | 29 | 574 | 52 | 88 | 47 | 1202 | 419 | 229 | 744 | 425 | 1195 | 1016 |
| Rb | 1 | 2 | 45 | 6 | 4 | 2 | 68 | 2 | 4 | 57 | 58 | 77 | 62 |
| Sr | 98 | 88 | 634 | 205 | 234 | 151 | 662 | 148 | 236 | 463 | 117 | 298 | 292 |
| Zr | 48 | 61 | 131 | 55 | 50 | 35 | 223 | 30 | 64 | 331 | 304 | 341 | 364 |
| Y | 18 | 24 | 21 | 19 | 16 | 19 | 20 | 11 | 10 | 48 | 49 | 49 | 46 |
| Nb | 3.5 | 4.9 | 8.5 | 1.7 | 1.7 | 0.7 | 14.2 | 1.0 | 1.3 | 18.8 | 17.4 | 19.8 | 14.4 |
| Ga | 14 | 16 | 21 | 17 | 14 | 20 | 20 | 13 | 15 | 22 | 21 | 23 | 20 |
| Cu | 24 | 8 | 69 | 158† | 13 | 474† | 51 | 158† | 7 | 47 | 21 | 28 | 11 |
| An | 118 | 84 | 92 | 72 | 66 | 76 | 86 | 88 | 53 | 94 | 115 | 118 | 73 |
| Pb | 0 | 0 | 1 | 2 | 2 | 8 | 36 | 0 | 0 | 22 | 10 | 6 | 12 |
| La | 10 | 14 | 33 | 0 | 0 | 13 | 46 | 0 | 15 | 50 | 34 | 45 | 23 |
| Ce | 29 | 9 | 57 | 19 | 18 | 40 | 72 | 12 | 29 | 92 | 74 | 98 | 68 |
| Th | 2 | 0 | 3 | 3 | 3 | 1 | 5 | 2 | 2 | 6 | 6 | 7 | 4 |
| **Rock Type** | Basalt | Basalt | Basalt | B.Ands | Ands | Basalt | Ands | B.Ands | Dacite | Ands | B.Ands | Ands | Ands |

*CO=Cotocollao

LC=La Chimba

RT=RioTambo

†=anomalously high level—should be retested

texture to many of the archaeological specimens. Raw material collected from this outcrop comprises the bulk of the raw material used for the experimental tools. In a single experiment designed to evaluate the effect of variables such as fracture toughness on wear formation, performance, and durability, a variety of materials (metamorphosed basalt, orthoquartzite, and three cherts) are tested in addition to the andesite. All experimental tools are manufactured according to a series of standardized dimensions derived from the artifact data (e.g., Figures 2.3 and 2.4). For most tests (e.g., those designed to investigate wear formation, performance efficiency, durability), the tool blanks are cut with a geologic slab-and-trim saw and ground to the final shape using a lap polisher with a series of abrasives.

## ENGINEERING ANALYSIS

Engineering analyses, together with distributional descriptions of traits in time and space, are necessary to distinguish patterns of variation structured by selection from those explicable in terms of other processes. The concepts of cost and performance (defined below) are the source of hypotheses about the engineering fitness of variants. Engineering fitness can only be evaluated within a specific use context (what enhances fitness in one context may be detrimental in another). Thus, cost and performance parameters cannot be measured prior to demonstrating that variants being compared are subject to the same conditions (i.e., used for similar work). This can be accomplished using wear and design analyses, discussed in this context below. Also in this section, I briefly examine the different aspects of stone tool technology for which cost and performance are being assessed, and consider some of the relevant variables.

### Some Definitions and Considerations

The form of an object is a function of many factors, including (but not limited to) the cost of producing the object and its performance requirements. The concepts of cost and performance address different aspects of energy expenditure. Cost is the amount of time and energy expended in constructing a component of the phenotype. Performance, assessed here in terms of efficiency and durability, is the relative effectiveness of alternative phenotypes in carrying out a specific kind of work. Detectable differences in cost or performance parameters are important because they are regarded as potential variations upon which selection may act. Among variants that perform a similar function, the lowest cost alternatives that accomplish a given task most efficiently will have the greatest positive effect on fitness and thus are most likely to be favored by selection under competition, all other things being equal (Dunnell and Feathers 1991; Feathers 1990; Jones et al. 1995; McCutcheon 1995; O'Brien et al. 1994; Pierce 1993).

An important aspect of cost and performance parameters is that they cannot be evaluated independently—variation in one part of the phenotype affects others.

An example specific to lithic technology illustrates this point. Stone tool manufacture and maintenance involves raw material discovery, acquisition and transport, production, and maintenance. The cost and performance of each step must be assessed with respect to the others. The potentially positive fitness effects of a low transport cost, for example, might be outweighed by higher performance efficiency and durability of tools made from a tougher material with substantially higher acquisition and manufacturing costs. Thus, it is the *interaction* of manufacturing with transport and raw material acquisition costs, and all costs with different aspects of performance, that is important for determining whether the potential for differential fitness exists among variants.

Another crucial methodological point is that the engineering analysis can only be undertaken with reference to a specific context of use. Cost and performance cannot be evaluated unless we have knowledge of the specific nature of the work involved. Assessing the efficiency of different kinds of temper to resist heat, for example, is only feasible if we are dealing with objects (such as cooking pots) that are designed for work in which they must withstand high temperatures (e.g., Dunnell and Feathers 1991; Feathers 1990; O'Brien et al. 1994). Regardless of the exact nature of the task, it is also essential to establish that the variants for which cost and performance are being assessed were actually used for the same work. Expanding upon the previous example, it would be fruitless to assess heat resistance of temper alternatives if some of the variants being compared were from vessels used as storage containers rather than cooking pots. Variation in cost and performance is only useful if demonstrated among alternative forms used for the same work; common use must be documented *prior* to undertaking the engineering analysis.

Identification of variants produced for a similar use can be accomplished using archaeological data on use context, through examination of traces of interaction of the tool with its environment (wear), and through design analysis. Since materials employed in this study were recovered from a variety of archaeological contexts, including burials, middens, house floors, and earthworks, the record indicates a range of use contexts. However, the quality of data necessary to provide a clear understanding of the relations between the archaeological (depositional) context and the use (primary) context (Schiffer 1987) is lacking. Thus, wear and design analyses must be used to identify variants with common uses and determine the nature of the use context.

## Wear and Design Analysis

Physical characteristics of a manufactured object are considered design features. The stone objects upon which this study is based share certain design features that minimally include a bit (broad, tapering portion that terminates in a sharpened cutting edge [ANSI 1991:2]), poll (a blunt end opposite the bit), and a body (the portion between the bit and the poll) (ANSI 1980, 1991; Dickson 1981; Semenov 1964; Sonnenfeld 1962). These criteria describe a wedge, one of five classical machine elements. A wedge differs from other machine elements in that its mechanics involve dynamic action (Cotterell and Kamminga 1992:97). Limiting the study to stone objects that display the descriptive attributes of a wedge is intended to be inclusive, but also has the effect of restricting the sample to those tools designed for a similar (at a very general level) kind of work. Work is regarded as mechanical work and defined as the product of the force exerted on a body and the distance it moves in the direction of that force (Cotterell and Kamminga 1992:33). Mechanical or chemical alterations that occur as a result of use in work are called wear or use-wear. Specifically, wear is defined as a set of attributes that results from the interaction of an object with its use (work) environment. Thus, attributes of wear provide a basis for identifying the nature of the physical and chemical conditions to which objects were exposed during use (Dunnell 1978a; Hayden 1979a; Keeley 1980; Pierce 1993; Semenov 1964).

Wear and design analyses are used together to accomplish three goals of the engineering analysis: 1. to identify alternative artifact forms (those variants used for similar work); 2. to make initial distinctions between functional and nonfunctional aspects of design; and 3. to determine the nature of the use context of alternative forms. The techniques used for accomplishing each objective are discussed below.

In addition to addressing objectives of the engineering analysis, the use-wear component is crucial to another concern of this study—understanding the formation and character of wear on groundstone. Despite a plethora of work on the formation of wear on chipped stone and its interpretation (for reviews see: Binning 1991; Cook and Dumont 1987; Gijn 1990; Jensen 1988; Olausson 1980, 1990; Unger-Hamilton 1989; Yerkes and Kardulias 1993), few studies have been conducted that deal with these questions in regard to groundstone tools (Gorman 1979; Mills 1987, 1993; Olausson 1983a, 1983b; Semenov 1964; Sonnenfeld 1962).

For this study, wear data are derived from two sources, analysis of archaeological forms and experimental work. The experimental aspect of the wear analysis is expected to contribute to our understanding of the formation of wear on groundstone materials, because forces exerted upon experimental tools under controlled conditions leave traces on the tool. Analysis of the wear (the traces of tool-environment interaction) allow me to assess how mechanical features of the stone interact with different motions (applied forces) to produce wear. In addition to generating new data on the formation of wear on groundstone, the experiments are designed to develop ways of distinguishing among use-wear, manufacture, and the effects of post-depositional diagenetic processes. The results of the wear and design analysis will be used as a source of specific hypotheses about the nature of the tool-environment interactions that produce wear on groundstone. With these data in hand, I will be in a position to discuss attributes that make an object an axe (or not) rather than simply assigning a functional name in the absence of any empirical warrant for doing so (Dunnell 1978a:66).

## Identification of Alternative Forms and Functional Aspects of Design

Identifying artifacts that are alternative forms used for similar work requires a hypothesis-testing procedure that brings together available contextual data, aspects of design, wear, and experimental data. The use-wear aspect of this process involves isolating variants with the same wear classes occurring in a similar position on the object relative to basic design features (bit, poll, and body). First, a "wear map" (e.g., Figure 2.5) is constructed for each artifact using scale drawings and photographs to prepare two-dimensional representations of the artifactual landscape. The occurrence and location of wear is plotted on the "landscape" space using grid coordinates. Each occurrence of wear on an object is assigned an analytic number and is described using a paradigmatic functional classification, altered only slightly from earlier iterations (Campbell 1981; Dunnell 1971; Dunnell and Beck 1979; Dunnell and Campbell 1977) to meet the specific needs of this study (Table 2.3). The functional classification creates categories by systematic reference to wear, thereby excluding the influence of style and ensuring that the resulting classes characterize artifacts only in terms of func-

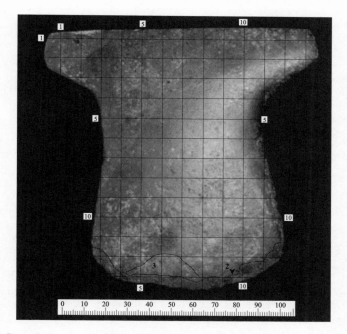

**Figure 2.5. Sample "wear map" of artifact from Cotocollao. Numbers in boldface (e.g., 2, 3) correspond to each area of wear identified; a separate number is assigned for each wear class. Area over which wear is visible is drawn and identified by the grid overlay (grid squares are named by the lower right corner, e.g., top left square is 1, 1).**

**Table 2.3**
**Paradigmatic Functional Classification of Macroscopic Wear (Based on Campbell 1981; Dunnell and Campbell 1977; Dunnell and Lewarch 1974)**

---

**Dimension I: Kind of Wear**
1. *chipping:* small, conchoidal fragments broken from edge, evidenced as flake scars
2. *abrasion:* striations with or without gloss
3. *crushing:* irregular, usually overlapping fragments removed
4. *polishing:* smooth and glossy without striations characteristic of abrasion
5. *none:* no wear apparent

**Dimension II. Location of Wear**
1. *edge:* wear occurs only at a single edge formed by the intersection of two (or more) planes
2. *unifacial edge:* wear occurs on an edge and extends onto the surface of one of the planes forming the edge
3. *multifacial edge:* wear occurs on an edge and extends onto the surfaces of the two or more planes forming the edge
4. *surface:* wear occurs on a single plane, not associated with or extending to any edge
5. *multiple surfaces:* wear occurs on multiple adjacent planes not associated with or extending to any edge

**Dimension III. Shape of Worn Area**
1. *convex:* an arc with a curve away from a flat surface
2. *concave:* an arc with a curve towards a flat surface
3. *straight:* a straight or flat surface
4. *point:* the intersection of three or more planes
5. *notch:* a convex edge or surface in which the lines or planes intersect at an acute angle

**Dimension IV. Orientation of Wear**
1. *parallel:* wear pattern axis does not intersect edge or intersects at an angle of less than 30°
2. *oblique:* wear pattern axis intersects edge at angle between 30° and 60°
3. *perpendicular:* wear pattern axis intersects edge at angle between 60° and 90°
4. *diffuse:* no direction is evident
5. *linear:* evidence of wear is aligned in a single direction on a surface and lacks edge referent
6. *multi-directional:* wear is oriented in two or more directions relative to the edge or surface

---

tion (Dunnell 1978a; Dunnell and Campbell 1977). After objects with similar macroscopic wear classes are identified, the wear maps are used to examine the distribution of the classes both in terms of relative position on the object (in relation to the basic design features of bit, poll, and body), and between objects.

The distribution of wear classes relative to certain design features is used to identify potential alternative forms and make initial distinctions between functional and stylistic attributes. If the wear analysis reveals a consistent correlation between a certain kind of wear pattern and a particular morphological feature, for example, I hypothesize that the feature is functional and that variability in certain attributes of the feature has an impact on the performance efficiency of the variant. Data generated during the experiments enable me to test such hypotheses.

The assumption that artifacts, displaying the same macrowear distributed in a similar manner relative to basic design features, were used for the same work is investigated using microscopic analysis. Wear patterns examined on a microscopic scale may exhibit variability that is simply not visible macroscopically. Microscopic analyses are conducted using the acetate peel replicas of macroscopically visible wear that were made during the museum collections analysis.

To make acetate peel replicas of wear patterns for microscopic analysis, a piece of cellulose acetate film is placed upon a surface moistened with acetone. The adhesive force developed at the acetate film-acetone-rock surface causes the acetate to "melt" and flow, binding with the rock surface. The acetate actually conforms to the relief of the specimen, thus replicating the microscopic textural and structural detail of the material (Knutsson 1982, 1988; Knutsson and Hope 1984; Kornbacher 1994; Young and Syms 1980). For each area replicated, the peel documents a portion of the wear. The orientation of the peel upon the tool can be reconstructed by means of a small arrow drawn upon the peel together with the scale drawing made of each peel while it is still adhering to the rock surface. Microscopic analyses of identical *macroscopic* wear classes that occur on different objects in similar positions relative to basic design features document variation in character and orientation of wear classes, resulting in a more secure assessment of alternative forms (variants used for the same work), as well as establishing the range of variation in wear of phenotypic variants.

### Identifying the Nature of the Tool-Environment Interaction

Experimental data must be generated to begin the process of identifying the nature of the object-environment interaction, because so little research has been conducted on the formation of wear on groundstone wedge tools. On a very general level, the basic design features of the tools included in this study imply they were constructed for a similar kind of work. The wear data have the potential to help us understand the *specific* nature of the work actually performed by providing information about the nature and direction of applied force, attributes of the body through which the tool moved, and which areas of the object exhibit evidence of different kinds of interaction. Before this potential can be realized, however, experimental work is necessary to clarify the relationship between the physical manifestations of use on groundstone wedge tools and varying aspects of the selective environment. The remainder of this section outlines the experiments designed to meet this objective.

Though wedge-based tools all have a bit working end, a poll, and a body, they may be assigned an array of functional names such as axe, hatchet, splitter, celt, adze, hoe, scraper, and chisel. The three main contextual variables upon which such appellations depend are: 1. the orientation of the tool bit in relation to the handle (if the tool is hafted); 2. the angle formed by the intersection of the bit and the workpiece (the angle of impact); and 3. the nature of the contact material or workpiece. An important aspect of determining the nature of the tool-environment interaction, therefore, involves using experiments to assess the effect that altering these variable values has on the character of the wear formed (Figure 2.6). The results can then be compared to the patterns of wear observed on the archaeological specimens.

Figure 2.6 diagrams the first series of experiments in which tool properties are held constant and conditions of use vary. For example, in Set A, Figure 2.6, tool geometry, raw material, surface roughness, contact material, and applied force are all held constant, and only the angle of impact (between the bit and the workpiece) is varied. This allows us to assess where a change in bit-handle orientation

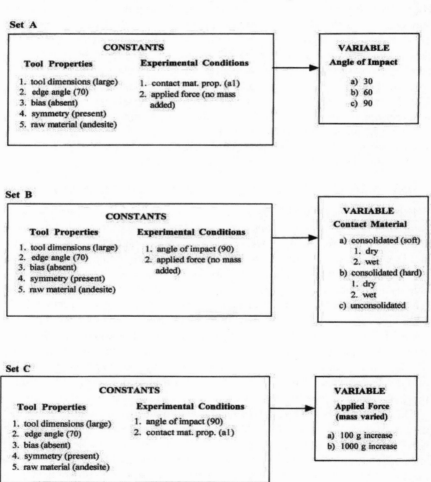

**Figure 2.6. Experiment Series I: Variable Use Conditions: Wear Formation, Performance, and Durability.**

would be effective on the continuum of possible impact angles (cf., Olausson 1983a, 1983b; Steensberg 1980), since the bit-handle relationship cannot be investigated directly. The minimum (30° is the smallest angle practical, given the geometry of the tools and the testing equipment) and maximum (90°) angles between the bit edge and the workpiece are tested first. If a significant difference in the wear formed at these two angles of impact is recorded, then testing continues by adding other impact angles incrementally until the resulting wear patterns contribute no new information.

In the second set of experiments (Set B, Figure 2.6), tool properties, applied force, and angle of impact are held constant, and only the contact material is varied. Again, experiments are initially performed using materials that exhibit grossly different properties (consolidated/unconsolidated; hard/soft). Contact materials with intermediate properties are added and more experiments performed if the initial tests produce significantly different physical manifestations of the interaction. The same strategy is applied in the third experiment set (Set C) illustrated in Figure 2.6, but here tool mass is varied as a means of altering the amount of force applied to the workpiece at impact.

Properties of the tools themselves may also inform on the nature of the tool-environment interaction and aspects of wear formation. The second series of experiments (Series II, Figure 2.7) proceeds in much the same fashion as the first except that in these experiments the conditions of use are held constant and the tool properties varied. In Set A (Figure 2.7), for example, angle of impact, properties of the contact material, amount of applied force, tool geometry, raw material, and surface roughness are all held constant and only the edge angle of the experimental wedge tool is varied. The minimum and maximum values (50° and 90°, respectively) are determined by the artifact data. In Set B, the size of the tool is varied, in Set C, the raw material, and in Set D only bit shape is varied. As for all of the experiments, a minimum of three virtually identical tools are manufactured for each test in a set so error terms can be generated for each outcome. The results of the experiments are analyzed macroscopically and microscopically. On the macroscopic level, a wear analysis is undertaken using the same protocol employed for the museum collections study: a wear map is produced (e.g., Figure 2.5) and wear described using a paradigmatic classification (Table 2.3). The kind and distribution of wear classes are then compared to the kind and distribution of classes documented in the identification of alternative forms among the archaeological specimens.

For microscopic analysis, acetate peels are made of all worn areas of experimental tools that can be replicated. The range of variation within and between experimental groups is documented and the results compared to those generated in the analysis of the archaeological peels. The final results of the macro- and microscopic analyses are expected to: 1. contribute to our knowledge of the nature of tool-environment interactions that produce distinctive traces of wear on groundstone, and 2. enable us to empirically evaluate traditional assumptions about the function of Ecuadorian and Peruvian stone tools termed "axes."

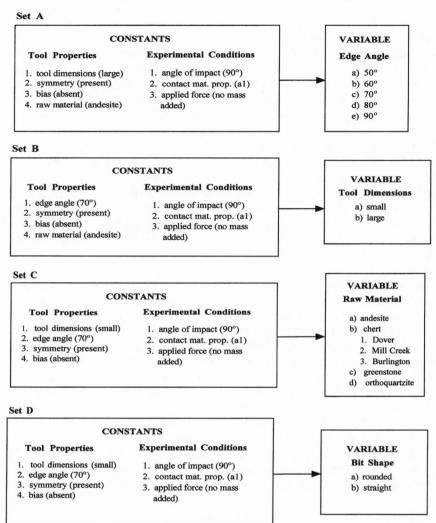

**Figure 2.7. Experiment Series II: Variable Tool Properties: Wear Formation, Performance, and Durability.**

## Cost of Production

As noted previously, cost and performance address different components of the energy required to complete a specific task. Variation in cost and performance during any aspect of tool production and use (raw material discovery, transport, manufacture, use, maintenance, recycling, etc.) provides an opportunity for selection to favor a lower cost variant at the expense of others. However, there are no data currently available on cost of raw material discovery and transport for the manufacture of groundstone wedge tools in northern South America. The cost analysis of this study must therefore be restricted to production activities. Aspects of use that can be evaluated are considered in the discussion of performance that follows.

Costs are incurred during several stages of tool production, including raw material acquisition, raw material transport, and tool manufacturing. The cost of each of these activities depends upon a host of variables. For example, transport costs are dependent upon the distance the material must be moved, the kind of technology available for transporting materials, specific characteristics of the materials being transported, as well as aspects of the environment within which transport occurs, such as topography, number and kind of physical barriers, etc. (Pierce 1993). The more contextual data available to the researcher, the greater the chance of identifying and thoroughly investigating the essential variables upon which various costs depend. For this study, data can be generated to evaluate cost of raw material acquisition and tool production.

### Raw Material Acquisition

Andesite and similar tough volcanic materials were frequently used in the manufacture of groundstone wedge tools prehistorically. Flows of such material have an extremely wide distribution in the Ecuadorian and Peruvian Andes and little lithic provenance research has been undertaken (but see Asaro et al. 1981, Asaro et al. 1994; Burger 1994; Burger and Asaro 1979; Burger et al. 1994; Salazar 1985 for obsidian provenance studies). In addition, andesite is a commonly occurring stone in stream-beds flowing from the western cordillera to the Ecuadorian coast. Thus, identifying the geologic source of raw materials typically used to manufacture groundstone tools would be difficult at best and is currently beyond the scope of this research. It is, however, possible to distinguish tools made from quarried material from those made on materials from secondary sources (such as stream cobbles) if little modification of the original cobble has occurred and/or cortex is detectable. In this manner the archaeological specimens are ranked according to an ordinal scale measure of raw material acquisition cost (cobbles = lower cost, quarried rock = higher cost).

### Tool Production

The cost of manufacturing stone tools depends on three interrelated variables: the reduction technology employed, the degree of morphological complexity, and physical properties of the raw material. Evaluating the production costs of phenotypic variants requires a combination of experimental and artifact analyses to examine each of these variables.

Studies indicate that axes, adzes, and other wedge-based tools are usually made by flaking and grinding, or pecking and grinding, or some combination of these three kinds of reduction (e.g., Clough and Cummins 1979; Dickson 1972, 1981; Mackie 1995; Mills 1987, 1993; Olausson 1983a, 1983b; Sonnenfeld

1962). Preliminary data from the analysis of the museum collections are corroborative: most artifacts are pecked and ground or ground only; some are flaked, pecked, and ground; and some simply flaked. The kind of reduction (grinding, flaking, or pecking) and the number of reduction techniques employed directly affect the cost of production. Few quantitative data have been generated about the cost of pecking versus grinding, although most archaeologists have an intuitive impression that pecking is more time-consuming than grinding, and that both require vastly more time to remove a given amount of material than flaking. Some researchers report direct personal or observational experience on this matter (e.g., Dickson 1972, 1981; Evans 1897; Harding 1987; Hayden 1977, 1979b; McCarthy 1967; Mills 1987; Olausson 1983a, 1983b; Pond 1930; Steensberg 1980), but results are usually described qualitatively or are conducted under non-replicable conditions. Thus, part of the experimental aspect of this study involves generating quantitative data on the cost of different reduction strategies, holding raw material properties constant.

Morphological complexity of the end product is another important aspect of production cost. The degree of complexity of a tool may be a reflection of the work it is designed to do, or it may be a result of factors unrelated to function. Regardless, the more complex the tool form, the higher the production costs, other things being equal. For this study, morphological complexity of the archaeological specimens is measured ordinally by presence or absence of bilateral symmetry in the plan view, number of acute angles, and the number of beveled surfaces, with the assumption that as the number of angles and beveled surfaces or edges increase, production costs also increase. The number of acute angles and the number of planes of symmetry of the artifacts is documented using a paradigmatic classification of shape (Campbell 1981). This information is to be combined with new documentation on the number of beveled surfaces or edges to produce an ordinal measure of morphological complexity.

Properties of the raw materials from which the tools are manufactured have a profound impact on production costs (Dickson 1981; Olausson 1983a, 1983b). The kind of reduction technique(s) used and the relative cost of different techniques depends to a large extent upon the mechanical properties of raw material used in tool manufacture. Hardness (resistance of a material to abrasion or penetration) and fracture toughness (resistance of a material to crack propagation) are the principal variables that have an impact upon cost and also affect the choice of reduction strategies. Thus, the impact of each manufacturing technique on production cost with respect to these two properties is investigated experimentally (Figure 2.8). The artifact data on raw material hardness were generated using a standard Moh's scale and are displayed in Figure 2.4. Although no direct measure of raw material toughness was made of the artifacts, mechanical properties that affect toughness (texture and structure) were described, and an ordinal scale of toughness is derived from those descriptions.

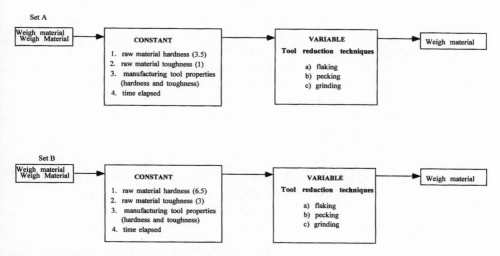

**Figure 2.8. Experiment Series III: Production Cost.**

## Experiments for Evaluating Cost of Production

The Series III technological experiments diagrammed in Figure 2.8 are conducted without the aid of a machine. These experiments are limited in that they test only two different raw materials of varying values of hardness and toughness (andesite and serpentine). For both hardness and toughness, the minimum and maximum values of the artifacts are used to specify the values to be tested to assess the relative cost of different reduction techniques. For example, Experiment Set A assesses the relative cost of grinding, flaking, and pecking (measured in terms of mass removed in a given amount of time) using rocks with a Moh's hardness of 3.5 and a toughness value of 1. In Set B, the same test is conducted using rocks with Moh's hardness of 6.5 and a toughness value of 3, and the results compared. (Moh's 3.5 and 6.5 and toughness 1 and 3 are the minimum and maximum hardness and toughness values represented by the archaeological materials.) Despite the limited number of materials tested, these experiments allow a general assessment of the relative cost of each manufacturing technique. Using the experimental data, together with artifact data on hardness and toughness and on the number and kind of reduction technologies exhibited, an initial production cost value (ordinal level) can be generated for most archaeological variants. Production cost cannot be assessed in this manner for all variants, since some reduction techniques obliterate evidence of others. A tool may be shaped into its initial form by flaking, for example, but subsequent pecking and grinding may eliminate visible indications of flaking.

A separate but important consideration for production costs is the effect of varying physical properties (hardness and toughness) of secondary materials used in the manufacturing process. For example, Dickson (1981:41) notes: "In experiments using slate as a substrate I have found that the task of grinding a basalt head which could have been done in an hour and a half on sandstone took two and a half hours." Thus, the properties of materials used in tool manufacture potentially have a large effect on the production cost. While this cannot be assessed for materials used in the manufacture of the artifacts, the effect of physical properties of the stone used for grinding, the "substrate" stone used in grinding, and the physical properties of the hammer used in pecking or flaking are held constant in the experimental work, since each has a potential impact on the cost of producing tools with different reduction technologies.

## Performance

Within the context of this study, performance is evaluated with respect to two aspects of stone tool use: efficiency and durability. Efficiency refers to the time and energy required by alternative forms to accomplish a given quantity of work, while durability concerns the amount of time alternative forms can be used before maintenance and/or replacement is necessary. Relevant variables for assessing both aspects of performance are determined by definition, design, and experiment. Recall that the operation of wedge tools involves dynamic impact and that mechanical work is defined as the product of the force exerted on a body and the distance it moves in the direction of that force (Cotterell and Kamminga 1992:33). Together with the functional limitations dictated by the basic design features objects must possess to be included in the study, and the results of engineering (ANSI 1980, 1991) and archaeological (Dickson 1981; Kamminga 1978; Mills 1987; Olausson 1983a, 1983b) experiments with wedge tools, these definitions allow identification of tool properties that affect performance efficiency and durability under a range of conditions.

### Efficiency

According to American National Standards Institute engineering publications on safety requirements for hand tools (ANSI 1980:4, 1991:2), wedge tools (axes and hatchets) must have bit cutting edges that are "sufficiently sharp to be used in cutting, notching, splitting, shaping, and trimming wood or wood products." Cutting edges must be parallel to the handle length, and the head of the tool "shall be free of nonfunctional sharp edges, points and surface roughness." Mechanical properties requirements include a hardness (Rockwell) of not less than C45 or more than C60 for a distance of not less than 12.7 mm from the edge. Although these standards are based on results of tests using modern steel axes and hatchets, they are indicative of important attributes of similar stone wedge tools. From the engineering requirements we can deduce, for example, that the bit edge is a functional feature of the artifacts and that important variables are bit sharpness, smoothness, and hardness. In addition to the variables identified from the engineering bulletins, experimental studies performed using tools modeled on artifact materials and dimensions (Crabtree 1974; Dickson 1981; Kamminga 1978; Mills 1987; Olausson 1983a, 1983b; Pond 1930) indicate that tool mass, bilateral symmetry, edge angle (of the bit), and degree of bias or symmetry about the median plane may also affect performance efficiency. Some variables have an impact on tool performance but are aspects of the conditions of use rather than measurable properties of artifacts. These include the angle at which the force is applied to the workpiece, the amount of force applied, and properties of the worked material. The effect of all of these variables on the performance efficiency of archaeological tool variants can be evaluated experimentally.

### Efficiency Experiments

Since efficiency is regarded as the energy required to complete a certain task, it can be assessed in terms of work by measuring the distance a tool moves in the direction of applied force after initial contact with the workpiece (if the contact material is a solid), or by measuring the amount of material displaced (if the contact material is unconsolidated). Using the analyzed prehistoric artifacts to specify the values of each property to be tested, one variable is changed and others are held constant. Any changes in the work accomplished are documented. Figure 2.7 (Series II experiments) illustrates the procedure for evaluating the effect of edge angle (Set A), tool size (Set B), raw material (Set C), and bit shape (Set D) on performance efficiency. These experiments are the same as those conducted for the purpose of understanding wear formation processes, but here the results are evaluated in terms of performance. As before, the minimum and maximum values tested for each variable are those obtained from the initial analysis of the artifacts.

After the completion of each test set, the differences in efficiency are evaluated quantitatively in terms of the amount of work accomplished in a given amount of time. If efficiency measures are the same or similar, the test is considered complete. Significant differences in efficiency measures indicate a greater range of values must be tested to thoroughly document the variability in efficiency of variant forms. In this event, I use the artifact data (e.g., Figures 2.3 and 2.4) to guide the selection of additional values (or range of values), and additional experimental tools exhibiting those values are produced and tested.

A similar strategy is applied to test the effects of different use conditions on the performance efficiency of a given variant (Series I, Figure 2.6), though in this case the value ranges are specified by general design requirements of a wedge rather than values of the artifacts. As described in the section on wear and design analysis, the experiments in Figure 2.6 hold tool properties constant and vary different aspects of the conditions of use, such that a different condition is varied in each experiment set while all other variables remain constant. For example, recall that in the first experiment set in Figure 2.6, the angle of applied force is varied using two extreme value ranges (e.g., 30° and 90°), while other conditions of use (amount of applied force and properties of the contact material) and tool geometry, mass, surface roughness, and raw material are held constant. In Sets B and C (Figure 2.6) contact material and amount of applied force are varied, respectively. If the difference in the amount of work accomplished with a given tool is great, then more tests are conducted across a range of angles and contact materials between these extremes in order to document more fully the range of variation in performance efficiency under certain conditions. Using experiments in this manner enables me to generate quantitative data on the effects of tool properties and use conditions on the time and energy required to accomplish a given amount of work. Since the range of variation of tool properties tested is dictated by the archaeological specimens, the results contribute directly to an understanding of how different artifact forms vary in terms of performance efficiency, given specific conditions of use.

### Durability

Since this research is concerned with work performed under impact conditions (Cotterell and Kamminga 1992:100), an assessment of durability must focus upon properties that affect the capability of an object to withstand stresses that result from dynamic load. Under such conditions, durability is a function of raw material properties (Atkinson 1989; Cotterell and Kamminga 1979, 1992; Crabtree 1974; Goodman 1944; Greiser and Sheets 1979; Kamminga 1982; Lawn and Marshall 1979; Luedtke 1992; Rabinowicz 1995; Semenov 1964; Tsirk 1979) and object geometry (especially edge angle [ANSI 1980, 1991; Dickson 1981]), as well as a number of variables extrinsic to the tools that result from the conditions of use, such as the amount of applied force, the angle of impact, and properties of the contact material (Dickson 1981; Kamminga 1982; Luedtke 1992; Olausson 1983a, 1983b). The interaction of all of these variables affect the amount of time a tool can be used before it must be maintained or replaced, as well as the probability that it will break during manufacture.

#### Resistance to Fracture

Two manifestations of applied force and resulting stresses affect durability—fracture (or breakage) and abrasion. Fracture refers to crack initiation and propagation. Of relevance, then, is the ability of objects to resist fracture under dynamic load. Researchers (Goodman 1944; Greiser and Sheets 1979; ISRM 1988; Kamminga 1982; Luedtke 1992; Tsirk 1979) refer to this aspect of strength as "fracture toughness." Toughness can be measured a number of ways and each is likely to yield a value specific to the technique employed (Atkinson 1989; Greiser and Sheets 1979). Here fracture toughness is defined as the resistance of a material to crack propagation; it is considered a measure of ductility versus brittleness (Greiser and Sheets 1979:294). Materials that break at or near yield stress (the point at which materials become ductile) without inelastic deformation are considered brittle (e.g., obsidian). Materials that are capable of undergoing deformation without breaking are referred to as ductile, or tough (Luedtke 1992:83).

Since wedge tools are subjected to high stress under dynamic load, the raw materials used must be tough, not brittle. The factors that control fracture toughness are varied (Dickson 1981; Greiser and Sheets 1979; Kamminga 1982; Koifman and Senatskaya 1963; Luedtke 1992) and include: 1. the hardness of constituent materials; 2. the presence and proportion of inclusions, voids, pores, fissures, and other structural flaws; 3. grain size and number of grains (e.g., the more grains around which a crack must travel, the tougher the material; the smaller the grains, the tougher the material); and, 4. the orientation of the crystal or granular structure (strength and elasticity increase with more effective interlocking and articulation of the crystals).

Based on this list of factors, the raw material properties classification (Table 2.4) employed during the initial collections analysis is used to develop ordinal toughness measures for the artifacts to determine whether a correlation between toughness and patterns of breakage is indicated. A more direct assessment of the effect of fracture toughness is undertaken experimentally. Raw materials that are used in the manufacture of wedge tools prehistorically but exhibit variable mechanical properties are compared in Experiment Series II, Set C (Figure 2.7). Fracture toughness of each material type is measured directly with a pendulum indenter and durability assessed within the context of each test (Dunnell et al., in prep.).

*Resistance to Abrasion*

Abrasion refers to the removal of material that occurs when a tool edge or surface comes into frictional contact with another surface and/or hard particles (Kamminga 1982:vii) and is another manifestation of applied stress important for evaluating durability. Abrasion removes material from the rock surface by microfracture, through adhesion, and separation of chemical bonds that allows individual molecules to break free (Del Bene 1979; Luedtke 1992; Rabinowicz 1995).

The greater the friction between surfaces or particles, the lower the resistance to abrasion. Friction is a function of a number of factors, including the compatibility of materials that come into contact (how similar they are), the amount of applied force, and the presence or absence of lubricants (Bowden and Tabor 1954; Kim and Suh 1991; Rabinowicz 1995). In work involving stone tools, friction may be greatly increased by sand or smaller-sized particles that adhere to the worked material and/or by small particles or flakes that are detached from the contact surfaces of the tool (Kamminga 1979:151). Important raw material properties affecting the value of friction and thus resistance to abrasion are surface roughness and hardness (Rabinowicz 1995:198). Hardness as a measure of resistance to abrasion depends not only on the properties of constituent materials, but also on the degree of bonding between the grains. Materials composed of small ions with high electrical charges that can be packed tightly have a greater resistance to abrasion (Luedtke 1992:91). Surface roughness is a variable property of unmodified stone surfaces, but is also a result of technological processes, such as grinding and polishing. For this study, artifact roughness values are derived from interferometer analysis of the acetate peels.

**Table 2.4**
**Paradigmatic Raw Materials Classification (based on McCutcheon 1997 and Thorpe and Brown 1993)**

---

**Dimension I. Grain Size**
*fine-grained:* few or no crystal boundaries distinguishable with the aid of a 10X handlens: mean grain size <1mm
*medium-grained:* most crystal boundaries distinguishable with the aid of a 10X handlens; mean grain size = 1-5mm
*coarse-grained:* virtually all crystal boundaries distinguishable with the naked eye; mean grain size >5mm

**Dimension II. Structure**
*uniform:* a consistent and unvarying color, texture, and/or luster
*bedding planes:* linear striae superimposed upon and/or parallel to one another; individual striae may be distinct in color and/or texture
*concentric banding:* concentric layers of varying color and/or texture
*mottled:* abrupt and uneven variations in color (e.g., swirled or clouded) or texture
*oolitic:* the matrix is composed of small round or ovoid shaped grains

**Dimension III. Solid Inclusions (particles distinct from the rock groundmass)**
*present*
*absent*

**Dimension IV. Void Inclusions (cavities or cracks devoid of material)**
*present*
*absent*

**Dimension V. Distribution of Solid Inclusions**
*random:* distribution is irregular with no discernible pattern
*uniform:* the distribution is unvarying and homogeneous throughout the rock body
*structured:* the distribution is patterned or isolated within the rock body
*none:* inclusions are absent

**Dimension VI. Distribution of Void Inclusions**
*random:* distribution is irregular with no discernible pattern
*uniform:* the distribution is unvarying and homogeneous throughout the rock body
*structured:* the distribution is patterned or isolated within the rock body
*none:* inclusions are absent

---

Based on these data and the raw materials analysis of the artifacts, an ordinal measure of "abrasion resistance" is determined for each artifact and combines Moh's hardness with measures of surface roughness, grain size, and structure. For an experimental assessment of the effect of these variables on surface roughness, a single experiment set (Figure 2.7, Set C) is undertaken in which raw materials are varied while all other variables are held constant. In addition to the ordinal measure of abrasion resistance, all materials are tested using a pendulum indenter to derive an interval-scale measure of fracture toughness (Dunnell et al., in prep.).

*Other Properties Affecting Durability*

Since wedge tools work by impact upon the workpiece and are subjected to a great deal of stress, the bit edge must be robust to be durable (Dickson 1981; Hayden 1979b; Olausson 1983a, 1983b; Sonnenfeld 1962). Thus edge angle and bit surface area affect the amount of time a tool can be used before it must be maintained or replaced. Variables specific to the context of use that have an impact on durability are the properties of the contact material and the introduction of lubricants (e.g., water, grease, or other fluids) or sediment into the system (Kamminga 1979; Rabinowicz 1995), the amount of applied force, duration of use, and the angle of impact. The values of abrasion resistance and fracture toughness and geometric aspects of the tool measured to assess durability also interact with similar properties of the contact material. Since these variables may also affect the amount of work that can be accomplished in a given amount of time, the experiments overlap with those designed for evaluating performance efficiency, as displayed in Figures 2.6 and 2.7. In a manner similar to the previous experiments, the first values tested in each set are the minimum and maximum values dictated by the artifacts. If significant differences in durability are documented between minimum and maximum values, a greater range of values is tested to ensure that the variation in durability of variant artifact forms is represented and can be thoroughly assessed.

## DISTRIBUTIONAL ANALYSIS

Distributional models are used to test the hypotheses derived from the engineering analysis concerning which aspects of phenotypic variation are explicable in terms of natural selection (function) and which sorted by transmission processes alone (style). Functional traits under selection have a distribution that is predictable in a general sense over time: the frequency increases rapidly once the feature comes under selection and then continues to increase at a decelerating rate until it reaches an asymptote. By contrast, the frequency distribution of stylistic traits is distinctively stochastic in the temporal dimension (Dunnell and Feathers 1991; O'Brien and Holland 1990). Because stylistic traits reflect homologous aspects of the phenotype that result from a single historical system of information transmission, their frequency distributions display a monotonic pattern over time, often referred to by archaeologists as a battleship-shaped (lenticular) curve (e.g., Dunnell 1970, 1978b, 1980, 1982; Hunt et al. 1995; Jones et al. 1995; Lipo et al. 1997; Neiman 1995; Teltser 1995).

Descriptions of the spatial distribution of phenotypic traits can also aid in the differentiation of functional and stylistic aspects of variation. From evolutionary theory, we expect the distribution of functional traits across space to correlate with changes in proximate ecological relations (Jones et al. 1995), "map on" to specific environments, or be tightly associated with particular environmental variables. If, for example, the engineering analysis indicates significant variation in the cost and/or performance values of alternative forms, we can hypothesize that the variable trait is functional. If the distributional data do not display non-random patterns in the spatial and temporal dimensions, the hypothesis is falsified. On the other hand, if no significant differences in engineering parameters are documented, and we hypothesize that the trait is stylistic, its distribution should display a monotonic pattern over time. Traits may be pleiotropic if no significant differences in relative cost and performance are discerned, yet the spatial and temporal distributions mirror those of a documented functional trait.

In addition to providing a test of hypotheses about whether variation is sorted by natural selection or stochastic processes, the distributions can be used to test additional hypotheses about the spatial and temporal occurrence of alternative forms. For example, I might hypothesize based on the results of the engineering analysis that objects exhibiting a particular suite of formal attributes are correlated with a particular environmental variable, such as altitude or soil type. The distributional data from the collections analysis can be used as an initial test. In the event that such hypotheses are not falsified, they can be tested more extensively as other collections become available for analysis. If hypotheses about the functional nature of attributes are not falsified, changes in the frequencies of functional attributes over time can be examined with respect to different aspects of the archaeology, environmental history, and regional ecology to begin the process of constructing explanations for the changes observed. Changes in frequencies of stylistic attributes over time will be examined to try and develop an understanding of the homologous relations between archaeological variants. Advances in this direction will be used to evaluate the veracity of assumptions about the equation of certain artifact forms with interaction (information transmission) between human populations of different environments.

## PRELIMINARY ASSESSMENT OF THE RESEARCH DESIGN

The research design developed in the preceding pages cannot be thoroughly evaluated without a full presentation of the results of its application. Obviously, such a presentation is beyond the scope and objective of this work (Hunt, Lipo, Sterling, this volume). However, an example of a portion of the work and findings should demonstrate that the research design is consistent with Bettinger and Richardson's (1996:223) call for paradigmatic case studies that address "real data" within the larger conceptual structure of evolutionary theory, and will, I hope, also illustrate the value of such an approach.

One aspect of the variation of wedge tool morphology documented while studying Ecuadorian collections is bit shape (Figure 2.9). Some of the artifacts examined have rounded bits while others form an angle (usually 90° or less) with the sides of the body. In the terms outlined in this study, is this a functional or stylistic attribute? Artifacts of otherwise similar morphology (e.g., T-shaped provision for hafting as in Figure 2.9a and 2.9b) exhibit differences in bit shape. Can

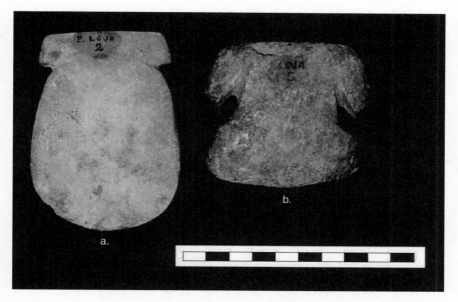

**Figure 2.9. T-shaped tools from the collection of Emil Estrada, Banco Central del Ecuador, Guayaquil. Note variation in bit shape.**

we conclude, therefore, that this is a stylistic attribute which, used in conjunction with other neutral traits, can be used to trace ancestor-descendent relations or document interregional interaction? Looking into the matter further, it becomes apparent that some artifacts with different bit shapes are *dissimilar* with respect to other aspects of their morphology (Figure 2.10). Bit shape is an aspect of the tool usually regarded as the "business end," an assessment supported by ethnographic observations, consideration of engineering-design constraints, and documentation of chipping and abrasive wear concentrated on this area of the tool. Perhaps it is reasonable to assume the attribute bit shape is functional since it is an aspect of the bit. Can we safely conclude on this basis, then, that tools with different bit shapes were actually used for different tasks?

The first step in answering these questions is to assess in a preliminary fashion whether objects that exhibit variation in bit shape are "alternative forms" or phenotypic variants in the terms of this study (see pp. 39–43). Using contextual, design, use-wear, and engineering data, I attempt to falsify the hypothesis that the objects are alternative forms. Both of the objects depicted in Figure 2.10 are from Salango, on the coast of Ecuador, both are cataloged and referred to as axes, or "hachas." Figure 2.10a is from an excavated context, and the larger object (Figure 2.10b) was surface-collected nearby. Thus the distribution of the objects does not in itself imply functional differences. Information about the Salango excavation (Lunniss 1985; Norton et al. 1983) indicates that the excavated artifact is

**Figure 2.10. Wedge tools from Salango, Ecuador. Note variation in bit shape: a) relatively straight; b) relatively rounded.**

probably associated with a residential structure, but no information is available about the tool depicted in Figure 2.10b. Beyond this general level of information (insufficient for falsifying the hypothesis), there are no data about the use-contexts of the tools.

Turning to the tools themselves for a means of assessing whether these objects are alternative variants, the morphology of the bit in cross section is examined. However, both objects are symmetrical about the median plane (Dickson 1981), a feature indicative of similar functional designs. In addition, there is a difference of only 8° in the edge angles. While this may be important from an engineering standpoint (Kornbacher 1999, in prep.), it is a small difference in terms of the range of angles represented by the artifacts, certainly not sufficient in itself to falsify the hypothesis that the artifacts are alternative variants. In this case, neither can the question be resolved by examining the character and distribution of wear. Both tools exhibit the same class of wear, multidirectional abrasion striations occurring on multiple surfaces, including the bit. The nature and distribution of the striations indicates that these features are caused by grinding during manufacturing, rather than during use of the objects. No other wear traces were observed on either tool microscopically that might inform on use context or the importance of bit shape. At this point, it might seem reasonable to conclude that variation in bit shape, ranging from straight to extremely rounded or cambered, is a stylistic attribute and can be used as a temporal marker at Salango and elsewhere.

Prior to drawing any conclusions of this nature, however, the engineering analysis is undertaken to investigate the particular attribute of bit shape, as outlined in the research design. Bit shape is initially examined at two extremes: highly cambered and straight. Figure 2.7, Set D specifies the use conditions and tool properties that are held constant while the two values of bit shape are tested. Under these experimental conditions, variation observed in the accumulation of wear and durability of the tools can be attributed to differences in bit shape. An analysis of variance (one-way ANOVA) of the results (Table 2.5) of weight loss of the experimental tools after 400 impacts shows a significant difference between the tools with camber and those with straight bit edges. In addition, the tendency of the straight-edged tools to develop camber through attrition of the bit is rather strikingly apparent as illustrated in Figure 2.11. The upper portion of this figure (Figure 2.11a) depicts the edge of a 70° experimental tool prior to testing. After 200 impacts, many of the straight-edged tools exhibit camber (e.g., Figure 2.11b). These findings indicate that within the context (given amount of applied force, angle of impact, and contact material) of the experiments, a cambered bit shape is selectively advantageous.

Can we generalize from this example and claim that all variation in bit shape is functional? No, obviously not. Then what have we learned? We know that a straight bit used at a 90° angle on a soft wood with dynamic impact of a given

**Table 2.5**
**ANOVA (Single Factor Analysis of Variance) of the Effect of Bit of Shape on Weight Loss (after 400 impacts)**

ANOVA: Single Factor
   SUMMARY

| Bit Shape Category | Count | Sum (Total Wt Loss) | Average | Variance |
|---|---|---|---|---|
| Straight | 3 | 0.9730 | 0.3243 | 0.0259 |
| Rounded | 3 | 0.1260 | 0.0420 | 0.0001 |

| Source of Variation | SS | df | MS | F | P-value | F crit |
|---|---|---|---|---|---|---|
| Between Groups | 0.1196 | 1 | 0.1196 | 9.1953 | 0.0387 | 7.7087 |
| Within Groups | 0.0520 | 4 | 0.0130 | | | |
| Total | 0.1716 | 5 | | | | |

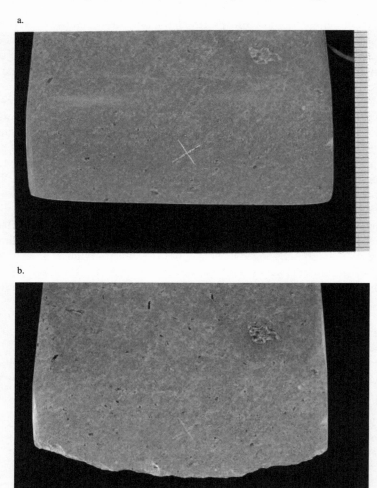

**Figure 2.11. Illustrates change in bit shape of 70-degree experimental tool from straight (a, after 0 impacts) to rounded (b, after 200 impacts).**

force would not stay straight for long. Thus, we know that if the wedge tool in Figure 2.10b was used, it was not used under these kinds of conditions. With the engineering data in hand, we can say with some assurance that the objects from Salango depicted in Figure 2.10 have a low probability of being alternative variants used for the same work. We have a sound basis for forwarding the hypothesis that bit shape is a functional or non-neutral attribute.

Before much more can be said, however, we need to understand other aspects of the design and morphology that interact with bit shape. Experiments that document a full range of variation (rather than simply the effects of the extreme values) must be undertaken to assess the engineering implications of this variable. A variety of use conditions must be introduced to see whether the effects of bit shape observed initially with extreme values persist when the tools are tested at different angles of impact using different contact materials. Once it is understood how bit shape articulates with other variables (such as edge angle, tool mass, raw material, and poll design), we can examine the distributions of suites of attributes in time and space to begin to understand the evolutionary history of these objects.

The actual use-histories of stone wedge tools are complex and cumulative phenomena. That is, the tools are durable, apparently designed to sustain many impacts and to be used over long periods of time. Confounding aspects of study include the fact that resharpening may obliterate traces of previous use and significantly alter tool morphology (DeBoer 1998). And, the function of the tools may actually change over the life-span of the tool. This may in fact be the case with the tools illustrated in Figure 2.9. The wear patterns of these wedge tools differ quantitatively but not in terms of character and distribution. Thus, it is likely that tools a and b depicted in Figure 2.9 may have exhibited a more similar bit shape at an earlier point in the use history of artifact b in Figure 2.9. In this case, variation in bit shape may reflect a change in function over the life of the tool.

It is apparent that in answering one question about the nature of a particular attribute of wedge tools, I have raised many others and identified paths for further work. This is an outcome that characterizes nearly all of the findings of this work so far. However, because it is theoretically derived, the research design outlined in these pages easily accommodates new questions and the testing procedures required to answer them. Within such a framework the work can continue, building a cumulative product and increasing our understanding beyond the accomplishments of a single researcher. As so eloquently expressed by Robert Dunnell (pers. comm.), "If it doesn't lead to other questions, it's not worth doing."

## CONCLUDING REMARKS

### Substantive Potential

It is no doubt the case that if pressed on the general issue, most archaeologists would not say they assume a *single* use for wedge tools. Nevertheless, studies that specifically identify various wedge tools as "axes" and interpret their prehistoric function as land-clearing in the complete absence of supporting functional data are common worldwide (e.g., Care 1979; Coles 1979; Metraux 1952; Morris 1939; Petrequin and Jeunesse 1995). The objects studied here (and in DeBoer's [1998] recent work) are variable in terms of morphology, size, and edge angle (e.g., Figures 2.3 and 2.4) and display a complex array of wear patterns. Laying the foundation for constructing explanations of such variation is the major goal of this work. Using use-wear, design, engineering, and distributional analyses within an evolutionary framework enables the initial distinction of functional, stylistic, and pleiotropic attributes among artifact variants, and generates an empirical means of investigating traditional assumptions about the prehistoric function and history of groundstone tools. Developing an understanding about how different forms were actually used in different environmental contexts and tracing the historical relations between variant artifact forms will have a substantial impact on traditional interpretations of wedge tools and their role in South American prehistory.

## Methodological Potential

It is now widely accepted that using the physical manifestations of use (use-wear) to study the function of stone tools involves generating experimental data that inform on the processes, motions, and materials that lead to the formation of wear. For chipped stone tools made of brittle materials, a large body of such experimental work exists. The study of wear on groundstone tools manufactured from tough stone, however, is in its infancy. Sufficient data are not available in the extant literature to impart an understanding of the relations between various motions and materials for which wedge tools are used and the characteristic traces left by such work. Through the program of controlled experimentation outlined in the previous pages, these data are being generated.

Archaeologists interested in stone tool function have typically rejected the use of mechanical testing for wear studies (e.g., Dickson 1981; Keeley 1980; Mackie 1995; Vaughan 1985; see articles in Hayden 1979c; Pelcin 1997a, 1997b for exceptions). Instead, most experimental designs attempt to replicate unknowable aspects of prehistoric conditions or behavior by incorporating more "human" variables into the work. This general tendency is exemplified by Lawrence Keeley's (1980:15) description of an aspect of his own design: "Many of the experiments were done with dirty hands, since the ancient users of these tools were unlikely to wash their hands once a week, let alone several times a day."

Since it is simply not possible to duplicate the exact conditions under which prehistoric tools were used, adherence to a reconstructionist agenda has hindered the development of a program of controlled experimentation in which the effects of different variables can be evaluated quantitatively. We have the tools to accomplish this at hand—we can employ the laws of physics. Unlike historically contingent behaviors and conditions, such laws are time-transgressive, as true now as they were in the prehistoric past (Dunnell 1980, 1992). As long as we are committed to retaining the "human" element in our experiments, however, we will be unable to control for such (controllable) variables as the amount of applied force or the angle of impact. Consequently, we will be unable to evaluate the effects that such variables may have had on the formation of wear patterns prehistorically.

Developing an effective experimental program for the engineering study of wedge tools and beginning to generate a widely applicable data base are the primary methodological goals this study is designed to address. They have the potential to advance the study of artifact function by increasing our knowledge of the processes of wear formation *and* our ability to identify specific kinds of work from physical traces on groundstone artifacts.

The results of the engineering analyses, together with the documentation of trait distributions in time and space, form the foundation upon which evolutionary narratives are constructed (Lipo and Madsen 1998; O'Hara 1988). As more engineering and distribution data are generated and used in concert, we will be able to build this kind of narrative and begin to develop an understanding of the evolutionary history of wedge tools and the people who made and used them in northern South America.

## REFERENCES CITED

American National Standards Institute, Inc. (ANSI)
    1980    American National Standard Safety Requirements for Hatchets. B173.7:1–8.
    1991    American National Standard Safety Requirements for Hand Tools—Axes. HTI B173.4:1–12.
Asaro, F., E. Salazar, H. V. Michel, R. L. Burger, and F. Stross
    1994    Ecuadorian Obsidian Sources Used for Artifact Production and Methods for Provenience Assignment. *Latin American Antiquity* 5:257–277.
Asaro, F. H., W. Michel, and R. L. Burger
    1981    *Major Sources of Archaeological Obsidian and Provenience Assignment of Artifacts.* Technical Information Department, Lawrence Berkeley Laboratory, University of California Berkeley, No. LBL-13246, 1981, Berkeley.
Atkinson, B. K. (Editor)
    1989    *Fracture Mechanics of Rock.* Academic Press Geology Series. Academic Press, San Diego.
Bettinger, R. L. and P. J. Richerson
    1996    The State of Evolutionary Archaeology: Evolutionary Correctness, or The Search for the Common Ground. In *Darwinian Archaeologies*, edited by H. D. G. Maschner, pp. 221–231. Plenum Press, New York.
Binning, J. D.
    1991    *Microscarring on Flaked-Stone Objects.* Ph.D. Dissertation, Department of Anthropology, University of California Riverside, Riverside.
Bowden, F. P. and D. Tabor
    1954    *The Friction and Lubrication of Solids.* Clarendon Press, Oxford.
Burger, R. L.
    1992    *Chavin and the Origins of Andean Civilization.* Thames and Hudson, London.
Burger, R. L. and F. Asaro
    1979    Analisis de rasgos significativos en la obsidiana de los Andes Centrales. *Revista del Museo Nacional* 43:281–325.
Burger, R. L., F. Asaro, H. V. Michel, F. H. Stross, and E. Salazar
    1994    An Initial Consideration of Obsidian Procurement and Exchange in Prehispanic Ecuador. *Latin American Antiquity* 5:228–255.
Campbell, S. K.
    1981    *The Duwamish No. 1 Site: A Lower Puget Sound Shell Midden.* University of Washington Office of Public Archaeology, Seattle.

Care, V.
1979 The Production and Distribution of Mesolithic Axes in Southern England. *Proceedings of the Prehistoric Society* 45:93–102.

Carneiro, R. L.
1961 Slash-and-Burn Cultivation Among the Kuikuru and its Implications for Cultural Development in the Amazon Basin. In *The Evolution of Horticultural Systems in Native South America*, edited by J. Wilbert, pp. 46–67. Fundacion La Salle de Ciencias Naturales, Caracas.
1974 On the Use of the Stone Axe by the Amahuaca Indians of Eastern Peru. *Ethnologische Zeitschrift Zurich* 1:107–122.
1979a Tree Felling with the Stone Ax: An Experiment Carried Out Among the Yanomamo Indians of Southern Venezuela. In *Ethnoarcheology: Implication of Ethnography for Archeology*, edited by C. Kramer, pp. 21–58. Columbia University Press, New York.
1979b Forest Clearance Among the Yanomamo, Observations and Implications. *Antropologica* 52:39–76.

Clough, T. H. M. and W. A. Cummins (Editors)
1979 *Stone Axe Studies: Archaeological, Petrological, Experimental, and Ethnographic*. Research Report No. 23. Council for British Archaeology, London.

Cole, J. R.
1977 *Stone Tools from Ceramic Period Cultures of Southwest Ecuador*. Ph.D. Dissertation, Department of Anthropology, Columbia University.
1983 Lithic Evidence for Trans-Andean Contact in Preceramic South America. In *Archaeological Investigations in Peru, Selected Papers I*, Occasional Publications in Anthropology Archaeology Series No. 17. Museum of Anthropology, University of Northern Colorado, Greeley, Colorado.

Coles, J.
1979 An Experiment with Stone Axes. In *Stone Axe Studies: Archaeological, Petrological, Experimental, and Ethnographic*, edited by T. H. M. Clough and W. A. Cummins, pp. 106–107. Research Report No. 23. Council for British Archaeology, London.

Cook, J. and J. Dumont
1987 The Development and Application of Microwear Analysis Since 1964. In *The Human Uses of Flint and Chert: Proceedings of the Fourth International Flint Symposium Held at Brighton Polytechnic 10–15 April 1983*, edited by G. d. G. Sieveking, G. and M. H. Newcomer, pp. 53–62. Cambridge University Press, Cambridge.

Cotterell, B. and J. Kamminga
1979 The Mechanics of Flaking. In *Lithic Use-Wear Analysis*, edited by B. Hayden, pp. 97–112. Academic Press, New York.
1992 *Mechanics of Preindustrial Technology*. Cambridge University Press, Cambridge.

Crabtree, D. E.
1974 Grinding and Smoothing of Stone Artifacts. *Tebiwa* 17:1–6.

Dawkins, R.
1990 *The Extended Phenotype: The Long Reach of the Gene*. New edition. Oxford University Press, Oxford.

DeBoer, W. R.

1998 *Axes of Variability in the Upper Amazon.* The 1998 Emeriti Lecture in Honor of Professor John H. Rowe, Depart of Anthropology, The University of California at Berkeley, Berkeley.

Del Bene, T. A.

1979 Once Upon a Striation: Current Models of Striation and Polish Formation. In *Lithic Use-Wear Analysis*, edited by B. Hayden, pp. 167–177. Academic Press, New York.

Denevan, W.

1974 Campa Subsistence in the Gran Pajonal, Eastern Peru. In *Native South Americans: Ethnology of the Least Known Continent*, edited by P. J. Lyon, pp. 91–110. Little, Brown, and Company, Boston.

1993 Stone vs. Metal Axes: The Ambiguity of Shifting Cultivation in Prehistoric Amazonia. *Journal of the Steward Anthropological Society* 20(1–2):153–165.

Dickson, F. P.

1972 Ground Edge Axes. *Mankind* 8:206–211.

1981 *Australian Stone Hatchets: A Study in Design and Dynamics.* Academic Press, Sydney.

Drachmann, A. G.

1963 *The Mechanical Technology of Greek and Roman Antiquity: A Study of the Literary Sources.* Munksgaard, Copenhagen.

Dunnell, R. C. and D. Lewarch

1970 Seriation Method and Its Evaluation. *American Antiquity* 35:305–319.

1971 *Systematics in Prehistory.* Free Press, New York.

1974 *Archaeological Remains in Home Valley Park, Skamania County, Washington.* Portland U.S. Army Corps of Engineers, Portland, Oregon.

1978a Archaeological Potential of Anthropological and Scientific Models of Function in Archaeology. In *Archaeological Essays in Honor of Irving B. Rouse*, edited by J. R. C. Dunnell and E. S. Hall, pp. 41–73. Mouton, The Hague.

1978b Style and Function: A Fundamental Dichotomy. *American Antiquity* 43:192–202.

1980 Evolutionary Theory and Archaeology. In *Advances in Archaeological Method and Theory*, edited by M. B. Schiffer, pp. 35–99. Academic Press, New York.

1982 Science, Social Science, and Common Sense: The Agonizing Dilemma of Modern Archaeology. *Journal of Anthropological Research* 38:1–25.

1983 Aspects of the Spatial Structure of the Mayo Site (15-JO-14), Johnson County, Kentucky. In *Lulu Linear Punctated: Essays in Honor of George Irving Quimby*, edited by R. C. Dunnell and D. K. Grayson, pp. 109–165. Anthropological Papers, No. 72. Museum of Anthropology, University of Michigan, Ann Arbor.

1989 Aspects of the Application of Evolutionary Theory in Archaeology. In *Archaeological Thought in America*, edited by C. C. Lamberg-Karlovsky, pp. 35–49. Cambridge University Press, Cambridge.

1992 Archaeology and Evolutionary Science. In *Quandries and Quests: Visions of Archaeology's Future*, edited by L. Wandsnider, pp. 209–224. Center for Archaeological Investigations, Occasional Paper No. 20. Board of Trustees, Southern Illinois University, St. Louis.

Dunnell, R. C., K. D. Kornbacher, and A. M. Araujo

In prep. Raw Material Physical Properties and the Effect on Groundstone Wedge Tools. (Manuscript.)

Dunnell, R. C. and S. K. Campbell
  1977  *Aboriginal Occupation of Hamilton Island, Washington.* University of Washington Department of Anthropology Reports in Archaeology No. 4. Department of Anthropology, University of Washington, Seattle.

Dunnell, R. C. and J. K. Feathers
  1991  Late Woodland Manifestations of the Malden Plain, Southeast Missouri. In *The Late Woodland Southeast*, edited by N. S. Nassaney and C. R. Cobb, pp. 21–45. Plenum Press, New York.

Dunnell, R. C. and C. Beck
  1979  *The Caples Site, 45-SA-5, Skamania County, Washington.* University of Washington Reports in Archaeology No. 6. University of Washington, Department of Anthropology, Seattle.

Evans, J.
  1897  *The Ancient Stone Weapons and Ornaments of Great Britain (2nd ed.).* Longmans, London.

Feathers, J. K.
  1990  *An Evolutionary Explanation for Prehistoric Ceramic Change in Southeast Missouri.* Ph.D. Dissertation, Dept. of Anthropology, University of Washington, Seattle.

Gijn, A. L. V.
  1990  *The Wear and Tear of Flint: Principles of Microwear Analysis Applied to Dutch Neolithic Assemblages.* Analecta Praehistorica Leidensia 22. University of Leiden, Leiden.

Goodman, M. E.
  1944  The Physical Properties of Stone Tool Materials. *American Antiquity* 9:415–433.

Gorman, F. J. E.
  1979  An Inventory System Perspective of Groundstone Artifact Use-Wear at the Joint Site. In *Lithic Use-Wear Analysis*, edited by B. Hayden, pp. 39–56. Academic Press, New York.

Greiser, S. T. and P. D. Sheets
  1979  Raw Materials as a Functional Variable in Use-Wear Studies. In *Lithic Use-Wear Analysis*, edited by B. Hayden, pp. 289–296. Academic Press, New York.

Harding, P.
  1987  An Experiment to Produce a Ground Flint Axe. In *The Human Uses of Flint and Chert: Proceedings of the Fourth International Flint Symposium Held at Brighton Polytechnic 10–15 April 1983*, edited by G. Sieveking and M. H. Newcomer, pp. 37–42. University of Cambridge Press, Cambridge.

Harding, A. and R. Young
  1979  Reconstruction of the Hafting Methods and Function of Stone Implements. In *Stone Axe Studies: Archaeological, Petrological, Experimental, and Ethnographic*, edited by T. H. M. Clough, pp. 102–105. Research Report No. 23. Council for British Archaeology, London.

Hayden, B.
  1977  Sticks and Stones and Ground Edge Axes: The Upper Paleolithic in South East Asia? In *Sunda and Sahul: Prehistoric Studies in Southeast Asia, Melanesia, and Australia*, edited by J. G. J. Allen and R. Jones, pp. 73–109. Academic Press, New York.

1979a Snap, Shatter, and Superfractures: Use-Wear of Stone Skin Scrapers. In *Lithic Use-Wear Analysis*, edited by B. Hayden, pp. 207–230. Academic Press, New York.

1979b *Palaeolithic Reflections: Lithic Technology and Ethnographic Excavations Among Australian Aborigines.* Australian Institute of Aboriginal Studies, Canberra, Australia. Humanities Press Inc., New Jersey.

Hayden, B. (Editor)

1979c *Lithic Use-Wear Analysis.* Academic Press, New York.

Hull, D.

1965 The Effect of Essentialism on Taxonomy—2000 Years of Stasis. *British Journal for the Philosophy of Science* 15:314–326; 16:1–18.

1978 A Matter of Individuality. *Philosophy of Science* 45:335–360.

Hunt, T., M. Madsen, and C. Lipo

1995 Examining Cultural Transmission Using Frequency Seriation. Paper presented at the 60th Annual Meeting of the Society for American Archaeology, Minneapolis.

ISRM Commission on Testing Methods

1988 Suggested Methods for Determining the Fracture Toughness of Rock. *International Journal of Rock Mechanics, Mineral Science, and Geomechanics Abstracts* 25:71–96.

Izumi, S. and T. Sono

1963 *Andes 2: Excavations at Kotosh, Peru, 1960.* Kadokawa Publishing Company, Tokyo.

Izumi, S. and K. Terada

1971 *Excavations at Kotosh, Peru. A Report on the Third and Fourth Expeditions 1963–1966.* University of Tokyo Press, Tokyo.

Jensen, H. J.

1988 Functional Analysis of Prehistoric Flint Tools by High-Power Microscopy: A Review of West European Research. *Journal of World Prehistory* 2(1):53–88.

Jones, G. T., R. D. Leonard, and A. L. Abott

1995 The Structure of Selectionist Explanations in Archaeology. In *Evolutionary Archaeology: Methodological Issues*, edited by P. A. Teltser, pp. 13–32. University of Arizona Press, Tucson.

Jørgensen, S.

1953 Forest Clearance with Stone Axes. *Fra Nationalmuseets Arbejdsmark* 109-10:36–43.

Kamminga, J.

1978 *Journey into the Microcosms: A Functional Study of Certain Classes of Prehistoric Australian Stone Tools.* Unpublished Ph.D. Dissertation, University of Sydney, Sidney.

1979 The Nature of Use-Polish and Abrasive Smoothing on Stone Tools. In *Lithic Use-Wear Analysis*, edited by B. Hayden, pp. 143–157. Academic Press, New York.

1982 *Over the Edge: Functional Analysis of Australian Stone Tools.* Occasional Papers in Anthropology. Anthropology Museum, University of Queensland, Queensland.

Keeley, L. H.

1980 *Experimental Determination of Stone Tools: A Microwear Analysis.* University of Chicago Press, Chicago.

Keller, C. M.

1966 The Development of Edge Damage Patterns in Stone Tools. *Man* 1:501–511.

Kim, D. E. and N. P. Suh
   1991   On Microscopic Mechanisms of Friction and Wear. *Wear* 149:199–208.
Kimura, M.
   1983   *The Neutral Theory of Molecular Evolution.* Cambridge University Press, Cambridge.
Knutsson, K.
   1982   *Analysis and Documentation of Use-Wear: Two Experiments Using Acetate Peels.* B.A. Thesis, Institute of Archaeology, University of Uppsala, Uppsala.
   1988   *Patterns of Tool Use: Scanning Electron Microscopy of Experimental Quartz Tools.* AUN 10. Societas Archaeologica Upsaliensis, Uppsala.
Knutsson, K. and R. Hope
   1984   The Application of Acetate Peels in Lithic Usewear Analysis. *Archaeometry* 26:49–61.
Koifman, M. I. and G. S. Senatskaya
   1963   Elementary Fracture and Mineralogical and Petrographical Peculiarities of Rocks. In *Mechanical Properties of Rocks*, edited by M. M. Protod'yakonov and M. I. Koifman, pp. 101–108. Academy of Science of the U.S.S.R., Israel Program for Scientific Translation, Jerusalem.
Kornbacher, K. D.
   1994   *Acetate Peels and Functional Analysis: A Replicative Technique for the Study of Wear on Ground Stone.* Department of Anthropology, University of Washington, Seattle.
   1995   Axes as Indicators of Agriculture and Interregional Interaction: Evaluating the Empirical Evidence. Paper Presented at the 60th Annual Meeting of the Society for American Archaeology, Minneapolis.
   1999   The Role of Controlled Experiments in Archaeology: An Example Using Groundstone. Poster Presented at the 64th Annual Meeting of the Society for American Archaeology, Chicago.
   In prep.   The Effect of Edge Angle on the Performance and Durability of Wedge Tools. Manuscript.
Lathrap, D. W.
   1962   *Yarinacocha: Stratigraphic Excavations in the Peruvian Montana.* Unpublished Ph.D. Dissertation, Dept. of Anthropology, Harvard University.
   1970   *The Upper Amazon.* Thames and Hudson, Southampton.
   1973   Gifts of the Cayman: Some Thoughts on the Subsistence Basis of Chavín. In *Variation in Anthropology: Essays in Honor of John C. McGregor,* edited by D. W. Lathrap and J. Douglas, pp. 91–105. Illinois Archaeological Survey, Urbana.
Lathrap, D. W., D. Collier, and H. Chandra.
   1975   *Ancient Ecuador: Culture, Clay, and Creativity 3000–300 B.C.* Field Museum of Natural History, Chicago.
Lawn, B. R. and D. B. Marshall
   1979   Mechanisms of Microcontact Fracture in Brittle Solids. In *Lithic Use-Wear Analysis*, edited by B. Hayden, pp. 63–82. Academic Press, New York.
Leechman, D.
   1950   Aboriginal Tree-Felling. *National Museum of Canada Bulletin* 118:44–49.
Leonard, R. D. and G. T. Jones
   1987   Elements of an Inclusive Evolutionary Model for Archaeology. *Journal of Anthropological Archaeology* 6:199–219.

Lewontin, R. C.
1970   The Units of Selection. *Annual Review of Ecology and Systematics* 1:1–18.
Lipo, C. and M. E. Madsen
1998   Comment on: The Goals of Evolutionary Archaeology: History and Explanation, by L. Lyman and M. J. O'Brien. *Current Anthropology* 39(5):637–638.
Lipo, C., M. E. Madsen, R. C. Dunnell, and T. Hunt
1997   Population Structure, Cultural Transmission, and Frequency Seriation. *Journal of Anthropological Archaeology* 16:301–34.
Luedtke, B. E.
1992   *An Archaeologist's Guide to Chert and Flint.* Archaeological Research Tools 7. UCLA Institute of Archaeology, Los Angeles.
Lunniss, R.
1985   Matrix and the Mound: An Empirical Approach to Complex Stratigraphy at a Late Formative and Regional Development Ceremonial Centre in Manabí. Paper Presented at the 45th International Congress of Americanists, Bogota.
Lyman, L. and M. J. O'Brien
1998   The Goals of Evolutionary Archaeology: History and Explanation. *Current Anthropology* 39(5):615–652.
Mackie, Q.
1995   *The Taxonomy of Ground Stone Woodworking Tools.* BAR International Series 613. TEMPVS REPARATVM Archaeological and Historical Associates, Ltd., Oxford.
Mathieu, J. R. and D. A. Meyer
1997   Comparing Axe Heads of Stone, Bronze, and Steel: Studies in Experimental Archaeology. *Journal of Field Archaeology* 24(3):333–351.
Mayr, E.
1959   Darwin and the Evolutionary Theory in Biology. In *Evolution and Anthropology: A Centennial Appraisal,* edited by B. J. Meggers, pp. 409–412. Anthropological Society of Washington, Washington.
1982   *The Growth of Biological Thought: Diversity, Evolution, and Inheritance.* The Belknap Press of Harvard University Press, Cambridge, Massachusetts.
1988   *Toward a New Philosophy of Biology: Observations of an Evolutionist.* Harvard University Press, Cambridge, Massachusetts.
McCarthy, F. D.
1967   *Australian Aboriginal Stone Implements (Including Bone, Shell, and Teeth Implements).* Trustees of the Australian Musuem, Sydney.
McCutcheon, P. T.
1995   Evolutionary Fitness of Stone Tool Heat-Treatment Technology. Paper presented at the 60th Annual Meeting of the Society for American Archaeology, Minneapolis.
1997   *Archaeological Investigations of Stone Tool Heat-Treatment in Southeast Missouri: An Experimental Approach.* Ph.D. dissertation, University of Washington, University Microfilms, Ann Arbor.
Metraux, A.
1959   *The Revolution of the Ax.* Diogenes 25:28–40.
Mills, P. R.
1987   *Use-Wear Analysis of Stone Axes from Sand Canyon Pueblo Ruin (5MT765), Southwestern Colorado.* M.A., Thesis, Department of Anthropology, Washington State University.

1993    An Axe to Grind: A Functional Analysis of Anasazi Stone Axes from Sand Canyon Pueblo Ruin (5MT765), Southwestern Colorado. *Kiva* 58:393–413.

Morris, E. H.
1939    *Archaeological Studies in the La Plata District, Southwestern Colorado and Northwestern New Mexico.* The Carnegie Institution, Washington, D.C.

Neiman, F. D.
1995    Stylistic Variation in Evolutionary Perspective: Inferences from Decorative Diversity and Interassemblage Distance in Illinois Woodland Ceramic Assemblages. *American Antiquity* 60:7–36.

Norton, P., R. Lunniss, and N. Nailing
1983    Excavaciones en Salango, Provincia de Manabí, Ecuador. Miscelánea Antropológica Ecuatoriana. Boletín de los Museos del Banco Central del Ecuador 3:9–72. Guayaquil, Ecuador.

O'Brien, M. J. (Editor)
1996    *Evolutionary Archaeology: Theory and Application.* University of Utah Press, Salt Lake City.

O'Brien, M. J. and T. D. Holland
1990    Variation, Selection, and the Archaeological Record. In *Archaeological Method and Theory*, edited by M. B. Schiffer, pp. 31–79. University of Arizona Press, Tucson.
1995    The Nature and Premise of a Selection-Based Archaeology. In *Evolutionary Archaeology: Methodological Issues*, edited by P. A. Teltser, pp. 175–200. University of Arizona Press, Tucson.

O'Brien, M. J., T. D. Holland, R. J. Hoard, and G. L. Fox
1994    Evolutionary Implications of Design and Performance Characteristics of Prehistoric Pottery. *Journal of Archaeological Method and Theory* 1:259–304.

O'Hara, R. J.
1988    Homage to Clio, or, Toward an Historical Philosophy for Evolutionary Biology. *Systematic Zoology* 37:142–55.

Olausson, D. S.
1980    Starting from Scratch: The History of Edge-Wear Research from 1838 to 1978. *Lithic Technology* 9(2):48–60.
1983a   *Flint and Groundstone Axes in the Scanian Neolithic: An Evaluation of Raw Materials Based on Experiment.* Scripta Minora, Regiae Societatis Humaniorum Litterarum Lundensis. CWK Gleerup, Leiden.
1983b   Lithic Technological Analysis of the Thin-butted Flint Axe. *Acta Archaeologica* 52:1-87.
1990    Edge-wear Analysis in Archaeology: The Current State of Research. *Laborativ Arkeologi* 4:5-14.

Petrequin, P. and C. Jeunesse
1995    *La Hâche de Pierre.* Éditions Errance, Paris.

Phillipson, L. and D. Phillipson
1970    Patterns of Edge Damage on the Late Stone Age Industry from Chiwemupala, Zambia. *Zambia Museums Journal* 1:40-75.

Pierce, C.
1993    *Evolutionary Theory and the Explanation of Formal Variation: An Application to Poverty Point Objects from the Lower Mississippi Valley.* M.A. Thesis, Dept. of Anthropology, University of Washington, Seattle.

1995 Theory, Measurement, and Explanation. In *Unit Issues in Archaeology: Measuring Time, Space, and Material*, edited by A. Ramenofsky and A. Steffen, pp. 163–190. University of Utah Press, Salt Lake City.

Pelcin, A.

1997a The Effect of Core Surface Morphology on Flake Attributes: Evidence from a Controlled Experiment. *Journal of Archaeological Science* 24(7): 613–621.

1997b The Effect of Indentor Type on Flake Attributes: Evidence from a Controlled Experiment. *Journal of Archaeological Science* 24(8):749–756.

Pond, A. W.

1930 *Primitive Methods of Working Stone Based on Experiments of Halvor L. Skavlem.* The Logan Museum, Beloit College, Beloit, Wisconsin.

Rabinowicz, E.

1995 *Friction and Wear of Materials.* Second Edition, John Wiley & Sons, New York.

Richardson, J. B. I.

1969 *The Preceramic Sequence and Pleistocene and Post-Pleistocene Climatic Change in Northwestern Peru.* Unpublished Ph.D. Dissertation, Department of Anthropology, University of Illinois, Urbana.

Rindos, D.

1984 *The Origins of Agriculture: An Evolutionary Perspective.* Academic Press, San Diego.

Salazar, E.

1985 Investigaciones Arqueologicas en Mullumica (Provincia del Pichincha). *Miscelanea Antropologica Ecuatoriana* 5:129–160.

Saraydar, S. and I. Shimada

1971 A Quantitative Comparison of Efficiency Between a Stone Axe and a Steel Axe. *American Antiquity* 36:216–217.

Schiffer, M. B.

1987 *Formation Processes of the Archaeological Record.* University of New Mexico Press, Albuquerque.

Schmidt, M.

1974 Comments on Cultivated Plants and Agricultural Methods of South American Indians. In *Native South Americans: Ethnology of the Least Known Continent*, edited by P. J. Lyon, pp. 60–68. Little, Brown and Company, Boston.

Semenov, S. A.

1964 *Prehistoric Technology.* Cory, Adams, and Mckay, London.

Sober, E.

1980 Evolution, Population Thinking, and Essentialism. *Philosophy of Science* 47:350–383.

1984 *The Nature of Selection: Evolutionary Theory in Philosophical Focus.* MIT Press, Cambridge, Massachusetts.

1993 *Philosophy of Biology.* Dimensions of Philosophy Series. Westview Press, Boulder.

Sonnenfeld, J.

1962 Interpreting the Function of Primitive Implements. *American Antiquity* 28:56–65.

Steensberg, A.

1980 *New Guinea Gardens: A Study of Husbandry with Parallels in Prehistoric Europe.* Academic Press, London.

Stothert, K.
  1985  The Preceramic Las Vegas Culture of Coastal Ecuador. *American Antiquity* 50:613–637.
Tello, J. C.
  1960  *Chavin: Cultura Matriz de la Civilizacion Andina (Primera Parte)*. Imprenta de la Universidad de San Marcos, Lima.
Teltser, P. A.
  1995  Culture History, Evolutionary Theory, and Frequency Seriation. In *Evolutionary Archaeology: Methodological Issues*, edited by P. A. Teltser, pp. 51–68. University of Arizona Press, Tucson.
Thorpe, R. S. and G. C. Brown
  1993  *The Field Description of Igneous Rocks*. John Wiley & Sons, Chichester.
Tsirk, A.
  1979  Regarding Fracture Initiations. In *Lithic Use-Wear Analysis*, edited by B. Hayden, pp. 83–96. Academic Press, New York.
Unger-Hamilton, R.
  1989  Experimental Microwear Analysis: Some Current Controversies. *L'Anthropologie* 93:659–672.
Up de Graff, F. W.
  1974  Jivaro Field Clearing with Stone Axes. In *Native South Americans: Ethnology of the Least Known Continent*, edited by P. J. Lyon, pp. 119–121. Little, Brown and Company, Boston.
Vaughan, P. C.
  1985  *Use-Wear Analysis of Flaked Stone Tools*. University of Arizona Press, Tucson.
Villalba, M.
  1988  *Cotocollao: Una Aldea Formativa de Quito*. Miscelanea Antropologica Ecuatoriana Serie Monografica 2. Museo del Banco Central del Ecuador, Quito.
Yerkes, R. W. and P. N. Kardulias
  1993  Recent Developments in the Analysis of Lithic Artifacts. *Journal of Archaeological Research* 1:89–119.
Young, H. R. and E. L. Syms
  1980  The Use of Acetate Peels in Lithic Analysis. *Archaeometry* 22:205–208.
Zalles-Flossbach, C.
  1989  Analsis de los Artifactos Liticos. In *Excavciones en Cochasquí Ecuador 1964–1965,* edited by U. Oberem and W. Wurster, pp. 218–229. Materialen zur Allgemeinen und Vergleichenden Archäologie Band 12. Verlag Phillip Von Zabern, Mainz am Rhein.

# 3

# The Engineering and Evolution of Hawaiian Fishhooks

*Michael T. Pfeffer*

## INTRODUCTION

A variety of artifacts, including objects commonly described as "fishhooks," have played an important role in attempts to understand the settlement history of Pacific Island populations. Researchers have used gross similarities in fishhook morphology to propose broad patterns of descent and interaction throughout the Pacific (e.g., Anell 1955; Emory et al. 1959; Heizer 1949; Landberg 1965; Sinoto 1967, 1968). Following Green (1961), Polynesian researchers have also used lashing device variability to construct chronological sequences and infer cultural affinities (Allen 1992; Davidson 1971; Emory and Sinoto 1964; Sinoto 1962, 1966, 1991). Others have argued however, that many fishhook design similarities may be independently derived through convergence due to similar environmental conditions (Crain 1966; Kirch 1980:116–117; Nordhoff 1930; Reinman 1967, 1970).

Despite these discrepancies, it has been generally accepted that some fishhook design attributes (notably hook curvature) are *functional*, while others (such as lashing device) are *stylistic*, and hence diagnostic of cultural affinity or chronological change (Allen 1996). Unfortunately, aside from preliminary research on fishhook function conducted by Crain (1966) and Reinman (1967, 1970), few researchers have rigorously evaluated these hypotheses. Indeed, Allen (1996:97) has recently called for a systematic reassessment of fishhook attributes to evaluate their use as indicators of cultural affinity, chronological change, or adaptive response.

To understand how these evolutionary processes govern the distribution of discrete fishhook attributes through time and across space, we must understand how each fishhook attribute, and/or combination of attributes interacts with its environment through use. Understanding fishhook use requires engineering experiments to identify those attributes with detectable performance and/or cost differences (Cotterell and Kamminga 1992). For prehistoric fishhooks however, engineering analyses are almost nonexistent (but see Crain 1966). Also lacking are distributional analyses, needed to assess which performance differences covary with the distribution of environmental variables through time and across space. Such analyses are required to demonstrate selective change.

## THEORETICAL CONSIDERATIONS

In archaeology researchers have demonstrated the value of applying an evolutionary approach to the study of human prehistory (e.g., Lipo et al. 1997; Neiman 1995; Teltser 1995). Within an evolutionary approach, the archaeological terms "style" and "function" are subsumed within evolutionary theory under the definitions of neutral theory and drift, and selection, respectively (Dunnell 1978a; Neiman 1995). In addition to style and function, pleiotropy may also be an important evolutionary mechanism. Pleiotropy is a process whereby a neutral trait is mechanically linked to a trait whose distribution is governed by selection. Thus, the distribution of the first trait is a consequence of the selective processes acting on the second trait.

Stylistic trait distributions are a consequence of a particular transmission system within a given environment; hence they are diagnostic of homology. On the other hand, selective processes govern pleiotropic and functional trait distributions; therefore they may, or *may not* be homologous. This ambiguity precludes using functional or pleiotropic traits as a priori indicators of transmission patterns within and between interacting populations. Therefore, stylistic traits are best used to identify cultural affinities and chronological change, while functional traits identify adaptive response to environmental conditions. Thus, as Allen (1996:97) notes, "before fishhooks can be reliably used to elucidate cultural patterns and evolutionary processes, stylistic and functional traits must be explicitly separated."

Elucidating cultural patterns and evolutionary processes using discrete attributes requires that we systematically and scientifically evaluate artifact morphology, raw material properties, and mechanical functions (Allen 1996; Crain 1966: 17). Until these analyses are undertaken, researchers have not, and cannot identify which artifact attributes are stylistic, and which are functional in a given environment. Therefore, for fishhooks, we must systematically reassess variability in artifact and attribute form, use, distribution, and mechanical function. A necessary step in such an analysis is an understanding of the mechanics underlying artifact use, performance, and cost.

## MECHANICS AND ENGINEERING

*Function* is definable as the relationship that obtains between an attribute and its environment (Dunnell 1978a). *Tool* is defined as the maximal set of co-occurring functional attributes associated within the boundaries of an individual object (Dunnell 1978b:55). Tool function (*use*) is the relationship that obtains between a tool and its environment. Engineering and mechanics are concerned with evaluating how raw material and design differences contribute to a tool's potential failure through use (Johnson and Sherwin 1996:1–10). In other words, engineering analyses enable researchers to understand how tools operate and how well they perform under specified external conditions. Mechanics enables researchers to understand why tools fail or break (Anderson 1994). Thus, mechanics and engineering provide the necessary methods to define and quantify functional variance in tool use within a specified environment or set of external conditions.

### Terms and Conditions

When a solid material is subjected to an external force, there is a change in its length (Johnson and Sherwin 1996:157–160). For example, by pulling the free end of an anchored bar, the bar increases in length and is under tension. If pressure is applied to the free end, the bar decreases in length, and is under compression. If force is applied by twisting the bar around its short axis, the object is subjected to shear forces. At some point, the force applied (either compressive, shear, or tensile) will be sufficient to initiate collapse and the object will break. Objects that increase greatly in length before breaking are ductile. Alternatively, materials that fail with little change in length are brittle. Typically, very few materials are very ductile or very brittle, and most lie somewhere in the middle.

When force is applied to a solid object, it results in stress. For an applied force ($F$), on an object with cross-sectional area ($A$), stress ($\sigma$) is equal to the applied force divided by the cross-sectional area ($\sigma = F/A$) (Johnson and Sherwin 1996:159). The magnitude of stress determines a change in the length of the bar ($\Delta L$). A change in bar length from $L$ to $\Delta L$ is referred to as the strain ($\varepsilon$), providing a dimensionless measure ($\varepsilon = \Delta L/L$).

Elasticity refers to a material's ability to deform under load (where stress is proportional to strain), but return to equilibrium when the force is removed. Plasticity is the amount of permanent deformation an object undergoes when under load before it fractures. Finally, the point at which a material fails is referred to as the ultimate tensile strength ($\sigma_y$) (Johnson and Sherwin 1996:161–162). Consequently, to evaluate fishhook function, attributes must be described and experiments designed in these terms. In particular, I focus on the physical properties of materials. Only when the physical properties of materials are known can an object's response to use be accurately gauged.

## Cost

Manufacturing *cost* is a measure of the amount of energy expended, either directly or indirectly, in raw material acquisition, manufacturing investment and failure, and fishhook durability. Raw material acquisition is a measure of four variables, *abundance, form, transport distance,* and *risk.* Variation in abundance affects the amount of energy expended in searching for suitable materials. Material form affects a material's suitability as a source for a tool requiring a given size and strength. Further, some raw materials require more preparation to render them suitable for tool manufacture. Variable transport distances affect acquisition costs for different raw materials, so distance from source to manufacturing/use area must be considered. Risk involved with material acquisition is also an issue.

Manufacturing cost includes the amount of energy required to create a finished fishhook from a piece of raw material. The energy expended in manufacturing, maintaining, and replacing associated tools of production must be considered as well. Manufacturing failure may result from variability in raw material physical properties. Typically, failure results from internal flaws, anisotropic internal structure, production error, or material brittleness. Increases in the rate of failure for a given raw material or tool form increase the amount of energy required to produce a usable fishhook.

Fishhook durability is a measure of the amount of time that a fishhook can be used before it requires maintenance or replacement. Durability is a measure of a tool's physical properties and object geometry (Cotterell and Kamminga 1992). Variables that must be measured include the amount of external stress needed to initiate fracture for a given raw material, hook attribute, or hook design. In addition, differences in raw material brittleness and ductileness must also be considered. Fishhooks that are more durable should be lower in overall cost relative to other hooks.

## Performance

*Performance* measures the amount of work done. Here, work is measured as a fishhook's ability to attract, retain, and retrieve prey from water. Hence, we must identify how variability in fishhook design and raw material affects prey attraction, retention, and retrieval. Prey attraction is a function of the ability for a given set of hook properties to entice prey to attack the hook. As others have noted (Crain 1966; Reinman 1967, 1970), the primary variable influencing prey retention is hook geometry. For prey retrieval, the dominant variable is hook strength, or ability to withstand stresses imposed when a prey is suspended and retrieved from water.

The kinds of performance data needed to complete these experiments can be obtained with the following analyses: raw materials must be identified for each hook examined. Experiments are needed to identify relevant internal structural properties, strength values, and measures of elasticity and plasticity for each raw material. Planimetric measures must be gathered for each hook. Using photography and digital image processing reduces the amount of time required to measure each hook, and increases precision and reliability (making it easier to generate error terms). Further, digital images can be loaded directly into a finite element analysis (FEA) program (an engineering program used to evaluate hook performance through two- and three-dimensional modeling). In cases where digital imaging precludes generation of a three-dimensional model, additional metric measures can be taken using standard calipers to fill in the necessary values.

## RESEARCH

Fishhooks have played an important role in Oceanic culture history. Attributes of their form have been used to identify cultural continuities in time and space. This use, however, presumes variations in form are stylistic (i.e., neutral), and thus faithful measures of homology. But an attribute that is functional at one point in time and space may be stylistic at another. It is apparent that previous analyses have failed to adequately consider these possibilities (Allen 1996), leaving many questions unanswered. Several archaeological assemblages are needed to begin addressing these concerns, as well as to take an initial step in explaining fishhook variability. The assemblages selected for analysis must contain large numbers of fishhooks, manufacturing debris, and well-described faunal assemblages. They should also represent contrasting environmental situations.

The sites at Nu`alolo Kai on Kaua`i and South Point (Ka Lae) on Hawai`i meet these conditions (Figure 3.1). Both assemblages have been pivotal in attempts to reconstruct historical relationships for Hawai`i and Polynesia (Emory et al. 1959; Emory and Sinoto 1964; Goto 1986; Sinoto 1967). Each assemblage contains abundant fishhooks, related manufacturing debris and tools, as well as associated marine faunal remains (Goto 1986; Soehren and Kikuchi n.d.). The locations differ in their marine environments. These factors make each assemblage well suited to comparative analyses necessary to examine functional relationships between fishhook variability and marine ecological zones and prey exploited in each area.

### Nu`alolo Kai, Kaua`i, Hawai`i

As the oldest main Hawaiian island, Kaua`i has the most well developed near-shore reefs and reef slopes. Located along Kaua`i's northwest coast, the Nu`alolo Kai valley lies adjacent to shallow near-shore reef and reef slope conditions. Abundant reef species, including a variety of wrasses (*Labridae*), parrot fish (*Scaridae*), goat fish (*Mullidae*), and surgeon fish (*Acanthuridae*) inhabit the reef and reef slope, as do predatory jacks (*Carangidae*) and snappers (*Lutjanidae*) (Randall 1985). Nu`alolo Kai was first excavated from 1958 to 1964 (Soehren

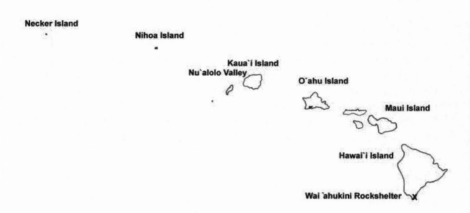

**Figure 3.1. Main Hawaiian Islands showing archaeological locations mentioned in the text.**

and Kikuchi n.d.). T. L. Hunt (personal communication 1998) conducted additional excavations in 1990. The materials from Nu`alolo Kai span a period from about 1450 A.D. to 1750 A.D., and can be divided into three chronological units (Moniz-Nakamura et al. n.d.). A wealth of materials, including fishhooks, fishhook-manufacturing debris, and marine faunal remains, has been recovered from Nu`alolo Kai. To date, over 1,620 fishhooks, fishhook fragments, and hook-manufacturing materials have been examined from the archaeological materials recovered in the K-3 locality. Preliminary analysis of these materials has identified differences between raw material use and fishhook classes (Pfeffer in press).

### South Point, Hawai`i, Hawai`i

Hawai`i Island has little reef development, with small patches occurring primarily along the western coastline. The South Point area lies at the southernmost tip of the island, adjacent to deep pelagic waters; shallow reef development is lacking. A variety of reef slope, benthic, and pelagic species occur in near-shore waters of South Point. These include various tuna (*Scombridae*), *mahi-mahi* (*Coryphaenidae*), marlin (*Istiophoridae*), jacks (*Carangidae*), and snappers (*Lutjanidae*).

The South Point (Site H-1) assemblage was excavated during the 1950s and early 1960s (Emory et al. 1959). Subsequently, Goto (1986) analyzed the South Point materials, including fishhooks and much of the available faunal materials.

More recently, T. L. Hunt and M. S. Allen (personal communication 1999) began a systematic (re-)analysis of materials from the early excavations. Despite the significance of this site and its large artifactual and faunal assemblages, little has been published (Emory et al. 1959; Goto 1986; Kirch 1985). While the initial research yielded early dates (Emory et al. 1959), subsequent radiocarbon dates (and analyses of the dates) suggest the site was occupied after A.D. 1400, and then for a relatively brief duration (Dye 1992). A series of new radiocarbon dates on wood charcoal and shell from the site appear to confirm a late chronology (T. L. Hunt, personal communication 1999). Assemblages that include approximately 1,710 fishhooks, 12,300 coral and sea-urchin abraders, other manufacturing debris, and associated marine faunal remains come from the H-1 Site (Kirch 1985:81). Preliminary analysis has been performed on approximately 2,173 fishhooks, fishhook fragments, and hook-manufacturing materials from the H-8 site (Wai`ahukiui) near South Point (Pfeffer in press).

## FISHHOOKS

Fishhooks are relatively simple devices, easily recognized the world over (Figure 3.2; Anell 1955; Hurum 1977; Rohan-Csermak 1963). Here, fishhooks are defined as curved beams, or long structural members generally subjected to transverse loading that produce significant bending effects as opposed to twisting or axial effects (Logan 1993:152). Curved beams can be modeled as cantilevers, consisting of an anchored arm or "shank limb," a connecting bend, and a free arm or "point limb" (Gere and Timoshenko 1997:267–391; Johnson and Sherwin 1996:177–206). Other devices, not falling in the "fishhook" category in English, may have done the same work. What is important is that all items included do the same task at a given scale.

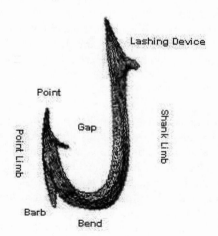

**Figure 3.2. Fishhook model showing commonly named attributes.**

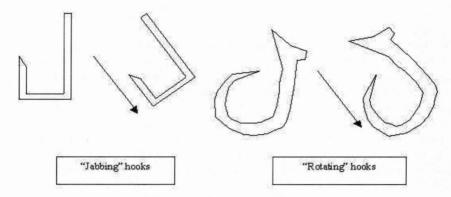

Figure 3.3. "Jabbing" and "Rotating" hooks at rest and under load.

### Hook Variability

In Polynesian archaeology, two fishhook classes are commonly differentiated (Figure 3.3). "Jabbing hooks" have a point limb oriented between 91° and 180° to the shank limb, while "rotating hooks" have a point oriented between 181° and 360° to the shank. In the Pacific, the broad distinction between "rotating" and "jabbing" fishhooks was first made by Nordhoff (1930:155–156), who proposed a relationship between hook curvature and prey retention.

The primary distinction between each category lies in the curvature, or orientation, of the point limb relative to the shank limb. While this distinction is important, and may significantly affect prey retention (Crain 1966), a tremendous amount of additional variability exists within these two hook categories (Hurum 1977). Distinguishing fishhook variability solely on this criterion may obscure other potential selective variance in hook design and use (particularly variance relating to prey attraction and retrieval). Indeed, it remains unclear whether observed differences between "rotating" and "jabbing" hooks are due to variability in hook curvature alone or to influence by a combination of other hook attributes.

### Angling

To catch fish, fishhooks must accomplish *prey attraction, prey retention*, and *prey retrieval*. For example, two methods are typically used to facilitate prey retention. Either constant tension is maintained between hook and prey to preclude escape, or hook curvature interacts with prey movement to prevent the prey from escaping once it has engaged the hook. Prey retrieval, on the other hand, involves suspending and pulling prey from the end of the hook. Therefore, raw material strength and hook designs are the relevant retrieval attributes. Isolating and defining the relationship(s) between each hook design attribute and angling task is required to evaluate how variable attributes affect hook cost and performance, singly, and in concert.

**Table 3.1**
**Dimensions Used to Classify Fishhook Attributes**

| Dimensions | 1 | 2 | 3 | 4 | 5 | 6 | 7 | 8 | 9 |
|---|---|---|---|---|---|---|---|---|---|
| Modes | Head Shape | Lashing device | Shank angle | Point limb angle | Point angle | Shank Barb | Point barb | Cross section | Material |
| 1 | Flat | Interior notch | Parallel | Straight (parallel) | Parallel to Point Limb | None | None | Circular | Human bone |
| 2 | Convex | Exterior notch | Angled inward | Angled inward | Acute angle | Interior | Interior | Ovate | Pig bone |
| 3 | Interior angle | Interior protrusion, or "knob" | Angled outward | Angled outward | Obtuse angle | Exterior | Exterior | Rectangular | Dog bone |
| 4 | Exterior angle | Exterior protrusion, or "knob" | | | | Multiple Interior | Multiple Interior | Square | Dog tooth |
| 5 | Inward angle | Interior notches | | | | Multiple Exterior | Multiple Exterior | Diamond | Whale bone |
| 6 | Concave | Exterior notches | | | | | | | Whale tooth |
| 7 | Interior stepped | Drilled hole | | | | | | | Turtle shell |
| 8 | Exterior stepped | Groove | | | | | | | Basalt |
| 9 | | Multiple Grooves | | | | | | | Pearl shell |
| 10 | | None | | | | | | | Turbo shell |
| 11 | | | | | | | | | Wood |
| 12 | | | | | | | | | Metal |

The following terminology is used to define hook design attributes as they relate to the application of stress during prey retention and retrieval (see Table 3.1 for a list of related fishhook attributes). The shank limb is the beam attached to a suspension device. The point limb is the load-bearing beam. Hook bend is the area of attachment between the shank and point limbs. Lashing device is any structure or mechanism enabling the shank limb to be attached to a suspension device. Gap is the distance between hook point and shank limb.

### Prey Attraction

*Prey attraction* is facilitated by various factors. One method involves using raw material coloration to mimic the appearance of smaller prey (e.g., small fish commonly eaten by larger predators). A second method uses bait placed on the hook, while a third method includes design elements to attract and provoke predators to attack the hook (e.g., Buck 1932; Nordhoff 1930; Pfeffer 1995; Reinman 1967). Typically, one or more of these processes accomplishes prey attraction. For example, a possible attraction element is the color and iridescence of pearl shell— thought to attract a variety of prey (e.g., Buck 1932, 1957; Kahaulelio 1902; Kamakau 1976). This minimizes the need for bait or other prey attraction elements, reducing costs relative to hooks made of nonattractive raw materials. Therefore, the relative effectiveness of a given raw material as a prey attractant may be important in analyzing hook performance and cost for different raw materials.

### Prey Retention

Researchers have studied *prey retention* more than prey attraction or retrieval (e.g., Crain 1966; Goto 1986; Nordhoff 1930; Reinman 1970). Three primary mechanisms have been identified that contribute to prey retention: constant tension between hook point and prey, hook curvature, and the presence of a barb or barbs.

#### Tension

Several fishhook classes require that the angler apply constant *tension* to the line to maintain contact between prey and hook. Commonly described as "jabbing hooks," these hooks have a point orientation between 90° and 180° to the shank limb (Figure 3.3). Jabbing hooks serve several dynamic procurement strategies. Trolling uses a baited jabbing hook or lure trailed behind a moving vessel. Cast/retrieval methods also use a baited jabbing hook or lure, which is thrown out on the surface of the water and retrieved quickly. With jigging strategies, a jabbing hook or lure is let down to the bottom and quickly retrieved once a fish has taken the hook. Importantly, even with modern trolling gear, dynamic strategies employ only one hook per angling line.

To work, jabbing hooks maximize angler leverage while limiting prey leverage. For jabbing hooks, the best prey retention is attained when the point limb is coincident with the shank limb and the vector of the force applied to the point is 180° to the angler's pull (Crain 1966). As long as this angle is maintained, the prey cannot exert enough leverage to free itself. This ideal angle can be achieved by creating a "U"-shaped hook, where a downward force is applied to the point limb and distributed up the shank and angling line. Because it is attached to a flexible line however, the hook pivots at the point of attachment when struck. This reduces the penetration angle to less than 180°, increasing the likelihood that the fish will get off the hook. Increasing the length of the shank limb relative to the point limb, or altering the presentation angle of the hook will counteract this problem, but impose other strength restrictions on the hook (Crain 1966). For example, lengthening the shank limb increases the likelihood of structural failure of the shank limb when under load.

### Hook Curvature

A geometric solution to prey retention is afforded by increasing the *curvature* of the shank and point limbs relative to each other. Commonly referred to as "rotating hooks," curved fishhooks are characterized by having a point/point limb oriented between 181° and 360° to the shank limb (Figure 3.3). By altering hook curvature, rotating hooks minimize the amount of interaction required between angler and prey. Further, increased curvature reduces the ability of prey to exert enough leverage to escape, even if the angler does not maintain tension on the line (Crain 1966; Nordhoff 1930). Johannes (1981:113–115) demonstrated that "rotating hooks" are useful when it is difficult or impossible for the angler to set the hook into the prey's mouth. This occurs when the distance between angler and hook is great, thereby allowing the angling to "bow out" and form a curve. When an angler jerks a bowed line, he/she only take up the slack, and the hook is not properly set.

When prey moves away with a rotating hook in its mouth, it gradually takes up the slack line and the hook pulls to the side of the the mouth. The hook point catches on the corner of the prey's mouth and pivots. This forces the hook to rotate around its axis, pushing the point limb through the corner of the mouth. The more the prey pulls on the hook, the further the hook rotates through its mouth, until it becomes lodged at the hook bend. Due primarily to the curvature of the hook and the ratio between the point and shank limb lengths, the prey cannot exert enough leverage to rotate itself back off the hook (Crain 1966; Johannes 1981). This enables multiple hooks to be used on a single line at one time without supervision. Procurement strategies favoring rotating hooks include several bottom-angling techniques.

### Barbs

On some hooks, an additional design element, the *barb*, is used to enhance a hook's retention capabilities (Figure 3.2). Barbs are ancillary retention devices that accomplish two purposes. First, barbs facilitate bait placement and retention. This is important, as fish will often nibble at bait, quickly removing it from the hook. Adding "bait barbs" increases the length of time that bait remains on the hook, thereby reducing maintenance and increasing the amount of time that the hook is in the water (presented to potential prey) before it must be checked. Second, barbs also retain prey on a hook once it has been snagged. Retention barbs occur on both the interior and exterior surfaces of the shank and point limbs (Anell 1955). On point limbs, barbs are oriented opposite to the hook point's direction. This forms a wedge, or barrier, that reduces the fish's ability to leverage itself back off the hook. Internal shank barbs generally face downward and toward the point limb and bend. These barbs point into the fish's body when it reaches the hook bend, again acting as a wedge to reduce a fish's ability to leverage itself further up the hook. External point limb barbs operate on a similar principle, and form a "stop" that keeps the fish from moving back up the point limb and off the hook.

### Prey Retrieval

Unlike prey retention, where the geometry of the hook is the critical variable, *prey retrieval* is primarily a mechanical problem, where the hook must be capable of suspending and retrieving a given prey load without breaking. The dominant factor limiting prey retrieval is hook strength or the ability to withstand stresses imposed when a hook is subjected to loading. Here, mechanics are used to evaluate how stresses are distributed throughout different combinations of shape and material attributes. As with prey retention, a successful solution to the problem of distributing stress through a fishhook is a consequence of the interaction of a set of variables under specific circumstances. Altering one or more variables will alter both the failure point for a given hook, as well as the utility of the hook for a given procurement strategy (e.g., dynamic/static strategies).

#### Hook Bend

The *bend* is required to enable the fish to bite down on the point. However, the bend is also the focal point for stress applied on the point limb as it is distributed through the hook. One way to increase the tensile strength of the hook bend is to spread the applied force over a greater area. Increasing the size of the point of attachment from a sharp focused angle to a gradual curve distributes stress over a larger area and reduces the amount of stress at any individual point along the hook. Curving the area over which the applied force is distributed also increases the surface area, thereby increasing hook strength. There is, however, a trade off. If the bend is lengthened too far, it effectively becomes a second cantilever. Force now concentrates at the new "bend" and may cause the first cantilever arm to fail. In such cases, failure is likely to occur along its length or at the apex of the new bend. Therefore, geometry and material properties are the critical variables that need to be measured to evaluate hook bend variability.

#### Lashing Device Form and Placement

With prey retrieval, failure can also occur when stress is applied to the point of attachment. Modern metal fishhooks are lashed to the angling line using an "eye" formed by bending the top of the shank limb into a loop (Hurum 1977). Oceanic hooks commonly used a variety of notches (reduced edges), knobs (protruding edges), encircling grooves, and drilled holes as attachment devices (Figure 3.4). Archaeological and ethnographic specimens show that angling line was wrapped and woven around a given lashing device (Buck 1957). A notch, knob, drilled hole, grooves, or combination thereof, changes the point at which a material breaks when subjected to stress (Anderson 1994; Broek 1989:41). Therefore, to examine potential functional differences in the tensile strength of different lashing forms, hafting locations and materials are the relevant variables.

Notching a bar of material concentrates stress applied to the bar at the apex of the notch, reduces the cross-sectional area of the bar, and can result in expansion loading, factors that reduce the bar's tensile strength (Broek 1989:23–25). Creating a series of connected notches to make a groove further exacerbates the problem and reduces bar strength. Drilling a hole through a bar also focuses stress around the hole, reduces bar area, and may interfere with hook presentation by allowing the hook to pivot freely when struck. Knobs protrude from the shank and may increase hook strength. Stress concentrates at the apex between the knob and shank, but cross-sectional area is not reduced for the shank. However, the knob may act as a lever arm, which may increase stress concentration at the knob/shank apex. Experiments will be required to evaluate more fully the distribution of stress applied to variable lashing attributes, their locations (e.g., interior/exterior), and materials.

## EXPERIMENTAL DESIGN AND ANALYSIS

Two related parameters, cost and performance, are relevant to measuring functional variability in fishhook use. I have outlined the relationship between descriptive variables and potential functional differences for prey retention and retrieval. As procurement tools, potential selective pressures on fishhooks include variability that enhances a hook's ability to attract, retain, and retrieve prey. Variables influencing fishhook use (prey attraction, retention, and retrieval) include raw material properties, hook geometry, and hook size.

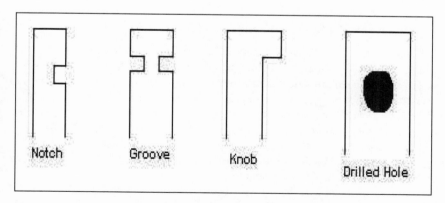

**Figure 3.4. Lashing devices commonly used on Oceanic fishhooks.**

## Raw Material Identification

Researchers believe that pig (*Sus scrofa*), human (*Homo sapiens*), and dog (*Canis familiaris*) bone, pearl oyster (*Pinctada margaritifera*) shell, and turbo (*Turbo spp.*) shell are commonly used to construct Oceanic fishhooks (Allen 1992; Emory et al. 1959; Sinoto 1967; Suggs 1961). In addition, rare materials include turtle shell (ascribed to *Chelonia mydas*), lithics (primarily basalt), wood, bird bone, fish bone, and teeth of sea mammals (commonly ascribed to *Kogia breviceps, Stenella longirostris,* or *Delphinus delphis*) or dog (*Canis familiaris*). In Hawai`i, hooks made of turbo shell seem to have been rare, but pearl shell and bone (including bone attributed to dog, human, and pig) were common (Emory et al. 1959; Goto 1986; Moniz-Nakamura et al. n.d.). The basis for material identification is not always clear, yet accurate determination is critical for the analyses that follow.

Preliminary analysis by the author suggests that pearl oyster (*Pinctada margaritifera*) shell is distinct enough from other materials to enable visual identification from comparative specimens. Different kinds of mammal bone on the other hand, are less easily discriminated. Research is underway on human, pig, and dog bones using a scanning electron microscope (SEM) to identify microscopic structural differences between each kind of bone (Diana Greenlee personal communication 1999). Preliminary analysis has identified multiple characteristics unique to each species. These characteristics may provide an unambiguous means to distinguish between each raw material, at least in relation to the impoverished mammalian fauna of Hawai`i. As the SEM research develops, it may prove possible to use a polarizing light microscope to distinguish pig, dog, and human bone on their unique characteristics for the fishhooks from the Nu`alolo Kai and South Point assemblages. Pearl oyster and other materials can be identified for each assemblage using comparative specimens or microscopic analysis as needed.

## Raw Material Physical Properties

Based on previous research (Emory et al. 1959; Goto 1986), pig, dog, human, and pearl oyster were chosen for strength testing. A detailed literature on the physical and mechanical properties of mammal bone provides the necessary values and research for this analysis (e.g., Cowin 1989; Evans 1973). Since the 1960s, extensive research has been conducted on macro- and microscopic bone structure, bone strength along all dimensions (tensile, compressive, and shear forces), and the physical properties of bone's constituent raw materials. These analyses provide the necessary values for evaluating bone strength, brittleness, and other physical property attributes relevant to fishhook use.

Using the protocol specified by the ASTM (American Society for Testing and Materials; Gere and Timoshenko 1997:11–15) for evaluating a raw material's physical properties, pearl oyster and turbo shells were analyzed by Melinda Allen and her colleagues. Each material was subjected to tensile and compressive strength tests using a standard test machine. Because the materials being tested are anisotropic in structure, they may be stronger along one dimension than another. Therefore, tests were performed both parallel and normal to the long axis of each specimen. Tests were also performed parallel and normal to the internal growth patterns of each species (M. Allen personal communication 1999). Relevant variables obtained from these analyses include data on pearl shell's internal structure (e.g., isotropic, anisotropic, orthotropic), as well as measures of elasticity, plasticity, and strength (tensile, compressive, shear). Results of these analyses will be used to specify empirical measures for each of the variables needed to accomplish the engineering analyses.

### Cost Experiments

Cost of acquisition includes raw material abundance and availability (search time), as well as the risk involved with procuring each material (e.g., killing a pig or diving for pearl oysters). Accurate identification of these variables will be derived through analysis of unused materials in the middens related to each assemblage. If there is unmodified bone or pearl shell in each midden, then it is likely that food acquisition or other needs are responsible for their presence. If this is the case, then using these materials to manufacture hooks is actually lowering the acquisition cost for some other activity, and acquisition costs for fishhooks are negligible. Alternatively, if unmodified pearl shell is rare or absent in each midden, then it is reasonably assumed that pearl oysters were sought specifically to manufacture hooks (or other artifacts). Therefore, less any dietary value, acquisition costs can be ascribed to fishhooks or other pearl shell artifacts (if present). If this is the case, then information on raw material habitat, distribution, and habits will be explored.

For example, the use of pearl oysters as a source of material for various artifacts (including fishhooks) is well attested (e.g., Emory et al. 1959). Two kinds of pearl oyster occur in Hawaiian waters. *Pinctada radiata* is a very small oyster and rarely measures over 5 cm in length (Walther 1997). *Pinctada margaritifera*, on the other hand, is much larger than its smaller cousin and reaches well over 20 cm in length. Pearl oysters (both species) live amidst the reef, along the reef slope, and in lagoons (Walther 1997). The only area in Hawai`i known to have contained large beds of pearl oysters (almost entirely the smaller *Pinctada radiata*) was Pearl Harbor on O`ahu Island (Walther 1997:15–17).

Large *Pinctada margaritifera* beds were almost certainly never found in Hawai`i, although individuals do occur with some frequency on the reefs, reef slopes, and lagoons surrounding O`ahu and Kaua`i. They seem, however, to have been rare on Hawai`i Island, particularly in the South Point area where reef and lagoon development is lacking. In his examination of Hawaiian fishing, Goto (1986), noted significant differences between the relative abundance of pearl shell fishhook from Hawai`i and Kaua`i. He found that pearl shell hooks are much more abundant on Kaua`i, and that they are rare in most Hawai`i Island localities (Goto 1986:198–201). This research is supported by recent reanalysis of the Nu`alolo Kai (K-3) and Wai`ahukini (H-8, near South Point) materials, which has identified statistically significant differences in the preferential use of pearl shell and mammal bone for different fishhook classes (e.g., one- and two-piece fishhooks; Pfeffer in press).

### Manufacturing Cost

Manufacturing costs include the amount of energy expended in making a fishhook from bone, shell, or other raw material. The manufacturing process of Oceanic fishhooks is relatively well known (e.g., Allen 1992, 1996; Sinoto 1991). Fishhooks are made through a reduction process, whereby files are used to cut blanks out of pieces of raw material. Each blank is cut by abrading a sharp, V-shaped cut into a piece of raw material until two pieces are formed. Each blank is then drilled and abraded into a finished hook using various abraders. While not exhaustive, archaeological evidence suggests that tools commonly used in fishhook manufacture include coral (primarily *Porites lobata*, although several species of *Pocillopora* may have also been used) and slate pencil urchin spine (*Heterocentrotus mammillatus*) files (Sinoto 1991).

Abrasion rate (T) is controlled by several factors: tool physical properties and hardness; hook material hardness (Moh's) and physical properties; as well as forces exerted both parallel and perpendicular to tool action. While the forces cannot be estimated accurately after the fact, they should be similar for all combinations (e.g., a pair of hands). Differential hardness is thus the dominant variable at the microscale. However, as McCutcheon and Dunnell (1991) point out for lithics, macrostructure (friability, voids, inclusions, etc.) may dominate processes at the scale at which fabrication takes place. This is especially so as the materials used to create fishhooks are composites. Consequently, it was necessary to construct a machine to quantify resilience to abrasion. This provided a measure of how much energy and material were consumed in tool manufacture. Here, a similar machine is employed to quantify the amounts of energy and materials used to cut fishhook raw materials with coral and urchin tools.

To ensure comparability and minimize the influence of external conditions, these tests will be performed under controlled laboratory conditions. Following a protocol developed by Allen et al., (personal communication 1999) for pearl and turbo shell, comparable pieces of each raw material and manufacturing file will be cut, dried, and placed in a box containing desiccating crystals. Once dried, each piece will be removed from the box, immediately weighed, and allowed to acclimate to the laboratory conditions. Weight, corrected for specific gravity, will be used to measure the amount of work done on both tool and hook material.

Each raw material blank will be placed in a vice. Likewise, a coral or urchin spine file will also be removed from the desiccating box, acclimated and weighed, and placed in a horizontal motion machine. A small motor (providing uniform motion force) and a uniform weight (to keep file and hook material in contact) will be used to control extraneous variation. Rates of abrasion will be measured between file and hook material. The surface area is held constant to ensure comparability between experiments. Then, the file will be rubbed against the hook material in a series of episodes (e.g., 2 minutes, or until significant differences can be detected for each material and tool combination). Each raw material will be cut both parallel and normal to the long axis of the bone to identify potential cost differences for different angles of orientation.

## Performance

Once manufacturing cost and acquisition cost tests have been performed, mechanical models will be used to identify potential performance differences between fishhook attributes and classes. As shown above, mechanics identifies a range of potentially significant strength differences in fishhook design. Adding notches, altering hook curvature, and changing hook size all affect the strength of a hook, or amount of stress it can withstand before failure.

To obtain a more detailed picture of how variability in hook material, geometry, design, and size affect performance, a finite element analysis (FEA) computer program will be used to construct two- and three-dimensional fishhook models. A second computer program will apply stresses to each fishhook model to isolate and identify performance differences for individual attributes as well as hook classes. Two kinds of fishhook models will be used. Idealized models will be constructed to identify performance differences for each design attribute. Fishhooks recovered from each archaeological assemblage will also be modeled and used to analyze the distribution of each hook attribute or class through time, across space, and as in relation to associated ecological, faunal, or other variables. Data necessary to accomplish these analyses will have been obtained by the experiments described above (see section on material identification and physical analysis).

## Finite Element Analysis (FEA) and Performance Tests

Reducing any tool to a simplified cantilever model will provide a relative measure of how stress is distributed throughout a tool under load. However, a more robust approach to understanding how stresses are distributed through a loaded hook is afforded through application of FEA. With simple cantilever models, a measure of the failure point is obtained by applying stress to the tip of the model. While this provides a single measure of the strength of the hook, it does not allow researchers to isolate and examine how variability in a single attribute can affect hook strength. The FEA method provides a means to isolate and examine a myriad of attributes, both singly and in concert, to evaluate variability in fishhook attribute and class performance.

FEA provides a numerical solution to engineering and mathematical physics (Logan 1993). This method is particularly appropriate for the solution of complex structural analyses, such as the distribution of stresses through a fishhook when subjected to loading. FEA programs model a given body by dividing it into equivalent units, or finite elements, each of which is attached at nodes. By solving for each of the individual elements simultaneously, FEA builds up a solution for the entire body (Logan 1993). Altering any attribute will result in a different solution, enabling researchers to evaluate very small changes in tool design. This analytic feature is crucial because various fishhook attributes may have significant performance differences. In addition, combinations of attributes may influence hook performance, further bolstering the need for a method such as FEA capable of isolating both individual attributes and groups of attributes. Variables needed to construct an FEA analysis include physical property (internal structure, tensile strength, etc.) measures for each raw material, as well as planimetric values for each attribute or attribute combination examined.

## TESTING HYPOTHESES ABOUT THE CAUSES OF VARIATION

Once the engineering experiments have been completed, distributional analyses are required to evaluate whether variability in fishhook design and distribution covary with environmental conditions, raw material abundance, or resource exploitation (including shifts in prey taken).

Variability in raw material abundance and availability must be measured through examination of hook materials, associated manufacturing debris, and related marine faunal remains. The abundance of unmodified pieces of raw material, as well as variability in the amount/kind of manufacturing debris associated with each raw material will be examined. For example, if pearl shell fishhooks decline in abundance on Kaua`i, then we should see a reduction in unmodified pearl oyster shells in archaeological middens. Further, pieces of pearl shell fishhook manufacturing debris should decrease in size as more and more of each shell is used.

Changes in the kind of prey exploited will be examined through analysis of marine faunal remains recovered from each locality. Various researchers have proposed a relationship between hook size and prey type (e.g., Goto 1986; Johannes 1981; Reinman 1970). Identifying different species, their habitat, and feeding habits can provide a means to assess this issue. In addition, analysis of changes in the abundance and size of individual species through time at each locality may identify changes in prey abundance/availability. For example, if near-shore reef fauna become less abundant through time, then we may see a shift from near-shore marine exploitation to reef slope/pelagic angling. Concomitant changes in fishhook design, size, and perhaps raw material should accompany this shift.

Previous research suggests that the materials needed to evaluate possible causes for fishhook variability are available in assemblages recovered from each locality (Goto 1986; Soehren and Kikuchi n.d.). Abundant marine faunal remains are available for analysis from each locality. Goto (1986) analyzed the marine faunal remains from both localities, providing a useful database for further analysis. Marine fauna will be identified to genera or species where possible, and to family when a finer distinction is not possible. The relatively limited number of marine fauna occurring in Hawaiian waters renders generic or family-level distinctions useful as indicators of habits and habitat. Changes in raw material abundance will be explored through analysis of manufacturing debris and related midden materials. Analysis of datable materials and other kinds of artifacts recovered from each locality will be used to evaluate possible shifts in dietary focus at each locality.

## SUMMARY

Fishhooks are an abundant artifact class in many Polynesian archaeological deposits, particularly in the Society, Marquesas, and Hawaiian Islands. Similarities in their attributes of form have been used to hypothesize patterns of interaction and chronological change within and between island populations. While some variance in fishhook design has long been recognized as potentially functional, few researchers have addressed the broader implications. My research should distinguish sources of similarity for fishhook design and identify functional aspects with respect to hook performance and cost. I propose to use engineering and cost analyses with distributional studies to evaluate which fishhook attributes are functional, stylistic, or pleiotropic for assemblages from Nu`alolo Kai and South Point. Although restricted to analysis of two Hawaiian assemblages, my research raises wider issues such as our understanding of fishhook use in Hawaiian prehistory and elsewhere in the Pacific. Finally, distinguishing functional and stylistic variance in fishhook attributes will contribute to our understanding of the use that fishhooks have as indicators of cultural affinity or chronological change.

## SIGNIFICANCE

Archaeologists have used a range of artifact attributes in attempts to reconstruct patterns of cultural affinity, historical change, and adaptive response. But in many cases, researchers have simply assumed that artifact similarities are stylistic, thus reflecting homologous patterns in time and space. In other cases, archaeologists have attributed functional differences to artifacts, but with little empirical support for their suppositions. These often-intuitive assessments of style and function undermine attempts to infer cultural affinity, chronological change, or adaptive response. This problem points to the need for systematic research that integrates engineering analyses within an evolutionary framework (e.g., Brandon 1990; O'Brien and Holland 1990). Engineering and mechanical studies will delineate processes underlying a given artifact's or attribute's function in an ecological context (Brandon 1990).

While focused on Hawaiian fishhooks, this research identifies analyses to distinguish stylistic and functional traits. In sum, I have outlined the analyses needed to begin a systematic reassessment of our understanding of fishhook technology and its role in understanding Polynesian prehistory. Second, this research protocol should enable archaeologists to differentiate stylistic and functional variance by assessing performance and cost differences within a given set of external conditions for any kind of artifact. I hope that this research will augment not only our understanding of Polynesian prehistory, but also the methods used by archaeologists to address similar issues in other contexts.

## REFERENCES CITED

Allen, M. S.
　1992　Temporal Variation in Polynesian Fishing Strategies: The Southern Cook Islands in Regional Perspective. *Asian Perspectives* 31:183–204.
　1996　Style and Function in East Polynesian Fish-hooks. *Antiquity* 70:97–116.
Anderson, T. L.
　1994　*Fracture Mechanics: Fundamentals and Applications.* Second edition. CRC Press, Boca Raton.
Anell, B.
　1955　*Contribution to the History of Fishing in the Southern Seas.* Studia Ethnographica Upsaliensia 9.
Brandon, R.
　1990　*Adaptation and Environment.* Princeton University Press, New Jersey.
Broek, D.
　1989　*The Practical Use of Fracture Mechanics.* Kluwer Academic Publishers, London.
Buck, P.
　1932　*Ethnology of Tongareva.* Bernice Pauahi Bishop Museum Special Bulletin 75, Honolulu.
　1957　*Arts and Crafts of Hawai'i, Section VII, Fishing.* Bernice Pauahi Bishop Museum Special Publication 45, Honolulu.
Cotterell, B., and J. Kamminga
　1992　*Mechanics of Pre-industrial Technology.* Cambridge University Press, Cambridge.
Cowin, S. C. (Editor)
　1989　*Bone Mechanics.* CRC Press, Boca Raton.
Crain, C.
　1966　Mechanical Aspects of the Single-piece Curved Shell Fishhook. *Kroeber Anthropological Society Papers* 34:17–29.
Davidson, J. M.
　1971　*Archaeology on Nukuoro Atoll: A Polynesian Outlier in the Eastern Caroline Islands.* Bulletin no. 9. Auckland Institute and Museum, Auckland.

Dunnell, R. C.
 1978a Style and Function: The Fundamental Dichotomy. *American Antiquity* 43:192–203.
 1978b Archaeological Potential of Anthropological and Scientific Models of Function. In *Archaeological Essays in Honor of Irving B. Rouse,* edited by R. C. Dunnell and E. S. Hall, Jr., pp. 41–73. Mouton, The Hague.

Dye, Tom
 1992 The South Point Radiocarbon Dates Thir[t]y Years Later (sic*). New Zealand Journal of Archaeology* 14:89–97.

Emory, K., W. Bonk, and Y. H. Sinoto
 1959 *Fishhooks.* Bernice Pauahi Bishop Museum Special Publication 47, Honolulu.

Emory, K. and Y. H. Sinoto
 1964 East Polynesian Burials at Maupiti. *Journal of the Polynesian Society* 73:143–160.

Evans, F. G.
 1973 Mechanical Properties of Bone. Charles C. Thomas, Springfield.

Gere, J. and S. Timoshenko
 1997 *Mechanics of Materials.* Fourth edition. PWS Publishing Company, Boston.

Goto, A.
 1986 Prehistoric Ecology and Economy of Fishing in Hawaii: An Ethnoarchaeological Approach. Department of Anthropology, University of Hawai'i, University Microfilms, Ann Arbor.

Green, R.
 1961 Review of Hawaiian Archaeology: Fishhooks, by Emory, Bonk, and Sinoto. *Journal of the Polynesian Society* 70:139–144.

Heizer, R. F.
 1949 Curved, Single-piece Fishhooks of Shell and Bone in California. *American Antiquity* 15(2):89–97.

Hurum, H. J.
 1977 *A History of the Fishhook: And the Story of Mustad, the Hook Maker.* Winchester Press, New York.

Johannes, R.E.
 1981 *Words of the Lagoon: Fishing and Marine Lore in the Palau District of Micronesia.* University of California Press, Berkeley.

Johnson, A. and K. Sherwin
 1996 *Foundations of Mechanical Engineering.* Chapman Hall, London.

Kahaulelio, A. D.
 1902 *Fishing Lore, Ka nupepa ku'o'koa.* Bishop Museum Press, Honolulu.

Kamakau, S. M. (Editor)
 1976 *The Works of the People of Old: Na Hana a ka Poe Kahiko.* Bishop Museum Press, Honolulu.

Kirch, P. V.
 1980 The Archaeological Study of Adaptation: Theoretical and Methodological Issues. *Advances in Archaeological Method and Theory* 3:101–156.
 1985 *Feathered Gods and Fishhooks: An Introduction to Hawaiian Archaeology and Prehistory.* University of Hawaii Press, Honolulu.

Landberg, L. C. W.
  1965   Tuna Tagging, and the Extra-Oceanic Distribution of Curved, Single-piece Shell Fishhooks in the Pacific. *American Antiquity* 3(4)485–493.
Lipo, C., M. Madsen, R. Dunnell, and T. Hunt
  1997   Population Structure, Cultural Transmission, and Frequency Seriation. *Journal of Anthropological Archaeology* 16:301–333.
Logan, D.
  1993   *A First Course in the Finite Element Method.* International Thomson Publishing, Cambridge.
McCutcheon P. and R. C. Dunnell
  1991   Mississippian Lithic Exchange, Heat Treatment, and Fracture Toughness. Paper presented at the 48th Annual Meeting of the Southeastern Archaeological Conference, 6–9 Nov., Jackson, Mississippi.
Moniz-Nakamura, J., M. S. Allen, and M. Graves
  n.d.   Methodological Issues in Artifact Analysis: Stylistic Variability in Hawaiian Fishhooks. Manuscript, Department of Anthropology, University of Hawaii.
Neiman, F.
  1995   Stylistic Variation in Evolutionary Perspective: Inferences from Decorative Diversity and Interassemblage Distance in Illinois Woodland Ceramic Assemblages. *American Antiquity* 60:7–36.
Nordhoff, C.
  1930   Notes on the Off-Shore Fishing of the Society Islands. *Journal of the Polynesian Society* 39:137–173.
O'Brien, M. and T. Holland
  1990   Variation, Selection, and the Archaeological Record. In *Archaeological Method and Theory*, vol. 2, edited by M. B. Schiffer, pp. 31–79. University of Arizona Press, Tucson.
Pfeffer, M. T.
  In press.   Implications of Hawaiian Fishhook Variability for Our Understanding of Polynesian Settlement History. In *Style and Function: Conceptual Issues in Evolutionary Archaeology*, edited by G. Rakita and T. Hurt. Greenwood Press, Westport.
Randall, J.
  1985   *Guide to Hawaiian Fishes.* Treasures of Nature, Honolulu.
Reinman, F. M.
  1967   *Fishing:* An Aspect of Oceanic Economy: An Archaeological Approach. *Fieldiana: Anthropology* 56:94–208.
  1970   Fishhook Variability: Implications for the History and Distribution of Fishing Gear in Oceania. In *Studies in Oceania History*, pp. 47–60. Pacific Anthropological Records No. 11, R. C. Green and M. Kelly, editors. Bernice Pauahi Bishop Museum, Honolulu.
Rohan-Csermak, G.
  1963   *Sturgeon Hooks of Eurasia.* Aldine Publishing Company, Chicago.
Sinoto, Y. H.
  1962   Chronology of Hawaiian Fishhooks. *Journal of the Polynesian Society* 71:162–166.
  1966   A Tentative Prehistoric Cultural Sequence in the Northern Marquesas Islands as a Dispersal Center in East Polynesia. *Pacific Anthropological Records* 11:105–132.

1967    Artifacts from Excavated Sites in the Hawaiian, Marquesas, and Society Islands: A Comparative Study. In *Polynesian Culture History: Essays in Honor of Kenneth P. Emory*, pp. 341–361. Special Publication 56, G. Highland et al., editors. Bishop Museum Press, Honolulu.

1968    Position of the Marquesas Islands in East Polynesian Prehistory. In *Prehistoric Culture in Oceania*, edited by I. Yawata and Y. H. Sinoto, pp. 111–118. Bishop Museum Press, Honolulu.

1991    *A Revised System for the Classification and Coding of Hawaiian Fishhooks.* Bishop Museum Occasional Papers 31:85–105. Bishop Museum, Honolulu.

Soehren, L. and Kikuchi, W.

n.d.    *Nua`olo Kai.* Department of Anthropology, Bishop Museum, Honolulu.

Suggs, R. C.

1961    *The Archaeology of Nuku Hiva, Marquesas, French Polynesia.* Anthropological Papers of the American Museum of Natural History, New York.

Teltser, P. A.

1995    Culture History, Evolutionary Theory, and Frequency Seriation. In *Evolutionary Archaeology: Methodological Issues*, edited by P. A. Teltser, pp. 51–68. University of Arizona Press, Tucson.

Walther, M.

1997    *Pearls of Pearl Harbor and the Islands of Hawai'i: The History, Mythology, and Cultivation of Hawaiian Pearls.* Natural Images of Hawai'i, Honolulu.

# 4

# Building the Framework for an Evolutionary Explanation of Projectile Point Variation: An Example from the Central Mississippi River Valley

*Kris H. Wilhelmsen*

## INTRODUCTION

Second only to ceramics, projectile points are the most abundant shaped artifact in the archaeological record, thus constituting one of the largest artifact classes available for the study of change. They have played an enormous role in North American archaeology generally, and in the Eastern United States in particular, projectile points have structured much of our understanding of prehistory. They are the basis of cultural chronologies before the development of ceramic technology (e.g., Brown and Vierra 1983; Broyles 1966; Coe 1964; Lewis and Lewis 1961; Morse and Morse 1983), and continue to play a role in chronology building even after the advent of pottery (e.g., George and Scaglion 1992; Litfin et al. 1993; Lynott 1991; O'Brien and Warren 1983). The temporal and spatial distributions of certain projectile point "types" are frequently used to infer the general north to south diffusion of bow and arrow technology in the East. Since arrows have a greater range and accuracy than casting projectiles and darts, the inferred replacement of the atlatl by the bow and arrow is considered by many to play a causal role in subsistence and settlement changes (e.g., Christenson 1981; Odell 1988; Shott 1993), and even in social changes such as increased intergroup conflict and warfare (e.g., LeBlanc 1997; Seeman 1992; Smith 1993).

Despite their importance to our understanding of prehistory, the extent of projectile point variation is poorly documented, and the explanatory potential untapped. Only quite recently has this situation begun to change (e.g., Beck 1995; Bradbury 1997; Knecht 1997; LeBlanc 1997; Shott 1996). Several aspects of previous research are notably problematic. The traditional use of projectile point "types" involves the assignment of objects to groups (e.g., Bell 1958; Perino 1968; Scully 1951; Suhm et al. 1954). Assignments are made on the basis of an archetype that is taken to represent the "essential" form and is often associated, either explicitly or implicitly, with untested functional inferences (e.g., Goodyear 1974; Price and Griffin 1979). It is thus not uncommon to find variation explained as "noise" or as the result of "atypical or unskilled manufacture," "rejuvenation," or "recycling." In addition, morphological similarity is characteristically treated as a measure of historical relatedness, when in fact, it may be a result of other factors. Objects may be contemporaneous, for example. Or they may share characteristics derived from recent common ancestry (divergent relation). Similarity may be a result of selection in a similar environment operating on otherwise unrelated forms (convergent relation). Finally, objects may share characteristics due to chance alone, particularly when the number of shared characteristics are few. Conflating these causes of similarity confounds the deduction and explanation of historical and functional relations among projectile points. Thus, "explanations" advanced for variation in projectile points are typically circular—the activities *inferred from* projectile point form are also considered the *causes of* the form. As a result of problematic classification and circular interpretation, very little progress has been made toward an increased understanding of the nature and causes of projectile point variation.

In the Central Mississippi Valley, as is true of most other regions in North America, these two related assumptions about projectile point variation are common. First, it is assumed that projectile points in general get smaller over time, presumably due to functional and technological changes. Second, and more specifically, the "transition" from dart to arrow technology is thought to be marked by a decrease in projectile point size and a standardization of point morphology. Demonstrating whether these generalizations are correct is an empirical task that requires understanding functional and morphological variation in projectile points and how they change over time and space. Explaining the changes requires an evolutionary perspective to integrate the functional and historical data into a single explanatory framework.

Projectile points are surviving parts of more complex tools. Thus, to understand functional and morphological variation in projectile points it is necessary to know how points are integrated with other components of the projectile and the launching device. This requires building a model for projectile point function using Newtonian mechanics. Fortunately, the long history of projectile technology combined with antiquarian interest has resulted in a vast body of experimental data generated in mechanics, ballistics, aerodynamics, and sports. An analysis of these data using Newtonian mechanics provides the basic explanatory framework for the interaction of launch, flight, and impact characteristics of a projectile and its various components. This engineering analysis identifies attributes that are useful for describing projectile point form and function.

Understanding why projectile point form and function changes over time and space requires a theory that provides a means for studying the relationship between functional and historical change. Evolutionary theory offers a robust means for integrating and explaining functional and historical processes and does so using the method of empirical falsification (Popper 1972). As a consequence, increasing attention has focused on integrating the scientific evolutionary paradigm in American Archaeology (e.g., Dunnell 1980, 1989, 1995; Feathers 1990; Jones et al. 1995; Lyman and O'Brien 1998; O'Brien and Holland 1995). As part of this larger effort, this chapter focuses on two critical issues: 1. the development of counting units relevant to processes explained by evolutionary theory; and 2. the development of a method for chronologically ordering these units. This will allow not only the evaluation of common, untested assumptions about projectile point form and function, but also elucidation of historical processes that have structured projectile point evolution in the Central Mississippi Valley.

## THEORETICAL FRAMEWORK

Darwin (1859) referred to evolution as "descent with modification." Through the notion of descent, Darwin recognized that information is transmitted to offspring from parents, and that offspring show greater resemblance to their parents than to offspring of other parents. Because no two organisms are identical and because space and energy are finite, there is competition among individuals that vary in their ability to acquire these resources (Dunnell 1989). Darwin provided a set of mechanisms to account for differential reproductive success, the most important being natural selection. Two processes can explain change in an evolutionary framework: selection and drift. Selection is objectified as the differential reproduction of organisms which, at the scale of population, results in a directional change in trait frequencies over time that correlates to external environmental conditions.

All things being equal, when alternative traits perform the same function in the same selective environment, those traits that cost less to produce and/or perform more efficiently eventually attain higher frequencies in a given population than other traits. The term "non-neutral" is applied to traits having distributions through time and space that are shaped by natural selection, while those not shaped by selection and having no measurable affect on fitness are selectively "neutral" (Brandon 1990; Kimura 1983; Sober 1984). Relative reproductive costs and performance characteristics within a given environment affect the frequency of non-neutral trait transmission (Dunnell 1980; Mayr 1988). The frequency of neutral trait transmission, on the other hand, is explained by drift, which consists of sampling error and the stochastic patterns of transmission (Lipo et al. 1997; Neiman 1995). Using the terms "function" and "style" in place of non-neutral and neutral, Dunnell (1978a:199) was first to note the critical theoretical role of these mutually exclusive terms for evolutionary explanation in archaeology.

Building explanations for changing trait frequencies requires distinguishing between neutral and non-neutral traits, each of which are subject to distinct evolutionary processes. One way to evaluate the role of traits in the reproductive success of an individual is to use an engineering design analysis and distributional tests. An engineering analysis for projectiles identifies, in mechanical terms, the traits or design features relevant to one or more of a projectile's functions. For example, a mechanical description of projectile flight can be used to identify projectile point traits that affect trajectory and distance, while the mechanics of cutting and piercing can be used to identify traits that affect penetration. Traits, however, that are non-neutral in one context of use may be neutral in another; thus, traits identified by the engineering design analysis are treated as *potentially* non-neutral. Non-neutral traits may originate through a common phylogenetic background (homologies) or from convergent evolution in similar selective environments (analogies). Because non-neutral traits are subject to selection, they have temporal distributions that map onto structure in the selective environment, and they increase or decrease in frequency over time with the reproductive success of individuals. Neutral traits also arise through transmission due to a common phylogenetic background but cannot arise through convergence, particularly when they are defined by a complex set of traits. Because neutral traits are unaffected by selection, they have temporal distributions that are stochastic and spatial distributions that map onto interacting lineages (Lipo et al. 1997). The distribution of neutral and non-neutral traits is modeled in Figure 4.1 using hypothetical data (see also Gould et al. 1977; O'Brien and Holland 1990; Raup and Gould 1974). These distributional models are distinct given the effects of selection and drift.

As Sober (1984:97–102) points out, the persistence of traits can result from both the "*selection of*" and "*selection for*" traits. Selection *for* a trait describes the causes of a selection process in which the reproductive success of the individual is enhanced by possession of the trait. Selection *of* a trait, on the other hand, describes the effects of a selection process in which the frequency of a given trait is increased with no effect on fitness. This is important because the phenotype is a complex network of physical and behavioral traits. Selection *for* a complex network of traits results in the selection *of* a particular phenotype, which contains both non-neutral and neutral traits. Neutral traits that have no actual effect on reproductive success, but increase with the reproductive success of individuals rather than going extinct, are referred to as pleiotropic traits. A pleiotropic trait is architecturally linked within the network that is selected *for*, and therefore exhibits an r-shape distribution as a result of reproductive success.

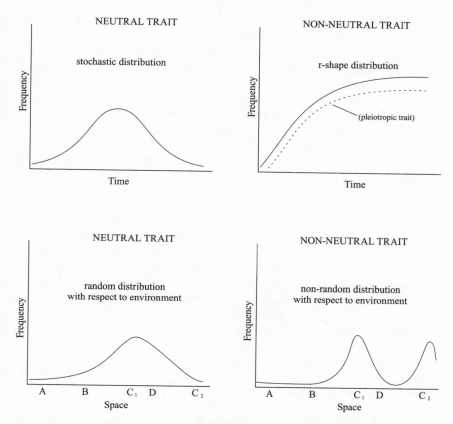

**Figure 4.1. Hypothetical frequency distributions of neutral and non-neutral traits over time and space. A–D represent different environments whereas C1 and C2 represent similar environments.**

Environmental variation plays a significant role in the selective conditions of projectile use with regard to resource availability across space and time. Resources include both organic and inorganic materials for manufacturing projectile components, as well as the animal resources acquired through projectile use. At any point in time and space the characteristics of a projectile technology, such as those involved in atlatls and darts, are the outcome of an engineering solution to a specific task, utilizing a given technology for manufacturing projectile components, and applied to an available set of raw materials. While the primary architect of such an engineering solution is natural selection, it is important to distinguish between an ecological solution and an evolutionary solution. Engineering designs are ecological solutions because they involve the interrelation of functional variables within a set of ecological parameters specific to a given point in time or space. On the other hand, an evolutionary solution involves the interrelation of functional variables across engineering solutions through time, and links temporal variation in functional variables to changing ecological parameters. In this way, an evolutionary solution explains the differential persistence of ecological solutions over time and space as the result of natural selection. To understand how and why selection results in a particular engineering solution, it is essential to link the differential persistence of non-neutral traits across variable selective environments through space and time.

The engineering design analysis is used to make the initial distinction between neutral and non-neutral traits and is the basis for constructing classifications that describe variation. The next step is to construct appropriate counting units that can be used to group empirical entities that together constitute a sample of the phenotype from a single lineage over a given range of time. Assemblages, as traditionally defined, are inappropriate counting units because they are aggregates of objects derived from a variable number of individual organisms over a variable amount of time (Dunnell 1995). Such "assemblages" are often referred to as mixed or multiple component assemblages because they contain historically unrelated objects (Dewar 1991; Ebert 1994). Because neutral traits are transmitted homologously within a single lineage, similarity of objects in terms of neutral traits is an indication of their common phylogeny. Thus, neutral traits provide the key to building appropriate counting units with which to examine differential persistence. First, a temporal order for projectile point classes is established using the occurrence seriation method. The classes are defined by the co-occurrence of manufacturing traits suspected to be neutral on the basis of engineering. This process identifies groups of projectile points having identical manufacturing attributes. Each group belongs to a different *period of manufacture* that is defined by a chronologically unique set of homologously transmitted attributes acquired at the time of manufacture. The "occurrence law" (Dunnell 1981:68) of seriation provides a test of the neutrality of traits, as well as a relative chronological order for projectile point classes.

To determine the absolute range of counting units and the amount of time represented by an individual counting unit, a method of chronologically anchoring units is necessary. The traditional method for assessing the age of a projectile point is by association with some other datable substance, such as organic material dated by radiocarbon (Feathers 1997). This method is problematic, however, because of questionable associations, and because of uncertainty in relating the actual dated event to the event of interest, or target event. Consequently, there is an unknown amount of error in association dating. To avoid this problem, thermoluminescence dating is used for chronologically ordering counting units, and for determining when projectile points were manufactured.

Building and ordering counting units in time and tabulating the frequency of non-neutral traits across these units provides data on the differential persistence of variant forms through time and across space. Explaining the differential persistence of variant forms over time and space is based on identifying correlations between functional variants and environmental variables. Since selection also operates on the relative cost of maintaining projectile components for different functional variants and their relative performance, it is also necessary to account for variation in manufacturing costs and performance differentials. Only by combining these sources of information can traditional assumptions about projectile point variation be evaluated and evolutionary explanations of variation be constructed.

The work outlined here will generate data that can be used to test common assumptions about projectile point variation over time. Distinguishing the causes of variation and building groups of historically related projectile points are beginning to provide the necessary foundation on which to build evolutionary explanations. Subsequent sections of this chapter address each aspect of this analytical work in greater detail.

## RESEARCH ASSEMBLAGES, SELECTIVE ENVIRONMENT, AND FORMATION PROCESSES

### The Research Assemblages

I examine 37 projectile point assemblages derived from surface clusters in Southeast Missouri and Northeast Arkansas in this research (Figure 4.2). Eight assemblages result from long-term academic research, while the remaining 29 belong to a long-time amateur collector in Southeast Missouri. Most of the surface clusters were repeatedly collected over a period of up to 25 years and contain a total of approximately 3,700 virtually complete projectile points, several thousand point fragments, and a wide variety of other lithic and non-lithic artifact types. Culture historical projectile point types as well as the geomorphic history of the area indicate temporal coverage of at least 11,000 years.

The presence of site records distinguishes this private collection from other "amateur" collections that are typically comprised of artifacts from unknown locations having unknown sample bias. While actively surface collecting, the owner of the collection sequentially numbered each surface cluster. Nearly all artifacts were individually labeled with cluster numbers. In addition, surface cluster provenience was described in terms of Township, Range, section quarter, sketch maps, and verbal descriptions for accessing the surface clusters via designated county roads. Twenty-one of the 29 surface clusters have been relocated in the field using these records, allowing the assemblages to be related back to their archaeological context. Most of the surface clusters are located in agricultural fields that are plowed several times annually, although a few fields are periodically left fallow or have been destroyed by land leveling. At least three clusters have been subject to previous analysis for a recent cultural resources management study (Walters 1988), and 16 clusters have been previously recorded and reported to the Missouri Archaeological Society.

Virtually all of the assemblages contain a wide range of artifacts such as chipped and groundstone tools and fragments, cores, tested cobbles, ceramics, faunal remains, and projectile points in various stages of manufacture. This richness of

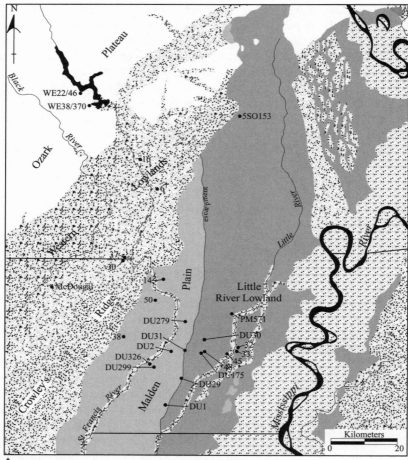

<sup>†</sup> note that location 6 represents the approximate provenience of 11 assemblages.

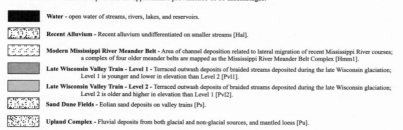

**Water** - open water of streams, rivers, lakes, and reservoirs.

**Recent Alluvium** - Recent alluvium undifferentiated on smaller streams [Hal].

**Modern Mississippi River Meander Belt** - Area of channel deposition related to lateral migration of recent Mississippi River courses; a complex of four older meander belts are mapped as the Mississippi River Meander Belt Complex [Hmm1].

**Late Wisconsin Valley Train - Level 1** - Terraced outwash deposits of braided streams deposited during the late Wisconsin glaciation; Level 1 is younger and lower in elevation than Level 2 [Pvl1].

**Late Wisconsin Valley Train - Level 2** - Terraced outwash deposits of braided streams deposited during the late Wisconsin glaciation; Level 2 is older and higher in elevation than Level 1 [Pvl2].

**Sand Dune Fields** - Eolian sand deposits on valley trains [Ps].

**Upland Complex** - Fluvial deposits from both glacial and non-glacial sources, and mantled loess [Pu].

**Figure 4.2. Map of Southeast Missouri and Northeast Arkansas showing physio-graphic provinces, surface geomorphology, and surface cluster locations (after O'Brien and Dunnell 1998); alphanumerics are Smithsonian numbers for surface clusters registered with the Archaeological Survey of Missouri and numerals are Miles Collection numbers for nonregistered surface clusters. See legend for explanation of shading; square brackets in legend contain designations of Saucier and Snead (1989).**

artifact types suggests that most assemblages are derived from domestic contexts and that collection bias is potentially minimal. Morphological and technological analyses have shown that the projectile points from these assemblages include manufacturing rejects, unfinished points, finished points, and use-fractured points. Since each cluster location was repeatedly surface collected over many years, the few assemblages that exhibit low richness of artifact types are likely to be representative of nondomestic contexts. Four of the assemblages were collected by people using a protocol to ensure sample representation of all objects greater than 4.0 mm (Dunnell n.d.).

Surface assemblages having accurate provenience records are used in this study because they are more well suited than excavated assemblages when evaluated in terms of: 1. statistical representation; 2. spatial autocorrelation; 3. resource depletion; and 4. assemblage size. Surface assemblages tend to be more statistically representative of artifact classes than are excavated assemblages because mechanical plowing randomizes artifacts on and within the plowzone (Ammerman 1985; Lewarch and O'Brien 1981). A small but representative percentage of artifacts are exposed on the surface at any given time, which means that in conditions of good surface visibility, systematic surface collections are statistically representative of subsurface assemblage composition. Depletion of the surface population through collection is also a gradual process, since only a small percentage of plow-zone material is present on the surface at any given time (Madsen and Dunnell 1989). As a result, surface clusters can typically be relocated even after tens of years of collection, providing extended fieldwork opportunities for resampling or for studying formation processes.

Another type of sample representativeness to be considered is spatial structure. Experimental studies demonstrate that very little lateral displacement takes place as a result of tillage (e.g., O'Brien and Lewarch 1981), suggesting that site structural data may be obtained at low cost through the systematic collection of entire surface clusters. This situation contrasts markedly with most excavations because the latter tend to recover artifacts from only small portions of subsurface deposits. As a consequence, excavated samples are not representative of entire subsurface deposits. In terms of spatial structure, they provide limited information at best. Thus, many excavated samples suffer from spatial autocorrelation wherein artifact frequencies tend to correlate with excavation location rather than assemblage structure or spatial structure.

Finally, surface collections tend to be larger than excavated collections in terms of numbers of objects simply because sample size can be increased at very low cost over many years. Thus, surface collections tend to be less subject than excavated collections to problems resulting from small sample size, such as sample size and richness correlations (Grayson 1989). For these various reasons, it is obvious that surface-collected assemblages with accurate provenience records meet the necessary conditions of this research.

### Characteristics of the Selective Environment

Environmental variation across the research area is largely a result of the ancient braided and meandering stream systems of the ancestral Mississippi and Ohio rivers (Saucier 1974; Smith and Saucier 1971). Evidence of these fluvial systems includes valley trains, relict stream channels, sloughs, flat to slightly undulating interfluves, swales, backswamps, floodplains, and levees. On a regional scale, four physiographic provinces are represented across which surface clusters of artifacts are located (Figure 4.2). These provinces include the Malden Plain, the Western Lowland, the Little River Lowland, and the Ozark Plateau.

The Malden Plain is an area of relatively high braided stream alluvium dating to the early Holocene (Fisk 1944). In general, the surface is approximately 10,850 years old and has been relatively unaffected by either erosion or deposition. At a local level, surface ages are variable; this variability is reflected in differences in topography, soil type, and drainage. The western boundary of the Malden Plain is marked by the north-to-south-trending Crowley's Ridge, which is composed of Tertiary-age gravels mantled by Quaternary loess deposits dating to approximately 13,000 B.P. (Guccione et al. 1988; Saucier 1974). The ridge extends from Commerce, Missouri, in the north, where it averages 12 miles wide, to Helena, Arkansas, in the south, where it averages 3 miles wide.

To the west, between Crowley's Ridge and the Ozark Plateau, lies the Western Lowlands. The Western Lowlands is also an area of braided stream alluvium and is comprised of five terrace sub-levels deposited prior to 30,000 years ago during the end of the Early Wisconsin glaciation (Saucier 1974). Many of these terraces are capped with a veneer of contiguous sand dunes formed by material blown from braided channels onto adjacent bars and interfluves between 20,000 and 25,000 years ago (Schiffer and House 1975). The oldest and highest stream terrace is situated adjacent to the western margin of Crowley's Ridge, where it is mantled by a thin and locally discontinuous layer of Peoria Loess that has an approximate surface age of 13,000 years B.P. (Rutledge et al. 1985). The archaeological assemblages derived from the Western Lowlands, therefore, are potentially older than those from the Malden Plain.

The Little River Lowland lies to the east of the Malden Plain and separates it from the Recent Mississippi floodplain. The Little River Lowland is composed of braided and meandering stream alluvium of the ancestral Mississippi and Ohio rivers, reworked and eroded by the modern Mississippi, as well as more modern features and alluvium associated with Little River and its tributaries. Except for erosional remnants, all of the Lowland is covered with a veneer of recent, fine-grained (Gumbo) sediments dating to approximately 6,000 B.P. For most of the Holocene, the Lowland was comprised of a levee-and-point-bar landscape punctuated by vast backswamp and open water lakes.

In this region, the history of environmental change is typically assessed through pollen profiles used to reconstruct past vegetation communities (e.g.,

Delcourt and Delcourt 1985). Given the dynamic fluvial history of the Central Mississippi Valley (hereafter CMV), however, pollen cores from one location may have little bearing on the actual conditions that existed in another location (O'Brien 1994). Fortunately, chemical and mechanical properties of soil, and geomorphic features on the landscape play an enormous role in the distribution and composition of floral and faunal communities. Geomorphic features also played an important role in structuring prehistoric land use in the CMV, offering the only high and dry places for settlement (Guccione et al. 1988). Soil characteristics and geomorphic features are more precise, if less accurate, surrogates for characterizing prehistoric environmental variation.

Each surface cluster location is confirmed in the field and plotted on USGS 7.5-minute topographic maps. These maps are overlain with both USDA General Soil Maps and photomosaics to quantify the relation between surface cluster location, soil types, and geomorphic features. This work is then supplemented with a large body of geomorphological data synthesized from recent research in the region (e.g., Guccione 1987; Guccione et al. 1988; Royall 1988; Royall et al. 1991; West and Rutledge 1987).

It is important to note that the utility of the environmental data varies depending on the formation processes responsible for the creation of individual assemblages. For example, assemblages formed in domestic contexts provide important information about manufacture and maintenance, whereas assemblages formed in use-contexts are more informative with regard to subsistence and land use. Thus, distances between domestic locations and raw material sources are an important measure of raw material acquisition costs, while distances between use-contexts and raw material sources generally are not. Consequently, it is important to understand how projectile point assemblages formed in order to determine how to interpret environmental variables with which they are associated.

## The Formation of Projectile Point Assemblages

Projectile points enter the archaeological record in a variety of ways. These "formation processes" can affect spatial associations traditionally recognized as "assemblages," in addition to affecting the richness and diversity of the assemblages. A discussion of how projectile point assemblages form is important in two respects: 1. to illustrate why traditional "assemblages" are inappropriate units of analysis; and 2. to outline formal and contextual properties that can be used, with engineering data and distributional models, to split assemblages and build appropriate historically related groups.

### Assemblages Formed in Use-Contexts

Projectile points lost in use typically occur as isolates in the landscape. Because these occurrences are low in density, individually lost points are not likely to be recovered in amateur surface collections or "site"-based research unless they are dropped near previously or subsequently deposited artifacts. In some environments, resources are clumped due to geomorphic constraints that affect local soil moisture, elevation, or water distribution. Since these areas may receive preferential utilization, the frequency of lost points over time will be high compared to the surrounding landscape. The assemblages produced in this manner contain historically unrelated points (Dancey 1973) and are often typified by a large number of distinct stylistic types relative to the overall number of points.

Whether points lost in use are recovered archaeologically as isolates, or as groups of historically unrelated artifacts, they often exhibit distal impact fractures that reach highest frequencies in use-contexts. Projectile points recovered from use-contexts, regardless of how they are related to each other, are invaluable because they provide direct evidence of the environmental context of projectile use. When relatively ephemeral geomorphic features, such as drainage bottoms or sloughs characterize these contexts, an important component of the selective environment of projectile use can often be inferred.

### Assemblages Formed in Special Activity Loci

Assemblages of projectile points may also result from historically related events of deposition. Some may represent special activity loci, such as hunting camps that are associated with the activities serviced by points. These projectile point assemblages are often dominated by broken parts and rejuvenated and/or recycled points. Such assemblages are traditionally distinguished by the low diversity of artifact types (including non projectile artifacts), and their historical integrity results in a low number of distinct stylistic types defined by historically related attributes.

Projectile points are also found as part of large, diverse assemblages traditionally identified as domestic loci. These assemblages can be identified because points in these contexts will be dominated by manufacturing rejects, rejuvenated points, and recycled points. When the raw material for projectile point manufacture is nearby, acquisition costs are minimal and the assemblage is likely to be dominated by a high frequency of debitage related to manufacture. As distance to the raw material source increases, however, increasing acquisition costs eventually put a premium on rejuvenation and recycling. These contrasting circumstances affect the structure of projectile point assemblages in several ways. Perhaps most obvious is the effect on the ratio of finished points to manufacturing rejects and debitage. Less obvious is the tendency for recycling to increase the complexity of a projectile point's use-history, particularly in assemblages far from lithic sources. In lithic-poor regions, for example, the use-history of a projectile point may span several millennia during which it may be found, utilized, rejuvenated, and lost by several unrelated lineages. Subsequent functions can obscure previous ones, while at the same time alter morphology. Thus, projectile points with complex use-histories must be interpreted in terms of the most recent function. Since this is not always easy to discern, projectile points with complex use-histories may be problematic.

Functional points will always be a small fraction of projectile point assemblages from domestic loci. Thus, their presence in such contexts is ambiguous, i.e., they may be historically related to other cluster elements or they may be part of the "in use" rain of isolated and historically unrelated projectile points in the landscape. Domestic loci that exhibit evidence of projectile point manufacture and maintenance provide an important source of information on manufacturing costs. For example, the amount of energy expended in lithic raw material acquisition scales directly (all else being equal) with distance between the source and the domestic locus where projectile point manufacturing occurs. Other costs that may be inferred from the content of a domestic assemblage are discussed in greater detail in subsequent sections.

Artifact caches represent another kind of special activity locus containing projectile points. Caches of projectile points are found either as burial goods, or as early stage manufacturing preforms and finished points. Because these points are historically related, they are stylistically and technologically similar, and are often devoid of distal impact fractures. Depending on whether they come from burial or nonburial contexts, cached points provide a variable amount of information about the selective context of projectile use, manufacturing, or performance. Manufacturing "preforms" and finished points provide information about manufacturing costs but nothing about the context of projectile use or projectile performance.

### Assemblage Formation and Collection Techniques

Collection techniques can also affect the spatial associations regarded as assemblages or the richness and diversity of artifact classes that an assemblage contains. This is true not only for amateur-collected surface assemblages but for professionally derived assemblages as well. Since domestic loci are "rich" in artifacts compared to other special activity loci, they are more obtrusive on the landscape and have long been the focus of extensive investigations, including surface collection and excavation. Thus, materials collected by amateurs are typically biased toward large, relatively whole, projectile points in the late stages of manufacture. Professionals may collect a wider range of materials, including manufacturing rejects and debitage, but detailed analysis is often restricted to virtually complete points. As a result, use-fractured points and early-stage manufacturing rejects are under-represented in collections and analyses. Small points may be under-represented as well, simply because they are less obtrusive than larger points. Thus, as samples for estimating population parameters, existing projectile point assemblages are often poor regardless of who undertook the collection or excavation.

Representativeness can also be biased by inadequate spatial control during surface collection. Spatially distinct surface clusters may be collected as one cluster resulting in a "mixed" assemblage containing historically unrelated projectile points. Alternatively, a single cluster may be collected as two or more assemblages separated arbitrarily on the basis of general location and date of collection.

Fortunately, these problems can sometimes be resolved through relocating and recollecting a surface cluster (or clusters) along spatially controlled transects.

Of the many contexts in which projectile point assemblages are formed, few provide unambiguous groups of historically related points useful for the analytical purposes outlined in this research. However, understanding the formation processes responsible for these assemblages provides information about which assemblages are likely to contain historically related points. This information can be used in conjunction with engineering and distributional models to build and test appropriate analytical units. In addition, an understanding of formation processes is necessary to determine how to evaluate projectile point data against the different environmental contexts in which the assemblages are found.

## REDEFINING PROJECTILE POINTS FOR ANALYSIS

Most archaeologists are aware that the morphological class "projectile point" is not functionally homogeneous and, consequently, some of the variation in form may arise from differences in projectile variants or features resulting from secondary use. By projectile technologies, I refer to various kinds of projectiles including: thrusting projectiles, hand-held casting projectiles, and projectiles launched using either an atlatl or bow. The primary function of all these projectile point variants is piercing. Developing a means to identify tools used for a piercing function is accomplished by constructing an explicitly defined class for grouping functionally related tools.

Tools are grouped based on similarity in engineering design. In the manufacture of projectile points, energy is expended in a complex bifacial manufacturing process resulting in the following engineering design features: longitudinal axial symmetry, a pointed termination at one end of the longitudinal axis, and a relatively nonpointed termination at the other end of the longitudinal axis. These design features are selected for, or "engineered" by selection, for a piercing function. Secondary functions, such as controlling the weight distribution of a shaft or cutting to enlarge a hole, depend upon the way in which objects interact with the environment of use and other mechanical components. Design features relating to these functions are more variable than features related to piercing. Thus, design characteristics related to piercing are more suitable for defining a class of objects having a high degree of functional coherence. This class is referred to as *Pointed Lithic Biface* (*PLB*), and the engineering characteristics required for membership include: 1. pointed and less-pointed ends at opposite extremes of the longitudinal axis; and, 2. longitudinal axial symmetry (Figure 4.3).

Some objects that satisfy the requirements for membership to *PLB* may have served both piercing and nonpiercing functions. For the most part, these include objects traditionally referred to as "drills," though some objects referred to as "knives" or "scrapers" may be included as well. Significantly, projectile points may serve other "nonpiercing" functions and, as long as they satisfy the engineering criteria listed above, they remain a member of the class *PLB*. A

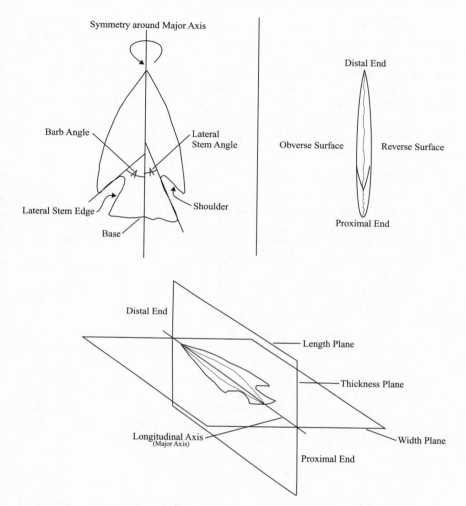

**Figure 4.3. Diagram showing terms and planes of reference for pointed lithic bifaces.**

projectile point can therefore be a multifunctional tool which remains serviceable as a projectile point for a period of time that is affected by both projectile and nonprojectile functions.

## ENGINEERING DESIGN ANALYSIS

Experimental data on aerodynamics and penetration identify the functional traits that need to be documented and provide a source of hypotheses about projectile evolution. Manufacturing cost and performance are concepts derived from evolutionary theory. When two or more non-neutral traits perform the same function, those which cost less to produce and/or perform more efficiently eventually attain higher frequencies than higher-cost, lower-efficiency alternatives. In this way, natural selection builds an engineering solution to a given task by favoring the persistence of traits that are more cost-effective in providing a solution and/or perform more efficiently. Thus, subsequent to the design analysis, manufacturing cost and performance parameters are outlined with the eventual goal of using them to construct evolutionary explanations of the differential persistence of trait frequencies.

### Projectile Design Considerations

Early in their history, projectiles may have been propelled at low velocity because relatively little selection against nonaerodynamic forms had taken place. Selection against forms with poor balance and insufficient penetration at low velocities may have favored innovations such as dense foreshafts and blade-edge serration. In fact, the repeated appearance of serrated blades in the archaeological record may be tied to changes in biface technology in general; changes that periodically reduced projectile velocity such that selection favored serrated blade edges with a similar periodicity. Selection against nonaerodynamic projectiles over time may have been the result of changes in resource structure, both in terms of resources necessary for building projectiles and in the animal species exploited through projectile use. These changes may also have been linked to changes in acquisition strategies, such as ambush versus stalking strategies (Waselkov 1978). Although these processes may be unknown at present, the cause lies in selection operating on preexisting variation. As projectile velocity increased through changes in propulsion technology, decreased projectile mass and increased projectile equilibrium would result in greater range and accuracy than low-velocity projectiles. Since penetration at high velocities is largely the result of kinetic energy, bifaces may have become smaller and more variable.

Projectile stability in flight is also maintained more effectively at higher velocities by decreasing projectile size and adding light surfaces such as fletching to the rear (proximal) end of the shaft. In some contexts, these changes may have had the added benefit of requiring less raw material for projectile manufacture and less frequent maintenance and replacement of projectile components. Before turning to a more detailed examination of projectile physics, however, it is important to note again that Newtonian mechanics provides only a functional explanation of projectile variation by specifying the interaction of functional traits. To explain trends in projectile evolution, it is necessary to document the differential persistence of these traits within the environmental context of projectile use over time and space.

### Physics of Flight

A projectile is a linear, rod-shaped object comprised of two or more interrelated components such as a biface, foreshaft, and mainshaft. Hand-held casting spears, atlatl darts, and arrows are flight projectiles delivered from predator to prey by propulsion through air. Two kinds of energy are involved in projectile propulsion. Potential energy (V) is the energy of a projectile due to its position or state of strain and is stored in the human musculature (O'Connell and Gardner 1972). When potential energy is released, it is converted into kinetic energy (T), which is the energy of a projectile due to its motion, and is transferred from the human musculature to the projectile either directly or through an intermediate device such as an atlatl or bow. The quantity of projectile motion is called momentum (P) and is the product of projectile mass and linear velocity (Tillery 1992). Mass (m) is a measurement of the quantity of matter in a projectile and is expressed as weight in kilograms, whereas linear velocity (v) is the rate of change in spatial location. All of these variables are functionally related, since different combinations of mass and velocity affect projectile flight, biface penetration, and breakage.

When the angle between a projectile and its flight-path tangent approximates zero, the projectile is considered to be in equilibrium. When a projectile is in equilibrium at the moment of impact, kinetic energy is most effectively translated into energy available for cutting and penetration (Huckell 1982). The equilibrium of a projectile is affected by the relative positions of the center of gravity (CG) and the center of pressure (CP) (Cotterell and Kamminga 1992). The center of gravity is the point in a projectile through which the force of gravity acts, and the center of pressure is the point through which aerodynamic forces act (Cotterell and Kamminga 1992) (Figure 4.4).

The probability of a projectile stalling or tumbling during flight increases with the angle between a projectile and its flight-path tangent. Two methods are available to increase projectile equilibrium and control stalling and tumbling: 1. increasing the mass of the projectile near the tip (distal end) so that the center of gravity is in front of the center of pressure; and 2. changing the shape of the projectile so that the center of pressure is moved toward the rear (proximal end), behind the center of gravity. The first method requires that 75% of the projectile's mass be concentrated in the distal 25% of its length in order to achieve a suitable relationship between the centers of pressure and gravity (Cundy 1989).

Although such a design has been used, it presents limitations on how energy is transferred to the projectile from the human musculature. Propulsion devices such as the bow or atlatl, for example, transfer energy through the proximal end of the projectile. This requires that the proximal section of the shaft be durable yet flexible, and have lower mass than the distal section—a configuration that can lead to bending and shaft fracture, particularly in higher-velocity projectiles. Consequently, this means of increasing equilibrium is more efficient for projectiles in which energy is transferred near the center of gravity, as is the case for relatively low-velocity spears or darts fitted with dense foreshafts or bifaces having large mass.

The second method of increasing equilibrium is to add light surfaces such as feathers to the proximal end to increase the surface area and move the center of pressure behind the center of gravity. The addition of feathers, i.e., fletching, is

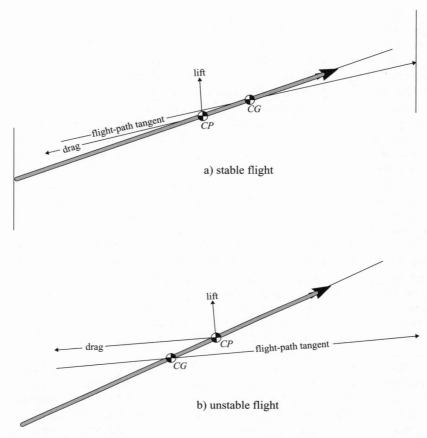

a) stable flight

b) unstable flight

**Figure 4.4. The relationship between the centers of pressure (*CP*) and gravity (*CG*) and their effect on projectile equilibrium: a) stable flight; b) unstable flight (after Cotterell and Kamminga 1992:171).**

common in modern arrows and has been extensively documented ethnographically (e.g., Cundy 1989; Palter 1977; Pope 1923). In addition to increasing projectile equilibrium, fletching placed obliquely to the projectile long axis imparts a rotation about the longitudinal axis that reduces wobble much like the rotational effect on a bullet caused by a rifled gun barrel.

During flight, the gravitation force causes projectiles to travel in an arched trajectory. When propelled horizontally the trajectory of a high-velocity projectile follows a large parabolic curve, whereas that of a low-velocity projectile follows a small parabolic curve. A low-velocity projectile such as a spear must therefore be cast upward so its arched trajectory overcomes the gravitational effect. This arched trajectory requires the point-of-aim to be between the thrower and a close target, or beyond a distant target. In general, greater consistency and accuracy is achieved when the trajectory of a projectile is flatter (Christenson 1986a, 1986b; Klopsteg 1939), and this is accomplished by an increase in velocity (Beyer 1962; Cundy 1989). A decrease in mass or an increase in kinetic energy achieves an increase in velocity. Arrows, for example, have relatively low mass and a minimal amount of potential energy is lost during transfer through the bow staves to the arrow shaft as kinetic energy. Thus, arrows are propelled at relatively high velocities of up to 50 m/sec. (Bergman et al. 1988) and the arrow remains almost perfectly aligned with the flight path throughout flight. The kinetic energy of low-velocity projectiles such as spears and darts can be increased by increasing projectile mass, although this is much less effective than increasing potential energy directly. Adding mass in the form of a heavier foreshaft or biface moves the center of gravity forward of the center of pressure and increases projectile equilibrium. However, the addition of mass increases drag and decreases lift so that low-velocity projectiles reach equilibrium much later in the course of flight than do high-velocity projectiles.

Blade surface area and longitudinal cross section are biface variables that also influence projectile aerodynamics. As the blade surface area of a biface increases, the center of pressure moves forward (distally) on the projectile and instability increases as the center of pressure eventually moves forward of the center of gravity. When the longitudinal cross section of a biface is not bilaterally symmetrical, a "steering effect" also pulls the projectile away from the flight path (Klopsteg 1943:189). The steering effect results from differential air pressures on each surface of the blade. Although the aerodynamic effects of blade surface area and longitudinal cross section increase with projectile velocity, the effects of each variable can also cancel each other out. In relatively high-velocity arrows, for example, the irregular longitudinal cross section of a biface may have no significant steering effect if the blade surface area is small relative to the cross-sectional area of the projectile shaft.

## Physics of Penetration

Data from wound ballistics and experimental studies have shown that penetration is a function of striking velocity, mass, tip sharpness, and blade-edge design. All else being equal, increasing velocity increases the amount of kinetic energy dissipated in a wound, eventually creating an explosive effect that shears skin and tissue leaving a wound cavity larger than the projectile dimensions (Jauhari and Bandyopadhyay 1976). Most prehistoric projectiles had an average velocity ranging from 18 m/sec to a maximum of perhaps 50 m/sec (Bergman et al. 1988; Cundy 1989; Pope 1923; Van Buren 1974). Within this range, arrows are high-velocity projectiles relative to atlatl darts and hand-held casting projectiles that are likely to have decreased in average velocity, respectively. Kinetic energy ($T$) is calculated as:

$$T = mv^2/2 \hspace{5cm} \text{(Equation 1)}$$

(where $m$ = mass and $v$ = velocity). Consequently, doubling mass yields only half the increase in kinetic energy that doubling velocity yields (Mattoo et al. 1974). This suggests that an inverse relation between mass and velocity contributes to enhanced penetration. Thus, the kinetic energy available for penetration at the moment of impact may be raised by increasing the mass of lower-velocity projectiles or by decreasing the mass of higher-velocity projectiles. The mass/velocity relationship also suggests that improvements in projectile equilibrium may be more efficiently achieved, in specific contexts, by increasing velocity rather than increasing mass.

Skin is a difficult substance to penetrate because it is a compliant material that undergoes relatively large deformations under applied stress before it actually yields (Friis-Hansen 1990). Because spears and darts are relatively low-velocity projectiles, penetration is affected more by tip sharpness and blade-edge configuration than by kinetic energy. A sharp tip concentrates downward force on the substrate resulting in compressional stresses, while tensional stresses develop as the substrate below the tip is depressed beyond the adjacent substrate. The result is a complex of principle stresses working within the substrate that generate shearing stresses in several planes midway between the principle stresses (Prindle and Walden 1976). The sharper the tip, the greater the disparity between compression and tension and the greater the potential shear, resulting in penetration.

Both archaeological and experimental work has been used to suggest that needle-sharp tips on bifaces enable low-velocity projectiles to achieve the penetration needed to immobilize large prey (Fischer 1985; Frison 1989, 1993; Frison et al. 1976; Frison and Todd 1986; Larralde 1990). Tip sharpness contributes to penetration largely by opening a hole (Frazzetta 1988; Knight 1975). After a hole is opened, however, it must be enlarged to facilitate penetration of the remainder of the biface and shaft. Drag on the biface is caused by the work of cutting and by the size of the maximum perimeter of the biface ($P_p$) which must pass through the hole and displace tissue (Friis-Hansen 1990) (Figure 4.5). Drag on the shaft comes from friction between the skin tissue and internal organs that close around the shaft upon entry. Experimental data suggest that some projectiles, particularly arrows, penetrate to a depth of 18–24 cm (Frison 1989; Huckell 1982; Odell and Cowen 1986). Holding velocity and mass constant, the deepest penetration is obtained when the maximum perimeter of the biface ($P_p$) is slightly larger than the maximum perimeter of the shaft ($P_s$) within 20 cm of the biface, so that friction between the shaft and wound opening is minimized (Figure 4.5). This configuration yields a $P_p{:}P_s$ ratio of slightly more than one. In archaeological specimens lacking shafts, shaft diameter is often approximated by the minimum stem width for stemmed bifaces, or as maximum base width for stemless bifaces (cf. Friis-Hansen 1990; Huckell 1982; Hughes 1995; Thomas 1978).

The function of enlarging the hole or wound may be served by blade edges that expand from the tip toward the proximal end. Given the same normal force ($N$), i.e., force applied normal to the cutting plane, a smooth blade drawn across a compliant substrate will cut more effectively than when it is simply pressed into

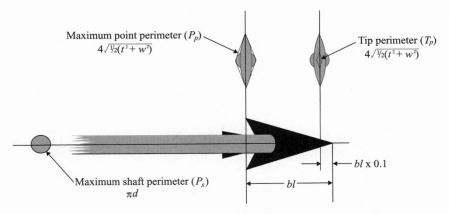

Figure 4.5. Locations for measuring maximum point perimeter (*Pp*), maximum shaft perimeter (*Ps*), and tip perimeter (*Tp*) (after Friis-Hansen 1990:498).

the substrate (Frazzetta 1988). Thus, the delta wing configuration of most bifaces is well suited to cutting because the blade edge is forced into the substrate at an angle. Edge friction against the substrate produces strain deformations of the affected material resulting in damaging shear stresses. The cutting value of a biface is greatest when the forces of stress are most concentrated, i.e., when the edge is sharpest. Increasing the normal force (*N*) increases friction directly and this also enhances the cutting value (Abler 1992). The cutting value of a smooth-edged blade is markedly limited, however, because of its dependence upon friction to produce shearing stresses. A useful cutting force will often be far smaller than the normal force (*N*), and never take full advantage of a potentially large drawing force (*D*); thus, in smooth-bladed cutting, the drawing force (*D*) has a maximum useful value that can never be greater than the frictional force (*f*) (Frazzetta 1988). Figure 4.6 illustrates the principle stresses created by smooth blades and serrated blades.

Unlike smooth blades, serrated blades have edges developed as a series of small projections or scallops. A serrated edge pressed against a compliant substrate can push a row of projections into the substrate, with very little yielding or even puncture. In fact, there is no need for an excessively large normal force (*N*) to push the projections into a compliant substrate such as skin and tissue. The drawing force (*D*) therefore functions nearly alone when a blade is serrated, and only a minimal normal force (*N*) just large enough to hold the projections in contact with the substrate is necessary (Frazzetta 1988). As the blade is drawn across the compliant substrate, each projection pulls against the material into which it is depressed, and tears it directly. Thus, all of the drawing force (*D*) is useful up to the yielding of the substrate rather than being limited by the frictional force (*f*). Finally, empirical studies have also demonstrated that both the degree of serration and evenness of serrations have an affect on cutting (Abler 1992; Frazzetta

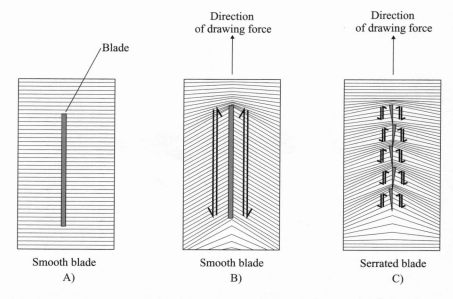

**Figure 4.6. Schematic plan view of complex strain deformations resulting in cutting: a) a smooth blade with normal force applied but no drawing force; b) a smooth blade with normal and drawing forces applied; c) a serrated blade with normal and drawing forces applied. Thin lines represent general strain deformations to substrate and thick lines represent complex localized strain deformations at region of blade/substrate contact.**

1988). Degree of serration refers to the overall size of serrations, while evenness of serrations refers to size changes over the length of an edge.

## Empirical Studies of Biface Fracture

Distinguishing biface fractures resulting from projectile use and manufacture, as well as nonprojectile functions, is important for several reasons. Bifaces fractured as a result of projectile use provide evidence of the physics of projectile use. When found in a use context, they also provide a link to the systemic and ecological contexts of projectile use. Catastrophic fractures resulting in manufacturing failure provide information on the quality of raw material, as well as the amount of energy invested in the production of bifaces. Bifaces prone to failure during manufacture, whether as a result of poor raw material or complex morphology, necessarily cost more to produce than bifaces that fail less often. Finally, fractures resulting from nonprojectile use constitute a source of information about the multifunctional nature of some biface forms. Bifaces that remain serviceable for projectiles while also performing other functions also cost less to produce, since their production costs are distributed across more than one function.

Experimental research on the fracture characteristics of lithic bifaces during use (Bergman and Newcomer 1983; Fischer 1985; Fischer et al. 1984; Huckell 1982; Odell and Cowen 1986; Titmus and Woods 1986; Towner and Warburton 1990; Woods 1988) and manufacture (Austin 1986; Flenniken and Raymond 1986; Titmus 1985; Woods 1987) is relatively recent. Nonetheless, fracture mechanics and experimental data suggest that use and manufacturing breakage can be distinguished by the location and orientation of flake scars and fractures (Atkinson 1989; Cotterell and Kamminga 1992; Fischer 1985; Titmus and Woods 1986). Flake propagation during manufacture results from tensile stresses applied near an edge, resulting in a partial Hertzian cone. Flake trajectory is at an angle to the longitudinal axis (Faulkner 1972; Speth 1972). Only this mode of flake propagation results in the characteristic bulb of percussion (Cotterell and Kamminga 1987:687). During use, flake propagation results from in-plane shear initiated at a point and flake trajectory tends to be in line with the longitudinal axis. These flakes, referred to as distal impact fractures, have small or nonexistent bulbs of percussion (Atkinson 1989; Cotterell and Kamminga 1979). Distal impact fractures originate at the distal terminus of the longitudinal axis and terminate proximally. Variation from these general characteristics is due to impact angle, substrate properties, material homogeneity, voids, and incipient fractures.

In addition, the orientation of use-related fractures can differ with projectile velocity, since velocity affects the direction of force at impact. High-velocity projectiles reach equilibrium quickly and the direction of force at impact is in line with the longitudinal axis of the projectile. In contrast, low-velocity projectiles can take much longer to reach equilibrium, often striking their target at large and quite variable angles, so the direction of force at impact is variable. Consequently, when distal impact fractures occur on bifaces mounted to high-velocity projectiles, they tend to be initiated by in-plane shear and are in line with the longitudinal axis (Atkinson 1989). Bifaces mounted to low-velocity projectiles tend to have distal impact fractures initiated by compression or bending, and the orientation of the crack is often normal to the longitudinal axis, or at oblique angles (Atkinson 1989; Faulkner 1972).

## Manufacturing Cost and Performance

To understand the differential persistence of variation in projectiles, it is necessary to examine not only engineering design but manufacturing cost and performance as well. Manufacturing cost refers to the energy invested in building a given phenotypic structure comprised of one or more traits. Energy is invested in the manufacture of all traits and structures, whether they are neutral or non-neutral in terms of reproductive success. According to the definition of a neutral trait, the energy invested in manufacture has no effect on reproductive success. If a neutral trait comes under selection, however, it becomes non-neutral by definition because the energy invested in its manufacture and/or its performance relative to functionally equivalent traits affects reproductive success. In other words, selection sorts heritable traits in terms of their manufacturing cost and relative performance to a given engineering solution in a given environment.

### Manufacturing Cost

The manufacturing cost of lithic bifaces is a function of the amount of energy expended directly or indirectly on raw material acquisition, manufacturing investment, manufacturing failure, and biface durability. Knowledge of the engineering design of projectiles and the physical properties of raw materials used to manufacture bifaces can be used to identify the traits relevant to these variables. However, due to the complex interaction of these traits, there is no optimal configuration that minimizes manufacturing costs. The overall manufacturing cost will be a function of geographic structure and distance between manufacturing locations and raw material sources, variation in the physical properties of the various raw materials, the selective environment of projectile use, etc. Consequently, it is the cumulative cost of these variables that must be evaluated over time and space. In general, manufacturing costs (*MC*) can be calculated as:

$MC = f$(raw material acquisition, manufacturing investment, manufacturing failure, biface durability).        (Equation 2)

Variables for calculating manufacturing cost are a function of other variables for which the values must be determined. These are discussed in the following sections and illustrated in Figure 4.7.

#### Raw Material Acquisition

Raw material acquisition cost is a function of material abundance, material physical properties, and transport distance. For secondary sources such as gravel deposits, lithic heterogeneity affects the amount of energy devoted to searching for raw materials. Average cobble dimensions vary among different gravel sources even within the same fluvial system, since gravel weathering in active systems is affected by flow velocity, transport distance, and material hardness (Plumley 1948). While fluvial transport tends to remove brittle material quickly, the age of a gravel deposit has a further affect on the physical properties of gravel due to in situ weathering. Material acquisition costs can therefore be high for secondary gravel sources because of their complex origin and transport history, even though they may be close to manufacturing locations. Tool size and shape requirements, heat treatment response, and fracture predictability interact with the physical properties of raw material in such a way as to increase search time for cobbles having particular characteristics.

By comparison, the physical properties of primary source materials tend to be more homogeneous. Thus, the cost of raw material acquisition from a primary source may be relatively low, even though it may be further from the manufacturing location. In general, the greater the distance between a lithic raw material source and the location of manufacture, the more energy is expended to transport raw materials. In its simplest expression, transport cost can be measured in terms of linear distance. However, variation in geography and mode of transport increase the complexity of measuring transport cost, because they can result in disparate energy expenditures for similar linear distances.

Material acquisition is evaluated in my research by examining the frequency of different material types in each domestic assemblage and the distance to known sources. Gravels derived locally from Crowley's Ridge account for at least 95% of the raw materials in the assemblages, and these are accessible in the cut banks of major streams flowing off the ridge. Biface size is evaluated against the size distribution of cobbles using previous research on the physical properties of Crowley's Ridge gravels (Bangs 1991; McCutcheon 1997).

*Manufacturing Investment*

Manufacturing investment also entails an expenditure of energy through a combination of manufacturing procedures. Among other things, heat treatment, blade serration and beveling, notching, lateral and basal grinding, and the amount of flaking necessary to produce a functional biface all contribute to the amount of energy invested in manufacturing. In general, the greater the number of manufacturing procedures the greater the manufacturing investment. However, energy expended during one procedure can reduce the energy expended during another procedure, or it may offset the energy expended in the procedure by increasing performance efficiency. Heat treatment, for example, lowers fracture toughness and increases fracture predictability, thereby reducing the incidence of failure during manufacture.

Energy expended in the process of manufacturing a biface is an investment if the finished product contributes to future energy returns, i.e., hunting success. This can be accomplished by reducing the overall manufacturing investment, increasing performance efficiency, or reducing the potential for manufacturing failure. Manufacturing investment is being assessed for finished bifaces by documenting the kind and invasiveness of notching, and the presence of blade serration and serration characteristics, blade-edge beveling, lateral and basal grinding, and heat treatment. In addition, the relative amount of flaking necessary to produce a finished biface is assessed by noting the number of overlapping flake sets, which are analogous to primary, secondary, and tertiary flake sets.

*Manufacturing Failure*

Manufacturing failure results when the manufacturing process is terminated prior to completion due to a catastrophic fracture or inability to satisfy design requirements. Manufacturing failure may result from nonhomogeneity of material, incipient flaws, or production errors. Failure during the manufacturing process results in an unrecoverable loss of energy investment. The rate of failure during manufacture increases the total energy necessary to produce lithic bifaces by increasing the frequency of manufacturing events necessary to reproduce a projectile technology. The rate of failure also interacts with material acquisition costs because, for a given failure rate, the energy expended in raw material acquisition increases linearly with distance to the source, regardless of geography and transport mode. The rate of manufacturing failure is being assessed by the ratio of finished bifaces to manufacturing rejects. However, manufacturing rejects tend to be recycled more often as distance to the raw material source increases, which may skew this ratio.

### Biface Durability

Biface durability is the length of time a biface can be used before requiring maintenance and eventual replacement. This affects the number of bifaces that are necessary to perform a given amount of work. Durability is a function of fracture toughness and physical properties. In general, a biface made from a brittle raw material will break upon impact more frequently than a biface made from a relatively less brittle material. In addition, physical properties such as voids and inclusions sometimes reduce fracture toughness, but they can also increase toughness by inhibiting fracture propagation. A more durable biface has a longer use-life and needs to be replaced less often than a less durable biface. Up to a point, however, brittleness facilitates manufacture and, thus, material choice is a compromise. In the case of lithic bifaces, the latter criterion outweighs the former so that many brittle materials like obsidian, almost never used for scrapers, are readily used for some kinds of lithic bifaces. The extensive use of heat treatment, which makes cherts more brittle, also suggests that durability is outweighed by other manufacturing or performance costs. Biface durability is assessed by characterizing lithic materials using a raw material typology and physical property paradigm that have been developed for the research area (McCutcheon 1997). The raw material typology distinguishes Crowley's Ridge gravel and various nonlocal materials from known sources such as Burlington, Mill Creek, Dover, and Pitkin cherts, as well as Arkansas Novaculite and St. Francois Mountain Rhyolite. The physical property paradigm characterizes these materials in terms of bedding structures and the occurrence and distribution of solid and void inclusions.

### Performance

The performance of lithic bifaces is a function of the effectiveness of penetration, biface retrogression, and angle of impact. The engineering design analysis allows identification of traits relevant to each of these variables. Again, however, it is important to note that since trait neutrality is context dependent, there is no optimal combination or value for these traits that will maximize performance. A neutral trait in one selective context may be non-neutral in another. Consequently, it is the differential persistence of these traits for a given environment, over time, that must be evaluated against the distributional models for neutral and non-neutral traits. Holding environmental context constant, however, it is possible to evaluate the relative performance ($P$) of different biface forms by the following measurement:

$P = f$(effectiveness of penetration, retrograde resistance, angle of impact).

(Equation 3)

Like manufacturing costs, the variables from which performance is evaluated are each a function of other variables for which the values must be determined. These are discussed in the following sections and also illustrated in Figure 4.7.

### Effectiveness of Penetration

Effectiveness of penetration is a function of kinetic energy; the ratio of maximum point perimeter to maximum shaft perimeter ($P_p$:$P_s$); tip perimeter ($T_p$) (Figure 4.5); blade-edge angle; and blade-edge sharpness and configuration. Unfortunately, the kinetic energy of a projectile cannot be estimated archaeologically from bifaces alone. Tip perimeter is a measure of tip sharpness, while the ratio of maximum point perimeter to maximum shaft perimeter affects how much the hole has to be enlarged for the biface and shaft to pass through. The effectiveness of penetration in this research is being assessed by documenting maximum point perimeter ($P_p$), maximum shaft perimeter ($P_s$), tip perimeter ($T_p$), blade-edge sharpness, and the incidence of blade serration. Serration configuration is measured ordinally using the degree and evenness of serration. Blade-edge sharpness is also measured using a goniometer and is averaged from several locations along the blade edge.

### Retrograde Resistance

Retrogression refers to movement in an opposite or backward direction. Projectile retrogression is the movement of a projectile in a direction generally opposed to that necessary for penetration. Barbs are often added to a biface as part of the manufacturing process to increase retrograde resistance and inhibit biface removal from the wound cavity. The addition of barbs increases the probability of a projectile shaft or fore shaft remaining within the wound cavity after impact. During an animal's flight, a biface with barbs will move around within the wound cavity due to the weight of the shaft or to resistance from obstacles such as brush or trees. In conjunction with the contraction and expansion of muscle tissues, this movement increases the amount of damage to tissues, blood vessels, and arteries (Friis-Hansen 1990). As a result, the animal dies from shock induced by hemorrhaging.

Three variables are important for retrograde resistance: 1. angle of the barbs; 2. depth of the barbs; and, 3. angle of the lateral stem edges. The angle of the barb is measured between the barb, often referred to as the shoulder, and the longitudinal axis of the biface. By decreasing barb angle, the potential for retrograde resistance increases as tissue becomes bunched between the barb and the lateral edge of the stem. Increasing the distance between the distal terminus of the lateral stem edge and the proximal terminus of the blade edge increases the depth of the barb. Increasing this distance causes even more tissue to become bunched within

MANUFACTURING COST

| Raw Material Acquisition | *function of:*<br>material abundance<br>transport distance<br>material form relative to tool form | *measured by:*<br>abundance of raw material at source<br>meters to raw material source<br>cobble:biface size ratio |
|---|---|---|
| Manufacturing Investment | *function of:*<br>number of manufacturing<br>procedures | *measured by:*<br>number of overlapping flake sets<br>kind and invasiveness of notching<br>blade-edge beveling<br>heat treatment<br>degree and evenness of serration<br>lateral and basal grinding |
| Manufacturing Failure | *function of:*<br>material homogeneity<br>material flaws<br>production errors | *measured by:*<br>physical property paradigm<br>physical property paradigm<br>finished:reject ratio |
| Biface Durability | *function of:*<br>fracture toughness<br>physical properties | *measured by:*<br>fracture toughness<br>physical property paradigm<br>raw material typology |

PERFORMANCE

| Effectiveness of penetration | *function of:*<br>point:shaft perimeter ratio<br>tip perimeter<br>blade-edge angle<br>blade-edge sharpness<br>blade-edge configuration | *measured by:*<br>point:shaft perimeter ratio<br>tip perimeter<br>blade-edge angle<br>blade-edge sharpness<br>degree and evenness of serration |
|---|---|---|
| Retrograde Resistance | *function of:*<br>presence of barbs<br>depth of barbs<br>expanding lateral stems | *measured by:*<br>angle relative to longitudinal axis<br>blade terminus to stem depth<br>proximal stem angle |
| Angle of Impact | *function of:*<br>projectile balance | *measured by:*<br>kind of impact fracture<br>orientation of impact fracture |

**Figure 4.7. Variables that affect the manufacturing cost and performance of bifaces and how they are measured archaeologically.**

the area of the barb and also increases friction by increasing the surface area of the blade edge in contact with the tissue. Retrograde force is also transferred to the haft area, however, where the biface is secured to the shaft or fore shaft. Resistance to retrograde motion at this point is facilitated by expanding lateral stem edges. Resistance to retrograde movement is therefore assessed by measuring all three of these variables.

*Angle of Impact*

The angle of a projectile with respect to a contact material during impact can also affect both penetration and breakage. To penetrate, a projectile must impact the contact material at a low angle with respect to the flight-path tangent, probably less than 5° (Cotterell and Kamminga 1992). The angle of impact depends on throwing skill and projectile balance. On impact, if the direction of force at the biface tip is in line with the longitudinal axis, the stress system is primarily compressive and a flake may or may not initiate, depending upon the material's fracture toughness and the physical properties of the target. These flakes, called distal impact fractures, generally travel down one surface of the blade and are more or less in line with the longitudinal axis of the biface. Often these flakes remove so little material that the biface remains serviceable or can be returned to service with minimal rejuvenation.

When the direction of force is at an angle to the longitudinal axis, secondary tensile stresses along one surface normally initiate a flake through bending (Tsirk 1979). Either the tip is truncated by the fracture or one blade edge may be partially or entirely removed by a burin-like fracture. Bifaces fractured in this manner are less likely to be returned to service through rejuvenation, since bending typically results in the loss of a relatively large portion of the blade, if not the entire blade segment. Instead, they may be discarded where used or recycled as "end scrapers." In general, however, as biface thickness approaches biface width, the potential for fracture initiation decreases, regardless of the angle of impact. Angle of impact can be assessed for bifaces exhibiting distal impact fractures by documenting the kind and location of fractures.

## BUILDING COUNTING UNITS FOR THE ANALYSIS OF DIFFERENTIAL PERSISTENCE

Information generated from the engineering design analysis and the discussion of manufacturing cost and performance have been used to develop classifications that describe biface variation in terms of potentially neutral and non-neutral traits. After characterizing this variation, it is necessary to build counting units in which to evaluate the differential persistence of these traits over time and space. Since neutrality is context dependent it is also necessary to test which of these traits are *actually* non-neutral given their environment of use. These goals are being accomplished using the occurrence seriation method and thermoluminescence (TL) dates.

### Counting Unit Requirements

The explanation of evolutionary change is the explanation of changes in frequencies. Generating frequencies that are explained by evolutionary theory requires counting units populated by objects or observations derived from historically related individuals, or lineages. Traditional "assemblages" are aggregates of objects derived from a variable number of individual organisms over a variable amount of time (Dunnell 1995). Consequently, these aggregates often represent "mixed assemblages" containing objects derived from historically unrelated events of occupation. The use of assemblages as counting units therefore is problematic for understanding evolutionary processes. Engineering design, paradigmatic classification, and occurrence seriation are used to build appropriate units for examining the differential persistence of variants. To ensure that members of a counting unit are from the same lineage, they must be homologously related. Homologously related members are defined as a class of objects that share an identical configuration of traits acquired during manufacture. These classes fulfill the counting unit requirements necessary for building evolutionary explanations.

The order of biface classes established by seriation provides a temporal framework in which to track the differential persistence of traits. This involves tabulating the relative frequencies of non-neutral variants within each biface class and examining frequency changes through time. For example, tabulating the frequencies of alternative variants for the class *Evenness of Blade Serration* involves counting the occurrence of the following traits: *Unserrated, Even, Uneven, Even Increase, Even Decrease*, and *Missing*. By examining how these frequencies change over chronologically ordered classes, it is possible to test whether a trait is actually non-neutral, and to track the differential persistence of such traits.

### Occurrence Seriation

The archaeological record is a contemporary phenomenon consisting of objects and groups of objects dating to the present. To yield relevant archaeological dates, the record must be conceived as events rather than objects. Events are defined as the time at which a set of traits assumes a particular configuration (Dunnell in press). Since age is important, the particular set of traits should be relevant to a chronological event such as the event of deposition or the event of manufacture. If a configuration of two or more traits occurs more than once, the first and last occurrence are never simultaneous. As a consequence, an event sums the history of the trait configuration by which it is defined. Occurrence seriation is an ordinal method for ordering events of variable duration. Ensuring that the order of events is chronological depends upon choosing the correct kind of traits for defining the events.

When building chronologies, the events ordered by occurrence seriation must be defined by: 1. neutral traits; 2. a combination of neutral and non-neutral traits; or 3. a combination of non-neutral traits. When events are defined by a combination of neutral and/or non-neutral traits, however, the particular combination must have a unique occurrence in time. When these conditions are met, the events will be ordered continuously in time. Traditionally, this distributional property has been specified by the "occurrence law," which states that events ordered by occurrence seriation must exhibit continuous distributions (Dunnell 1971). The occurrence law is a general statement about the temporal distribution of neutral traits as a consequence of cultural transmission, and it also applies to combinations of neutral and non-neutral traits having a unique occurrence in time.

Neutral and non-neutral traits have both temporal and spatial distributions, however, and spatial influences must be eliminated to assume that a seriation order is chronological. Eliminating spatial variation ensures that all seriated events are populated by groups of objects that constitute samples of the same lineage. Traditionally, this has been accomplished by adherence to the criterion of "same local tradition," which specifies that all seriated groups should be samples of the same historical sequence (Dunnell 1971). One way to accomplish this is to limit the seriation to objects derived from the same local area. Another means is to build multiple seriation orders of a single event, such as an event of manufacture, each time using a different combination of traits to define the event. Only those events that are ordered identically by the different seriation orders can then be interpreted as chronological.

## Evaluation of Sample Size

In addition to the error introduced by spatial variation, the influence of chance in seriation must also be considered. The probability of getting a seriation solution by chance alone depends upon two factors: 1. the number of traits used in the description of an event; and 2. the number of descriptions contained in the seriation order. As the complexity of a description increases, the probability that it will reoccur at another point in time or space decreases. The same is true for increasing the number of descriptions in the seriation solution. Consequently, the probability of getting a solution by chance alone can be decreased by using as many traits as possible to define events, and by using large sample sizes, so that a large percentage of the total number of possible trait combinations actually have membership. Quantifying the probabilistic relationship between these factors and chance for occurrence seriations of varying size is a necessary component of this research.

When the frequency of traits, i.e., richness, is correlated with sample size, the frequencies of traits cannot be treated as population estimates. Consequently, it is necessary to examine the relationship between the number of objects in a class, i.e., sample size, and the number of non-neutral traits tabulated. One way of evaluating this relationship is to use a resampling technique known as bootstrapping (Lipo et al. 1997; Kintigh 1989). The bootstrapping technique involves creating a series of richness distributions constructed from samples of systematically increasing size, drawn at random from a class. Biface classes with sample sizes large enough to adequately estimate the richness of variants display both asymptotic richness as resample size increases, and decreased sampling variance as

larger samples converge on the best estimate of richness. Classes having problematic sample sizes may reach an asymptote as sample size increases, but without the decrease in sampling variance that indicates a precise estimation, or they
may still be accumulating new variants as resample sizes reach the total sample
size for the manufacturing event (Lipo et al. 1997). In the research presented
here, problematic classes identified by the bootstrapping technique are being
dropped from certain analyses. However, since surface assemblages are being
used, it will always be possible to increase sample size by re-collecting surface
clusters at a later date.

### Developing a Chronology for the Research Region

Since evolutionary theory explains differential persistence of traits over time,
it is essential that the units in which trait frequencies are tabulated can be ordered
chronologically. While a general chronology has been established for the CMV
(Chapman 1947, 1948a, 1948b; Morse and Morse 1983), a detailed local
chronology is entirely lacking and the status of culture-historical projectile point
types is uncertain. The two most frequent methods for determining when a biface
was used or manufactured are typological cross-dating and radiocarbon dating of
associated organic material. Due to the paucity of stratified sites in the CMV, the
cross-dating technique is based primarily on projectile point types defined from
deeply stratified rock shelter and alluvial deposits outside of the CMV (e.g., Bray
1956; Logan 1952; McMillan 1966). Radiocarbon dating is, therefore, prefer-
able, but depends upon secure associations between preserved organic remains
and bifaces. Such associations are relatively rare in the CMV, and in the author's
research area in particular, because most archaeological clusters occur in plow-
zone contexts and because high soil acidity inhibits organic preservation.

An even more pervasive problem than poor association and preservation is the
disparity between the target event and the actual event that is "dated" by these techniques. In typological cross-dating, the target event is actually a time range coincident with somewhat arbitrarily bracketed culture-historical periods. Thus,
characteristics of points may be used to assign an assemblage to the Middle or Late
Archaic Period. Since traditional-type definitions conflate neutral and non-neutral
traits, the actual event is a space/time unit of unknown magnitude. The actual event
dated by radiocarbon, on the other hand, is the isolation of organic material from
the atmospheric carbon[14] reservoir, which may or may not overlap with when a
biface was used, and is most likely not coincident with when it was manufactured.

Because of the disparity between actual events and target events in dating, and
the conflation of neutral and non-neutral traits, existing projectile point chronologies are inherently error prone. The magnitude of this error and its distribution
over ten to twelve thousand years are not likely to be resolved until a method is
developed to date the duration of manufacture for individual classes of biface,
and for ordering these in time. The most promising method for accomplishing
this goal utilizes both seriation and TL dating.

## TL Dating

While the seriation method provides a relative order of events, an independent method is required for determining the direction of temporal change and the duration of manufacture. The method used in this research is the application of TL dating to thermally altered bifaces (Wilhelmsen and Miles 1998; Wilhelmsen and Feathers in press). The TL technique dates a heating event during which the temperature of a crystalline material last exceeded 450° centigrade (Aitken 1989; Feathers 1997). For lithics, this corresponds either to the event of manufacture, assuming heat treatment is part of the manufacturing process, or accidental heating subsequent to manufacture. Successful heat treatment can occur at temperatures lower than 450° centigrade, so that not all heat-treated bifaces can be used. The two problems that must be resolved in dating heated bifaces with TL are: 1. distinguishing bifaces that have been heated in excess of 450° centigrade; and 2. distinguishing between heating during manufacture and subsequent heating.

A resolution of the first problem is provided by the experimental heat treatment of cherts. Experimental heating has demonstrated that most cherts heated rapidly to between 350° and 400° centigrade either explode or exhibit features of "catastrophic" thermal alteration (Purdy 1974). Catastrophic thermal alteration implies that fracture properties such as fracture toughness and predictability (McCutcheon 1997) are so adversely affected that the probability of subsequent manufacture by percussion is significantly reduced (Griffiths et al. 1987). The mechanism responsible for catastrophic thermal alteration is most likely rapid heating beyond the maximum coefficient of expansion for water, which is 373° centigrade (Luedtke 1992). Beyond this temperature, water under pressure can no longer remain liquid and expands rapidly through vaporization, resulting in potlids, crazing, and crenulated fracture surfaces (Luedtke 1992; Purdy 1974, McCutcheon 1997). Cherts can be heated and cooled rapidly without exploding or exhibiting any of these characteristics as long as the maximum temperature does not exceed 350° centigrade (Luedtke 1992). Consequently, the appearance of potlids, crazing, and the crenulated fracture surfaces that result from crazing can be used to identify material that is likely to have been sufficiently heated for TL dating.

The second problem has a probabilistic rather than empirical solution. When heat treatment is part of the manufacturing process, assemblages containing manufacturing debitage are also likely to contain catastrophically heated bifaces. Given the effects of catastrophic heating on fracture properties, most of these bifaces will be rejected during the manufacturing process. Rejection due to catastrophic heating may occur at various stages of manufacture, depending on the amount and degree of crazing and/or potlids, though some bifaces may be successfully manufactured in spite of excessive heating. Successfully manufactured bifaces made from catastrophically heated chert will tend to exhibit potlids more often than crazing, since crazing results in more pervasive structure flaws. There is also potential for catastrophic heating to occur subsequent to manufacture when a biface falls into a hearth or is burned on a house floor. In this case, there is no relation between the event of manufacture and the event of catastrophic heating. However, catastrophic heating subsequent to manufacture is a chance occurrence and its frequency is likely to be insignificant relative to its occurrence during manufacture. Catastrophic heating from surface fires is also possible. However, the occurrence of these bifaces is also likely to be rare, because heat is generated for an insufficient amount of time to cause excessive heating. Furthermore, bifaces catastrophically heated after manufacture are more likely to be finished bifaces than manufacturing rejects.

The relation between the thermal event dated by TL and the *event of manufacture* is illustrated in Figure 4.8a for a single biface. The thermal event dated by TL occurs at a point in time relative to the *event of manufacture*, which begins with the primary shaping of a material, continues through heat treatment, and ends with completion of secondary shaping. The *period of manufacture*, on the other hand, has an even longer duration, because it includes the *event of manufacture*, as well as the use-history of the biface. The use-history has a range beginning after the biface is manufactured and ending at its final deposition. Within this range, there may be multiple episodes of use, rejuvenation, discard, or loss. For catastrophically heated bifaces, the beginning and ending of the event of manufacture closely bracket the TL event. In contrast, the use-history of a biface may be on the order of days or, when a lost or discarded biface is recycled at a later date, thousands of years. For a single biface, then, a TL event is a good estimate of when the *event of manufacture* occurred but provides no information about the duration of its *period of manufacture*.

As an estimate of the *duration of manufacture* for a particular class of biface, illustrated in Figure 4.8b, a single TL event is very poor for two reasons. First, all bifaces from the single class were not manufactured simultaneously, so the events of manufacture have a distribution beginning and ending when the first and last bifaces were catastrophically heated. Second, the use-history is summed for all bifaces, which increases the probability of error resulting from bifaces with problematic use-histories, including bifaces accidentally heated, reused, or recycled by unrelated individuals. Dating multiple bifaces from the same class, however, will eventually identify a range of time over which *events of manufacture* for the class occurred. Identifying this range will eliminate bifaces with problematic use-histories and increase the chronological accuracy provided by the combined use of seriation and TL.

While TL dates will be used to anchor the occurrence seriations with absolute dates, the combination of TL dates and seriation results will be used to calculate rates of change and to date critical functional and technological changes. It will then be possible to integrate this detailed chronological information with engineering design data, distributional data, and environmental data, to evaluate common assumptions about biface variation. Perhaps more importantly, this work will also provide the foundation for building explanations for the evolution of biface technology.

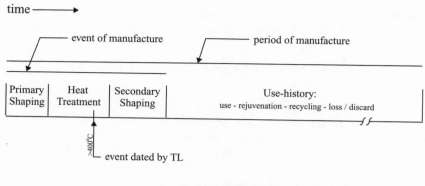

a) single biface

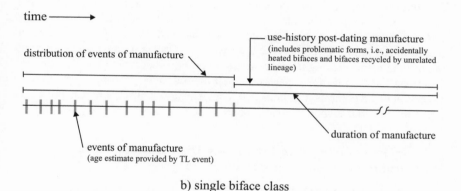

b) single biface class

**Figure 4.8. Relation between the event dated by thermoluminescence (TL), the event of manufacture, and the period of manufacture: a) relations illustrated for a single biface, b) relations illustrated for a single class of biface.**

## BUILDING EVOLUTIONARY EXPLANATIONS

Building explanations for changing trait frequencies begins by distinguishing between neutral and non-neutral traits, since each are subject to different evolutionary processes. After this distinction is made, it is necessary to examine the persistence of non-neutral traits with respect to the selective environment. The engineering design analysis discussed previously was used to identify traits that affect projectile function, and this served as a foundation for constructing morphological and technological classifications that yield relevant data. The following section outlines the complex iterative process for testing trait neutrality.

### Testing Trait Neutrality Using Engineering and Distributional Data

The process of distinguishing neutral and non-neutral traits using an engineering design analysis and seriation is modeled as a flowchart in Figure 4.9. The distinction is made through a series of three hypotheses that are tested using distributional data and engineering data. In this example, Hypothesis 1 tests whether Trait $X$ is neutral by comparing its distribution to the temporal distribution of a neutral trait. Rejection of Hypothesis 1 implies that Trait $X$ is non-neutral, pleiotropic, or poorly formulated. Poorly formulated traits are traits inadvertently defined by a combination of neutral and non-neutral traits and, as a consequence, they do not conform to either neutral or non-neutral distributions.

Hypothesis 2 then tests whether Trait $X$ is non-neutral by comparing its distribution to the temporal distribution of a non-neutral trait. Rejection of Hypothesis 2 implies that Trait $X$ is poorly formulated, and must therefore be reformulated on the basis of engineering data and submitted again to Hypothesis 1. Failure to reject Hypothesis 2, however, implies that Trait $X$ is either non-neutral or pleiotropic. Finally, Hypothesis 3 tests whether Trait $X$ is pleiotropic or non-pleiotropic using the engineering design analysis to determine which traits are functional and non-functional (i.e., non-neutral and neutral, respectively). Rejection of Hypothesis 3 implies that Trait $X$ is non-neutral, whereas failure to reject implies that Trait $X$ is pleiotropic.

### Correlating Changes in Frequency Distributions with Environmental and Engineering Data

Correlating non-neutral trait frequencies and environmental parameters is a complex process that must take into consideration formation processes and environmental variation. The primary source of information about the environmental context of projectile use must come from isolated bifaces lost in the context of use or clusters of historically unrelated bifaces formed in use-contexts. The occurrence and frequency distribution of non-neutral traits in these contexts will map onto environmental structure both temporally and spatially due to the influence of changing resource structure. Changes in resource structure are described in terms of differences in soil characteristics and geomorphic features, including lakes, backswamps, sloughs, interfluves, floodplains, and uplands. In the research region, for example, bifaces lost in use are often found along relict slough margins either as isolates or as clusters resulting from the long-term exploitation of faunal resources associated with this wetland environment.

After determining the *duration of manufacture* for a given class of biface and mapping its specific use-context temporally and spatially, it will then be possible

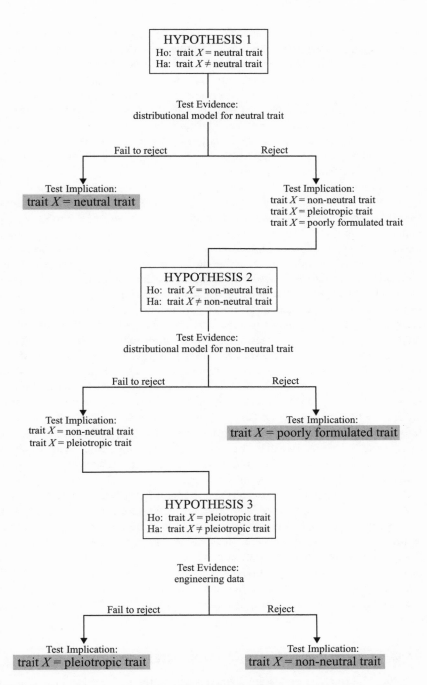

**Figure 4.9. Model for distinguishing neutral, non-neutral, and pleiotropic traits using nested hypotheses based on distributional models and engineering data.**

to associate palaeoenvironmental data on a local or regional scale to infer the range of possible resources exploited. To the extent that data from contemporaneous faunal assemblages are available, these will be used to test hypotheses about resource exploitation based on palaeoenvironmental data. Examining these data for different environments of projectile use will provide an ecological framework for explaining how different biface classes were functionally embedded in different resource exploitation strategies involving projectile technology. Examining changes in resource exploitation strategies in light of these same data will provide an historical framework for explaining the evolution of projectile technology within the research region.

In addition, bifaces found in domestic and manufacturing contexts are the primary source of information about manufacturing costs and other functions serviced by bifaces. Since selection operates on costs associated with producing and maintaining projectile components, this information is also critical to explaining the differential persistence of biface variants. Most bifaces in manufacturing contexts are rejects discarded at some time during the manufacturing process. Some bifaces discarded late in the manufacturing process have virtually complete proximal ends. When these bifaces share an identical combination of traits specified by an *event of manufacture*, as defined by occurrence seriation, they are historically related. The *duration of manufacture* for a particular group of historically related bifaces can also be determined where catastrophically heated bifaces are successfully dated using TL. This chronological information is then combined with data on manufacturing costs for particular classes of biface, including raw material acquisition costs and raw material characteristics that result in different rates of manufacturing failure, as well as energy invested in the manufacturing process and biface durability. Bifaces found in domestic contexts also provide information on other functions performed by bifaces both while they are still serviceable for projectiles and after they are serviceable. Such points may be favored by selection over other biface variants, since manufacturing and maintenance costs are averaged across all functions.

After determining the manufacturing costs for different classes of biface, these classes will be compared between domestic and manufacturing contexts both temporally and spatially. Examining these data for different environments of projectile use will provide an ecological framework for explaining engineering designs that represent a compromise between available raw materials for manufacturing bifaces and the functional requirements of a specific use-context. This will also provide an historical framework for explaining the evolution of projectile technology within the research region as an outcome of selection operating on both cost and performance.

## RESEARCH EXPECTATIONS AND SIGNIFICANCE

Although projectile points are abundant and commonly used to infer chronological position in the CMV, little progress has been made toward understanding the range of variation and causes of change in these tools. Archeologists remain unable to assess the role these tools played with regard to subsistence, settlement, and social conflict among the prehistoric populations that created them, despite a plethora of speculative works that draw conclusions of this nature.

In contrast to most previous work, this research documents variation in this important class of tools and attempts to distinguish and explain causes of variation. Completion of the former objective alone will provide a substantive contribution in that, once variation is documented, the data can be used to address a myriad of questions about projectile point form, function, and technological change. These data can also be used to evaluate traditional models of projectile point function, providing a greater understanding of the archaeological record of this region than we currently possess.

The latter objective of this work, distinguishing and explaining the causes of variation, attends the larger theoretical effort represented by the contributions to this volume—that of integrating/applying evolutionary theory to the explanation of archaeological phenomena. In this regard, this research stands to make both a methodological and theoretical contribution. A most problematic aspect of the application of evolutionary theory to archaeology involves the construction of counting units that can be used to track the differential persistence of phenotypic variants. Distinguishing between homologous and analogous similarities and neutral and non-neutral traits is the first step toward generating frequencies explicable by evolutionary processes. Through the iterative use of an engineering design analysis, metric documentation and paradigmatic classification, occurrence seriation, and TL dating, it is hoped that this research will contribute to the development of this process.

Since evolutionary theory explains differential persistence of traits over time, it is essential that the units in which trait frequencies are tabulated can be ordered in time. By far the most pervasive stumbling block to progress in this direction is the use of traditionally (intuitively) defined types that conflate neutral and non-neutral traits, making it impossible to distinguish temporal and spatial variation. This research directly addresses both of these problems. Through the combined use of seriation, TL dating, and an engineering analysis, data are being generated to build historically significant units instead of relying on traditional "types." In addition, a detailed regional chronology is being built.

The procedures outlined in this paper have a potential to make important, substantive, methodological, and theoretical contributions. Establishing a detailed regional chronology will do much to advance our understanding of local prehistory. We have much to learn about how projectile points change over time relative to other aspects of prehistoric adaptations before we can understand why these changes occurred. In addition, a detailed regional chronology will greatly increase the precision of relative dating in the region. Working on the development of the TL technique for dating lithic artifacts is an important methodological aspect of this research. A technique that enables direct dating of important archaeological (target) events rather than requiring researchers to rely on material of uncertain temporal association obviously has worldwide application. The chronology built through this iterative methodology will order units containing objects that are homologously related samples of the human phenotype. Developing these counting units and ordering them chronologically is critical to all evolutionary research, not just research on projectile technology. In concert with engineering and environmental data, these units will provide a solid foundation for both ecological explanations of how projectiles functioned in different use contexts, and explanations of the evolution of specific functional and technological changes which occurred in this important archaeological region of the CMV.

## REFERENCES CITED

Abler, W. L.
  1992   The Serrated Teeth of Tyrannosaurid Dinosaurs, and Biting Structures in Other Animals. *Paleobiology* 18(2):161–183.
Aitken, M. J.
  1989   Luminescence Dating: A Guide for the Non-Specialists. *Archaeometry* 31:147–159.
Ammerman, A. J.
  1985   Plow-zone Experiments in Calabria, Italy. *Journal of Field Archaeology* 12:33–40.
Atkinson, B. K. (editor)
  1989   *Fracture Mechanics of Rock.* Academic Press, London.
Austin, R. J.
  1986   The Experimental Reproduction and Archaeological Occurrence of Biface Notching Flakes. *Lithic Technology* 15:96–100.
Bangs, E.
  1991   Crowley's Ridge Gravels: An Archaeological Perspective. Unpublished Senior Honors thesis, University of Washington, Seattle.
Beck, C.
  1995   Functional Attributes and the Differential Persistence of Great Basin Dart Forms. *Journal of California and Great Basin Anthropology* 17(2):222–243.
Bell, R. E.
  1958   Guide to the Identification of Certain American Indian Projectile Points. *Oklahoma Anthropological Society, Special Bulletin* No. 1.
Bergman, C. A., E. McEwen, and R. Miller
  1988   Experimental Archery: Projectile Velocities and Comparison of Bow Performances. *American Antiquity* 62:658–670.
Bergman, C. A., and M. H. Newcomer
  1983   Flint Arrowhead Breakage: Examples from Ksar Akil, Lebanon. *Journal of Field Archaeology* 10:238–243.
Beyer, J. C.
  1962   *Wound Ballistics.* Medical Department, U.S. Army, Office of the Surgeon General. Department of the Army, Washington, D.C.
Bradbury, A. P.
  1997   The Bow and Arrow in the Eastern Woodlands: Evidence for an Archaic Origin. *North American Archaeologist* 18(3):207–233.

Brandon, R. N.
  1990   *Adaptation and Environment*. Princeton University Press, Princeton.
Bray, R. T.
  1956   The Culture-Complexes and Sequence at the Rice Site (23SN200), Stone County, Missouri. *The Missouri Archaeologist* 18:46–134.
Brown, J. A., and R. K. Vierra
  1983   What Happened in the Middle Archaic? Introduction to an Ecological Approach to Koster Site Archaeology. In *Archaic Hunter and Gatherers in the American Midwest*, edited by J. A. Phillips and J. A. Brown, pp. 165–195. Academic Press, New York.
Broyles, B. J.
  1966   Preliminary Report: The St. Albans Site (46KA27), Kanawha County, West Virginia. *West Virginia Archaeologist* 19:1–43.
Chapman, C. H.
  1947   A Preliminary Survey of Missouri Archaeology Part II: Middle Mississippi and Hopewellian Cultures. *Missouri Archaeologist* 10:57–94.
  1948a   A Preliminary Survey of Missouri Archaeology Part III: Woodland Cultures and the Ozark Bluff Dwellers. *Missouri Archaeologist* 10:95–132.
  1948b   A Preliminary Survey of Missouri Archaeology Part IV: Ancient Cultures and Sequence. *Missouri Archaeologist* 10:133–164.
Christenson, A. L.
  1981   *The Evolution of Subsistence in the Prehistoric Midwestern United States*. Unpublished Ph.D. dissertation, Department of Anthropology, University of California, Los Angeles.
  1986a   Projectile Point Size and Projectile Aerodynamics: An Exploratory Study. *Plains Anthropologist* 39:109–128.
  1986b   Reconstructing Prehistoric Projectiles from Their Points. *Journal of the Society of Archer-Antiquaries* 29:21–27.
Coe, J. L.
  1964   The Formative Cultures of the Carolina Piedmont. *Transactions of the American Philosophical Society* Vol. 54, Part 5. Philadelphia.
Cotterell, B., and J. Kamminga
  1979   The Mechanics of Flaking. In *Lithic Use-Wear Analysis*, edited by B. Hayden, pp. 97–112. Academic Press, New York.
  1987   The Formation of Flakes. *American Antiquity* 52:675–708.
  1992   *Mechanics of Pre-Industrial Technology*. Cambridge University Press, Cambridge.
Cundy, B. J.
  1989   Formal Variation in Australian Spear and Spearthrower Technology. *BAR International Series No. 546*.
Dancey, W. S.
  1973   *Prehistoric Land Use and Settlement Patterns in the Priest Rapids Area, Washington*. Ph.D. dissertation, University of Washington, University Microfilms, Ann Arbor.
Darwin, C.
  1859   *On the Origin of Species by Means of Natural Selection*. Reprint of second edition, 1935. Oxford University Press, London.
Delcourt, H. R., and P. A. Delcourt
  1985   Quaternary Palynology and Vegetational History of the Southeastern United States. In *Pollen Records of Late-Quaternary North American Sediments*, edited by

V. M. Bryant and R. G. Holloway, pp. 1–37. American Association of Stratigraphic Palynologists Foundation, Dallas.

Dewar, R. E.

1991   Incorporating Variation in Occupation Span into Settlement-Pattern Analysis. *American Antiquity* 56:604–620.

Dunnell, R. C.

1971   *Systematics in Prehistory.* Free Press, New York.

1978   Style and Function: A Fundamental Dichotomy. *American Antiquity* 43:192–202.

1980   Evolutionary Theory and Archaeology. In *Advances in Archaeological Method and Theory*, edited by M. B. Schiffer, pp. 35–59. Vol. 3. Academic Press, New York.

1981   Seriation, Groups, and Measurements. In *Manejos de Datos y Metods Matematicos Arquelogia*, edited by G. L. Cowgill, R. Whallon, and B. S. Ottaway, pp. 67–90. Union Internacional de Ciencias Prehistoricas y Protohistoricas, Mexico.

1989   Aspects of the Application of Evolutionary Theory in Archaeology. In *Archaeological Thought in America*, edited by C. C. Lamberg-Karlovsky, pp. 35–49. Cambridge University Press, Cambridge.

1995   What Is It That Actually Evolves? In *Evolutionary Archaeology: Methodological Issues*, edited by P. A. Teltser, pp. 35–50. University of Arizona Press, Tucson.

n.d.   *Field Manual for Southeast Missouri.* Manuscript on file, Department of Anthropology, University of Washington, Seattle (1996).

In press.   In *Archaeological Method and Theory: An Encyclopedia*, edited by L. Elliss. Garland Publishing, New York.

Ebert, J.

1994   *Distributional Archaeology.* University of New Mexico Press, Albuquerque.

Faulkner, A.

1972   *Mechanical Principles of Flintworking.* Unpublished Ph.D. dissertation, Department of Anthropology, Washington State University, Pullman.

Feathers, J. K.

1990   *Explaining the Evolution of Prehistoric Ceramics in Southeastern Missouri.* Unpublished Ph.D. dissertation, Department of Anthropology, University of Washington, Seattle.

1997   The Application of Luminescence Dating in American Archaeology. *Journal of Archaeological Method and Theory* 4:1–66.

Fischer, A.

1985   Hunting with Flint-Tipped Arrows. In *The Mesolithic Europe*, edited by C. Bonsall, pp. 29–39.

Fischer, A., P. V. Hansen, and P. Rasmussen

1984   Macro and Micro Wear Traces on Lithic Projectile Points: Experimental Results and Prehistoric Examples. *Journal of Danish Archaeology* 3:19–46.

Fisk, H. N.

1944   *Geologic Investigation of the Alluvial Valley of the Lower Mississippi River.* Publication No. 52. Mississippi River Commission, Vicksburg.

Flenniken, J. L., and A. W. Raymond

1986   Morphological Projectile Point Typology: Replication, Experimentation, and Technological Analysis. *American Antiquity* 51:603–614.

Frazzetta, T. H.
  1988   The Mechanics of Cutting and the Form of Shark Teeth (Chondrichthyes, Elasmobranchii). *Zoomorphology* 108:93–107.
Friis-Hansen, J.
  1990   Mesolithic Cutting Arrows: Functional Analysis of Arrows Used in the Hunting of Large Game. *Antiquity* 64:494–504.
Frison, G. C.
  1989   Experimental Use of Clovis Weaponry. *American Antiquity* 54:766–784.
  1993   North American High Plains Paleo-Indian Hunting Strategies and Weaponry Assemblages. In *From Kostenki to Clovis: Upper Palaeolithic Paleo Indian Adaptations*, edited by O. Soffer and N. D. Praslov, pp. 237–249. Plenum Press, New York.
Frison, G. C., and L. C. Todd
  1986   *The Colby Mammoth Site: Taphonomy and Archaeology of a Clovis Kill in Northern Wyoming.* University of New Mexico Press, Albuquerque.
Frison, G. C., M. Wilson, and D. Wilson
  1976   Fossil Bison and Artifacts from an Early Altithermal Period Arroyo Trap in Wyoming. *American Antiquity* 41:28–57.
George, R. L., and R. Scaglion
  1992   Seriation Changes in Monongahela Triangular Lithic Projectiles. *Man in the Northeast* 44:73–81.
Goodyear, A. C.
  1974   *A Techno-Functional Study of a Dalton Site in Northeastern Arkansas*, Arkansas Archeological Survey, Publications in Archeology, Research Series No. 7.
Gould, R. J., D. M. Raup, J. J. Sepkoski, T. J. M. Schopf, and D. S. Simberloff
  1977   The Shape of Evolution: A Comparison of Real and Random Clades. *Paleobiology* 3(23–40).
Grayson, D. K.
  1989   Sample Size and Relative Abundance in Archaeological Analysis: Illustrations from Spiral Fractures and Seriation. In *Quantifying Diversity in Archaeology*, edited by R. D. Leonard and G. T. Jones, pp. 79–84. Cambridge University Press, Cambridge.
Griffiths, D. R., C. A. Bergman, C. J. Clayton, K. Ohnuma, G. V. Robins, and N. J. Seeley
  1987   Experimental Investigation of the Heat Treatment of Flint. In *The Human Uses of Flint and Shert*, edited by G. d. G. Sieveking and M. H. Newcomer, pp. 43–52. Cambridge University Press, Cambridge.
Guccione, M. J.
  1987   Geomorphology, Sedimentation, and Chronology of Alluvial Deposits, Northern Mississippi County, Arkansas. In *A Cultural Resources Survey, Testing, and Geomorphic Examination of Ditches 10, 12, and 29, Mississippi County, Arkansas*, edited by R. H. Lafferty, M. J. Guccione, L. J. Scott, D. K. Aasen, B. J. Watkins, M. C. Sierschula, and P. F. Bauman, pp. 67–99. Mid-Continental Research Associates Report No. 86-5. Report submitted to the Department of the Army, Memphis District, Corps of Engineers.
Guccione, M. J., R. H. Lafferty, and L. S. Cummings
  1988   Environmental Constraints of Human Settlement in an Evolving Holocene Alluvial System. *Geoarchaeology* 3:65–84.

Huckell, B. B.
   1982   The Denver Elephant Project: A Report of Experimentation with Thrusting Spears. *Plains Anthropologist* 27:217–224.
Hughes, S. S.
   1995   *Getting to the Point.* Manuscript in author's possession.
Jauhari, M. and A. Bandyopadhyay
   1976   Wound Ballistics: An Analysis of a Bullet in Jel. *Journal of Forensic Sciences* 21:616–624.
Jones, G. T., R. D. Leonard, and A. L. Abbott
   1995   The Structure of Selectionist Explanations in Archaeology. In *Evolutionary Archaeology: Methodological Issues*, edited by P. A. Teltser, pp. 13–32. University of Arizona Press, Tucson.
Kimura, M.
   1983   *The Neutral Theory of Molecular Evolution.* Cambridge University Press, Cambridge.
Kintigh, K. W.
   1989   Sample Size, Significance, and Measures of Diversity. In *Quantifying Diversity in Archaeology*, edited by R. D. Leonard and G. T. Jones, pp. 25–36. New Directions in Archaeology. Cambridge University Press, Cambridge.
Klopsteg, P. E.
   1939   The Penetration of Arrows. *American Bowman-Review* 8.
   1943   Physics of Bows and Arrows. *American Journal of Physics* 11:175–192.
Knecht, H. (editor)
   1997   *Projectile Technology.* Plenum Press, New York.
Knight, B.
   1975   The Dynamics of Stab Wounds. *Forensic Science* 6:175–192.
LeBlanc, S.A.
   1997   Modeling Warfare in Southwestern Prehistory. *North American Archaeologist* 18(3):235–276.
Larralde, S. L.
   1990   *The Design of Hunting Weapons: Archaeological Evidence from Southwestern Wyoming.* Unpublished Ph.D. dissertation, Department of Anthropology, University of New Mexico, Albuquerque.
Lewarch, D. E., and M. J. O'Brien
   1981   Effect of Short-term Tillage on Aggregate Provenience Surface Pattern. In *Plowzone Archaeology: Contributions to Theory and Technique*, edited by M. J. O'Brien and D. E. Lewarch, pp. 7–49. Publications in Anthropology No. 27. Vanderbilt University, Nashville.
Lipo, C. P., M. E. Madsen, R. C. Dunnell, and T. Hunt
   1997   Population Structure, Cultural Transmission, and Frequency Seriation. *Journal of Anthropological Archaeology* 16:301–334.
Litfin, J. C., P. C. Jackson, and K. D. Vickery
   1993   A Chronological Seriation Approach to Fort Ancient Triangular Arrowpoints in the Central Ohio Valley. Paper presented at the 58th Annual Meeting of the Society for American Archaeology, St. Louis.
Logan, W. D.
   1952   *Graham Cave, an Archaic Site in Montgomery County, Missouri.* Missouri Archaeological Society, Memoir No. 2.

Luedtke, B. E.
  1992   *An Archaeologist's Guide to Chert and Flint.* Institute of Archaeology, University of California, Archaeological Research Tools No. 7, Los Angeles.

Lyman, R. E., and O'Brien, M. J.
  1998   The Goals of Evolutionary Archaeology: History and Explanation. *Current Anthropology* 39(5):615–652.

Lynott, M. J.
  1991   Identification of Attribute Variability in Emergent Mississippian and Mississippian Arrow Points from Southeast Missouri. *Midcontinential Journal of Archaeology* 16:189–211.

Madsen, M. E., and R. C. Dunnell
  1989   The Role of Microartifacts in Interpreting Low-density Plowzone Records. Paper presented at the 53rd Annual Meeting of the Society for American Archaeology, Atlanta.

Mattoo, B. N., A. K. Wani, and M. D. Asgekar
  1974   Casualty Criteria for Wounds from Firearms with Special Reference to Shot Penetration—Part II. *Journal of Forensic Sciences* 19:585–589.

Mayr, E.
  1988   *Toward a New Philosophy of Biology: Observations of an Evolutionist.* Harvard University Press, Cambridge, Massachusetts.

McCutcheon, P.
  1997   *Archaeological Investigations of Stone Tool Heat-Treatment in Southeast Missouri: An Experimental Approach.* Ph.D. dissertation, University of Washington, University Microfilms, Ann Arbor.

McMillan, R. B.
  1966   *Archaeological Investigations at the Rodgers Rockshelter Site, Kaysinger Bluff Reservoir, Missouri: The 1965 Field Season.* Report submitted to the National Park Service, Omaha.

Morse, D. F., and P. A. Morse
  1983   *Archaeology of the Central Mississippi Valley.* Academic Press, New York.
  1990   The Emergent Mississippian in the Central Mississippi Valley. In *The Mississippian Emergence*, edited by B. D. Smith, pp. 153–173. Smithsonian Institution Press, Washington, D.C.

Neiman, F.
  1995   Stylistic Variation in Evolutionary Perspective: Inferences from Decorative Diversity and Interassemblage Distance in Illinois Woodland Ceramic Assemblages. *American Antiquity* 60:7–36.

O'Brien, M. J.
  1994   *Cat Monsters and Headpots: The Archaeology of Missouri's Pemiscot Bayou.* Columbia University Press, Columbia.

O'Brien, M. J., and R. C. Dunnell, editors
  1998   *Changing Perspectives on the Archaeology of the Central Mississippi Valley.* The University of Alabama Press, Tuscaloosa and London.

O'Brien, M. J., and T. D. Holland
  1990   Variation, Selection, and the Archaeological Record. In *Archaeological Method and Theory*, edited by M. B. Schiffer, pp. 31–79. Vol. 2. University of Arizona Press, Tucson.

1995    The Nature and Premise of a Selection-based Archaeology. In *Evolutionary Theory: Methodological Issues*, edited by P. A. Teltser, pp. 175–200. University of Arizona Press, Tucson.

O'Brien, M. J., and D. E. Lewarch
1981    *Plowzone Archaeology: Contributions to Theory and Technique*. Publications in Anthropology No. 27. Vanderbilt University, Nashville.

O'Brien, M. J., and R. E. Warren
1983    An Archaic Projectile Point Sequence from the Southern Prairie Peninsula: The Pigeon Roost Creek Site. In *Archaic Hunters and Gatherers in the American Midwest*, edited by J. L. Phillips and J. A. Brown, pp. 71–98. Academic Press, New York.

O'Connell, A. L., and E. B. Gardner
1972    *Understanding the Scientific Bases of Human Movement*. Waverly Press, Baltimore.

Odell, G. H.
1988    Addressing Prehistoric Hunting Practices through Stone Tool Analysis. *American Anthropologist* 90:335–356.

Odell, G. H., and F. Cowen
1986    Experiments with Spears and Arrows on Animal Targets. *Journal of Field Archaeology* 13:195–212.

Palter, J. L.
1977    Design and Construction of Australian Spear-Thrower Projectiles and Hand Thrown Spears. *Archaeology and Physical Anthropology in Oceania* 12:161–172.

Perino, G.
1968    Guide to the Identification of Certain American Indian Projectile Points. *Special Bulletin No. 3, Oklahoma Anthropological Society*.

Plumley, W. J.
1948    Black Hills Terrace Gravels: A Study in Sediment Transport. *Journal of Geology* 56:526–577.

Pope, S. T.
1923    *A Study of Bows and Arrows*. University of California Publications, Vol. 13, No. 9, Berkeley.

Popper, K.
1972    *Objective Knowledge*. Oxford University Press, Oxford.

Price, J. E., and J. B. Griffin
1979    *The Snodgrass Site of the Powers Phase of Southeast Missouri*. Anthropological Papers, Museum of Anthropology, University of Michigan, No. 66. Ann Arbor.

Prindle, B., and R. G. Walden
1976    *Deep-sea Lines Fishbite Manual*. National Oceanographic and Atmospheric Administration. National Data Buoy Office, Bay St. Louis, Mississippi.

Purdy, B. A.
1974    Investigations Concerning the Thermal Alteration of Silica Minerals: An Archaeological Approach. *Tebiwa* 17:37–66.

Raup, D. M., and S. J. Gould
1974    Stochastic Simulation and the Evolution of Morphology—Towards a Nomothetic Paleontology. *Systematic Zoology* 23:305–322.

Royall, P. D., P. A. Delcourt, and H. R. Delcourt
1991    Late Quaternary Paleoecology and Paleoenvironments of the Central Mississippi Alluvial Valley. *Geological Society of America Bulletin* 103:157–170.

Rutledge, E. M., L. T. West, and M. Oamkupt
  1985   Loess Deposits on a Pleistocene Age Terrace in Eastern Arkansas. *Soil Science Society of America Journal* 49:1231–1238.
Saucier, R. T.
  1974   *Quaternary Geology of the Lower Mississippi Valley.* Arkansas Archaeological Survey Research Series No. 6.
Saucier, R. T., and J. I. Snead
  1989   Quaternary Geology of the Lower Mississippi Valley. Louisiana Geological Society Map. Geological Society of America, Boulder, Colorado.
Schiffer, M. B., and J. H. House
  1975   *The Cache River Archaeological Project: An Experiment in Contract Archaeology.* Arkansas Archaeological Survey, Publications in Archeology, Research Series No. 8.
Scully, E. G.
  1951   *Some Central Mississippi Valley Projectile Point Types.* Museum of Anthropology, University of Michigan, Ann Arbor.
Seeman, M. F.
  1992   The Bow and Arrow, the Intrusive Mound Complex, and a Late Woodland Jack's Reef Horizon in the Mid-Ohio Valley. In *Cultural Variability in Context, Woodland Settlements of the Mid-Ohio Valley,* edited by M. F. Seeman, pp. 41–51. *Mid-Continental Journal of Archaeology* Special Report Number 7.
Shott, M. J.
  1996   Innovation and Selection in Prehistory: A Case Study from the American Bottom. In *Stone Tools: Theoretical Insights into Human Prehistory,* edited by G. H. Odell, pp. 279–309. Plenum Press, New York.
Smith, F. L., and R. T. Saucier
  1971   *Geological Investigations of the Western Lowlands Area, Lower Mississippi Valley.* U.S. Army Corps of Engineers, Waterways Experiment Station Technical Report S-71-5, Vicksburg.
Smith, M. O.
  1993   Intergroup Violence Among Prehistoric Hunter/Gatherers from Kentucky Lake Reservoir. *American Journal of Physical Anthropology.* Supplement 16 pp. 183–184.
Sober, E.
  1984   *The Nature of Selection.* Bradford Bood, MIT Press, Cambridge, Massachusetts.
Speth, J. D.
  1972   Mechanical Basis of Percussion Flaking. *American Antiquity* 37:34–60.
Suhm, D. A., A. D. Krieger, and E. B. Jelks
  1954   An Introductory Handbook of Texas Archaeology. Bulletin of the Texas Archaeological Society 25.
Thomas, D. H.
  1978   Arrowheads and Atlatl Darts: How the Stones Got the Shaft. *American Antiquity* 43:461–472.
Tillery, B. W.
  1992   *Introduction to Physics and Chemistry.* William C. Brown Publishers, Dubuque.
Titmus, G. L.

1985    Some Aspects of Stone Tool Notching. In *Stone Tool Analysis: Essays in Honor of Don E. Crabtree*, edited by M. G. Plew, J. C. Woods, and M. Pavesic, pp. 243–264. University of New Mexico Press, Albuquerque.

Titmus, G. L., and J. C. Woods
1986    An Experimental Study of Projectile Point Fracture Patterns. *Journal of California and Great Basin Anthropology* 8:37–49.

Towner, R. H., and M. Warburton
1990    Projectile Point Rejuvenation: A Technological Analysis. *Journal of Field Archaeology* 17:311–321.

Tsirk, A.
1979    Regarding Fracture Initiations. In *Lithic Use-Wear Analysis*, edited by B. Hayden, pp. 83–96. Academic Press, New York.

Van Buren, G. E.
1974    *Arrowheads and Projectile Points: With a Classification for Lithic Artifacts.* Arrowhead Publishing Company, Garden Grove.

Walters, G. R.
1988    *A Phase I Cultural Resources Survey and Evaluation of the Otter Slough Wildlife Management Area, Stoddard County, Missouri.* Missouri Department of Conservation Project. Submitted to Missouri Department of Conservation by Triad Research Services, Columbia, Missouri.

Waselkov, G. A.
1978    Evolution of Deer Hunting in the Eastern Woodlands. *Mid-Continental Journal of Archaeology* 3:15–34.

West, L. T. and E. M. Rutledge
1987    Silty Deposits of a Low Pleistocene-age Terrace in Eastern Arkansas. *Soil Science Society of America Journal* 51:709–715.

Wilhelmsen, K. H., and T. Miles
1998    Thermoluminescence Dating of Catastrophically Heated Projectile Points. Paper presented at the 63rd Annual Meeting of the Society for American Archaeology, Seattle.

Wilhelmsen, K.H., and J.K. Feathers
In press    Dating the Manufacture of Projectile Points Using Thermoluminescence. In *Lithic Analysis of the New Millennia*, edited by M. Moloney and M. Shott. Institute of Archaeology, University of London.

Woods, J. C.
1987    *Manufacture and Use Damage on Pressure-Flaked Stone Tools.* Unpublished Master's thesis, Department of Sociology, Anthropology, and Social Work, Idaho State University, Pocatello.
1988    Projectile Point Fracture Patterns and Inferences About Tool Function. *Idaho Archaeologist* 11:3–7.

# 5

# Social Complexity in Ancient Egypt: Functional Differentiation as Reflected in the Distribution of Standardized Ceramics

## Sarah L. Sterling

## INTRODUCTION

The Egyptian archaeological record for the period between 3300–2100 B.C., like the primary old and new world states of China, Mesopotamia, the Indus Valley, Mesoamerica, and Peru, is often included in studies devoted to global explanations of the emergence of complexity (e.g., Trigger 1993, 1997; Wenke 1981, 1989, 1997). Generally, archaeologists have defined "complexity" as social systems that share similarity in monumental architecture, writing systems, trade in luxury goods and subsistence technology, and specialization (with resulting standardization) in crafts and artistic motifs (Trigger 1993, 1997; Wenke 1981, 1997). Craft specialization suggests the presence of large-scale labor organization and full-time specialists whose subsistence is provided by another portion of the population. That craft specialization appears to go hand in hand with social complexity has intrigued scholars working in a variety of global settings (e.g., Brumfiel 1980; Brumfiel and Earle 1987a; Rice 1981, 1991; Peregrin 1991; Stein 1998; Underhill 1991). From 3300–2100 B.C., distinctions between the previously localized ceramic traditions of Upper and Lower Egypt are sharply reduced and these local traditions are replaced by a unified national style. This change is taken as evidence of craft specialization. The "standardized" pottery of the Old Kingdom is one of a larger suite of traits that mark Old Kingdom Egypt as a complex society (Wenke 1989, 1997; Wilkinson 1996).

Explanations posited for the development of craft specialization in general have grown out of the tradition of providing global explanations for the emergence of complexity, wherein the commonalties held across complex societies are the focus of analysis (e.g., Carneiro 1970; White 1959; Wittfogel 1957). Particularly common to these kinds of explanations is the implicit assumption that populations will ascend from simple to complex through a preordained series of steps. Craft specialization studies tend to follow the same path, often seeking to explain a progression from household production to industrial production distributed by market systems (Lebo 1992:1). Studies of craft specialization have tended to focus on reconstructing the nature of the relationship between craft specialists and those that control the resources that facilitate the production of commodities (e.g., Brumfiel and Earle 1987b; Rice 1981, 1991). In many studies of general cultural evolution, the concentration of wealth in a small percentage of the population is part of a larger mechanism used to explain how state-level societies form.

Such studies do not pause to ask why a complex society emerges from a simple society, but rely on the implicit assumption that people will progress toward a modern level of complexity (Dunnell 1996; Dunnell and Wenke 1979; Rindos 1984; studies summarized in Stein 1998). This assumption of progress as a mechanism has limited our understanding of the particular historical and functional factors that led to the emergence of complexity in Egypt (Kemp 1989). More important for the purposes of this study, the need to explain why craft specialization systems evolve is obviated by assuming craft specialization to be a manifestation of differential control of resources (Stein 1998:6). Consequently, craft specialization has yet to be described in theoretically meaningful terms (Lebo 1992:12). It is argued here that attributes of products that are potentially the result of craft specialization can provide information about larger-scale distributive networks crucial to a complex, or "functionally differentiated" society. Since degree of functional differentiation provides information about the scale of selection in evolutionary terms, social complexity is an appropriate focus for evolutionary study. Evolution, therefore, can potentially provide the theoretical framework that has been lacking in traditional studies of craft specialization.

All complex societies are characterized by a degree of functional differentiation, wherein members of a given society no longer produce all the resources they need, and are, therefore, dependent on non-kin based relations for survival (White 1949; Dunnell 1996; Dunnell and Wenke 1979). For this condition to exist, there must be a network in place that moves resources and ideas throughout the polity (Dunnell 1996:13). These networks can be clearly demonstrated in the case of city-states such as Mesopotamia, wherein settlements on the floodplains of the Tigris and Euphrates rivers were dependent on the exchange of raw materials from the highlands for products manufactured in urban areas (Algaze 1993:1).

The question of degree of centralization in pottery production during the Old Kingdom in Egypt remains unanswered, however. It has been suggested that pottery production in Ancient Egypt was a local phenomenon, with pottery types thus reflecting local needs and fashions (Bourriau 1981:14). However, Old Kingdom pottery exhibits notable similarities over a broad area (e.g. Ballet 1987; Wenke 1997; Wilkinson 1996), suggesting consolidation, if not centralization of production. The mechanism driving these observed similarities, however, remains undetermined. The Nile River doubtless provides a conduit for moving goods and ideas through Egypt, but the scale of interaction between areas of Egypt is unclear.

The degree of functional differentiation in Egypt during the Old Kingdom is reflected in the scale of craft specialization, because the distribution patterns of specialized crafts provides evidence of the scale of integrative mechanisms extant in Egypt. If actual goods are moving, then there is evidence of craft specialization because commodities are made in one part of the polity and distributed to others. If the ideas for making the goods are moving rather than the objects themselves, however, then the similarity that has been taken to be the result of craft specialization may really be the result of diffusion of ideas along the Nile.

Much has been written about how to characterize the scale of craft specialization from a more traditional culture evolutionary perspective (e.g., Brumfiel and Earle 1987a; Rice 1981, 1991). In such explanations, the emphasis on the study of craft specialization tends to rely on variables that are not part of the archaeological record, and are thus of questionable explanatory utility (e.g., how labor is conscripted, the status of the individual involved in specialized production). But such studies do outline a particular variable of interest, namely that of standardization, which *can* be measured archaeologically (e.g., Rice 1991). Rice (1991: 268) defines standardization as ". . . a relative degree of homogeneity or reduction in variability in the characteristics of the pottery." Contemporary Old Kingdom illustrations (e.g., Bourriau 1981:15, Figures 1–3) of pottery manufacture provide a basis to hypothesize the existence of craft specialization. To begin to test whether Old Kingdom pottery is the work of craft specialists, however, this study will use the distribution of "standardized" ceramics to determine whether codes for manufacture or actual items are moving through Egypt. This information will provide part of an answer to a larger evolutionary question about how Egypt's trade networks are organized.

Distribution across paradigmatic classes of rim morphologies of an apparently standardized type, referred to as a Meidum bowl, will be used to determine the scale of craft specialization. Within this type, there is substantial variation in rim morphologies (Figure 5.1). Local-scale craft production is indicated if a given variant appears significantly earlier in one place and later in others (see Table 5.1). If a given variant appears more or less synchronously across Egypt, on the other hand, mass production at one or a few sites with large-scale distribution is indicated. If this is the case, absolute dates can be used to assess the potential simultaneity of the variants.

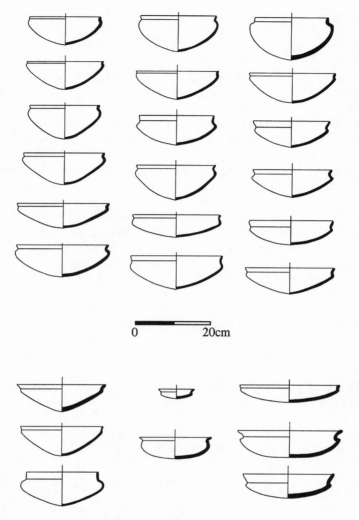

0            20cm

**Figure 5.1. Meidum Bowl variants identified by Reisner (1955).**

Timing and distribution of particular variants can provide a "map" of the network in place that moved these items or ideas about their construction through Upper and Lower Egypt. Mapping this network provides a crucial piece of the larger picture of how Egypt was organized functionally, in the sense that one portion of the population provides resources for another portion of the population, during the Old Kingdom (see also Wenke 1997).

Bowl variants will be distributed in one of four ways, based on the table. If variants tend to be randomly distributed without any chronological pattern (cases

**Table 5.1**

**Expectations of Global- Versus Local-scale Craft Manufacture**

|  | Variant | Distribution | Timing |
|---|---|---|---|
| 1. | Global Specialization | Global | Global |
| 2. | Local Specialization | Local | Local |
| 3. | Indeterminate | Global | Local |
| 4. | Indeterminate | Local | Global |

3 and 4), then there is a strong case for diffusion being the primary mechanism behind this supposed craft specialization, such that the widespread diffusion of the idea of the s-shaped rim is the mechanism of transmission rather than large-scale craft specialization. If, however, there is some structure to the distribution of the variants (cases 1 and 2), then there is warrant to infer the existence of a large-scale commodities network (case 1) or that variants are transmitted with some degree of heritability and are thus useful chronological markers (case 2).

Local timing means a particular variant appears early in a particular place and later in others. Global timing refers to a particular variant appearing more or less synchronously across Egypt. Global distribution refers to the area covered by the Nile Valley and Delta. Local distribution refers to territories within that area. Categories exhibiting a combination of attributes indicate that the scale of interaction is not global, but that the role of diffusion as opposed to trade is indeterminate.

This research tests the long-held hypothesis that Meidum bowls are examples of mass produced crafts, and provides a framework for doing so derived from theoretical principles based in evolutionary theory. The proposed study has the potential to accomplish two things important to the larger issue of understanding the functional scale of interaction during the Old Kingdom period. First, this research provides a way to test for the degree of craft specialization. Second, if the bowl variants demonstrate a large degree of heritability, then further work might allow for a finer chronological resolution using types created in this study.

## HISTORICAL BACKGROUND: A BRIEF HISTORY OF CERAMIC CHANGES IN EGYPT FROM 3500–2100 B.C.

### Late Predynastic (3500–3300 B.C.)

Upper Egyptian pottery from the Late Predynastic, known alternatively as the Gerzean in Petrie's time sequence (Petrie 1899, 1901) or Nagada II in Kaiser (1957), is characterized by imitations of Palestinian and Mesopotamian pottery, as well as red-painted ceramics decorated with patterns, representations of sacred boats, trees, birds, and animals. These latter decorated vessels are found distributed throughout Upper and Lower Egypt (Trigger 1983:32–33). This kind of pottery is typical from Badari in the north to Hierakonpolis in the south (Wilkinson 1996:5–7; see Figure 5.2 for locations of these sites).

The Late Predynastic is the first period during which we see the rapid change that precedes the emergence of the suite of characteristics that comprise the Old

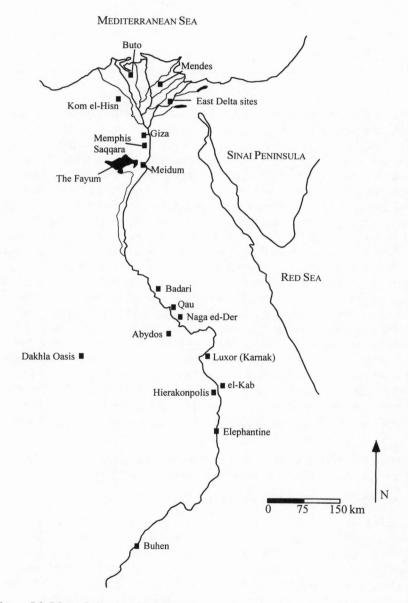

**Figure 5.2. Map of sites mentioned in text.**

Kingdom. Recent discoveries suggest that the distributions of distinctive types of ceramics present a more complex picture of interaction between Upper and Lower Egypt than the earlier conquest model indicates (O'Connor 1997; Wenke 1991, 1997; Wilkinson 1996). Ceramics by themselves do not necessarily reflect cultural boundaries, but they do reflect interaction. Therefore, the distinctive pottery traditions of Upper and Lower Egypt, and changes in their distribution over time, provide some information about the movement of goods and ideas through Egypt during this critical period (Conkey 1990:11, Wilkinson 1996:5).

Less is known about the pottery from the area north of the mouth of the Fayum to the Nile Delta. (See Figure 5.2 for a map of Egypt and the sites discussed in this text.) During the first half of the 4th millennium B.C., pottery from this region is distinct from the pottery of Upper Egypt and has been identified as the Maadi complex, or more recently, the Buto-Maadi ceramic complex (Rizkana and Seeher 1987, 1990; summarized in Wilkinson 1996:5). Maadi ceramics tend to be made of light-colored brown paste with occasional painted decorations. The type site of Maadi, now located under a suburb of modern Cairo, also contains a considerable amount of Early Bronze Age (3000–2700 B.C.) pottery from Syro-Palestine, as well a few pieces of decorated Upper Egyptian pottery (Kantor 1992:6; Trigger 1983:26). Buto, a site on the western side of the Nile Delta, is interesting in that it appears to be an enclave of Upper Egyptian ceramic technology, wherein wares with fabrics typical of Upper Egypt increase in frequency over time, yet appear to be locally made (Kohler 1993:254, Wilkinson 1996:7). Buto also contains some examples of the Maadian pottery and a Buto variant of the Maadian pottery with distinctive decorative motifs not known at the type-site of Maadi (Kantor 1992:6–7).

There is some evidence that Lower Egyptian cultures expanded into Palestine during the Late Predynastic (Joffee 1991; Wenke 1989). This is indicated by the large number of imported ceramics found in Lower Egyptian sites at this time, suggesting a trade network. In general, one can say with certainty that communication between Mesopotamia, Syro-Palestine, and Egypt increased during this time.

## Archaic (Early Dynastic) (3300–2600 B.C.)

The Archaic period is distinct from the later stages of the Predynastic in that there is more apparent uniformity in ceramic types and there seems to be a cessation of influences from Mesopotamia, but an increase in the intensity of relations with Syro-Palestine (Kantor 1992:19). Pottery from Syro-Palestine starts to appear in the form of oil or wine containers. In addition to an increase in distinctive Syro-Palestinian oil and wine containers, there is also a large percentage of "Abydos Ware" (which Petrie called "Late Ware") reflecting what many ceramicists consider a "degradation" (referring to apparent decreased care in the production of ceramics) of styles observed in the Predynastic (Bourriau 1981:44–45; Friedman 1994:37–38; Kantor 1992:19). Unlike ceramics from earlier periods characterized by more or less distinct Upper and Lower Egyptian traditions, there is less disparity between the two regions during this period.

## Old Kingdom (2600–2100 B.C.)

The unification of Egypt is reflected strongly in the apparent standardization of pottery known from the Old Kingdom. Pottery styles change dramatically from the more heterogeneous assemblages of the late Predynastic. The variety of decoration known from the Predynastic is replaced by a more homogeneous decorative style featuring red-slipped polished surfaces (Bourriau 1981:51; Reisner 1955). The pottery of the Old Kingdom in general is characterized by low frequencies of imported wares, relative to the plethora of imported wares known from the Predynastic (Bourriau 1981:51; Reisner 1955).

The Meidum bowl, the focus of this study, is part of this larger corpus of standardized ceramics. The bowl is described as being a high-quality Nile silt or Marl shallow bowl with a beveled rim, rounded base, and red polish. The bowls were first described by Petrie at Meidum (Petrie et al. 1910) and later by Reisner at Giza (1955) but are now shown to have a distribution from the southernmost regions of Egypt to the Nile Delta (Ballet 1987; Bourriau 1981:53; Wenke 1997:126; Wenke and Brewer 1995:281; see Figure 5.2).

## CULTURAL VS. DARWINIAN EVOLUTION: JUSTIFICATION OF THEORETICAL FRAMEWORK

### Cultural Evolution

During the Predynastic/Archaic/Old Kingdom transition, classes of artifacts ranging from ceramics to residential architecture show increased stylistic similarity over the extent of the Nile Valley and Delta from Syro-Palestine to Nubia. These similarities are often taken to indicate degree of functional integration as they reflect the scale of social interaction, and concomitant social complexity. Cultural evolution and its later variants have been the dominant paradigms used to describe the emergence of state-level societies. Cultural evolutionism has provided useful, descriptive typologies based on political and social commonalties observed across complex societies.

Much has been written about how and why state-level societies emerge. Until recently, many scholars have studied complex societies from a cultural-evolutionary perspective and have used a typological approach, emphasizing stages of "progress," to explain the appearance of state-level societies (e.g., Sahlins and Service 1960; White 1949, 1959). Starting with Spencer, Tyler, and Vico, typological approaches to state formation have assumed that state-level social organization is an empirical part of the natural world to which scientific methods can be applied (Wenke 1981:82). The traditional cultural evolutionary paradigm categorizes kinds of social organizations as bands, tribes, chiefdoms, and states. Change results in the transformation of one kind of social organization into another.

Based on ethnographic observation, each stage is attributed a variety of social, economic, and political attributes. Thus, from attributes of the archaeological record such as monumental architecture, writing systems, craft specialization, and complex settlement patterns, inferences are made about the nature of the political organization of that society. Stages are problematic as analytical units, because they embody the particular history of the data set from which they were drawn (Dunnell 1980; Stein 1998). Stages, therefore, cannot be applied to other data sets, because these data will deviate from the ethnographic model used to construct the unit (Dunnell 1980:46). Athens (1977:361) points out that paradigms that assume a state to be some real measurable entity lend an "unrealistic boundedness" to the phenomena in question. Such reification is consistent with the typological conceptions of cultural evolution.

Many scholars have criticized the typological approach on the grounds that it is a limiting perspective. Binford (1968:322) argues that trends observed in the archaeological record are phenomena to be explained, and thus cannot be used as explanations in and of themselves. He further argues that such conceptions of the archaeological record postulate causal factors that are incapable of being tested. McGuire (1983) provides global examples that do not meet the expectations of a typological model of cultural evolution and argues for specifying variables relevant to the social structure in question. Post-processualists, such as Shanks and Tilley (1992) and Hodder (1986), argue that our own cultural experiences influence our explanations of the past and prevent us from understanding the role a given artifact or feature played in the society that created it. Leonard and Jones (1987:201) argue that the scale of culture-evolutionary studies is too inclusive to understand the mechanisms behind culture change, rendering progress as the primary reason for change and prime movers as the only explanation that can thus be posited for change. Recent discussions of "heterarchies" have discussed power structures as not simply hierarchical (progressive) but capable of taking many forms depending on "juxtaposition of cognitive and ecological liminality" (e.g., Crumley 1995:3).

Lebo (1992) provides an excellent discussion of how craft-specialization models constructed under the same rubric as general culture-evolutionary studies are untestable, because the variables employed in such studies are not chosen for any particular theoretical purpose. She emphasizes the problems with such studies is that, in the absence of a theory of specialization, there is no accepted definition of what specialization is or how it can be identified in the archaeological record (Lebo 1992:283). Rice (1981), for example, focuses on recognizing a reduction in relative variation of artifact attributes and noting changes in the distribution of production loci relative to finished products. Rice does not consider stylistic attributes such as vessel form and decoration or style important variables for recognizing craft specialization, because these are more vulnerable to factors not related to specialized production (Lebo 1992; Rice 1981).

Lebo argues that studies of craft specialization tend to fail on explanatory grounds because of the burden of untestable assumptions derived from a culture-evolutionary perspective (1992:288). Specifically, these types of studies use the distribution of pottery-manufacturing technology in attempts to identify full- or part-time specialists who provide for either elites or commoners (Lebo 1992:288). This is problematic because such a focus "attach(es) superfluous elements to the distribution model to the detriment of empirical examination of specialization" (Lebo 1992:288).

The study proposed here employs ceramic standardization to answer questions relating to the scale of social organization using an evolutionary framework. It is argued that this perspective allows a theoretically justified link between social complexity and apparent standardization and thus can begin to address Lebo's general criticisms by providing a theoretical justification for describing the phenomenon of craft specialization.

## Social Complexity from a Darwinian Perspective

The problems entailed in culture-evolutionary studies call for a more empirically and dynamically sufficient theoretical framework that explains why ancient Egypt looks the way it does. If we are committed to an empirical standard for explaining the past, then historical science is our goal. Explaining change in the archaeological record over time is problematic, because historical data only offer the results of change rather than the process itself. Change is, therefore, inferred from these results (Gould 1986:62). Since we cannot observe change, we must look for changing frequencies (i.e., variation) in temporally ordered phenomena. Changing frequencies of selectively neutral traits (meaning traits that confer no selective advantage or disadvantage to the organism) and selectively advantageous traits (non-neutral traits that can confer an advantage to the organism) inform as to issues of relatedness and issues of fitness. Measurement of the frequencies of these traits quantify the history (relatedness to previous generations) and the fitness benefits of specified traits of a phenotype at any given time under certain environmental conditions.

Just as organisms consist of traits that are selectively adaptive and selectively neutral, human technology consists of neutral and non-neutral traits (Dunnell 1978, 1980, 1989, 1996; O'Brien and Holland 1990). The quantification of traits identified as neutral and non-neutral can provide historical and functional information. Measurement of the frequency and distribution of neutral traits informs as to interaction because the factors that drive the transmission of those traits are purely the result of communication. Communication is equivalent to the inheritance of neutral traits in genetics wherein traits that confer no advantage persist in a population through such mechanisms as drift and mutation (or innovation) (Neiman 1995). Neutral traits measure relatedness, therefore, because their presence in any population is the result of inheritance in the case of genetic transmission, or interaction in the case of cultural transmission (Dunnell 1978; Neiman 1995). Transmission of functional attributes indicates how that group interacts with its environment because the distribution of these attributes is driven by natural selection, wherein inheriting a certain attribute confers a selective advantage on an organism in a given environmental setting (Dunnell 1978; O'Brien and Holland 1990).

Both kinds of attributes (neutral and non-neutral) have distinctive distributions that can be represented by monotonic frequency curves through time. The distribution of variability in stylistic descriptions is represented statistically by a unimodal curve, the shape of which is the result of stochastic transmission events (Dunnell 1978, 1980, 1997; Neiman 1995). In contrast, variability in functional attributes, though often unimodal as well, is driven by natural selection and has a distribution that is the result of differences in relative fitness at particular times.

The principles of evolutionary biology can be applied to the archaeological record if culture is recognized as a mechanism of transmission acting in parallel with genetic transmission. Cultural transmission differs from genetic transmission only in that inheritance occurs continuously rather than just during biological reproduction. Thus, in cultural transmission there is no difference between reproduction and growth over any particular time scale and, consequently, change can occur faster. In addition, cultural transmission is not constrained by parent-offspring relationships (Boyd and Richerson 1985; Dunnell 1996).

This last quality of cultural transmission can change the scale of selection, because transmission is not tied to simple interactions between two individuals or within a particular lineage. Thus, in Darwinian evolutionary terms, the difference between a simple and complex society is the scale at which selection operates. In a simple society, the individual contains nearly all the information necessary to reproduce biologically and culturally. Therefore, individuals in such populations are functionally redundant, and selection operates to sort out differences between individual organisms. A complex society can be characterized by functional specialization, wherein organisms can no longer reproduce all the information necessary for survival. Selection thus operates to sort out differences between individuals comprised of several single organisms, since changes in some of the organisms have fitness consequences for all others in that system (Dunnell 1996:13; Dunnell and Wenke 1979:28; Lipo, this volume).

From this perspective, social organization is critical to the survival of a complex system, because it acts as a "glue" that holds together the organism comprised of multiple individuals. Networks that control the distribution of critical resources and the technologies for utilizing those resources are crucial for a socially complex system. Functional specialization is often manifested as large-scale movement of resources in exchange networks. In such cases, a small percentage of the population is responsible for producing food, while other parts of the population manufacture subsistence items such as farming tools and pottery. Thus, the degree of functional differentiation in a complex society as such is defined here is reflected in the extent of the networks that move these resources throughout the larger individual comprised of multiple organisms.

## Craft Specialization and Functional Differentiation

Patterns of interaction (of which the distribution of standardized crafts is a subset) reflect functionally redundant or functionally differentiated populations, in other words, the scale of social complexity. In a functionally redundant society, interaction among individuals can be viewed as a simple function of distance (Dunnell 1995; Lipo, this volume). In a complex society, individuals are not functionally redundant, but interdependent on others for subsistence or critical activities necessary for survival. Degree of interaction in a complex society reflects more than simple distance; it is a consequence of the functional structure of this larger integrative unit (Dunnell 1995; Lipo, this volume).

The distribution of particular variants of Meidum bowls, classified using attributes hypothesized to be neutral (or homologous), can potentially measure interaction among individuals. Since neutral trait frequencies are driven by inter-action (Dunnell 1978; Lipo, this volume; Neiman 1995), the distribution in time and space of these particular variants provides a critical dimension for mapping community structure in Egypt during the Old Kingdom.

From an evolutionary perspective, the stylistic traits used by culture historians to build historical classes are neutral traits whose distribution through time is driven by transmission and random processes such as drift and innovation rather than selection (Dunnell 1997:17; Neiman 1995:12). Therefore, the traditionally chronological tool, seriation, maps patterns of transmission or lineages of inter-acting individuals whose interaction results in the transmission of homologous traits (Dunnell 1997:17; Lipo et al. 1997).

Distributions of particular artifact styles do not represent an immutable set of boundaries for social groups (Conkey 1990; Lipo, this volume). Therefore, it is more accurate to think of social groups as being composed of individuals who interact frequently and whose interaction results in the material and behavioral patterns that we recognize as social organization in the archaeological record (Lipo and Madsen 1997:2). Degree of interaction, therefore, provides insights into social organization. Understanding the change in scale of craft specialization provides one line of evidence to answer larger questions about degree of interac-tion during the Old Kingdom. Within an evolutionary framework, change in the variability of homologous traits has the potential to identify change in degree of craft specialization.

## FUNCTIONAL DIFFERENTIATION IN CERAMIC PRODUCTION: MEIDUM BOWLS

Meidum bowls are made primarily from Marl or Nile clay, with thick red-slip on interior and exterior surfaces. They are highly polished with a large mouth, rounded bottom, and flared rim (Bourriau 1981; Petrie et al. 1910; Reisner 1955; see Figure 5.1 for illustration of variations within this type). Meidum bowls are widely distributed in large volumes across Egypt from Elephantine and Buhen to the Nile delta (see Figure 5.2 for locations of these sites). The "s"- shaped rim (see Figures 5.1 and 5.3) is hypothesized here to be a homologous trait, and the distri-bution of vessels displaying this trait could result from trade or diffusion of ideas.

When trade moves an object, all the attributes of the object are foreign relative to local conditions (Dunnell and Whittaker 1990). In diffusion, only some of the attributes will be foreign, while others will be local (Dunnell and Whittaker 1990). Trade (as defined above) is the mechanism of transmission for global-scale craft specialization, while diffusion (as defined above) is the mechanism of transmission for local or indeterminate craft production. Although Meidum bowls share many attributes (see Figure 5.1), they are also highly variable. The distribution of these variables across particular classes will indicate how this variation is transmitted. Therefore, the types will be subdivided into paradigmatic classes to determine whether attributes display distributions consistent with trade or diffusion (see the table).

This study would benefit from knowing clay sources used in the manufacture of the bowls. Such studies are only informative, however, if the precision with which one identifies a clay source matches the resolution required by the scope of the problem. Arnold et al. (1991:84) note that many ceramics analyzed compositionally cannot be attributed to a particular source, because the size of the geographic area to which clay is sourced is largely a function of local environmental conditions. The Nile Valley is one regional source in that sediments are difficult to distinguish regionally within the floodplain, based on elemental composition. Widespread homogeneity in Nile clays thus complicates provenance studies (Hamroush 1992; Hamroush et al. 1992).

Recent work, however, by Mallory-Greenough and Greenough (1998) is promising in that compositions of Nile silt pottery from Karnak and Mendes (see Figure 5.2 for locations of these sites) can be distinguished using high-precision, inductively coupled plasma, mass spectrometry. The authors were able to demonstrate that samples made from Nile silts from Mendes could be distinguished from samples made from Nile silts from Karnak, based primarily on relative concentrations of 30 elements, with lead being the most statistically powerful discriminator (Mallory-Greenough and Greenough 1998:86). The ceramics discriminated were from two different time periods (the First Intermediate Period, ca. 2100–2000 B.C., and the New Kingdom, ca. 1500–1000 B.C.) This suggests the possibility that post-depositional conditions may have been a factor in the differential elemental composition noted (Mallory-Greenough and Greenough 1998:86). Lead has a high ionic potential (meaning high ionic charge/ionic radius) due to variable solubility in groundwater. Therefore, amounts of lead will reflect local external conditions at least as much as elemental differences between clays from different parts of the Nile floodplain (Brooks 1972; Mallory-Greenough and Greenough 1998). Since the research proposed here deals primarily with ceramics not widely separated in time relative to the Mallory-Greenough and Greenough study, that factor might not be an issue in ICP analysis. Thus, it may be possible to distinguish clays originating from distant sites using this technique. If distributions consistent with craft specialization are identified, then locational hypotheses derived from these distributions can potentially be tested using ICP.

Traditionally, construction of artifact types in Egypt has largely been for chronological purposes. Formation of such types has been largely intuitive

(Wenke 1997:122–123; Wenke and Brewer 1995), thus, "types" used for relative dating are defined by a series of implicitly selected variables. Wenke (1997) argues that while these traditional types are temporally sensitive at coarse scale, more information about chronology and interaction could be gained by subdividing each type into a series of paradigmatic classes (Ballet 1987). These classes would include variables that reflect interaction between populations and, by extension, test for the presence of craft specialization.

## ATTRIBUTE SELECTION AND UNIT CONSTRUCTION

Classifications used to describe interaction must be constructed to best measure stylistic (neutral) variability, rather than functional attributes. Attributes identified with potential functions of the bowls, therefore, should be eliminated from the explicitly constructed classes.

### Functional Attributes

The role Meidum bowls played in the context of Egyptian daily life is unknown. Some have suggested they were serving vessels, while others have suggested they were ornamental, used for floating lotus blossoms (summarized in Bourriau 1981:51). They have been found in a variety of settings, perhaps the most prominent of which is a collection of 38 complete vessels from the tomb of Hetepheres at Giza (4th Dynasty, ca. 2600 B.C.; Reisner 1955). This particular collection of bowls was found sealed intact, and this context suggests that one aspect of the manufacture of the bowls was ceremonial. They are thus cultural elaborations rather than direct functional components of the subsistence system.

Tests must be undertaken, however, to determine whether the bowls exhibit any attributes that could potentially affect their performance under certain environmental conditions. Ceramic attributes that are most likely to confer a selective advantage are those that affect the vessel's "ability to perform the basic cooking, carrying, and storage needs for the social unit within which it is made and used" (Neff 1992:173). Therefore, there are three basic functional contexts in which the form of a ceramic vessel affects performance: storage, cooking, and carrying (Neff 1992:173; O'Brien et al. 1994:270). It should be noted that function is not necessarily equivalent to use. At times, any of these bowls may have been *used* for storage, cooking, and carrying. However, *function* refers to how the vessel potentially affects the fitness of the organism and is identified by examining the development of attributes that enhance the vessel's performance under certain environmental conditions. Vessel function is an analytical description that may or may not be related to how particular bowls were used in the past.

The lips of Meidum bowls indicate carrying is the most likely use of these vessels. Meidum bowls have beveled or grooved rims, suggesting the possibility that the groove is for a more effective attachment for a rope or strap of some kind. However, if one considers the amount of variability in the rim morphologies of these bowls (see Figure 5.1), one can see that sometimes the bevels are quite deep and sometimes they are barely visible.

Changes in the rim bevel of Meidum bowls can be used to assess whether Meidum bowls were used for carrying. If earlier variants of the bowls demonstrate more pronounced rims and later variants show increased variability and less pronounced bevels, one has reason to suggest at least an early carrying use for the bowls. If the opposite is true, that highly variable rim morphologies collapse into less variable rim morphologies over time, one has warrant to suggest the convergence represents an exaption (sensu Gould and Vrba 1982) of a stylistic element into a functional element (Wenke, personal communication).

Thus, preliminary evidence suggests that transporting food, liquid, or other material is the most likely use of the bowls. That most bowls have diameters in the range of 20 centimeters suggests the volume of the bowls may have been significant (Wenke and Brewer 1995; see Figure 5.4).

## Rim Morphology as a Set of Potentially Heritable Attributes

The Meidum bowl has distinctive rim morphology with significant variation that could potentially be homologous (Ballet 1987:3; Bourriau 1981:52; Reisner 1955; Wenke 1997; Wenke and Brewer 1995). Two studies of the rim morphology of Meidum bowls warrant further research as to whether Meidum bowl rims are truly neutral rather than random traits. Ballet (1987) argues that the attributes of Meidum bowls depicted in Figure 5.3a are stylistic and has demonstrated some overall temporal trends in bowl morphology from sherds collected at Dakhla Oasis, generally noting that the height of the shoulder increased over time (see measurement 7, Figure 5.3a).

Wenke and Brewer (1995:281–282) applied Ballet's artifact measurements at Kom el-Hisn and Mendes in Lower Egypt and found some comparability with Ballet's findings. Samples collected at Mendes were found in strata under a 5th-Dynasty mastaba. Since the 5th Dynasty represents the middle of the Old Kingdom, the underlying strata likely date to the early Old Kingdom. Previous work at Kom el-Hisn indicates occupation during only the 5th and 6th Dynasties (Wenke 1986; Wenke et al. 1988). There is also radiocarbon information from Kom el-Hisn dating the occupation of the site to about 2500 B.C. (Wenke et al.1988. This slightly predates the 5th or 6th Dynasties, see Haas et al. [1987] for discussion of discrepancies between historical and radiocarbon chronologies in Egypt.)

Using a technique outlined by Read (1982), Wenke and Brewer (1995) compared the metric measurements of Meidum bowls described in Figure 5.3 to determine which attributes specified by Ballet (1987) displayed frequencies consistent with the definitions of stylistic attributes. Read (1982:78–79) observes that for a series of measurements on a sample of artifacts there will be a unimodal distribution of values about a mean. Large, multimodal distributions of measurements suggest that variation in the attribute in question is not driven by functional

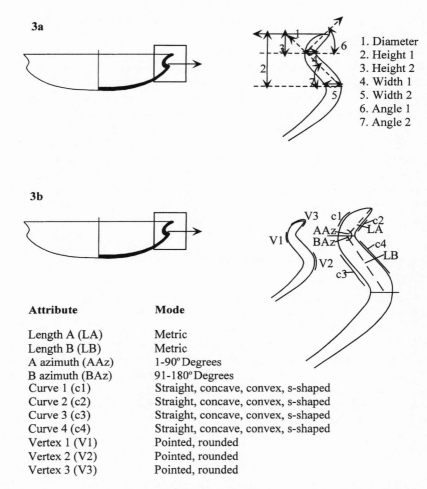

| Attribute | Mode |
|---|---|
| Length A (LA) | Metric |
| Length B (LB) | Metric |
| A azimuth (AAz) | 1-90° Degrees |
| B azimuth (BAz) | 91-180° Degrees |
| Curve 1 (c1) | Straight, concave, convex, s-shaped |
| Curve 2 (c2) | Straight, concave, convex, s-shaped |
| Curve 3 (c3) | Straight, concave, convex, s-shaped |
| Curve 4 (c4) | Straight, concave, convex, s-shaped |
| Vertex 1 (V1) | Pointed, rounded |
| Vertex 2 (V2) | Pointed, rounded |
| Vertex 3 (V3) | Pointed, rounded |

**Figure 5.3. Two examples of paradigmatic classifications designed to characterize the shape of Medium Bowl rims. Figure 3a after Ballet (1987, Figures 5 and 7).**

change but rather drift, and thus reflects the stochastic nature of attributes described as stylistic. These modes will not be used as breaking points for the paradigmatic classifications but merely as heuristic devices to compare the variance of the particular attributes of bowls to isolate those that might be constrained by more than random factors.

Sterling and Wenke (1997) undertook a preliminary study of bowl measurements from four sites in Lower Egypt (see Figures 5.2 and 5.4). We observed that bowl diameter measurements showed little variation across these four sites, suggesting that diameter is constrained by conditions beyond the stochastic factors constraining other measurements (see Figure 5.4). Diameter is a reflection of

Diameter in centimeters, horizontal line represents mean for
each sample, vertical lines represent variance (Measurement 1, Figure 3a)

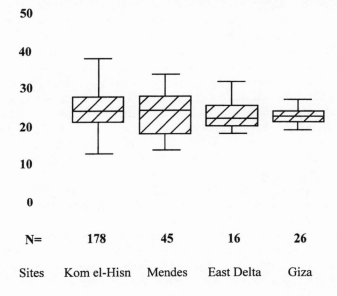

Angle 2 in degrees, horizontal line represents mean for
each sample, vertical lines represent variance (Measurement 7, Figure 3a)

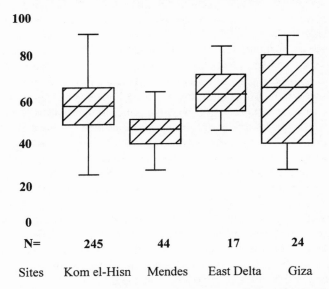

**Figure 5.4. Box plots of results of preliminary study of Meidum bowl measurements.**

vessel volume, and the consistency of the measurement across Mendes and Kom el-Hisn suggests that volume may have played a functional role. In contrast, our study showed significant differences between measurements of rim construction (see Figure 5.4) across the four sites, suggesting rim attributes without diameter might be homologous traits. Figure 5.3b is a modification of Ballet's original (1987) classification, designed to better characterize the shape of the rim bevel. As yet, results of analyses using this classification are pending.

Temporal trends in specified morphological attributes of these ceramics can be used to distinguish stylistic and functional distributions. Since a functional attribute is constrained by both communication and environmental factors and confers some performance enhancement, one should expect to see a lot of initial variation followed by a convergence of form. Stochastic processes, in contrast, will result in a lack of direction and convergence of form, thus indicating that variability in the attribute reflects neutral distributions.

The goal of this study is to describe how the defined stylistic attributes of Meidum bowls vary through time and across space. A paradigmatic classification (after Dunnell 1971) is appropriate because it makes no hierarchical assumptions about the attributes specified and the units constructed explicitly measure the phenomena of interest (in this case, stylistic similarity). Paradigmatic classifications are unambiguous as they are comprised of explicitly described mutually exclusive features, thus eliminating the intuitive decisions that are often made when assigning phenomena to more traditional typologies (Dunnell 1971: 73–74). Since analysts construct paradigmatic classifications to answer specific research questions, the classes measure phenomena of interest by definition, thereby making a given class comparable with all other classes. This is important when making statistical distinctions between groups of phenomena sorted into classes (Allen 1996:101, Dunnell 1971:74).

Traditional types can be intuitively or explicitly defined and are not necessarily comprised of only stylistic attributes (as discussed above). Intuitive and explicit types have both been used in seriation (Dempsey and Baumhoff 1963; Dunnell 1971). However, the use of intuition in archaeological type construction renders many classifications imprecise because the logic used to construct them is implicit (Read 1982:57). Egyptian archaeologists have often employed traditionally constructed types as units of analysis, and, thus, it is not possible to determine what kinds of attributes (stylistic or functional) are being seriated (Wenke 1997). In contrast, by applying a paradigmatic classification to the rim morphology of Meidum bowls, I can potentially construct a seriation based only on the stylistic attributes of the bowls.

Metric variables differ from the nominal variables often used in constructing a seriation in that they are continuous, and, thus, cannot be recorded as present or absent data, nor can they be directly converted to percentages of total "types" of artifacts represented at the archaeological unit under investigation. Therefore, the dimensions specified will be arbitrarily divided into equal units.

A type used in seriation can be a paradigmatic class of discrete objects defined by modes (Dunnell 1971:202). A paradigmatic classification is a non-hierarchical arrangement of objects wherein classes are formed by the intersection of modes and dimensions. Dimensions are mutually exclusive features and modes are intuitively defined characteristics of those features (Dunnell 1971:70–76, 200, 202; Rouse 1939:12). Once the distributions of all the attributes has been analyzed, those dimensions that display the most variation will be used to construct stylistic classes following from the notion that the variation displays suggest a trait the fidelity of whose construction is not constrained by anything in particular. Occurrence seriations (see also Wilhelmsen, this volume) will be used to test the chronological significance of these attributes and, by extension, whether they are neutral. Alternatively, the distribution of classes may be neither neutral nor functional, thus reflecting the possibility that the similarity observed is random. To seriate Meidum bowls, I will use the classes formed by the intersection of metric dimensions as the "types" used in more traditional seriations. These classes (here equivalent to types) represented at sites with known Old Kingdom occupations (see Figure 5.2) will be used to construct occurrence seriations.

### Occurrence Seriations

Occurrence seriations of types constructed will be used to test the hypothesis that variation in the dimensions outlined above can be explained as homologous or simply random. Graphical occurrence seriations are different from numerical seriations in that solutions are deterministic rather than probabilistic, i.e., solutions must conform to the first ordering generalization that hypothesized historical types should be continuously distributed through time (Dunnell 1981:68). However, to evaluate whether this continuous distribution is not the result of random factors or biases resulting from formation processes, the rate and duration of each assemblage employed must be assessed (Lipo and Madsen 1997:2).

Assemblages that are comparable by seriation must have roughly equivalent durations (Dunnell 1981; Lipo and Madsen 1997). Ceramic samples used in this study tend to come from the stratified cultural deposits that comprise tell-like settings (Rosen 1986:9). Structures are often built on older structures and these older structures are usually filled with ceramics and other debris to form foundations for new constructions (Rosen 1986:9). One occupation using mud brick structures can deposit several meters of cultural material in an individual's lifetime. Therefore, deposits with large volumes of ceramics tend to represent relatively rapid depositional events. Documentary evidence provides some relative dating information for determining how deposits are ordered in time (see above summary of the Wenke and Brewer [1995] study for an example of how dating is assessed in Egyptian cultural deposits). Further chronological refinement comes from stratigraphic association with historical landmarks (such as the known 5th-Dynasty mastaba at Mendes.) While it is difficult to assign absolute dates to particular dynasties with great accuracy (Haas et al. 1987), known associations with particular dynasties provides relative chronological information. Therefore, assemblage duration can be assessed on a case-by-case basis, using combinations of relative chronological markers.

Occurrence seriations must also conform to the generalization that seriated groups come from the same local area to ensure that samples are taken from the same historical tradition (Dunnell 1981). Chronological significance of types is partially assessed by comparing the order of particular groups of sherds classified as types from one deposit with the order of the same set of types at another deposit. If all sets of types in different locations form the same order, there is warrant to assume that some of the variability noted in these types is the result of cultural transmission of homologous traits.

Samples used for seriation must be large enough to ensure the variability measured reflects the phenomena of interest and not the idiosyncratic nature of the sample. Two factors drive the probability of getting seriation solution by chance alone: 1. the number of traits used in the description of the object; and 2. the number of descriptions contained in the seriation order (Wilhelmsen, this volume). Given the small number of attributes used here to define a Meidum bowl variant, large samples are required so that the number of classes represented is not a function of sample size (Lipo et al. 1997).

Sample size will be assessed using resampling (Lipo et al. 1997; Wilhelmsen, this volume). Resampling procedures involve drawing a series of random samples from a group of sherds assigned to paradigmatic classes. The sizes of these samples are increased systematically, and the mean and variance of frequency of membership in a particular class is tabulated. If the mean frequency reaches a richness asymptote before maximum sample size is reached, this indicates the sample size is an adequate estimate of the richness of the variants (classes) relative to the sample (Lipo et al. 1997; Wilhelmsen, this volume). If mean frequencies continue to increase as sample size increases, then sample size is not adequate (Lipo et al. 1997). Variance around the mean frequency is further employed to evaluate the precision of overall class richness. If the variances do not decrease, it is likely that the samples are problematically imprecise. Ideal samples are therefore also identified by a corresponding decrease in the variance around mean class frequency as sample size increases (Lipo et al. 1997:316; Wilhelmsen, this volume). Assemblages that conform to the latter case are adequately sized for the purposes of seriation. Therefore, all assemblages used will be subjected to a bootstrap analysis to evaluate sample size.

Occurrence seriations will be used to determine whether traits hypothesized to be neutral are distributed through time in a way that is consistent with the requirements of the ordering and local-area generalizations of seriation.

### *Interval-scale Thermoluminescence Dating*

Thermoluminescence (TL) provides absolute dates for the event of ceramic manufacture (Aitken 1985; Feathers 1992). Unlike radiocarbon dating, which measures the death of an organism associated with the archaeological material to be dated, the chronological measurements resulting from the use of TL require no bridging argument between the archaeological event and the actual event measured. Given that the data employed in this study are ceramic, therefore, TL has the potential to provide precise tests of relative ages of ceramics.

Ratio-scale TL provides absolute dates for ceramics, but the error terms involved are too large to resolve the chronological issues raised here (Feathers 1992). The Old Kingdom (2600–2100 B.C.) is about 500 years in duration and error terms for TL dates can approach that span. However, by relaxing the requirements of an absolute date, much of the error in TL can be reduced and high-precision relative dates that simply demonstrate whether one item is older or younger than another can be provided (Feathers 1992:3). For the purposes of this study, variants displaying distributions consistent with global-scale craft specialization widely separated in space can be tested to determine whether they are the same age or substantially younger or older.

If variant classes constructed reflect global-scale distribution, their relative ages can be assessed using interval-scale TL dating, which will allow an independent assessment of relative ages of classes hypothesized to be from similar time periods but different locations.

## DATA REQUIREMENTS

Data generated for this study will come from measurements of extant collections, scaled drawings, and material generated during excavations at Kom el-Hisn, Mendes, and Giza. In addition to known collections discussed below, there are also a large number of published scale drawings that can be suitably included in this study with some qualifications. Sites considered in this analysis are chosen based on their known representation in museum collections, whether the collection contains pottery spanning the Predynastic/Old Kingdom time period, and adequacy of sample. Figure 5.2 shows the locations of the sites to be considered.

### Ceramic Collections

Samples from sites in Lower Egypt include pottery from Mendes and Kom el-Hisn. Kom el-Hisn was possibly a provincial capital during part of the Old Kingdom, probably the later half of this period between 2400 and 2100 B.C. Therefore, samples collected are assumed to date to this time period. Samples from Mendes come from strata under a gypsum tomb that dates to the 6th Dynasty; we are therefore fairly certain the strata in question date to the 4th Dynasty (2600–2400 B.C.).

Other ceramics are held in collections at various museums. The Hearst Museum at the University of California at Berkeley contains material also excavated by Reisner from Naga ed-Deir, spanning the late Predynastic to the Old Kingdom (3500–2100 B.C.). The University of Pennsylvania houses material from excavations at Abydos with ceramics representing the Predynastic to the early Dynastic

(3500–2600 B.C.), as well as pottery excavated by Petrie at Meidum (the type-site for the bowls) representing the Old Kingdom (2600–2100 B.C.). Material held in collections from Qau and Badari at the British Museum is also incorporated, as is additional material from Qau, Meidum, and El Kab held by the Petrie Museum at University College, London. Additional collections will be incorporated as deemed relevant whenever possible; including anticipated 4th Dynasty material from Giza.

All sherds are photographed in two dimensions for two reasons. First, it is the rim profile that is meaningful in this investigation and measurement on a flat surface is more precise than measurement on the sherd itself. Second, by measuring the items in two dimensions, it becomes possible to compare data generated from published sources with actual objects. Published drawings of ceramic profiles can thus be used as data in this study.

### Published Drawings

Supplemental sample data can be gathered from published and unpublished sherd profiles from various excavations. Archaeological work in Egypt often entails housing artifact collections at the excavated site. As a result, it is often the case that there are scaled drawings of all excavated rim sherds from any given project. Since the attributes of importance here are in one plane of the artifact, all things being equal, measurements taken on scaled drawings should be equivalent to measurements taken on actual artifacts. The process of profile drawing is fairly simple once mastered. The rim sherd is oriented using a flat surface. The perimeter of the sherd is traced with the top of the sherd aligned on graph paper to reflect its proper orientation. There is some potential that the drawings do not accurately reflect the artifact they illustrate, but the risk in this particular case is small and should be random with respect to the variability of interest. Unfortunately, there is no way to quantify this error, since the published material is the product of several different illustrators working over the course of many years. This drawback is not sufficient enough, however, to abandon the wealth of already collected data available in sherd profile drawings.

All drawn images will be scanned and measured using the metric facilities of a computer-drafting program (Canvas). The use of the drafting program increases precision, because the act of measurement is not dependent on human dexterity and allows multiple measurements to be made quickly (see Pierce [1998] for discussion of the use of scaled drawings for measurement of Poverty Point objects). The graphics program also allows the object to be enlarged several times, thus increasing accuracy and precision of measurements.

## EXPECTATIONS AND IMPLICATIONS

### Expectations

Explaining the appearance and distribution of Meidum bowls using an evolutionary explanatory framework has empirical consequences. Lipo (this volume) argues that homologous similarities in a functionally differentiated population will have different distributions than homologies in a functionally redundant population. By mapping the distribution of Meidum bowl variants, I evaluate the degree of trade interaction in Egypt. These results inform as to the scale of craft specialization, which in turn informs as to the possible presence of a global-scale distribution system. A global distribution system must exist for the entire area represented by the Nile Valley and Delta to be functionally integrated.

It is possible that the observed similarities in ceramics across Egypt are simply the result of widespread sharing of ideas transmitted through simple interaction, rather than centralized production with global distribution. If this is the case, I expect to see geographic trends in the relative dates of particular variants, such that dates for a particular class of bowl are measurably earlier in one part of Egypt than in another. There is warrant for chronological inference if the classes generate the same order across several sites. Since similarity among individuals is driven by distance, local-scale craft manufacture should result in certain bowl variants originating in one location. These variants would then appear at slightly later times in locations further away from the center of origin.

Global-scale craft specialization, on the other hand, will result in a different distribution of bowl variants. In this case, I expect that similar classes from widely dispersed parts of Egypt will not have measurably different relative dates. Distance and the geography of the functionally interacting population, implying the existence of a large-scale interaction network, drive similarity in a functionally differentiated society. To demonstrate global-scale craft specialization, I expect to see evidence of similar variants appearing approximately synchronously at widely distributed centers.

## Implications

If the observed similarity of Meidum bowls is the result of global-scale craft specialization, there is further reason to follow other lines of evidence (e.g., architectural styles, stone vessels, faunal, and botanical remains) to see if they exhibit similar patterns of distribution. For example, the initial appearance of standardized ceramics occurs at approximately the same time as substantial changes in architectural styles during the Archaic period (3000–2500 B.C.). The broad distribution of niched and corbelled roof architecture in conjunction with the "national" ceramic styles suggests that information was easily transmitted throughout Egypt at that time. The distribution of stylistically similar structures in Egypt from Elephantine to the Nile Delta (see Figure 5.2) at given times could be used to map the boundaries of a communicating population along with the distribution of possibly standardized ceramics (Sterling 1995).

The processes that formed the Old Kingdom by uniting the two lands of Upper and Lower Egypt at the end of the Predynastic were doubtless a complex mix of population increase, erratic Nile flood patterns, foreign influences, and internal political and economic changes. It is unreasonable to expect that we can find a single cause for the emergence of social complexity at that time. Examining the distribution of classes of Meidum bowls makes it possible to begin mapping communication networks during this early, pivotal period in Egyptian prehistory and history.

## ACKNOWLEDGMENTS

Early versions of this chapter benefited greatly from the comments of Don Grayson, Robert Dunnell, and Angela Close. I am especially grateful to Kim Kornbacher, Carl Lipo, Terry Hunt, and Rob Wenke for reading multiple drafts and continuing to provide useful insights each time. Much of the preliminary research that went into this chapter was made possible by the Niles Fellowship maintained by the Department of Anthropology, University of Washington; thanks to the Archaeology faculty for awarding me this fellowship. Several museums have kindly granted me access to their collections: the British Museum; the Hearst Museum of Anthropology, University of California, Berkeley; and the University of Pennsylvania Museum of Archaeology and Anthropology. Thanks to Vivian Davies, Denise Doxey, Leslie Freund, Joan Knudsen, and Jeffrey Spencer for their time and help.

## REFERENCES CITED

Aitken, M.
    1985   *Thermoluminescence Dating*. Academic Press, New York.
Algaze, G.
    1993   *The Uruk World System: The Dynamics of Expansion of Early Mesopotamian Civilization*. The University of Chicago Press, Chicago.
Allen, M. S.
    1996   Style and Function in East Polynesian Fish-hooks. *Antiquity* 70:97–116.
Arnold, D., H. Neff, and R. Bishop
    1991   Compositional Analysis and "Sources" of Pottery: An Ethnoarchaeological Approach. *American Anthropologist* 93:70–90.
Athens, J. S.
    1977   Theory Building and the Study of Evolutionary Processes in Complex Societies. In *For Theory Building in Archaeology*, edited by L. Binford, pp. 353–384. University of New Mexico Press, Albuquerque.
Ballet, P.
    1987   Essai de classification des coupes type "Maidum-Bowl" du sondage nord de 'Ayn-Asil (Oasis de Dakhla): Typologie et evolution. In *Cahiers de la Ceramique Egyptienne*, edited by P. Ballet, pp. 1–17. Publications de l'institute Francais d'archaeologie orientale, Le Caire.
Binford, L. R.
    1968   Post-Pleistocene Adaptations. In *New Perspectives in Archaeology*, edited by S. R. Binford and L. R. Binford, pp. 313–341. Aldine, Chicago.
Bourriau, J.
    1981   *Um El-Ga'ab: Pottery from the Nile Valley before the Arab Conquest*. Cambridge University Press, Cambridge.

Boyd, R., and P. Richerson
1985   *Culture and the Evolutionary Process*. University of Chicago Press, Chicago.
Brooks, R. R.
1972   *Geobotany and Biogeochemistry in Mineral Exploration*. Harper and Row, New York.
Brumfiel, E.
1980   Specialization, Market Exchange, and the Aztec State: A View from Huexotla. *Current Anthropology* 21:459–478.
Brumfiel, E., and T. Earle (editors)
1987a   *Specialization, Exchange, and Complex Societies*. Cambridge University Press, Cambridge.
Brumfiel, E., and T. Earle
1987b   Specialization, Exchange, and Complex Societies. In *Specialization, Exchange, and Complex Societies*, edited by E. Brumfiel and T. Earle, pp. 1–9. Cambridge University Press, Cambridge.
Carneiro, R. L.
1970   A Theory of the Origin of the State. *Science* 169:733–738.
Conkey, M.
1990   Experimenting with Style in Archaeology: Some Historical and Theoretical Issues. In *The Uses of Style in Archaeology*, edited by M. Conkey and C. Hastdorf, pp. 5–17. Cambridge University Press, Cambridge.
Crumley, C.
1995   Heterarchy and the Analysis of Complex Societies. In *Heterarchy and the Analysis of Complex Societies*, edited by R. Ehrenreich, C. Crumley, and J. Levy, pp. 1–5. Archaeological Papers of the American Anthropological Association, Washington, D.C.
Dempsey, P., and M. Baumhoff
1963   The Statistical Use of Artifact Distributions to Establish Chronological Sequence. *American Antiquity* 28:496–509.
Dunnell, R. C.
1971   *Systematics in Prehistory*. The Free Press, New York.
1978   Style and Function: A Fundamental Dichotomy. *American Antiquity* 43:192–202.
1980   Evolutionary Theory and Archaeology. In *Advances in Archaeological Method and Theory*, edited by Michael B. Schiffer, pp. 35–99. Academic Press, Orlando.
1981   Seriation, Groups, and Measurement. In *Manejos de Datos Y Methods Mathematicos de Arqualogia*, edited by G. L. Cowgill, R. Whallon, and B. S. Ottaway, pp. 67–99. Union Internacional de Ciences Prehistoricas y Protohistoricas, Mexico DF.
1989   Aspects of the Application of Evolutionary Theory in Archaeology. In *Archaeological Thought in America*, edited by C. C. Lamberg-Karlovsky, pp. 35–49. Cambridge University Press, Cambridge.
1995   What Is It That Actually Evolves? In *Evolutionary Archaeology*, edited by P. Telser, pp. 33–50. University of Arizona Press, Tucson.
1996   Natural Selection, Scale, and Cultural Evolution: Some Preliminary Considerations. In *Evolutionary Archaeology: Theory and Application*, edited by M. J. O'Brien, pp. 24–29. University of Utah Press, Salt Lake City.

1997   The Concept Seriation. Paper presented at the Annual Meeting of the Society for American Archaeology, Nashville, Tennessee.

Dunnell, R. C., and R. J. Wenke
1979   An Evolutionary Model of the Development of Complex Society. Paper presented at the American Association for the Advancement of Science, San Francisco.

Dunnell, R. C., and F.H. Whittaker
1990   The Late Archaic of the Eastern Lowlands and Evidence of Trade. *Louisiana Archaeology* 17:13-36.

Feathers, J.
1992   Refining Archaeological Site Chronology through Relative Thermoluminescence Dating of Ceramics. Unpublished grant proposal.

Friedman, R. F.
1994   *Predynastic Settlement Ceramics of Upper Egypt: A Comparative Study of the Ceramics of Hemamieh, Nagada, and Hierakonpolis.* Ph.D. dissertation, University of California, Berkeley. University Microfilms, Ann Arbor.

Gould, S. J.
1986   Evolution and the Triumph of Homology, or Why History Matters. *American Scientist* 74:60–69.

Gould, S. J., and E. Vrba
1982   Exaptation—A Missing Term in the Science of Form. *Paleobiology* 8:4–15.

Haas, H., J. Devine, R. J. Wenke, M. Lehner, W. Wolfie, and G. Bonani
1987   Radiocarbon Chronology and the Historical Calendar in Egypt. In *Chronologies in the Near East*, edited by O. Aurenche, J. Evin, and F. Hours, pp. 585–606. BAR International Series, Lyon, France.

Hamroush, H.
1992   Pottery Analysis and Problems in the Identification of the Geological Origins of Ancient Ceramics. In *Cahiers de la Ceramique Egyptienne*, edited by P. Ballet, pp. 39–51. L'Institut Francais D'Archaeologie Orientale, Cairo.

Hamroush, H., M. Lockhardt, and R. Allen
1992   Predynastic Egyptian Finwares: Insights into the Ceramic Industry. In *The Followers of Horus: Studies Dedicated to Michael Allen Hoffman,* edited by R. Friedman and D. Holmes, pp. 45–52. Oxbow Books, Oxford.

Hodder, I.
1986   *Reading the Past.* Cambridge University Press, Cambridge.

Joffee, A.
1991   Early Bronze I and the Evolution of Social Complexity in the Southern Levant. *Journal of Mediterranean Archaeology* 4:3–58.

Kaiser, W.
1957   Zur inneren Chronologie der Naqadakultur. *Archaeologia Geographica* VI:69–77.

Kantor, H. J.
1992   The Relative Chronology of Egypt and its Foreign Correlations before the First Intermediate Period. In *Chronologies in Old World Archaeology*, edited by R. W. Ehrich, pp. 3–21. University of Chicago Press, Chicago.

Kemp, B.
1989   *Ancient Egypt: Anatomy of a Civilization.* Routledge, London.

Kohler, E. C.
   1993   *Tell el-Fara'in-Buto: Die Keramik der Schichten III bis VI. Untersuchungen zur Topfereiproduktion einer fruhen Siedlung des Nildeltas.* Unpublished Ph.D. dissertation, Heidelberg University, Heidelberg.
Lebo, S.
   1992   *Specialization: Stoneware Pottery Production in Northcentral Texas 1850–1910.* Ph.D. dissertation, University of Washington. University Microfilms, Ann Arbor.
Leonard, R., and G. Jones
   1987   Elements of an Inclusive Evolutionary Model for Archaeology. *Journal of Anthropological Archaeology* 6:199–219.
Lipo, C., and M. Madsen
   1997   The Method Seriation: Explaining the Variability in the Frequencies of Types. Paper presented at the Society for American Archaeology Meetings, Nashville.
   1997   Population Structure, Cultural Transmission, and Frequency Seriation. *Journal of Anthropological Archaeology* 16:301–333.
Mallory-Greenough, J., and J. D. Greenough
   1998   New Data for Old Pots: Trace-Element Characterization of Ancient Egyptian Pottery Using ICP-MS. *Journal of Archaeological Science* 25:85–97.
McGuire, R.
   1983   Breaking Down Cultural Complexity: Inequality and Heterogeneity. In *Advances in Archaeological Method and Theory, Volume 6,* edited by M. B. Schiffer, pp. 91–142. Academic Press, New York.
Neff, H.
   1992   Ceramics in Evolution. In *Archaeological Method and Theory*, edited by M. B. Schiffer, pp. 141–193. University of Arizona Press, Tuscon.
Neiman, F.
   1995   Stylistic Variation in Evolutionary Perspective: Inferences from Decorative Diversity and Interassemblage Distance in Illinois Woodland Ceramic Assemblages. *American Antiquity* 60:7–36.
O'Brien, M. J., and T. D. Holland
   1990   Variation, Selection, and the Archaeological Record. In *Archaeological Method and Theory*, edited by M. B. Schiffer, pp. 31–79. University of Arizona Press, Tuscon.
O'Brien, M. J., T. D. Holland, R. J. Hoard, and G. Fox
   1994   Evolutionary Implications of Design and Performance Characteristics of Prehistoric Pottery. *Journal of Archaeological Method and Theory* 1:211–258.
O'Connor, D.
   1997   Ancient Egypt: Egyptological and Anthropological Perspectives. In *Anthropology and Egyptology: A Developing Dialogue*, edited by J. Lustig, pp. 13–24. Sheffield Academic Press, Sheffield.
Peregrin, P.
   1991   Some Political Aspects of Craft Specialization. *World Archaeology* 23:1–11.
Petrie, W. M. F.
   1899   Sequence in Prehistoric Remains. *Journal of the Royal Anthropological Institute of Great Britain*, London 29:295–301.

1901    *Diospolis Parva: The Cemetaries of Abadiyeh and Hu.* The Egypt Exploration Fund, London.

Petrie, W. M. F., E. MacKay, and G. Wainwright
1910    *Meydum and Memphis.* British School of Archaeology in Egypt, London.

Pierce, C.
1998    Theory, Measurement, and Explanation: Variable Shapes in Poverty Point Objects. In *Unit Issues in Archaeology,* edited by A. Ramenofsky and A. Steffen, pp. 163–190. University of Utah Press, Salt Lake City.

Read, D. W.
1982    Toward a Theory of Artifact Classification. In *Essays on Archaeological Typology,* edited by R. Whallon and J. Brown, pp. 56–92. Center for American Archaeology Press, Evanston, Illinois.

Reisner, G.O.
1955    *A History of the Giza Necropolis.* Harvard University Press, Cambridge, Massachusetts.

Rice, P.
1981    Evolution of Specialized Pottery Production: A Trial Model. *Current Anthropology* 22:219–240.
1991    Specialization, Standardization, and Diversity: A Retrospective. In *The Ceramic Legacy of Anna O. Shepard,* edited by R. Bishop and F. Lange, pp. 257–279. University of Colorado Press, Niwot.

Rindos, D.
1984    *The Origins of Agriculture.* Academic Press, New York.

Rizkana, I., and J. Seeher
1987    *Maadi I. The Pottery of the Predynastic Settlement.* von Zabern. AVDAIK 64, Mainz am Rhein.
1990    *Maadi IV. The Predynastic Cemetaries of Maadi and Wadi Digla.* von Zabern. AVDAIK 81, Mainz am Rhein.

Rosen, A.
1986    *Cities of Clay: The Geoarchaeology of Tells.* University of Chicago Press, Chicago.

Rouse, I.
1939    *Prehistory in Haiti: A Study in Method.* Yale University Publications in Anthropology, New Haven.

Sahlins, M., and E. Service
1960    *Evolution and Culture.* University of Michigan Press, Ann Arbor.

Shanks, M., and C. Tilley
1992    *Re-constructing Archaeology: Theory and Practice.* Routledge, New York.

Stein, G.
1998    Heterogeneity, Power, and Political Economy: Some Current Research Issues in the Archaeology of Old World Complex Societies. *Journal of Archaeological Research* 6:1–44.

Sterling, S.
1995    Standardization as an Indication of Increasing Communication from Predynastic to Old Kingdom Egypt. Unpublished Master's paper, University of Washington, Seattle.

Sterling, S., and R. Wenke
1997 *Attribute Scale Seriation of Old Kingdom Ceramics.* Paper presented at the Society for American Archaeology Meetings, Nashville, Tennessee.

Trigger, B.
1983 The Rise of Egyptian Civilization. In *Ancient Egypt: A Social History,* edited by B. Trigger, B. Kemp, D. O'Connor, and A.Lloyd, pp. 1–70. Cambridge University Press, Cambridge.
1993 *Early Civilizations: Ancient Egypt in Context.* American University in Cairo Press, Cairo.
1997 Ancient Egypt in Cross-cultural Perspective. In *Anthropology and Egyptology: A Developing Dialogue,* edited by J. Lustig, pp. 137–143. Sheffield Academic Press, Sheffield.

Underhill, A.
1991 Pottery Production in Northern Chiefdoms: The Longshan Period in Northern China. *World Archaeology* 23:12–27.

Wenke, R. J.
1981 Explaining the Evolution of Cultural Complexity: A Review. In *Advances in Archaeological Method and Theory,* edited by M. B. Schiffer, pp. 79–127. Academic Press, New York.
1986 Old Kingdom Community Organization in the Western Egyptian Delta. *Norwegian Archaeological Review* 19:15–33.
1989 Egypt: Origin of Complex Societies. *Annual Review of Anthropology* 18:129–155.
1991 The Evolution of Early Egyptian Civilization: Issues and Evidence. *Journal of World Prehistory* 5:279–329.
1997 Anthropology, Egyptology, and the Concept of Culture Change. In *Anthropology and Egyptology: A Developing Dialogue,* edited by J. Lustig, pp. 117–136. Sheffield Academic Press, Sheffield.

Wenke, R. J., and D. J. Brewer
1995 The Archaic-Old Kingdom Delta: The Evidence from Mendes and Kom El-Hisn. In *Haus und Palast im alten Agypten,* edited by M. Bietak, pp. 265–285. Austrian Archaeological Institute, Vienna.

Wenke, R. J., P. E. Buck, H. Hamroush, M. Kobusiewicz, K. Kroeper, and R. Redding
1988 Kom el-Hisn: Excavation of an Old Kingdom Settlement in the Egyptian Delta. *Journal of the American Research Center in Egypt* 25:5–34.

White, L.
1949 *The Science of Culture: A Study of Man and Civilization.* Farrar Strauss, New York.
1959 *The Evolution of Culture.* McGraw Hill, New York.

Wilkinson, T.
1996 *State Formation in Egypt: Chronology and Society.* British Archaeological Report, Oxford.

Wittfogel, Karl
1957 *Oriental Despotism: A Comparative Study of Total Power.* Yale University Press, New Haven.

# 6

# Community Structures among Late Mississippian Populations of the Central Mississippi River Valley

*Carl P. Lipo*

## COMPLEXITY AND COMMUNITY ORGANIZATION

The developmental relation between "simple" and "complex" societies is a major transition in human history and has been the subject of extensive investigation and speculation (e.g., Childe 1925, 1941, 1958; Service 1975; Spencer 1883; Tylor 1865; Wright 1977, 1986). One feature, common to all views of complex society, is a quantum increase in the scale of organization and the concomitant appearance of specialization, especially craft specialization. This change has been described and explained using a wide array of theoretical stances including, among others, cultural evolution, cultural ecology, Marxist structuralism, and Darwinian theory. Each approach seeks to explain the profound changes that mark the emergence of complex society. My research uses an evolutionary approach to explain the origins of complex organizations using an empirically-testable, explanatory framework.

In evolutionary terms, the distinction between simple and complex societies is of fundamental importance and can be expressed alternatively as the scale at which selection operates on human populations or the scale of the "individual" (Dunnell 1978b; 1995). In simple societies, the scale of selection is that of the organism, i.e., persons (ignoring age and sex) who carry the full set of codes, genetic and cultural, to reproduce the human phenotype. Simple societies are aggregates of such units. Many other, less archaeologically-visible features (e.g., kin-based organization, intrasocietal competition, etc.) of simple societies are thus explained as well (Dunnell 1978b, 1980; Dunnell and Wenke 1979).

Complex societies are populations in which the scale of selection, the individual, is larger than the organism, i.e., persons do not carry the entire set of instructions for producing a human phenotype. Societies or units of similar scale are the individuals upon which selection acts. In complex societies, it is only at the scale of aggregates of organisms at which all of the functional requirements for reproduction of the society are met. Within complex societies, people perform different functions, each of which is necessary to the survival of the whole. Because each subpart performs only one of a few functions out of the total, subparts cannot survive on their own. This element is recognized archaeologically by such things as craft specialization, polity-based organization, wide-scale functional interaction, and intersocietal competition (Dunnell 1978b, 1980; Dunnell and Wenke 1979).

In simple societies, communities are independently organized and interaction is a local phenomenon between individuals and occurs between neighbors in proportion to their distance. In complexly organized communities, organisms are functionally dependent, and interaction occurs more often between people who are part of the same individual than persons in another functionally complete system of communities. While interaction between persons in a simple society is primarily a function of distance, many interactions between persons in complex societies are structured by community membership.

Differences between the degree of interaction are detected archaeologically by differences in the stylistic similarity of artifact assemblages assuming that, other things being equal, greater stylistic similarity among assemblages indicates a greater degree of relatedness or interaction. If traditional stylistic similarity is understood as homologous similarity (*sensu* Dunnell 1978a) then there is general warrant for this notion. Whether a set of persons is part of a single interacting group, or part of several functionally independent communities, however, is not simply a matter of identifying sharp discontinuities between otherwise homogenous distributions of artifacts. Communities "are not continuous integrated bounded entities that can be stopped in their space-time tracks as traditional ethnography has led us to believe" (Conkey 1990:11). The theoretical underpinnings for making these distinctions, as well as contemporaneity and measurement issues, must all be considered in the detection of changes in the scale and character of social organization. Most importantly, the data upon which measurements of interaction are made must be collected using strategies designed to produce information that reflects patterns of prehistoric interaction and not environmental constraints, collection strategies, sample size effects, and other measurement biases (Dunnell 1995).

At present there are 1. few reliable and detailed extant datasets that can be used to examine interaction between settlements; 2. few tools developed for detecting organizational change; and 3. no protocols for collecting the appropriate data by which changes in interaction can be observed and measured. In this chapter, I address these three deficiencies by collecting data and developing methods for examining variation in prehistoric intercommunity interaction. Employing these methods, I examine a set of artifacts likely to represent an early stage in the development of social complexity in the eastern United States.

## STUDY AREA

Acquiring data to document the initial phases of social complexity is usually hampered by explosive growth that typically follows a change in scale of the individual; complex cultural systems obscure evidence of their own development. In contrast to most complex societies, the Late Prehistoric communities (ca. 1400–1600 A.D.) of the Mississippi River valley exhibit clear movement to complexity but are terminated by disease (from European contact) before large scale growth ensues making them uniquely suited to research on the origins of social complexity.

Research by House (1991), Phillips (1970), D. Morse (1973, 1990), P. Morse (1981, 1990), and Williams (1954) suggests that changes occurring during the late Mississippian period are related to a change in social complexity. These changes appear as distinct shifts in settlement patterns that are archaeologically marked by cohesive deposits consisting of large, palisaded town sites, elaborately decorated pottery, and earthen mounds (Morse and Morse 1983). Since the Mississippi valley is primarily agricultural today, many of these archaeological deposits are easily accessible and relatively intact.

## ARCHAEOLOGICAL UNITS

Traditionally, archaeologists treat space as a nominal variable, employing "areas" as units of description. Variations of areas as units include "cultures" (e.g., Rouse 1955), phases (e.g., Phillips 1970; Phillips and Willey 1953; Willey and Phillips 1955, 1958; Williams 1954), provinces (e.g., Cordell and Plog 1979; F. Plog 1979, 1983) and polities (e.g., Hammond 1972; King and Freer 1995; Upham and Plog 1986). The unit termed "phase" has the longest history and is the most widely used with a spatial component (Phillips 1970; Phillips and Willey 1953; Willey and Phillips 1955, 1958; Williams 1954). The concept of phase has dominated the archaeology of the central Mississippi River valley (e.g., D. Morse 1973, 1990; P. Morse 1981, 1990; Smith 1990), where it was developed.

The phases of the central Mississippi River valley have their roots in the Lower Mississippi River Valley Survey conducted by Phillips, Ford, and Griffin (1951; hereafter, PFG) in the 1940s. The analytic focus of the PFG study is a series of seriations constructed by Ford. For the seriation, Ford divided the valley into a set of local areas (St. Francis, Memphis, Upper Sunflower, Lower Arkansas,

Lower Yazoo) recognizing that spatial variation in the frequencies of historical types was sufficiently large that no single seriation could be constructed for the entire survey area. Figure 6.1 shows these divisions. Although Ford (1952) broke with his co-authors to analyze spatial variability quantitatively, PFG took an essentialist view and broke each seriation into a series of chronological periods (A through G). These units became the phases of Phillips and Willey (1953).

Using these kinds of units as a foundation, Phillips and Willey proposed the phase concept to integrate both time and space and to replace the phenetic Midwestern Taxonomic System (Phillips and Willey 1953; Willey and Phillips 1955, 1958). Although Williams (1954) was first to apply the Willey and Phillips system, Phillips has had the greatest impact on the area by defining phases for the entire chronological sequence of the central Mississippi River valley (Phillips 1970). In his 1970 re-analysis, Phillips renamed the PFG periods in each area as phases. The assemblages assigned to periods A and B in the St. Francis area, for example, become the Parkin phase. The northern A-B assemblages in the Memphis area become the Nodena phase.

The phase is defined as "an archaeological unit possessing traits sufficiently characteristic to distinguish it from all other units similarly conceived, whether of the same or other cultures or civilizations, spatially limited to order of magnitude of a locality or region and chronologically limited to a relatively brief period of time" (Willey and Phillips 1958:22). Although it has been routinely suggested that "the equivalent of phase . . . *ought* to be 'society'" (Willey and Phillips 1958:49, emphasis added), early workers were sanguine about the culture/phase equivalence (e.g., Abbot 1972; McKern 1939; Willey and Phillips 1955) and realized that such equivalencies were accidental rather than structural. Pressure to be "anthropological" has tended to overwhelm such wisdom in many areas, including the central Mississippi River valley. Here, many archaeologists treat phases as if they are the material manifestations of ethnic, political, or linguistic units. As a consequence researchers in the central Mississippi River valley have tried to relate these phases to historical groups (e.g., Brain 1978, 1985; Brain et al. 1974; Hudson 1985; Morse and Morse 1983, 1990, 1996; Phillips 1970; Phillips et al. 1951; Rouse 1965; Willey and Phillips 1958). Not surprisingly, there is little discussion regarding their definition (e.g., Eighmy and LaBelle 1996:56). Indeed, Phillips (1970: 523-52), one of the main proponents of the phase concept, candidly admits that the procedures for constructing phases are "regrettably nonobjective." Most discussion centers on their interpretation.

Recently, however, the phase formulations have been criticized as too simplistic and it has been argued that neither ethnic, political, nor linguistic units have straightforward analogs in artifact distributions (Fox 1992, 1998; House 1991; O'Brien 1994, 1996). Mainfort (1995) has proposed that while "some previously defined late period phases represent relatively valid units (i.e., statistically reproducible). . . . others are much less robust, and some simply do not exist." Re-analyses suggest that phases may have little empirical basis. Fox (1992, 1998;

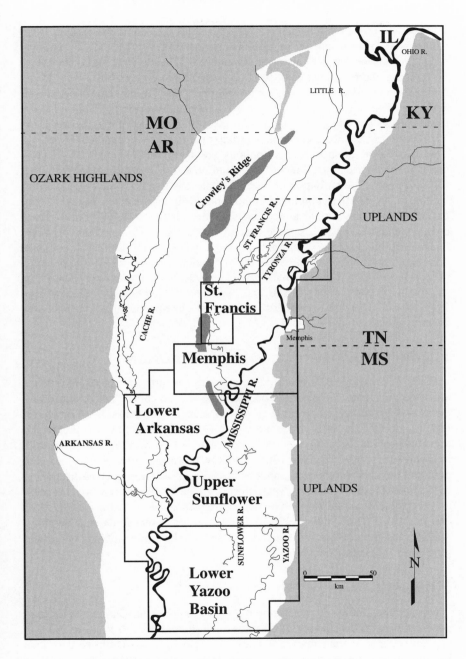

**Figure 6.1. Subdivision of the Mississippi River valley by Ford for purposes of building seriations.**

O'Brien and Fox 1994) characterizes the phases of the central Mississippi River valley as an inconsistent set of assemblages whose only rationale is historical usage. Fox (1998) has demonstrated that phases created by Williams (1954) have no defining characteristics and cannot be considered classes (i.e., there are no necessary and sufficient conditions for membership). At the same time, cluster analysis of the ceramic frequencies used to place assemblages in particular phases shows that phases are not groups (i.e., the members of one phase are not more similar to members of the same group than they are to members of others).

Phases, their locations and distributions, are inappropriate tools with which to describe the archaeological record when our goal is to construct evidence of the form, timing, and distribution of social complexity. Even if the phases, or similar constructs, had been employed in the central Mississippi River valley in a rigorous fashion, they would have been deficient on two grounds. First, phases create boundaries regardless of the structure of the record. And second, they were invented to build culture-historical sequences where time and space coherence (i.e., homology) is the objective, yet the distinction between simple and complex organization is plainly functional. Instead of phases, the appropriate focus is the occupation (Dewar 1991; Dewar and McBride 1992; Dunnell 1971; Madsen 1994), the minimal unit to which *both* time and spatial coherence and functional characteristics can be assigned.

## THEORETICAL FRAMEWORK OF INTERACTION

Eager to develop methods for investigating patterns of interaction in the archaeological record, the early processualists—the so-called "ceramics sociologists"—assumed that culture is a system of transmission and treated the distributions of artifact type frequencies as a direct reflection of prehistoric transmission intensity (Deetz 1965; Longacre 1970; S. Plog 1976a, 1976b; Redman 1977, 1978; Whallon 1968). Quickly, however, archaeologists began to point out that this assumption cannot be made because factors such as differences in time, subsistence strategies, vessel forms, exchange, and depositional process all play a role in the distribution of artifact frequencies (e.g., S. Plog 1978, 1980; Schiffer 1987; Stanislawski 1973). The relationship between the distribution of artifact type frequencies and transmission is complex and combines both theoretical and empirical considerations.

### Theoretical Background

Measurement of trait transmission frequency requires the examination of temporal and spatial distribution of attributes not affected by selection. In order to explain patterns of transmission, the archaeological record should be described in terms that have distributions not correlated with the environment (Cronin 1962; Dickens and Chapman 1978; Dunnell 1978a, 1978b, 1996; Whallon 1968). These terms produce descriptions of homologous, rather than analogous similarity. The failure to distinguish between analogous and homologous similarity has been a central problem in historical studies for more than a century (e.g., Binford 1968; Naroll 1960; Sahlins and Service 1960; Service 1962, 1975; White 1949). Evolutionary theory provides the tools with which it is possible to differentiate functional and stylistic attributes (Dunnell 1978a, 1978b, 1980, 1996) through the concept of neutrality and the contrastive distribution of the two in time and space.

## Style and Function

Due in part to their interests in building historical frameworks, culture historians assumed that stylistic similarity and interaction are directly related and used this assumption to order assemblages in time and to build chronologies and phases (Lyman et al. 1997). While the connection between interaction and similarity was often phrased in terms of behavior and common sense, the fact that there is a general relationship between interaction and homologous similarity allowed methods such as seriation to be used to create coarse chronologies.

The general shift in interest from questions of chronology toward function pushed the new archaeology to focus specifically on how "interaction" in the functionalist sense could be divined from spatial patterns of material similarity. S. Plog (1976a, 1976b, 1980), Longacre (1970:27–28), Whallon (1968:223), and others (e.g., Deetz 1965; Redman 1977:51, 1978: 172–173, 175) have argued that the degree to which designs or attributes are shared between individuals, social segments, or villages is directly proportional to the amount of interaction between them. Differences in interaction, as measured by the similarity of assemblages produced in several localities, are the basis for analyses of "communities," or "polities" (Engelbrecht 1971; Leone 1968). Significantly, the new archaeologists did not explicitly recognize the importance of homology or style in this operation, but simply used traditional culture-historical units.

Traditional archaeological approaches to the relationship between similarity and interaction can be summarized as follows:

Culture Historians: Stylistic Similarity = f(*time* )        (Equation 1)

New Archaeologists:(Stylistic) Similarity = f(*interaction* )        (Equation 2)

While neither culture history nor new archaeology often used the word, both approaches are founded in a *transmission* theory, i.e., neither position makes sense unless one assumes that similarity is understood as homologous similarity. In the case of culture history, the chronological claims were testable (e.g., stratigraphy and, later, chronometric dating); those of the new archaeology were not. Both equations, however, grossly oversimplified the causes of similarity as measured empirically, with the result that only crude and variable approximations were possible under the best of circumstances.

The problem can best be explored by examining basic components of a transmission model. At a population scale, the frequency of any particular trait, as measured by homologous similarity ($S_h$), is determined by the configuration of the population ($P$), the process of transmission ($T$) and the characteristics of the space between the transceivers and receivers ($D$) (Cavalli-Sforza and Feldman 1981). Other, nontransmission-related components that can impact the frequency of traits include chance ($C$) and formation processes ($FP$).

We can now imagine that a better description of the relationship can be summarized by a schematic equation:

$$S_h = f(D, P, T, C, FP)$$  (Equation 3)

In evolutionary terms, the culture historical approach either ignored or attempted to control nontemporal factors such as formation processes and spatial distance in order to produce a chronological method, seriation. The early new archaeology, in contrast, simply ignored the nonspatial factors. Overall, confusion as to why culture historians succeeded in producing knowledge about cultural interaction and why they failed in other respects, hindered the new archaeologists from solving significant problems for the discipline. While the new archaeologists were keenly aware that culture historians had relatively narrow interests, their overall rejection of culture-historical methods was theoretically and empirically unwarranted. Thus, in order to understand how these robust methods can provide information about past interaction in areas other than chronology, we need to specify each of the theoretical terms with a set of variables that are measurable in the archaeological record. By breaking down the theoretical model into a series of conceptual variables, it is possible to understand how the culture-historical model can produce information about interaction and artifact similarity.

Culture historians eliminated the effects of chance similarity being mistaken as homologous similarity by using types or combinations of attribute classes. The likelihood of the accidental recurrence of a suite of conjoined elements is vastly smaller than for a single element. Consequently, so long as one describes the archaeological record as the frequencies of types, similarity arising by chance ($C$) can be minimized or virtually eliminated in the parameters contributing to similarity (contra Duff 1996; LeBlanc 1975). Therefore,

$$S_h = f(D, P, T, FP)$$  (Equation 4)

so long as $S_h$ is measured by the frequency of multidimensional types.

This theoretical relationship does not describe any particular dataset, because the record is the result of transmission *and* everything that has affected the record since the transmission event. Both the culture historians and the early new archaeologists uniformly ignored formation processes. Because the effects of formation processes enter in writing specific descriptions of the archaeological record (Schiffer 1987), I take them up later when I consider the mechanics of sample description. Thus,

$$S_h = f(P, T, D) \qquad \text{(Equation 5)}$$

so long as when $S_h$ is expressed, relative frequency of types and the formation of assemblages is comparable or corrected to be comparable.[1]

The characteristics of the population ($P$) that drive $S_h$ include population size ($P_n$) and the distribution of the population across the landscape ($P_d$). This can be expressed as:

$$P = f(P_n, P_d) \qquad \text{(Equation 6)}$$

The effect of increasing the number of transmitters and receivers ($P_n$), all other things being equal, is to increase the number of transmissions, and thereby the rate of change of diffusion and innovation. Decreases in $P_n$ result in a smaller number of transmissions, as well as decreases in the rates of change, diffusion, and a loss of variation. In general then, the effects of $P_n$ on $S_h$ are limited to absolute numbers of variants and, therefore, are negligible unless there are catastrophic changes in $P_n$ (e.g., founder's effects).

The components of transmission that influence similarity include the probability of transmission ($T_p$), technology used for transmission ($T_t$), and the duration of transmission ($T_{dt}$) and can be expressed as:

$$T = f(T_p, T_t, T_{dt}) \qquad \text{(Equation 7)}$$

Probabilities of transmission ($T_p$), distance between individuals ($P_d$), and geographic space ($D$) are not necessarily uniform through time and space. Both culture historians and new archaeologists were aware of temporal and spatial components of transmission, though in dramatically different ways. The culture historians recognized that "styles vary and trend toward those of other centers in rough proportion to the distances involved, subject of course to the ethnic distributions and geographic factors" and are thus not just a measure of temporal distance (Phillips et al. 1951:62). S. Plog's (1977, 1980) critique of ceramic sociology takes a different approach. He argues there are a number of empirical factors that can influence the relationship between ceramic similarity and interaction, including differences in settlement-subsistence systems, vessel shape and use, exchange of materials, and time. Plog cautions that these factors must be controlled before one can explain ceramic variation as interaction. Thus, while the culture historians treated time and space as components of a theoretical system of explanation, the new archaeologists were primarily interested in space and treated time as an empirical issue that must be treated during analysis. Unfortunately, the new archaeologists, in their zeal to address sociological and functional aspects of the past (e.g., settlement systems, land-use patterns, social relationships, subsistence, etc.), removed the implicit theoretical component that made culture history successful.

### Spatial Approaches

Despite fundamental limitations, the spatial focus of the new archaeologists has led to many interesting and potentially powerful applications. If it was possible to hold time and population size constant, a variety of geographic aspects of interaction could be investigated. Since interaction is not uniform between all individuals throughout space, and the farther the individuals are apart, the less frequently one would expect them to interact (e.g., Haynes 1974; Hodder and Orton 1976; Wilson 1971; Zipf 1949), I expect stylistic similarity to be proportional to degree of transmission, and thus inversely proportional to distance. This relationship has been the basis of numerous studies of community interaction (Carrothers 1956; Haggett 1966; Hodder and Orton 1976; Wilson 1971) and can be neatly expressed through the use of a gravity model where:

$$I_{ij} = \frac{aN_iN_j}{D_{ijb}} \qquad\qquad \text{(Equation 8)}$$

In Equation 8 $I_{ij}$ is the amount of interaction between two settlements $i$ and $j$, $N_i$ and $N_j$ are the population sizes of settlements, $D_{ij}$ is the distance between the two settlements, and $a$ and $b$ are constants. This relationship can take a number of forms (Renfrew 1977, 1984), including the Pareto model (e.g., G. Wright 1970), exponential distance decay, and Gaussian fall-off (e.g., Renfrew 1984). Examples of studies of geographic distance and stylistic similarity include research in the Southwest (e.g., Hill 1970; Longacre 1964, 1970; F. Plog 1979, 1983), the Midwest and Northwest (e.g., Deetz 1965; Whallon 1968), the Southeast and Northeast (e.g., Ford 1952; Deetz and Dethlefsen 1965), the South and Mesoamerica (e.g., S. Plog 1976b), and the Old World (e.g., Hodder 1974; Hunt 1987; Pollnac and Rowlett 1977; Renfrew 1977, 1984).

The use of a gravity model to explain interaction communities typically requires setting $a$ and $b$ to empirically determined values. The $b$ exponent, for example, is usually set to either 1 or 2 (Olsson 1965; Zipf 1949), and the $a$ value is set between 1 to 3.5 (Berry 1967; Chilsholm and O'Sullivan 1973). These studies, thus, simplify the transmission function to:

$$S_h = f(P_n, P_d) \qquad\qquad \text{(Equation 9)}$$

where $P_n$ is the population size, $P_d$ is the distance between interactors, and $a$ and $b$ are used to account for the spatial distribution of the population ($P_d$), differences in the probabilities of transmission ($T_p$) and technology ($T_t$) at some particular range in time. ($T_{dt}$ is assumed constant between assemblages.)

This relationship, however, is too simple. Not all paths of interaction are of equal cost. Space ($D$) affects similarity ($S_h$) by increasing or decreasing the probability of interaction along particular directions by enhancing interaction through watercourses or currents, or decreasing interaction through mountains, and swamps, (e.g., Irwin 1992). The effect of geographic structure, of course, depends upon available communication technology and transportation systems (Alonso 1964; Hodder and Orton 1976; Wilson 1971). Any change in interaction must be tested against innovations in communications systems. $D$, therefore, can be expanded to include linear distance ($D_{rq}$), geographic weighting according to direction ($a_q$) given a particular transmission technology ($T_t$), and can be expressed as:

$$D = f(D_{rq}, a_q) \text{ given } T_t \hspace{3cm} \text{(Equation 10)}$$

In many cases, such as among Late Prehistoric communities in the central Mississippi River valley, the effects of communication systems can be eliminated from consideration because of the lack of fundamental change in transmission technology over the period of analysis. Linear distances ($D_{rq}$) are easily measured. Approximation of geographic weighting ($a_q$), therefore, is critical to the analysis; the better $a_q$ is modeled, the closer the equation will fit the prehistoric case. McCutcheon (1996) has shown that distance weighting is of sufficient importance to have major impact on correlations and that a boat-transportation model is, at least for lithic raw material, appropriate for the central Mississippi River valley.

Increases in population density resulting from changes in $P_n$ and/or changes in $P_d$ will increase the probability of transmission events; decreases in population density will reduce the probability of transmission. Geometry plays a role, however. Populations are not randomly or uniformly distributed but are instead clustered to some extent. Increases and decreases in clustering distribution do not change the mean rate of transmission but rather have quantum effects (Glance and Huberman 1994; Green 1994; Huberman and Glance 1994).

The factors that drive the probability of transmission ($T_p$) are also important to consider. Within social groups, there is a greater-than-random chance of interaction between individuals considering distance ($P_d$ and $D$) and given a particular transmission technology ($T_t$) than between individuals in different social groups (Cook 1970:34, 47; Flannery 1976; S. Plog 1976b; Soja 1971). Functional interaction between individuals will also have to reflect a higher-than-random chance of transmission than distance alone would dictate. In other words, any one individual does not randomly transmit to other individuals in the population after distance is factored out. This can be explained in terms of the similarity equation. While stylistic class frequencies are free to vary (i.e., are neutral with respect to selection and have stochastic distributions), the *source* of the variation in stylistic attributes can be patterned. Therefore, if there is similarity between assemblages that cannot be accounted for by geography and the temporal-spatial patterning of the population (i.e., residual similarity), then interaction is being structured at a level greater than the simple organism. In essence, by accounting for other variables, we can solve the similarity equation for $T_p$ where $T_p$ is a measure of structured interaction:

$$T_p = \frac{S_h}{f(P_n, P_d, D, T_t, T_{dt})}$$
(Equation 11)

The terms that compose this equation and the means for measuring them are listed in Table 6.1. Solving the equation is fairly simple: similarity $(S_h)$ can be measured by calculating the frequencies of stylistic classes; distance $(P_d)$ can be measured as geographic distance between assemblages; population size $(P_n)$ and transmission duration $(T_{dt})$ and technology $(T_t)$ can be held constant; and geographic factors $(D)$ can be modeled. In this way, it is possible to detect structured transmission patterns and complex organization.

Most methods for examining the spatial component of transmission make use of the simplest case, wherein similarity is assumed to be a function of geographic distance (i.e., Equation 8). A simple plot of assemblage similarity (as measured by the Brainerd-Robinson coefficient) and interassemblage distance can be a first step in evaluating the relative effects of time and distance within a set of assemblages (Cowgill 1968, 1972). Other approaches make direct use of the gravity equation to explain patterns of similarity based on distance and estimates of population size (e.g., S. Plog 1976b; Renfrew 1969). A directional examination of assemblage correlation that accounts for differential interaction by direction is possible by directly mapping assemblage similarity. Geostatistical methods such as isotropic and anisotropic semivariance analysis can also be used to evaluate the degree to which similarity is autocorrelated to distance (Cliff et al. 1974; Isaaks and Srivastava 1989). Jackknife error estimates using a cross-validation technique permit the calculation of an average estimation error and, thus, the identification of meaningful differences.

**Table 6.1**
**Measurable Components in the Similarity Equation**

|  | Space ($D$) | Population ($P$) | Transmission ($T$) | Similarity ($S_h$) |
|---|---|---|---|---|
| Factors | $D$ Geographic space | $P_d$ Population distribution $P_n$ Population size | $T_t$ Transmission technology | $S_h$ Similarity |
| Measurability | $D$ Yes. Construct models about the costs of transmission over geographic space | $P_d$ Yes. Measure X and Y coordinates of assemblages $P_n$ Yes. Differences negligible unless catastrophic changes in population size | $T_t$ Yes. Can hold constant by looking at a short period of time with no changes in transmission technology | $S_h$ Yes. Measured frequencies of stylistic types |

The ultimate difficulty with the spatial approach to the study of interaction, however, is that transmission occurs simultaneously through time *and* space and that homologous similarity is, by definition, the product of both temporal and spatial interaction. It is never possible to eliminate variability in homologous similarity caused by the temporal component of transmission from its spatial component and *vice versa*.

## Seriation

The culture historians took a complementary tack in their analyses of transmission. By holding space and population size constant, a variety of temporal aspects of interaction can be investigated. Since $S_h$ depends upon the frequency of interaction, stylistic similarity is inversely proportional to distance between individuals in time (Brainerd 1951; Robinson 1951). Culture historians exploited this relationship in their development of seriation (Dunnell 1970, 1981). Three different families of techniques grew up around three different approaches to describing similarity: frequency, occurrence, and similarity seriation (Dunnell 1970; see also Cowgill 1972). In all cases, however, the "null hypothesis" was an empirical model ultimately derived from stratigraphy and not a model for transmission. Despite this misunderstanding, when a number of conditions are met, the product of seriation is a chronological ordering. The method has been proven to be tremendously robust. Its products are the fundamental chronological sequences upon which our understanding of prehistory has been built (e.g., Ford 1936, 1938, 1949; Kidder 1924; Mayer-Oakes 1955; Phillips et al. 1951).

In seriation, using the "local-area criterion" held space constant (cf. Dunnell 1970). In other words, assemblages must be derived from the "same local area" in order to seriate successfully (Deetz and Dethlefsen 1965; Dunnell 1970, 1981; Ford 1952; Lipo et al. 1997; Neiman 1995; Phillips et al. 1951). As transmission occurs through time and over space simultaneously, the "local-area criterion" is an essentialist attempt to minimize the continuous effect of transmission over space and maximize differences caused by transmission through time. Like the spatial case, seriation exploits the same general relationship detailed in Equation 5, except that the distance between individuals ($P_d$) is predominately temporal rather than spatial. Seriation as a "dating" method is just as theoretically defective as spatial analysis, but for a mirror-image reason; space and population size cannot be held constant.

The population distribution component of Equation 5 ($P_d$) can be decomposed into temporal distance ($P_{dt}$) and spatial distance ($P_{dxy}$):

$$P_d = f(P_{dt}, P_{dxy})$$

(Equation 12)

In seriation, the spatial variability ($P_{dxy}$) term is minimized by the "local-area criterion," thus maximizing variability in similarity through time ($P_{dt}$). Seriation can be used, however, as a general method for examining transmission (Lipo et al. 1997; Neiman 1995). If one uses a temporal model to order assemblages, for example, then residuals from that model may be explicable as spatial factors. By measuring each of the factors involved in spatial distance ($P_d$), including the distribution of the population ($P_{dxy}$) across a particular geographical configuration ($D = f (D_{rq}, a_q)$), it is possible to detect differences caused by population density and functional dependency. These differences measured through time are the components of interaction that define *lineages* (Cavalli-Sforza and Edwards 1967; Felsenstein 1982; Ridley 1986; Wiley 1981). Thus, seriation, when viewed as a tool for examining transmission, can be used to trace lineages entirely comparable to lineages in biology (Beals et al. 1945:89), just as if DNA were being used. Seriation, since it detects relative differences in composite frequencies of traits rather than simple presence and absence, has the potential to produce maps that trace inheritance with greater quantitative detail than can even be done by cladistics.[2]

The distribution of neutral traits measured in terms of relative frequencies has a "unimodal" distribution through time and space (Dunnell 1970, 1981; Kimura 1976; King and Jukes 1969; Lipo et al. 1997; Neiman 1995). Analysis of interaction using seriation consists of building seriations that are comprised of the largest number of assemblages possible, while simultaneously assembling them in an order that matches a unimodal or "battleship-shaped" pattern (Cowgill 1972). Assemblages are added in an iterative fashion with orderings treated as a hypothesis about their fit to a unimodal distribution. Testing the fit involves pairwise comparison of assemblages using confidence intervals for class frequencies calculated on the basis of sample size. Assemblages that fit the expectations of the unimodal curve are accepted into a given seriation group. Assemblages that do not fit within confidence limits are rejected and placed into different groups. In this way, the total group of available assemblages can be broken down into sets that produce consistent seriations within which frequencies scale by distance. These sets of assemblages can be treated as interacting populations. Assemblages that fit in multiple seriation solutions document assemblages that are part of *multiple lineages*.

Used in this fashion, seriation provides a method for measuring interaction across space and time by comparison of relative frequencies of stylistic types. Investigations of transmission can be complemented by spatial analyses. While strictly spatial analyses do not consider transmission through time, the spatial studies provide a means for evaluating the degree to which similarity can be accounted by a distance model. This information then provides a means to evaluate the order of assemblages produced in seriation. Transmission that occurred primarily through space, for example, can be quickly identified. Transmission that cannot be accounted for by distance alone and cannot be seriated identify populations of differentially interacting individuals.

## PRELIMINARY ANALYSES: SOCIAL ORGANIZATION AND INTERACTION IN THE CENTRAL MISSISSIPPI VALLEY

Along with Madsen, Dunnell, and Hunt (Lipo et al. 1997), I conducted a preliminary study to investigate the potential of the spatial and seriation methods to study prehistoric interaction using ceramic data collected in the 1940s by PFG from the Lower Mississippi Valley Survey. Using the frequency of Mississippian, decorated, shell-tempered ceramics collected from the surface (screened for sample size effects), we created seriation solutions in iterative testing of particular orderings. We found that the groups within which assemblages seriate without violations of unimodality are spatially cohesive sets. Strikingly, the spatial groups of assemblages, to a rough approximation, resemble the general shapes and positions of culture historical phases, i.e., the intuitive phases may represent lineages.

We also examined the effect of changing classification level on the patterns of "grouping." Using coarser classification created larger sets of assemblages, but did not change the general spatial configuration of groups. While this analysis suggests that our results might indeed reflect structure in the interaction history of the region, the exact boundaries of the groups depend upon the number of dimensions used to define classes.

This research used similarity $(S_h)$ as measured by the relative frequencies of stylistic types while controlling for variation in patterns of similarity of stylistic elements caused by the distance between individuals through space $(P_{dxy})$ and time $(P_{dt})$, in order to detect variation not predicted from simple distance and interaction functions. This process enabled us to identify potential variation that may be caused by the particular history of interaction among and between the demic structure of the late Mississippian populations.

Despite our apparent success, however, we were unable to make any substantive claims about gaining knowledge of the archaeological record. $S_h$ is calculated using class frequencies. Therefore, the process of data collection, measurement, and analysis must be controlled so that the methods used to gather data, the units used to make the measurements, the size of the samples, comparability between classes, and other abundance estimation procedures do not produce unestimated variability in the class frequencies. Each step of the measurement process has the potential to increase the error terms on the class frequencies, and if these terms become too large, or worse, are unknown, use of these frequencies to describe transmission processes is unwarranted. Since the PFG data were collected without controlling many potential sources of variation, and since the original collections no longer exist, we could not rule out other factors that may be responsible in their entirety for the variation we potentially identified as a consequence of community interaction. Without additional data, it was not possible to distinguish interaction patterns from variability caused by the way the sample was collected, the types defined, and the type frequencies calculated.

## DATA REQUIREMENTS

Further progress requires the controlled collection of new information that takes into account factors that can influence measures of similarity ($S_h$) (Table 6.1). This effort consists of the collection of enough new data on stylistic similarity ($S_h$) to evaluate this approach to investigating interaction specifically as it relates to measuring differences in the transmission probability ($T_p$). These new data will permit one to evaluate the PFG data biases and to incorporate them to varying degrees into an analysis of interaction.

### Selection of a Field Study Area

While the approach taken here makes no particular demands in terms of data distribution, its evaluation in the context of an efficient and reasonably scaled project demands some restrictions. Since current interests tend to be spatial rather than chronological, and since the methods employed are well-established as chronological tools, it is necessary to select a set of assemblages from a restricted area of approximately the same age, but which spans at least two phases. Four areas can be identified that are large enough to contain the record of several phases and that have intact surfaces old enough to contain the full archaeological record. These areas are the Fifteenmile Bayou area (St. Francis and Crittenden Counties, Arkansas), the southern end of Crowley's Ridge (Lee and St. Francis Counties, Arkansas), Nodena (Mississippi County, Arkansas), and the Sunflower River Basin (Bolivar and Washington Counties, Mississippi).

After extensive background research and several preliminary field visits, I concluded that the Fifteenmile Bayou area west of Memphis, Tennessee, is the best area for this research (Figure 6.2). Figure 6.3 details the Fifteenmile Bayou region. The study area consists of an east-west rectangle centered on Fifteenmile Bayou, extending from Crowley's Ridge to West Memphis, Tennessee. Fifteenmile Bayou is the center of a tangled maze of watercourses that stretches from the Mississippi River to the east, to the St. Francis River to the west, and from the Tyronza River to the north to the Mississippi to the south. At least fifteen large, late prehistoric settlements representing three traditional phases are known from this area (Table 6.2) including one, Holden Lake (3CT240), that has not been previously studied. The Fifteenmile Bayou area is a region of overbank deposition not affected by river migration. The minimum surface age of the Fifteenmile Bayou area is ca. 2500 years B.P., considerably older than the late prehistoric occupation (Autin et al. 1991).

### Assemblage Selection: Choosing Assemblages

The analysis of ceramic "decorations" potentially provides excellent information about interaction (Deetz 1965; Fewkes 1898, 1909; Hill 1970; Longacre

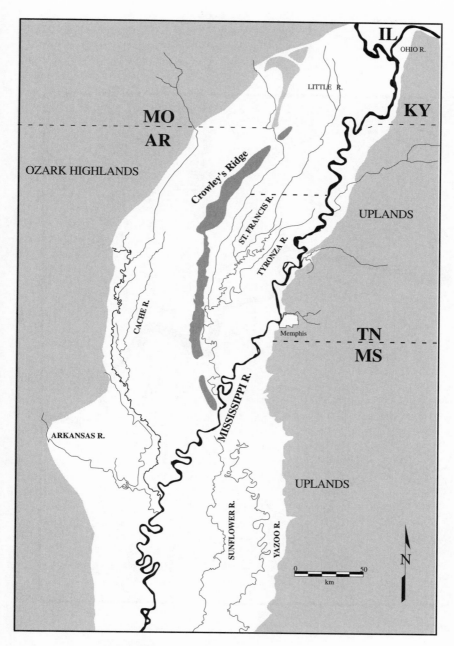

**Figure 6.2. The Central Mississippi River valley.**

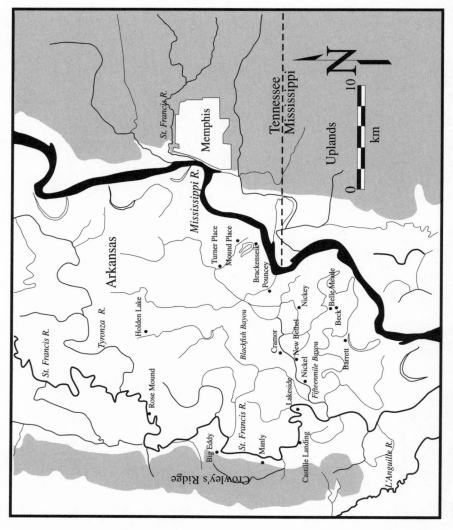

**Figure 6.3. Fifteenmile Bayou area.**

**Table 6.2**
**Large Mississippian Sites in the Fifteenmile Bayou Area**

| Name | PFG | Ceramics | Description | Age (PFG) | Sample Size (PFG) | Decorated Sherds Sample Size (PFG) |
|------|-----|----------|-------------|-----------|-------------------|-------------------------------------|
| Cramor Place | 12-O-5 | Shell-tempered ceramics | St. Francis-type site | C - B | 1014 | 144 |
| Nickel | 13-N-15 | Neeley's Ferry, Old Town Red, Parkin Punctated, Kent Incised | Large village site (12 acres) with rectangular platform mound and small mounds. | D - B | 481 | 382 |
| Belle Meade | 13-O-5 | Parkin Punctated, Old Town Red, Kent Incised, Barton Incised, Rhodes Incised, Walls Engraved | Large St. Francis-type site with large platform mounds and small mounds in plaza arrangement | B - A | 798 | 254 |
| Beck Plantation | 13-O-7 | Parkin Punctated, Old Town Red, Kent Incised, Barton Incised, Rhodes Incised, Ranch Incised, Owen's Punctated, Fortune Noded, Walls Engraved | Village site with mounds in plaza arrangement | B - A | 260 | 82 |
| Lakeside | 13-N-18 | Bell Plain, Parkin Punctated, Old Town Red, Mulberry Creek Cordmarked, Baytown Plain | Village site with large and small mounds. Mound (110 feet diameter x 9 feet high), 60 feet diameter mound, 50 feet diameter mound. | C - B | 335 | 106 |
| Sycamore Bend | | Shell-tempered ceramics | 4 low mounds on ridge joining each other | Miss.? | | |
| Nickey Mound | 13-O-4 | Neeley's Ferry, Baytown Plain, Bell Plain, Parkin Punctated, Old Town Red, Barton Incised, Mulberry Creek Cordmarked | Village site with large mound. | C - B | 543 | 31 |

(continued)

193

**Table 6.2 (continued)**

| Name | PFG | Ceramics | Description | Age (PFG) | Sample Size (PFG) | Decorated Sherds Sample Size (PFG) |
|---|---|---|---|---|---|---|
| Pouncey | 12-O-2 | Parkin Punctated, Kent Incised, Barton Incised, Wall Engraved, Hull Engraved | Large village site with large platform mounds and small mounds in plaza arrangement | E - B | 390 | 369 |
| Barrett Site | 13-O-1 | Shell-tempered pottery, grog tempered pottery | Large village site with large rectangular platform mound and small mounds | D - B | 1529 | 265 |
| Mound Place | 12-P-1 | Parkin Punctated, Kent Incised, Barton Incised, Ranch Incised, Fortune Noded, Walls Engraved | Village site with large platform mounds | A - B | 3203 | 193 |
| Brackenseed Place/ Rhodes Place | 12-O-6 | Parkin Punctated, Kent Incised, Barton Incised, Rhodes Incised, Fortune Noded | Large village site with large rectangular mound | A - B | 89 | 13 |
| Turner Place (Pierce Site) | 12-O-1 | Barton Incised, Fortune Noded, Parkin Punctated | Small mound and village site | C - B | 495 | 66 |
| New Hope Plantation | None | Shell-tempered pottery | House wall daub, oblong mound (75-100 feet in length) | Miss.? | | |
| Pouncey | None | Parkin Punctated, Old Town Red, Kent Incised, Barton Incised, Rhodes Incised, Owen's Punctated, Fortune Noded, Walls Engraved | Mentioned by Gerald Smith (1990) (in Horseshoe Lake Phase) | Miss? | | |
| Young | None | Includes Parkin Punctated, Barton Incised, Fortune Noded | Mentioned by Gerald Johnson (in Horseshoe Lake Phase) | Miss. | | |
| Claude Manley Place | 12-N-2 | Bell Plain, Neeley's Ferry, Old Town Red, Parkin Punctated | St. Francis village Site | B - A | 252 | 44 |

1970; S. Plog 1976a, 1978, 1980), since what we think of as decoration is frequently neutral. Ceramic assemblages provide an excellent source of data because ceramics 1. are abundant in late prehistoric settlements of the central Mississippi River valley; 2. their designs have a wide variety of potentially stylistic attributes; and 3. existing phases have been defined by ceramic type frequencies.

Assemblages must meet a set of criteria to ensure that frequencies of stylistic types are not caused by factors unrelated to the probabilities in transmission. First, assemblages must also come from functionally equivalent deposits. Choosing sites of similar function would reduce functional differences in assemblage composition. This criterion is met, in the present case, as only one kind of late Mississippian settlement is known, the so-called "St. Francis-type" settlement (Phillips et al. 1951). Second, the locations of assemblages must be distributed across the study region so that high similarity from tightly clustered assemblages in space do not overwhelm other factors. Third, the assemblages should be relatively contemporaneous to minimize the number needed. Unfortunately, there are few absolutes for any Mississippian deposits in the central Mississippi River valley. Since it is relatively easy to identify late prehistoric ceramics, analysis begins with information gathered through traditional methods, and the selection of sites that have stylistic markers of the latest prehistoric period. It is also necessary to choose assemblages that have a similar ratio of decorated/undecorated ceramics, since large differences in the frequency of decorated ceramics, not accounted for by differences in sample size, might indicate differences in contemporaneity or duration. While later analysis may refine these choices and change the selection of assemblages, this strategy provides a reasonable starting point.

The presence or absence of burials can influence the frequencies of ceramic types in domestic assemblages. Ceramics included in burials are biased toward smaller vessel sizes and do not typify the overall assemblages from which they are drawn (Childress 1992). Since the size of a ceramic vessel determines the range of decorations that can be applied, frequencies of decorative types in assemblages will be, in part, driven by the presence or absence of burial deposits with accompanying ceramics. Problems in comparability between assemblages can arise, therefore, if burial ceramic assemblages are not uniformly included. Comparability between the assemblages can be ascertained by examining each site for the presence of human skeletal remains—an indication of disturbed burials.

Based on these requirements and my initial field visits, investigations have focused on four late prehistoric sites in the Fifteenmile Bayou study area: Castile Landing, Nickel, Brackenseik Place, and Holden Lake (3CT240). Existing records and field studies suggest that these sites are closely contemporaneous, equidistant, large, and functionally similar. In addition, each site has evidence of human bones from disturbed burials, and decorated late prehistoric ceramics available for collection on the surface.

## Collection Considerations: Controlling Measurement Error in $S_h$

We can rephrase the question of whether the late prehistoric communities of northeastern Arkansas exhibit features of complex organization in analytic terms. The question thus becomes whether the phases identified by culture historians represent arbitrary divisions of roughly continuous spatial variation, or joints in the spatial structure of interaction. On one hand, it is possible that transmission was structured in late prehistoric populations of Fifteenmile Bayou. In this case, one would expect that the similarity $(S_h)$ between assemblages would not simply correlate with distance once differences in time $(P_{dt})$, space $(P_{dxy})$, and geography $(D)$ are considered. On the other hand, interaction may have been continuous across this area and the differences detected by archaeologists in similarity $(S_h)$ are simply the product of sampling and other collection procedures (Ford 1936). Biases resulting from collection techniques will contribute artificial variation that can potentially affect measurements of similarity $(S_h)$. Consequently, data must be gathered carefully to control as many of the measurement procedures as possible.

### Sample Size

Basic fieldwork consists of making large, representative collections of decorated ceramics that can be used to measure homologous similarity between assemblages. Similarity is a function of the richness or the number of different categories, the evenness or relative proportions of the categories, and, importantly, the number of things present (Jones et al. 1983; Kintigh 1984; Plog and Hegmon 1993; Rhode 1988; Shott 1989). Although it is possible that distinctions can be made at smaller sample sizes using resampling techniques (Efron and Tibshirani 1993; Kintigh 1984), a reasonable target assemblage size (all sherds) depends upon two factors: 1. the frequency of decorated ceramics in an assemblage; and 2. the statistical resolution needed in distinguishing frequencies. My analysis of the PFG data suggests that the frequency of decorated sherds (versus plain sherds) in late Mississippian assemblages ranges between 14% and 23% (Table 6.3). Since transmission is measured by frequency of stylistic types, the finer the differences between frequencies that can be statistically distinguished, the greater the resolution that obtained in mapping transmission.

Fine distinctions, however, have a steep price in terms of sample size. We can calculate the minimum sample size needed to distinguish the percentages of types in two populations at a particular significance (a) level using the equation:

$$N = \frac{(\hat{p}_1 + \hat{p}_2)(1 - (\frac{\hat{p}_1 + \hat{p}_2}{2})) * z^2}{(\hat{p}_1 - \hat{p}_2)^2} \qquad \text{(Equation 13)}$$

where $\hat{p}_1$ = the proportion of a class in sample one; $\hat{p}_2$ = the proportion of the same class in sample two; and $z$ is the z-score at the specified significance level $(a)$.

**Table 6.3**
**Percentage of Decorated Mississippian Ceramics in Sites of the Fifteenmile Bayou Area**

| Site Name | Site Number | Number of PFG Types | Mississippian Ceramics | Decorated Mississippian Ceramics | Percentage of Decorated Ceramics |
|---|---|---|---|---|---|
| Beck | 13-O-7 | 8 | 265 | 87 | 32.83% |
| Belle Meade | 13-O-5 | 10 | 804 | 260 | 32.34% |
| Nickel | 13-N-15/C,D,E | 10 | 739 | 165 | 22.33% |
| Castile Landing | 13-N-21 | 11 | 2037 | 402 | 19.73% |
| Nickel | 13-N-15/B | 7 | 120 | 21 | 17.50% |
| Manly | 12-N-2 | 6 | 249 | 41 | 16.47% |
| Pouncey | 12-O-2 | 7 | 445 | 66 | 14.83% |
| Cramor | 12-O-5 | 8 | 1016 | 146 | 14.37% |
| Barrett | 13-O-1 | 6 | 286 | 39 | 13.64% |
| Brackinseik | 12-O-6 | 7 | 84 | 8 | 9.52% |
| Pouncey | 12-O-2/D | 3 | 23 | 2 | 8.70% |
| Turner | 12-O-1 | 7 | 458 | 29 | 6.33% |
| Mound Place | 12-P-1 | 12 | 3201 | 191 | 5.97% |
| Lakeside | 13-N-18 | 4 | 236 | 7 | 2.97% |
| Nickey | 13-O-4 | 5 | 524 | 12 | 2.29% |

This calculation assumes that samples are of equal size. Table 6.4 shows the necessary sample sizes required to distinguish between differences in the percentage of classes in two populations; very fine distinctions (e.g., <1.0%) require extremely large sample sizes.

Based on an average of 14% decorated sherds in Mississippian assemblages, it is estimated that a representative sample of at least 20,000 total sherds provides sufficient basis to distinguish class frequencies of 2.0% at a significance of $\alpha = 0.05$. Surface collections, therefore, must consist of at least 10,000 sherds per assemblage so that 1,400 to 2,300 decorated sherds will be available from each assemblage for analysis.

### Spatial Variability

The selection of St. Francis-type settlements, a large component of which is redeposited refuse, will likely minimize spatial variability in stylistic similarity that could lead to nonrepresentative samples. This assumption may not be realized, however, so to evaluate spatial homogeneity and to detect multiple occupations, surface collections are made in 10-meter squares. While these units are too gross to describe spatial structure, analysis of within and between block variance

**Table 6.4**

**Sample Sizes Required to Make Distinctions of 1%, 2%, and 3% Differences in the Proportion of a Class in Two Samples (a = .05)**

| 1% Distinction | | | 2% Distinction | | | 3% Distinction | | |
|---|---|---|---|---|---|---|---|---|
| Type 1 % | Type 2 % | Sample Size Required | Type 1 % | Type 2 % | Sample Size Required | Type 1 % | Type 2 % | Sample Size Required |
| 5 | 6 | 2813 | 5 | 7 | 763 | 5 | 8 | 365 |
| 15 | 16 | 7088 | 15 | 17 | 1818 | 15 | 18 | 828 |
| 25 | 26 | 10282 | 25 | 27 | 2603 | 25 | 28 | 1171 |
| 35 | 36 | 12392 | 35 | 37 | 3117 | 35 | 38 | 1394 |
| 45 | 46 | 13421 | 45 | 47 | 3361 | 45 | 48 | 1496 |
| 55 | 56 | 13366 | 55 | 57 | 3334 | 55 | 58 | 1478 |
| 65 | 66 | 12230 | 65 | 67 | 3036 | 65 | 68 | 1340 |
| 75 | 76 | 10011 | 75 | 77 | 2468 | 75 | 78 | 1081 |
| 85 | 86 | 6710 | 85 | 87 | 1629 | 85 | 88 | 702 |
| 95 | 96 | 2326 | 95 | 97 | 520 | 95 | 98 | 203 |

in style frequencies can be used to evaluate the relevant sample characteristics. Homogeneous deposits display similar variance between and within blocks. In the case of multiple occupations or functionally discrete areas, between block variance would be much greater than within block variance and exhibit a spatial pattern.

### Controlled Collections

The undocumented, largely uncontrolled, and idiosyncratic manner in which PFG collected and counted artifacts make their data of limited value. It is impossible to determine, for example, if differences in frequencies are caused by differences in the archaeological record or by collection strategies. In field surveys, I collect *all* ceramics greater than 1 centimeter, and record surface visibility to calibrate differences caused by variability in collection conditions. I instruct assisting field workers to collect any objects that resemble a sherd (i.e., having the shape, color, and texture of ceramics) without making in-field decisions. In addition, groups of collectors are randomly rotated in order to minimize individual collector bias across units. Material collected by each worker is bagged separately. Analysis of the variance of collections made between collectors will permit one to determine if individuals biased their collections toward particular kinds of ceramics and, therefore, allow corrections for those assemblages.

### Castile Landing

Castile Landing (3SF12) presents a special case in this research design. This site is included in this study because it is considered part of the Parkin phase rather than Horseshoe Lake or Walls phases. Castile Landing was originally recorded by C. B. Moore (1910) and by PFG (1951) as a large St. Francis-type rectangular town. During the 1950s, it was nearly obliterated by backfill from the construction of the St. Francis floodway. Since the site is not plowed, collections must be made from subsurface deposits. Extensive coring and excavations at the site during the summer of 1996 by the University of Washington field school, however, revealed that a significant deposit remains intact and is accessible. During my initial excavations, I placed ten 1 x 1-meter units ten meters apart on the east and west sides of the levee. These units were excavated in arbitrary 20-cemtimeter levels. The number of the samples ultimately collected at Castile Landing will be determined by the spatial extent of the site and density of sherds.

Excavation samples are cluster samples and suffer from problems of autocorrelation. Frequencies of excavated ceramics are not normally comparable to surface collections, because samples collected from the same units are more likely to be derived from the same vessel; frequencies will be affected by processes of breakage. Local informants (M. Linn, personal communication) and my initial analysis of the Castile Landing excavation data, however, indicate that the site was plowed before it was buried. This suggests that the excavated collections will be comparable to collections made from tilled surfaces. In order to ensure that the sample collected from Castile Landing is comparable to the surface collections, I will refit the decorated ceramics taken from the same excavation unit. The presence of complicated design elements in late Mississippian ceramics should make this task relatively efficient. Analysis of between and within sample variance will be used to evaluate representativeness as in the case of the surface samples.

## Solving the Transmission Equation: Determining $T_p$ by Calculating Measures of $S_h$, $P_{dxy}$, $P_{dt}$, $D$, and $T_{dt}$

The research goal presented here is to determine whether interaction (as measured by $S_h$) between late Mississippian communities is explicable in terms of distance ($P_{dxy}$), geography ($D$) and time ($P_{dt}$) alone, or indicative of complex organization (i.e., $T_p$ is variable).

### Determining Homologous Similarity: $S_h$

#### *Building the Counting Units: Classification*

All meaningful measurement requires the construction of a classification (Dunnell 1971). In the present study, it is necessary to build a set of stylistic classes (Dunnell 1978a) that have distributions in time and space that are not affected by selection, and with which it is possible to measure interaction. Although culture historians were relatively adept at the construction of these kinds of classes (e.g., Ford 1952; Phillips et al. 1951), culture-historical classifications are often a mix of functional and stylistic attributes (Dunnell 1986). This is certainly the case in the PFG classification, which mixes decorative attributes such as incising and stamping with functional attributes such as temper (Dunnell and Feathers 1991). Bell plain ceramics, for example, are identified by the size of the shell inclusions used for temper. The size of shell particles, however, is a functional dimension, not a neutral one, and does not exhibit stochastic distributions (Dunnell and Feathers 1991; Feathers 1989, 1990; Feathers and Scott 1989). This dimension, therefore, is not useful for studying transmission structure.

It is difficult, however, to specify *a priori* what dimensions and classes will be useful, since this depends upon the composition of the assemblages and available sample size. In addition, there is no way to know in advance whether a particular dimension will be stylistic. In this analysis, it is useful to begin with "decorative" dimensions that have been treated as stylistic by the culture historians. These dimensions include the presence and absence of incising, engraving, punctuates, paint, and appliqué. Assemblages measured with types constructed of these dimensions have relative frequencies that do not covary with environmental variability, and were successfully used by Ford, at least in the broad sense, to build seriations for the central Mississippi River valley (Phillips et al. 1951).

Although published collections provide valuable information for the initial construction of an historical classification (e.g., Holmes 1884, 1886; Moore 1910; Phillips 1970; Phillips et al. 1951), additional dimensions will be added as the analysis proceeds. All dimensions will be used as hypotheses about the distribution of classes in time and space. If particular dimensions are found to covary with the environment or technological change, then they will be omitted. Overall, however, the classification that I employ includes decoration technique, decoration composition, and design element dimensions (Table 6.5).

Artifacts will be grouped using a hybrid classification scheme (*sensu* Dunnell 1971). Hybrid classifications are advantageous in this particular case, because they can be expanded and collapsed to examine the effects of the classification on the membership of the classified groups at a particular measurement level. These multiple classifications are necessary to evaluate how a particular kind and scale of classification affects the spatial configuration of interaction structure.

Degree of similarity is measured by comparing frequencies of historical classes between assemblages. Thus, the absolute results of both seriation and the spatial methods of investigating transmission are wholly dependent upon the classes used to measure variability in ceramic design. There is a relationship between the kinds of numbers of dimensions used in building historical classes used in measuring transmission (Dunnell 1970, 1981, 1986; Ford 1952; Phillips et al. 1951). The larger the number of dimensions used to construct classes, the more local the distribution in time and space. This feature of classification can be exploited in seriation and spatial analyses by systematically changing the number of dimensions that comprise classes used to measure cultural phenomena. As one decreases the number of dimensions used in classes, the distributions of types should increase smoothly in a geometric progression. Variability in the

**Table 6.5**
**Hybrid Classification Construction**

---

**Dimensions: Techniques, Decoration, Design**

**Dimension: Techniques**
Incised (PFG: Barton Incised), Punctated (PFG: Parkin Punctated), Engraved (PFG: Walls Engraved), Noded (PFG: Fortune Noded), Painted (PFG: Carson Red-On-White)

Incised/Punctated, Incised/Engraved, Incised/Noded, Incised/Painted, Punctated/Engraved, Punctated/Noded, Punctated/Painted, Engraved/Noded, Engraved/Painted

Incised/Punctated/Engraved, Incised/Punctated/Noded, Incised/Punctated/Painted, Punctated/Engraved/Noded, Punctated/Engraved/Painted, Engraved/Noded/Painted

Incised/Punctated/Engraved/Noded, Incised/Punctated/Engraved/Painted, Punctated/Engraved/Noded/Painted

Incised/Punctated/Engraved/Noded/Painted

**Dimension: Decorations**
Line
Zone
Line/Zone
Fill
Line/Fill
Zone/Fill
Zone/Fill /Line

**Dimensions: Decorations and Techniques**
Line - Incised, Line - Engraved, Line - Punctated, Line - Noded, Line - Painted
Zone - Punctated, Zone - Line, Zone - Noded, Zone - Engraved, Zone - Painted
Fill - Incised, Fill - Engraved, Fill - Punctated, Fill - Noded, Fill - Painted
Line - Incised/Zone - Engraved, Line - Incised/Zone - Punctated, Line - Incised/Zone - Noded,
Line - Incised/Zone - Painted
etc.

**Dimension: Designs**
Perpendicular Lines
Cross Hatching
Animorphic
Spiral
Chevron
Parallel Lines
etc.

**Dimensions: Technique, Decoration, and Design**
Line - Incised/Zone - Engraved/Cross Hatching
Line - Incised/Zone - Incised/Perpendicular Lines
Line - Punctated/Zone - Incised/Parallel Lines
etc.

---

changes of these distributions (as measured by $S_h$) can be used as a tool to measure the slope of transmission fall-off.

### Estimating Abundances: Making Measurements of Stylistic Type Frequencies

The methods by which abundances are generated and compared have been, for the most part, ignored in archaeology (Orton 1993). There are a number of factors to be considered when estimating ceramic frequencies. There is, for example, a necessary relationship between form and design composition, because the application of decorations may be functionally restricted during the manufacturing process to particular forms (Krause 1972). If a design element is produced only on jars and another is produced only on bowls, for example, comparisons between assemblages with differing frequencies of bowls and jars (caused by differences in function) will necessarily produce different frequencies of design elements. These differences in frequencies of decoration indicate differences in the functional composition of the assemblage rather than style. The first step in evaluating abundances is to undertake a formal analysis to determine the relationship between form and design elements (Krause 1972, 1990; Roe 1989). Formal analysis utilizes a grammatical technique to break the construction and decoration of vessels into a sequence that documents the order in which design elements become associated by physical constraints to other design elements of the vessel.

In addition, sherd size can greatly affect the frequencies of types where a design does not cover the entire surface. Further, if recognition of a particular design element is dependent upon the size of sherd, counts of that element will be biased. In these cases, therefore, it is necessary to evaluate the frequencies of identified types in assemblages based on sherd size. There may be a minimum sherd size that can be used for estimating abundances of particular types. In these cases, sample size will have to be sacrificed for confident estimation of abundances. The smaller the sherds, the more restrictive the classes that can be used. Larger sherds, on the other hand, have fewer constraints and more dimensions/attributes available for measurement.

### Sample Size Adequacy: Statistically Distinguishing $S_h$

While my research objective is to obtain a sample sufficient to investigate the distributions of most configurations of classes (ca. 10,000 sherds), I will also check for sampling error due to sample size for each particular comparison. As collections are made, each sample will be evaluated for changes in richness and evenness. Sufficient sample sizes will be detected by examining the plots of class richness as the sample size increases. When the richness reaches an asymptote, sufficient sample size has been reached to estimate the number of classes.

Similarly, as sample sizes increase, it is necessary to examine the assemblages for differences in variances between class frequencies. Sample sizes obtained when differences in frequencies of 2% can be statistically distinguished at

$\alpha = 0.05$ will be considered sufficient for this analysis. This calculation can easily be made using an approximation of the standard normal distribution:

$$z = \frac{(\hat{p}_1 - \hat{p}_2) - (p_1 - p_2)}{\sqrt{p_1(1 - p_1)/n_1 + p_2(1 - p_2)/n_2}}$$

(Equation 14)

where $n_1$ and $n_2$ are the totals of assemblage 1 and assemblage 2; $\hat{p}_1$ and $\hat{p}_2$ are the relative proportions of sherds out of a combined total ($N = n_1 + n_2$ total sherds, $\hat{p}_1 = n_1/N$, and $\hat{p}_2 = n_2/N$); and $p_1$ and $p_2$ are the proportions of a type in each assemblage in Equation 14.

If it is statistically impossible to distinguish proportions of types in assemblages at $\alpha = 0.05$, further collections will be necessary. Iterative evaluation of sample size and recollection ensures that frequencies are representative of the archaeological population.

### Evaluating $S_h$ for Assemblages Across the Study Area

If primary collections are made from four sites in this research, there are clearly too few cases to evaluate the research question. Except for Holden Lake, each of the fifteen potential sites used in this research were collected by PFG, thus facilitating comparisons between my data and PFG. Comparisons should be readily made between my data and those collected by PFG. Using chi-square analysis, it is possible to determine if the PFG assemblages are representative samples of my larger, controlled collections. If systematic differences exist, as I expect, it is necessary to examine the causes. In this way, the PFG data can be "corrected" using the new primary assemblage data. Consequently, it will then be possible to make reasonable hypotheses about interaction structure across the whole of the Fifteenmile Bayou area using all fifteen Late Mississippian assemblages.

## Distribution of Populations Through Time: $P_{dt}$

Distinguishing between differences measured in ceramic frequencies caused by spatial ($P_{dxy}$) structure and temporal distance ($P_{dt}$), will be independently assessed using thermoluminescence (TL) dating. Unlike radiocarbon, TL dating addresses the target event of *archaeological* interest (the manufacturing of the vessel) and does not require inferences of association. To calculate assemblage duration, TL measurements are needed for at least three samples from each assemblage. Samples will be chosen from assemblages to maximize the potential range of dates using the temporal distribution of PFG types as a guide.

## Transmission Over Time: $T_{dt}$

Controlling for assemblage duration ($T_{dt}$) is a critical component of a transmission analysis (Dunnell 1970, 1981). Differences in duration can be detected by noting differences in richness; excess richness probably represents a long span of time. Variance among assemblage duration, if large, can be detected by inspecting seriations for failure to meet the expectation of the unimodal distribution, but not caused by variability due to spatial structure.

It may be possible to subdivide assemblages with durations markedly longer than others using attributes sensitive to depositional history (Madsen 1994) or information on spatial variability. In this manner, assemblages may be divided into two or more assemblages of comparable duration. Regional seriations (e.g., PFG) can, to some degree, provide information on time-sensitive dimensions as they have in my own preliminary analyses (Lipo et al.1997).

## Spatial Analysis: Evaluating the Effects of $P_{dxy}$ and $D$

In the study of transmission, the first step is to isolate variability in stylistic similarity ($S_h$) that is explicable by transmission over distance alone. The factors of interest here are the distribution of populations across space ($P_{dxy}$) and the intervening geography ($D = f(D_{rq}, a_q)$). In order to address differences in accessibility, GIS data can be incorporated into the analysis for the St. Francis and Crittenden county areas. By coding GIS layers for the presence and absence of watercourses, and then weighting distance between assemblages by the amount of "connectivity" due to water, the linear distance ($P_{dxy}$) can be adjusted to compensate for realistic geography ($D$). Using this recalculated distance, the degree to which similarity ($S_h$) can be accounted for by distance can be explored.

## Seriation Analysis: Solving for $T_p$

Major portions of interaction analyses consist of the construction of seriations. Using the reliably generated frequencies of stylistic classes in comparable assemblages and estimates of $P_{dxy}$, $P_{dt}$, $T_{dt}$, and $D$, seriations are made by building the largest possible group of assemblages that meet the monotonic distribution criterion and are statistically-significant solutions. The process is initiated by starting with the largest group of assemblages and attempting to build a deterministic frequency seriation. Inability to produce a valid seriation solution at any step prompts a search for the assemblage (or assemblages) that does not match with the others and that can be best explained by the differences detected in $P_{dt}$, $P_{dxy}$, and $D$, using the principle that frequency change should scale with transmission distance. In this way, the total group of available assemblages can be broken down into sets that produce consistent seriations within which frequencies scale transmission (both $P_{dxy}$ and $P_{dt}$). Such groups represent interacting subpopulations that are the goal of this research.

## CONCLUSIONS AND EXPECTATIONS

Despite growing interest in the use of evolutionary theory in archaeology (e.g., Dunnell 1980, 1989, 1992, 1995; O'Brien 1995; O'Brien and Holland 1990,

1992; Rindos 1984, 1989; Teltser 1995), there have been few discussions about data requirements. As Lewontin (1974:8) has pointed out: "We cannot go out and describe the world in any old way we please and then sit back and demand that an explanatory and predictive theory be built on that description." It is clear that the early culture historians were well aware of this axiom in their constructions of types and culture-historical units (Lyman et al.1997). In building models for explaining patterns of stylistic similarity related to changes in organization, however, there have been few attempts to quantify the requirements for generating the descriptions of the archaeological record explicable by a theory of human cultural interaction. There have been many attempts to address issues of scale change in interaction patterns, but few models link data to explanatory theory. One goal of this research, therefore, is the explicit specification of requirements for collecting data pertaining to transmission history—a necessary component of all evolutionary explanations. The study of the evolution of complex societies, in particular, requires detailed information about changes in how populations interact and how those patterns of interaction changed through time. This research is an attempt to build a conceptual model of transmission, to outline the means by which transmission can be studied, and to identify the kinds and amounts of data necessary to test hypotheses about prehistoric interaction.

The late prehistoric village deposits of the central Mississippi River valley provide a unique opportunity to study interacting populations of complexly organized individuals. An inadequate understanding of the sampling and data collection methods necessary for acquiring reliable data has hampered previous work. The research design presented here shows how data pertaining to patterns of prehistoric transmission can be generated and used to evaluate claims of community structure, as well as produce a statistically defensible history of interaction. By using these methods and constructing the outlines of lineage relationships between interacting populations, this research illustrates that the collection of reliable data on prehistoric interaction is not only possible, but can form the basis of theoretically informed historical explanations.

## ACKNOWLEDGMENTS

The success of my research project rests primarily on the tremendous generosity of local landowners and residents, without whose help and kind permission the research could not have been conducted. In particular, I would like to thank Elly Beasley of Heth, Arkansas, for providing invaluable support, introductions, and information for all of the field seasons. Also integral to my research have been Margaret Linn, J. J. Meals, Frank Barton, the Zanone family, the Pouncey family, R. Dawson, Amanda Wise, Ed Cuples, Lan Letner, Kenn Thompson, Rush Harris, Bill Felty, Jim Pugh, Frank Reynolds, Buster Briggs, Thomas Beene, and David Wallace. In addition, Dr. John House has been instrumental in assisting, supporting, and encouraging my field project. This research was conducted while the author was on a George Franklin Dales Foundation scholarship. I would like to thank Barbara Dales for her never flagging and continued support of my work and progress toward my dissertation. The help of all of these individuals and many others has made this research possible; their contribution to my work is greatly appreciated. Finally, I thank Dr. Robert Dunnell for his inspiration, wisdom, unwavering support, and guidance in my research.

## NOTES

1. Correcting assemblages for differences in composition caused by formation processes is a data-specific operation and the details must be considered case by case.

2. In fact, seriation has a greater power to map lineage relationships because it makes none of the branching assumptions required in cladistics.

## REFERENCES CITED

Abbott, D. N.
    1972    The Utility of the Concept of Phase in the Archaeology of the Southern Northwest Coast. *Syesis* 5:267–278.

Alonso, W.
    1964    Location Theory. In *Regional Development and Planning: A Reader*, edited by J. Friedmann and W. Alonso, pp. 78-106. MIT Press, Cambridge, Massachusetts.

Autin, W. J., S. F. Burns, B. J. Miller, R. T. Saucier, and J. I. Snead
    1991    Quaternary Geology of the Lower Mississippi Valley. In *Quaternary Nonglacial Geology: Coterminous U.S.*, edited by R. B. Morrison, pp. 547–582. The Geology of North America, V. K-2. Geological Society of America, Boulder.

Beals, R. L., G. W. Brainerd, and W. Smith
    1945    Archaeological Studies in Northeast Arizona. *University of California Publications in American Archaeology and Ethnology*, Volume 4:1–236.

Berry, B. J. L.
    1967    *The Geography of Market Centres and Retail Distribution*. Prentice Hall, Englewood Cliffs, New Jersey.

Binford, L. R.
    1968    Archaeological Perspectives. In *New Perspectives in Archaeology*, edited by L. Binford, pp. 5–32. Academic Press, New York.

Brain, J. P.
    1978    The Archaeological Phase: Ethnographic Fact or Fancy? In *Archaeological Essays in Honor of Irving B. Rouse*, edited by R. C. Dunnell and E. S. Hall, pp. 311–318. Mouton Publishers, New York.
    1985    Introduction: Update of De Soto Studies Since the United States De Soto Expedition Commission Report. In *Final Report of the United States De Soto Commission*, edited by J. R. Swanton, pp. xi–xix. Smithsonian Institution Press, Washington, D.C.

Brain, J. P., A. Toth, and A. Rodriguez-Buckingham
    1974    Ethnohistoric Archaeology and the De Sota Entrada into the Lower Mississippi Valley. *Conference on Historic Archaeology Papers* 7:232–289.

Brainerd, G. W.
　1951　The Place of Chronological Ordering in Archaeological Analysis. *American Antiquity* 39:162–167.
Carrothers, G. A. P.
　1956　An Historical Review of the Gravity Model and Potential Concepts of Human Interaction. *Journal of the American Institute of Planners* 22:94–102.
Cavalli-Sforza, L. L. and A. W. F. Edwards
　1967　Phylogenetic Analysis: Models and Estimation Procedures. *Evolution* 32:550–570.
Cavalli-Sforza, L.L., and M.W. Feldman
　1981　*Cultural Transmission and Evolution: A Quantitative Approach.* Monographs in Population Biology 16, Princeton University Press, Princeton.
Childe, V. G.
　1925　*Dawn of European Civilization.* A. A. Knopf, New York.
　1941　*Man Makes Himself.* The New American Library, Inc., New York.
　1958　*The Prehistory of European Society.* Penguin Books, Harmondsworth.
Childress, M. R.
　1992　Mortuary Vessels and Comparative Ceramic Analysis: An Example from the Chucalissa Site. *Southeastern Archaeology* 11:31–50.
Chisholm, M., and P. O'Sullivan
　1973　*Freight Flows and Spatial Aspects of the British Economy.* Cambridge University Press, Cambridge.
Cliff, A. D., P. Haggett, and J. K. Ord
　1974　*Elementary Regional Structure: Some Quantitative Approaches to the Spatial Organization of Static and Dynamic Regional Systems.* Cambridge University Press, Cambridge.
Conkey, M.
　1990　Experimenting with Style in Archaeology: Some Historical and Theoretical Issues. In *The Uses of Style in Archaeology,* edited by M. W. Conkey and C. A. Hastorf, pp. 5–17. University of Cambridge Press, Cambridge.
Cook, T.
　1970　*Social Groups and Settlement Patterns in Basketmaker III.* Unpublished Master's thesis, Department of Anthropology, University of Chicago, Chicago.
Cordell, L., and F. Plog
　1979　Escaping the Confines of Normative Thought: A Reevaluation of Puebloan Prehistory. *American Antiquity* 44:405–429.
Cowgill, G.
　1968　Archaeological Applications of Factor, Cluster, and Proximity Analysis. *American Antiquity* 33:367–375.
　1972　Models, Methods, and Techniques for Seriation. In *Models in Archaeology,* edited by D. Clarke, pp. 381–424. Methuen and Company, London.
Cronin, C.
　1962　An Analysis of Pottery Design Elements, Indicating Possible Relationships between Three Decorated Types. In *Chapters in the Prehistory of Eastern Arizona I,* edited by P. S. Martin, pp. 105–114. Chicago Natural History Museum, Chicago.
Deetz, J.
　1965　*The Dynamics of Stylistic Change in Arikara Ceramics.* Illinois Studies in Anthropology, Urbana, Illinois.

Deetz, J. A., and E. Dethlefsen
    1965    The Doppler-effect and Archaeology: A Consideration of the Spatial Aspects of
            Seriation. *Southwestern Journal of Anthropology* 21:196–206.
Dewar, R. E.
    1991    Incorporating Variation in Occupation Span into Settlement-Pattern Analysis.
            *American Antiquity* 56:604–620.
Dewar, R. E., and K. A. McBride
    1992    Remnant Settlement Patterns. In *Space, Time, and Archaeological Landscapes*,
            edited by J. Rossignol and L. Wandsnider, pp. 227–255. Plenum Press, New York.
Dickens, R. S., and J. H. Chapman
    1978    Ceramic Patterning and Social Structure at Two Late Historic Upper Creek Sites
            in Alabama. *American Antiquity* 43:390–398.
Duff, A. I.
    1996    Ceramic Micro-Seriation: Types or Attributes? *American Antiquity* 61: 89–101.
Dunnell, R. C.
    1970    Seriation Method and its Evaluation. *American Antiquity* 35:305–319.
    1971    *Systematics in Prehistory.* Free Press, New York.
    1978a   Style and Function: A Fundamental Dichotomy. *American Antiquity*
            43:192–202.
    1978b   Archaeological Potential of Anthropological and Scientific Models of Function.
            In *Archaeological Essays in Honor of Irving Benjamin Rouse*, edited by R. C.
            Dunnell and E. S. Hall, pp. 41–73. Mouton, The Hague.
    1980    Evolutionary Theory and Archaeology. In *Advances in Archaeological Method
            and Theory Volume 3*, edited by M. B. Schiffer, pp. 35–99. Academic Press, New
            York.
    1981    Seriation, Groups, and Measurement. In *Manejos de Datos Y Methods
            Mathematicos de Arqualogia*, edited by G. L. Cowgill, R. Whallon, and B. S. Ottaway,
            pp. 67–90. Union Internacional de Ciences Prehistoricas y Protohistoricas, Mexico DF.
    1986    Methodological Issues in Americanist Artifact Classification. In *Advances in
            Archaeological Method and Theory, Volume 9*, edited by M. Schiffer, pp. 149–207.
            Academic Press, New York.
    1989    Aspects of the Application of Evolutionary Theory in Archaeology. In
            *Archaeological Thought in America*, edited by C. C. Lamberg-Karlovsky, pp. 35–99.
            Cambridge University Press, Cambridge.
    1992    Archaeology and Evolutionary Science. In *Quandaries and Quests: Visions of
            Archaeology's Future*, edited by L. Wandsnider, pp. 209–224. Center for
            Archaeological Investigations, Occasional Paper No. 20. Southern Illinois University
            Press, Carbondale.
    1995    What Is It That Actually Evolves? In *Evolutionary Archaeology*, edited by P. A.
            Teltser, pp. 33–50. University of Arizona Press, Tucson.
    1996    Natural Selection, Scale, and Cultural Evolution: Some Preliminary
            Considerations. In *Evolutionary Archaeology: Theory and Application*, edited by M.
            J. O'Brien, pp. 24–29. University of Utah Press, Salt Lake City.
Dunnell, R. C., and J. K. Feathers
    1991    Late Woodland Manifestations of the Malden Plain, Southeast Missouri. In
            *Stability, Transformation, and Variation: The Late Woodland Southeast*, edited by M.
            S. Nassaney and C. R. Cobb, pp. 21–45. Plenum Press, New York.

Dunnell, R. C. and R. J. Wenke
 1979 An Evolutionary Model of the Development of Complex Societies. Paper presented at the annual meeting of the American Association for the Advancement of Science, San Francisco.

Efron, B., and R. Tibshirani
 1993 *An Introduction to the Bootstrap.* Chapman and Hall, New York.

Eighmy, J. L., and J. M. LaBelle
 1996 Radiocarbon Dating of Twenty-Seven Plains Complexes and Phases. *Plains Anthropologist* 41:53–69.

Feathers, J. K.
 1989 Effects of Temper on Strength of Ceramics: Response to Brontisky and Hamer. *American Antiquity* 54:579–588.

 1990 *Explaining the Evolution of Ceramics in Southeast Missouri (Woodland Mississippian).* Unpublished Ph.D. Dissertation, Department of Anthropology, University of Washington, Seattle.

Feathers, J. K., and W. D. Scott
 1989 Prehistoric Ceramic Composition from the Mississippi Valley. *Ceramic Bulletin* 68:554–557.

Felsenstein, J.
 1982 Numerical Methods for Inferring Evolutionary Trees. *Quarterly Review of Biology* 57:379–404.

Fewkes, J. W.
 1898 Archaeological Expedition to Arizona, 1895. *Seventeenth Annual Report of the Bureau of American Ethnology, Washington, D.C.* Part 1:519–741.

 1909 Ancient Zuni Pottery. In *Putnam Anniversary Volume, Essays Presented to Frederick W. Putnam,* pp. 43–82. G. E. Stechert, New York.

Flannery, K. V.
 1976 Analysis of Stylistic Variation Within and Between Communities. In *The Early Mesoamerican Village,* edited by K. V. Flannery, pp. 251–257. Academic Press, New York.

Ford, J. A.
 1936 *Analysis of Indian Village Site Collections from Louisiana and Mississippi.* Department of Conservation, Louisiana State Geological Survey, Anthropological Study, 2. New Orleans.

 1938 A Chronological Method Applicable to the Southeast. *American Antiquity* 3:260–264.

 1949 Cultural Dating of Prehistoric Sites in Viru Valley Peru. *American Museum of Natural History, Anthropological Papers* 5:263–266.

 1952 *Measurements of Some Prehistoric Design Elements in the Southeastern States,* 44. Anthropological Papers of the American Museum of Natural History, New York.

Fox, G. L.
 1992 *A Critical Evaluation of the Interpretive Framework of the Mississippi Period in Southeast Missouri.* Unpublished Ph.D. Dissertation, Department of Anthropology, University of Missouri-Columbia, Columbia.

 1998 An Examination of Mississippian-period Phases in Southeastern Missouri. In *The Archaeology of the Central Mississippi River Valley,* edited by R. C. Dunnell and M. J. O'Brien, pp. 31–58. University of Alabama Press, Tuscaloosa.

Glance, N. S., and B. A. Huberman
    1994   The Dynamics of Social Dilemmas. *Scientific American* 270:76–81.
Green, D. G.
    1994   Connectivity and Complexity in Landscapes and Ecosystems. *Pacific Conservation Biology* 1:194–200.
Haggett, P.
    1966   *Locational Analysis in Human Geography*. St. Martin's Press, New York.
Hammond, N.
    1972   Location Models and the Site of Lubaantun: A Classic Maya Center. In *Models in Archaeology*, edited by D. L. Clarke, pp. 757–300. Methuen, London.
Haynes, R.
    1974   Application of Exponential Distance Decay to Human and Animal Activities. *Geografisker Annaler B* 56.
Hill, J. N.
    1970   *Broken K Pueblo: Prehistoric Social Organization in the American Southwest*. Anthropological Papers of the University of Arizona, Tucson.
Hodder, I.
    1974   Regression Analysis of Some Trade and Marketing Patterns. *World Archaeology* 6:172–189.
Hodder, I., and C. Orton
    1976   *Spatial Analysis in Archaeology*. Cambridge University Press, Cambridge.
Holmes, W. H.
    1884   Illustrated Catalogue of a Portion of the Ethnologic and Archaeologic Collections Made by the Bureau of Ethnology During the Year 1881. *Bureau of Ethnology, 3rd Annual Report for 1881–82*, pp. 433–506. Smithsonian Institute, Washington.
    1886   Ancient Pottery of the Mississippi Valley. *Bureau of Ethnology, 4th Annual Report for 1882–83*, pp. 367–436. Smithsonian Institute, Washington.
House, J. H.
    1991   *Monitoring Mississippian Dynamics: Time, Settlement, and Ceramic Variation in the Kent Phase, Eastern Arkansas*. Unpublished Ph.D. Dissertation, Department of Anthropology, Southern Illinois University, Carbondale.
Huberman, B., and N. S. Glance
    1994   Evolutionary Games and Computer Simulations. *Proceedings of the National Academy of Sciences of the United States* 90:7716–7718.
Hudson, C.
    1985   De Soto in Arkansas: A Brief Synopsis. *Arkansas Archeological Society Field Notes* 205:3–12.
Hunt, T. L.
    1987   Patterns of Human Interaction and Evolutionary Divergence in the Fiji Islands. *Journal of the Polynesian Society* 96:299–334.
Irwin, G.
    1992   *The Prehistoric Exploration and Colonisation of the Pacific*. Cambridge University Press, Cambridge.
Isaaks, E. H., and R. M. Srivastava
    1989   An Introduction to Applied Geostatistics. Oxford University Press, Oxford.

Jones, G. T., D. K. Grayson, and C. Beck
  1983   Artifact Class Richness and Sample Size in Archaeological Surface Assemblages. In *Lulu Linear Punctated: Essays in Honor of George Irving Quimby*, edited by R. C. Dunnell and D. K. Grayson, pp. 55–73. Museum of Anthropology, University of Michigan, Ann Arbor.

Kidder, A. V.
  1924   *An Introduction to the Study of Southwestern Archaeology with a Preliminary Account of the Excavations at Pecos*. Yale University Press, New Haven.

Kimura, M.
  1976   How Genes Evolve: A Population Geneticist's View. *Annales Génétique* 19:153–168.

King, A., and J. Freer
  1995   The Mississippian Southeast: A World-Systems Perspective. In *Native American Interactions: Multiscalar Analyses and Interpretations in the Eastern Woodlands*, edited by M. S. Nassaney and K. E. Sassaman, pp. 266–288. University of Tennessee Press, Knoxville.

King, J. L., and T. H. Jukes
  1969   Non-Darwinian Evolution: Random Fixation of Selectively Neutral Mutations. *Science* 164:788–798.

Kintigh, K. W.
  1984   Measuring Archaeological Diversity by Comparison with Simulated Assemblages. *American Antiquity* 49:44–54.

Krause, R. A.
  1972   Toward a Formal Account of Bantu Ceramic Manufacture. In *Archaeological Essays in Honor of Irving B. Rouse*, edited by R. C. Dunnell and E. S. Hall, pp. 87–120. Studies in Anthropology. Mouton Publishers, New York.
  1990   Ceramic Practice and Semantic Space—an Ethnoarchaeological Inquiry into The Logic of Bantu Potting. *Antiquity* 64:711–726.

LeBlanc, S. A.
  1975   Micro-Seriation: A Method for Fine Chronological Differentiation. *American Antiquity* 40:22–38.

Leone, M.
  1968   Neolithic Economic Autonomy and Social Distance. *Science* 162:125–132.

Lewontin, R. C.
  1974   *The Genetic Basis of Evolutionary Change*. Columbia University Press, New York.

Lipo, C. P., M. E. Madsen, R. C. Dunnell, and T. Hunt
  1997   Population Structure, Cultural Transmission, and Frequency Seriation. *Journal of Anthropological Archaeology* 16:301–333.

Longacre, W. A.
  1964   Sociological Implications of the Ceramic Analysis. In *Chapters in the Prehistory of Eastern Arizona, Volume 2*, pp. 155–167. Field Museum of Natural History, Chicago.
  1970   *Archaeology as Anthropology: A Case Study* 17. Anthropological Papers of the University of Arizona Press, Tucson.

Lyman, R. L., M. J. O'Brien, and R. C. Dunnell
  1997   *The Rise and Fall of Culture History*. Plenum Press, New York.

Madsen, M. E.
  1994   Problems and Solutions in the Study of Dispersed Communities. In *Ohio Hopewell Community Patterns*, edited by W. S. Dancey and P. J. Pacheco, pp. 85–104. Kent State University Press, Kent.
Mainfort, R. C.
  1995   Cluster Analysis and Archaeological Phases: An Example from the Central Mississippi Valley. Paper presented at the 39th Annual Midwest Archaeological Conference, Beloit.
Mayer-Oakes, W. J.
  1955   *Prehistory of the Upper Ohio Valley: An Introductory Archaeological Study*. Anthropological Series, No. 234, Carnegie Museum, Pittsburgh.
McCutcheon, P. T.
  1996   *Stone Tool Heat-Treatment Technology on the Malden Plain, Southeast Missouri: An Experimental Approach*. Unpublished Ph.D. Dissertation, Department of Anthropology, University of Washington, Seattle.
McKern, W. C.
  1939   The Midwestern Taxonomic Method as an Aid to Archaeological Study. *American Antiquity* 4:301–313.
Moore, C. B.
  1910   Antiquities of the St. Francis, White and Black River, Arkansas. *Journal of the Academy of Natural Sciences of Philadelphia* 14:255–364.
Morse, D. F.
  1973   *Nodena: An Account of 75 Years of Archaeological Investigation in Southeast Mississippi County, Arkansas*. Arkansas Archeological Survey Research Series, 4, Pine Bluff.
  1990   The Nodena Phase. In *Towns and Temples along the Mississippi*, edited by D. H. Dye and C. A. Cox, pp. 69–97. University of Alabama Press, Tuscaloosa.
Morse, D. F., and P. A. Morse
  1983   *Archaeology of the Central Mississippi Valley*. Academic Press, New York.
  1990   The Spanish Exploration of Arkansas. In *Columbian Consequences Vol. 2*, edited by D. H. Thomas, pp. 197–210. Smithsonian Institution Press, Washington, D.C.
  1996   Northeast Arkansas. In *Prehistory of the Central Mississippi Valley*, edited by C. H. McNutt, pp. 119–135. The University of Alabama Press, Tuscaloosa.
Morse, P. A.
  1981   *Parkin*. Arkansas Archeological Survey Research Series No. 13, Pine Bluff.
  1990   The Parkin Site and the Parkin Phase. In *Towns and Temples along the Mississippi*, edited by D. Dye and C. Cox, pp. 119–134. University of Alabama Press, Tuscaloosa.
Naroll, R.
  1960   Two Solutions to Galton's Problem. *Philosophy of Science* 28:15–31.
Neiman, F.
  1995   Stylistic Variation in Evolutionary Perspective: Inferences from Decorative Diversity and Interassemblage Distance in Illinois Woodland Ceramic Assemblages. *American Antiquity* 60:7–36.
O'Brien, M. J.
  1994   *Cat Monsters and Head Pots: The Archaeology of Missouri's Pemiscot Bayou*. University of Missouri Press, Columbia.

1996 Archaeological Research in the Central Mississippi Valley: Culture History Gone Awry. *The Review of Archaeology* 16:23–26.

O'Brien, M. J. (editor)
1995 *Evolutionary Archaeology: Theory and Application.* University of Utah Press, Salt Lake City.

O'Brien, M. J., and G. L. Fox
1994 Assemblage Similarities and Dissimilarities. In *Cat Monsters and Head Pots: The Archaeology of Missouri's Pemiscot Bayou*, edited by M. J. O'Brien, pp. 61–93. University of Missouri Press, Columbia.

O'Brien, M. J., and T. D. Holland
1990 Variation, Selection, and the Archaeological Record. In *Archaeological Method and Theory, Volume 2*, edited by M. B. Schiffer, pp. 31–80. Academic Press, New York.
1992 The Role of Adaptation in Archaeological Explanation. *American Antiquity* 57:36–59.

Olsson, G.
1965 Distance and Human Interaction. A Review and Bibliography. *Regional Science Research Institute, Bibliographic Series* 2.

Orton, C.
1993 How Many Pots Make Five?—an Historical Review of Pottery Quantification. *Archaeometry* 35:169–184.

Phillips, P.
1970 *Archaeological Survey in the Lower Yazoo Basin, Mississippi.* Peabody Museum, Cambridge, Massachusetts.

Phillips, P., J. A. Ford, and J. B. Griffin
1951 *Archaeological Survey in the Lower Mississippi Alluvial Valley, 1940–1947.* Papers of the Peabody Museum of American Archaeology and Ethnology 25. Harvard University, Cambridge, Massachusetts.

Phillips, P., and G. R. Willey
1953 Method and Theory in American Archaeology: An Operational Basis for Culture-historical Integration. *American Anthropologist* 55:615–33.

Plog, F.
1979 Prehistory: Western Anasazi. In *Handbook of North American Indians, Volume 9: Southwest*, edited by A. Ortiz, pp. 109–130. Smithsonian Institution, Washington.
1983 Political and Economic Alliances on the Colorado Plateaus, A.D. 400–1450. In *Advances in World Archaeology, Vol. 2*, edited by F. Wendorf and A. Close, pp. 289–330. Academic Press, New York.

Plog, S.
1976a The Inference of Prehistoric Social Organization from Ceramic Design Variability. *Michigan Discussions in Anthropology* 1:1–47.
1976b Measurement of Prehistoric Interaction between Communities. In *The Early Mesoamerican Village*, edited by K. V. Flannery, pp. 255–272. Academic Press, New York.
1977 *A Multivariate Approach to the Explanation of Ceramic Design Variation.* Unpublished Ph.D. Dissertation, Department of Anthropology, University of Michigan, Ann Arbor.
1978 Social Interaction and Stylistic Similarity: A Reanalysis. In *Advances in Archaeological Method and Theory, Volume 1*, edited by M. B. Schiffer, pp. 143–182. Academic Press, New York.

1980   *Stylistic Variation in Prehistoric Ceramics*. Cambridge University Press, Cambridge.

Plog, S., and M. Hegmon
1993   The Sample Size-Richness Relation—the Relevance of Research Questions, Sampling Strategies, and Behavioral Variation. *American Antiquity* 58: 489–496.

Pollnac, R. B., and R. M. Rowlett
1977   Community and Supracommunity within the Marne Culture: A Stylistic Analysis. In *Experimental Archeology*, edited by D. Ingersoll, J. E. Yellen, and W. Macdonald, pp. 167–90. Columbia University, New York.

Redman, C. L.
1977   The "Analytical Individual" and Prehistoric Style Variability. In *The Individual in Prehistory: Studies of Variability in Style and Prehistoric Technologies*, edited by J. N. Hill and J. Gunn, pp. 41–53. Academic Press, New York.
1978   Multivariate Artifact Analysis: A Basis for Multidimensional Interpretations. In *Social Archaeology: Beyond Subsistence and Dating*, edited by C. L. Redman, pp. 159–92. Academic Press, New York.

Renfrew, C.
1969   Trade and Culture Process in European Prehistory. *Current Anthropology* 10:151–69.
1977   Alternative Models for Exchange and Spatial Distribution. In *Exchange Systems in Prehistory*, edited by T. K. Earle and J. E. Ericson, pp. 71–90. Academic Press, New York.
1984   *Approaches to Social Archaeology*. Harvard University Press, Cambridge, Massachusetts.

Rhode, D.
1988   Measurement of Archaeological Diversity and the Sample-size Effect. *American Antiquity* 53:708–716.

Ridley, M.
1986   *Evolution and Classification: The Reformation of Cladism*. Longman Press, London.

Rindos, D.
1984   *The Origins of Agriculture: An Evolutionary Perspective*. Academic Press, New York.
1989   Darwinianism and its Role in the Explanation of Domestication. In *Foraging and Farming: The Evolution of Plant Exploitation*, edited by D. Harris and G. Hillman, pp. 27–41. Unwin Hyman, London.

Robinson, W. S.
1951   A Method for Chronologically Ordering Archaeological Deposits. *American Antiquity* 16:293–301.

Roe, P. G.
1989   A Grammatical Analysis of Cedrosan Saladoid Vessel Form Categories and Surface Decoration: Aesthetic and Technical Styles in Early Antillian Ceramics. In *Early Ceramic Population Lifeways and Adaptive Strategies in the Caribbean*, edited by P. E. Siegel, pp. 267–382. British Archaeological Reports, International Series 506, Oxford.

Rouse, I.
1955   On the Correlation of Phases of Culture. *American Anthropologist* 57:713–722.

1965   The Place of "Peoples" in Prehistoric Research. *Journal of the Royal Anthropological Institute* 95:1–15.

Sahlins, M. D., and E. R. Service (editors)
1960   *Evolution and Culture.* University of Michigan Press, Ann Arbor.

Schiffer, M. B.
1987   *Formation Processes of the Archaeological Record.* University of New Mexico Press, Albuquerque.

Service, E.
1962   *Primitive Social Organization: An Evolutionary Perspective.* Random House, New York.

1975   *Origins of the State and Civilization: A Process of Cultural Evolution.* Norton, New York.

Shott, M. J.
1989   Diversity, Organization, and Behavior in the Material Record. *Current Anthropology* 30:283–315.

Smith, G. P.
1990   The Walls Phase and Its Neighbors. In *Towns and Temples along the Mississippi,* edited by D. Dye and C. Cox, pp. 135–169. University of Alabama Press, Tuscaloosa.

Soja, E. W.
1971   The Political Organization of Space. *Association of American Geographers, Commission on College Geography,* Washington.

Spencer, H.
1883   *Social Statics.* Appleton, New York.

Stanislawski, M. B.
1973   Review of Archaeology as Anthropology: A Case Study. *American Antiquity* 38:117–122.

Teltser, P. A. (editor)
1995   *Evolutionary Archaeology: Methodological Issues.* University of Arizona Press, Tucson.

Tylor, E. B.
1865   *Researches into the Early History of Mankind and the Development of Civilization.* J. Murray, London.

Upham, S., and F. Plog
1986   The Interpretation of Prehistoric Political Complexity in the Central and Northern Southwest: Toward a Mending of the Models. *Journal of Field Archaeology* 13:223–238.

Whallon, R.
1968   Investigations of Late Prehistoric Social Organization in New York State. In *New Perspectives in Archeology,* edited by S. R. Binford and L. R. Binford, pp. 223–244. Aldine Press, Chicago.

White, L. A.
1949   *The Science of Culture: A Study of Man and Civilization.* Farrar Straus, New York.

Wiley, E. O.
1981   *Phylogenetic Systematics: The Theory and Practice of Phylogenetic Systematics.* John Wiley and Sons, New York.

Willey, G. R., and P. Phillips

   1955   Method and Theory in American Archaeology. II: Historical Developmental Interpretation. *American Anthropologist* 57:723–819.

   1958   *Method and Theory in American Archaeology.* University of Chicago Press, Chicago.

Williams, S.

   1954   *An Archaeological Study of the Mississippian Culture in Southeast Missouri.* Unpublished Ph.D. Dissertation, Department of Anthropology, Yale University, New Haven.

Wilson, A. G.

   1971   A Family of Spatial Interaction Models and Associated Developments. *Environment and Planning* 3:1–32.

Wright, G. A.

   1970   On Trade and Culture Process in Prehistory. *Current Anthropology* 11:171–173.

Wright, H.

   1977   Recent Research on the Origin of the State. *Annual Review of Anthropology* 6:379–397.

   1986   The Evolution of Civilizations. In *American Archaeology Past and Future*, edited by D. D. Fowler and S. A. Sabloff, pp. 323–365. Smithsonian Institution Press, Washington.

Zipf, G.

   1949   *Human Behavior and the Principle of Least Effort.* Addison-Wesley Press, New York.

# 7

# Dietary Variation and Village Settlement in the Ohio Valley

*Diana M. Greenlee*

## INTRODUCTION

Sedentary nucleated villages appear at different times in different places in the Eastern Woodlands of North America for apparently different reasons. Archaeologists have yet to unravel the cause(s) for the appearance, distribution, and persistence of nucleated villages. While most explanatory attempts rely on gradual, directional change toward increased settlement size, sedentariness, and permanence, this is not consistent with the archaeological record of many areas. Consider, for example, the settlement record of the middle and upper Ohio River valley during the Late Woodland and Late Prehistoric periods.

### The Late Woodland Period (400–1000 A.D.)

The initial appearance of nucleated, sedentary settlement systems in the Ohio Valley occurred at the beginning of the Late Woodland period. First appearing in about 400 A.D., these habitations were relatively large, dense concentrations of cultural debris generated by multiple contemporaneous households (Ahler 1987; Dancey 1992; Railey 1984; Shott 1990). Although occupied throughout the annual seasonal cycle, the occupations were of low permanence, inhabited for a few years only. Where enough of the deposit has been exposed to determine attributes like internal organization, mortuary treatment, and defensive posture, the settlements exhibit substantial variation. Some Late Woodland villages are disorganized in terms of household placement, with features such as encircling ditches that suggest a defensive posture. Others have structures arranged circularly around an interior plaza, with no identified defensive features. Some villages have associated burial mounds, some contain pit burials, and others are apparently devoid of human skeletal materials, the latter suggesting that mortuary and domestic functions are spatially separate as in earlier times. As further evidence of this, isolated burial mounds are known as well.

After about 700 A.D., a significant reorganization in settlement occurred with remains indicating a return to a dispersed system. Unfortunately, very few deposits of this age have been discovered, let alone systematically examined. Those that have been studied tend to be small, scattered with scanty cultural debris, and contain relatively few features compared to earlier villages (Carskadden and Morton 1989; Jones 1978, 1979; Morton 1984; Seeman 1992; Shott 1990). There is considerable variation among them, however. Some are short-term sedentary hamlets, while others appear to be more consistent with a dispersed, mobile settlement system.

Rockshelters in southeast Ohio and central Kentucky also provide occupational evidence dating to the Late Woodland period (Cowan 1979; Ormerod 1983; Prufer 1967, 1981; Prufer and McKenzie 1966). Indeed, while cultural debris indicates these contexts were used for short-term, possibly seasonal occupations over a great time span, the bulk of materials appears to be of Late Woodland age (Seeman 1980). It has been further noted (Seeman 1980) that rockshelters were used more heavily during the later, as opposed to earlier, portion of the Late Woodland period. These kinds of deposits by themselves do not shed much light on settlement systems, but that they were used more heavily during the late Late Woodland is consistent with an apparent settlement reorganization toward greater dispersion and perhaps mobility. Although these contexts are useful for subsistence studies because their environments are so conducive to excellent preservation of faunal and botanical remains, their status as locales of special use requires those remains be evaluated carefully for potential biases.

Subsistence systems of the Late Woodland period are also highly variable. Archaeobotanical assemblages from early Late Woodland contexts are similar to those of the Middle Woodland period, with continued reliance on several cultivated plants (squash, sumpweed, sunflower, maygrass, chenopod, and erect knotweed), with particular emphasis on the latter three, the starchy-seeded ones; these indigenous crops were supplemented by a diverse assortment of wild plant resources, particularly nuts, and occasionally maize (Watson 1989; Wymer 1992, 1993). By the end of the Late Woodland period, maize had largely replaced the native crops and wild plant resources in Ohio Valley archaeobotanical assemblages (Wagner 1983, 1987). Throughout the Late Woodland period, animal exploitation emphasized white-tailed deer and wild turkeys, although many other taxa (e.g., raccoon, rabbit, squirrel, woodchuck, duck, fish, and turtles) are represented as well (Breitburg 1992; Oetelaar 1990).

## The Late Prehistoric Period (1000–1650 A.D.)

By 1000 A.D., communities in the Ohio Valley were again organized as nucleated, sedentary villages (Cowan 1988; Graybill 1981; Hart 1993; Henderson 1992). These settlements were large, with a multitude of pits (for burial, storage, and refuse), hearths, house structures, and middens containing abundant food remains of both plants and animals. They show considerable variation in such attributes as settlement size and location, internal organization, mortuary treatment, and the presence of defensive features. Some villages are in bottomland settings, while others are in the uplands; some exhibit a radial arrangement of structures and other features around a central plaza, while others are linear; some have burial mounds, some have individuals buried inside houses, and others have individuals buried in pits outside houses; and some villages are surrounded by palisades while others are not.

Initial attempts to explain Late Prehistoric period settlement variation assumed it reflected functional differences between more-or-less contemporary habitations. While there is no evidence to support contentions about hierarchical settlement systems (contra Essenpreis 1978), almost certainly some of the variation is functional, reflecting different environmental situations and different uses (Brose 1982; Turnbow et al. 1983). There is also a strong temporal component to much of the settlement variation, although the specific timing and particular manifestation of changes seem to vary from region to region. The earliest villages tend to be small, their internal structure unorganized, with no evidence for defensive attributes. Later villages are larger and radially organized with central plazas. By 1450 A.D., villages are considerably larger, reduced in number, restricted in geographic distribution, and include more defensive attributes. By 1670 A.D., the region was essentially uninhabited as a result of the combined effects of introduced European disease and Iroquois raids.

When compared with those from earlier periods, Late Prehistoric-aged archaeobotanical assemblages in the Ohio Valley exhibit significantly higher frequencies of maize and lower frequencies of cultivated native and wild plant resources; beans, squash, sunflower, and chenopod contribute minor amounts to these assemblages (Rossen 1992; Wagner 1987). The same cannot be said for some other regions, where the indigenous plants apparently continued to contribute significant amounts to subsistence even after maize became a staple crop (Smith 1992). In contrast to the botanical record, faunal exploitation changed subtly (e.g., increased remains of turkey and opossum) from that of the Late Woodland period (Greenlee 2000).

## Implications

Much of the archaeological research relevant to explaining change in settlement systems has concentrated on identifying central tendencies in such things as settlement location and size. While this approach has laid the foundation for much of our current understanding of culture history in the Eastern Woodlands, it has failed to produce testable explanations. The archaeological record of the middle and upper Ohio River valley is not consistent with commonsensical notions of how settlement change *should* have occurred. Thus, models that rely on a gradual, directional change from small, mobile hunting/gathering camps to large, sedentary farming villages simply cannot account for the variation documented in the Ohio River valley during the Late Woodland and Late Prehistoric periods. An explanation of why nucleated sedentary villages appear when and where they did in the Ohio Valley must be able to accommodate the "on/off" quality of, as well as the great variation in, the settlement record.

To date, several explanations (e.g., migration, defense, climatic change, and maize agriculture) have been forwarded to account for specific aspects of the Ohio Valley settlement record. Each scenario emphasizes different characteristics of the settlement record and, as explanations, all suffer from a similar suite of problems. They are intuitive assertions about general patterns, relying on unwarranted assumptions (e.g., village settlement and maize agriculture are mere traits that can be diffused from one group to another) and variables that lack empirical relevance (e.g., social risk). Further, they fail to provide mechanisms for change. It is not enough to assume that, because people made settlement choices, that those choices explain why settlement systems were as they were. A new approach is warranted; one with an explicit theoretical framework that specifies variables of empirical relevance, that provides mechanisms for change, and that has as its goal explanation, not interpretation. Evolutionary theory provides such an approach.

## Theoretical Framework

I turn now to a theoretical consideration of settlement. In particular, I define the relevant terms and derive empirical implications from them. That explicit definitions are necessary is clear from a brief examination of the literature. For example, the term "sedentary" has several meanings (cf., Kelly 1992; Rafferty 1985), ranging from residentially less mobile (Bar-Yosef and Belfer-Cohen 1991), to residentially stationary throughout the annual cycle (Rice 1975), to residentially permanent through multiple annual cycles (Trigger 1968). Given this situation, it is frustrating when otherwise excellent contributions, such as Rosenberg's (1998) insightful piece on the evolution of sedentary populations, fail to define basic terms like "sedentary." Because readers are left to guess what is meant by such terms, these efforts are less effective than they could be.

## Settlement Systems

The term "settlement system" here refers to the physical organization of people, both through the annual seasonal cycle and across the landscape (Rice 1975; Whitlam 1981). In the temporal dimension, settlement systems may be characterized by how they respond to seasonal variation in resource abundance

(Rafferty 1985; Rice 1975; Whitlam 1981; cf., Binford 1980). Mobile communities respond by moving between environments; sedentary communities do not move in response to seasonal changes in resource kind and abundance. Thus, to be sedentary, a settlement must be occupied by at least some members of the community year-round. As such, sedentary settlement systems can only occur where food is available in amounts sufficient to support the population on a daily basis throughout the year. Where seasonal variation in productivity is high (e.g., the mid- and upper latitudes), storage technology may sometimes compensate for predictable food shortages during seasons of low resource availability (Hart 1995; Smyth 1989; Testart 1982). These two settlement systems place different demands on subsistence in terms of the seasonal availability and productivity of resources exploited.

In the spatial dimension, settlement systems may be characterized by the distribution of community members across the landscape (Dancey 1992; Fuller 1981; Nass 1995; Rafferty 1985). A dispersed settlement system consists of geographically separate, functionally interdependent and redundant, domestic units or households. Sometimes called hamlets, the several households constituting the functional community are not located in one place and, consequently, the entire settlement is manifest as several sites. Nucleated settlements are geographically clustered occupations, consisting of multiple, functionally redundant, and interdependent households. The entire settlement is manifest archaeologically as one site. Because all members of the community are located in one geographic place, the catchment area is considerably less than that of a dispersed community. Thus, these two settlement systems place different demands on subsistence in terms of the spatial distribution and productivity of resources exploited.

The four settlement classes created by the intersecting modes of these dimensions (i.e., dispersed mobile, dispersed sedentary, nucleated mobile, and nucleated sedentary) are similar to those used in traditional approaches to archaeology (e.g., Beardsley et al. 1955). That traditional units can be useful for partitioning archaeological phenomena in an evolutionary approach is not unprecedented (e.g., Lipo et al. 1997). I have simply attempted to place these intuitive divisions into a more explicit theoretical framework.

## Implications

Blanket statements are often made that certain configurations of settlement (e.g., sedentary nucleated villages) will, "all things being equal," confer greater fitness on the relevant populations and, thus, they are inevitable developments. From this position, when such a configuration is realized, it is because the opportunity presented itself and it happened "naturally"; when it is not evidenced, it is because environmental conditions did not "allow" it to happen. Obviously, the latter cases occur when "all things" are *not* equal. A more promising approach views the relative costs and benefits of different settlement alternatives as varying with the particular situation and evaluates them accordingly.

In Table 7.1, I list several potential costs and benefits of being sedentary (as opposed to mobile) and of being nucleated (as opposed to dispersed). Because the costs and benefits of being sedentary and/or nucleated will vary with the particular circumstance, these settlement systems will increase the reproductive fitness of populations under *some* conditions, but not under others. Thus, sedentary nucleated settlements must be viewed as one settlement option that may arise for several reasons (e.g., changes in climate, subsistence technology, or demographic structure). Such settlements might differ in structure and stability; these differences could be reflected in a variety of parameters including dietary composition, subsistence system, settlement structure, settlement location, and population size.

For example, one of the explanations advanced for settlement nucleation in this part of eastern North America can be thought of as the consequence of a shift from a generalized hunting and gathering, or, alternatively, a non-maize-specialized system involving the Eastern Agricultural Complex plants, to a specialized subsistence system specifically tied to maize agriculture (Cowan 1988; Ford 1974; Fuller 1981; Griffin 1967). In either case, the environmental carrying capacity of the local environment will increase, supporting greater local population densities and population sizes, and decreasing the size of catchment necessary to support the community. The structure and content of the subsistence system will be distinctly different, and dietary change will be clearly visible in bone chemistry. The

**Table 7.1**
**Potential Costs and Benefits of Being Sedentary and/or Nucleated**

|  | Costs | Benefits |
|---|---|---|
| Sedentary | ↑costs locating dispersed resources[a,b]<br>↑risk of resource depletion[c,k] | ↓transport costs[d]<br>↑fertility[f]<br>↑site-specific knowledge[b] |
| Nucleated | ↑risk of resource depletion[c,k]<br>↑risk of intragroup conflict[c,e,j,k]<br>↑disease load[l] | ↓communication costs[g,h,j,k]<br>↓defense costs[h,i,j,k]<br>↑spatial efficiency[h,i,j]<br>↑labor force[i,j,k] |

[a] Binford 1983
[b] Moran 1983
[c] Rosenberg 1998
[d] Cleland 1976; Dunnell 1998
[e] Lee 1972a
[f] Lee 1972b
[g] Heffley 1981
[h] Cashdan 1992
[i] Fuller 1981
[j] Jochim 1981
[k] Hames 1983
[l] Kent 1986

distribution of settlements across environments may be biased toward locations with conditions (e.g., frost-free days, moisture capacity) favorable to maize growth. Like many swidden systems, settlement permanence may decrease in response to weed growth and local succession in cultivated areas.

In contrast, characteristics of settlements established for defensive purposes, i.e., to reduce the risks associated with intercommunity competition, should differ in some key ways. Local population densities may increase due to the spatial reorganization of groups without a notable increase in population size. Expansion or intensification of the subsistence base may allow nucleation to be sustained for a short time, but without significant increases in resource productivity, populations will not grow and the occupations are likely to be unstable (impermanent). Settlement locations may be biased toward more "strategic" situations, with the construction of defensive structures (stockades, overlapping entries, bastions, and moats) and/or increased evidence for violent deaths.

The underlying mechanism(s) of change necessary to explain why settlement systems took the particular forms they did when and where they did can only be identified through an examination of temporal and environmental variation in relevant parameters (e.g., settlement structure and location, subsistence structure and content, diet, and demographic trajectory). With the exception of diet, these data are largely available in the archaeological literature. My research attempts to remedy this deficiency by emphasizing the collection of dietary information through chemical characterization of archaeological human bone. After briefly considering the concept of diet below, I outline my research design and analytical techniques. My goal is to document dietary variation as a crucial step in identifying the mechanism(s) responsible for the appearance, distribution, and persistence of sedentary nucleated settlements in the middle and upper Ohio River valley.

## Diet

It is necessary here to distinguish subsistence systems from diet. Subsistence, the acquisition of all manner of resources, both edible and inedible, is an attribute of the community; diet, the consumption of resources, is an attribute of individuals within the community. As such, different kinds of data are necessary to address questions of subsistence and dietary change. Aggregates such as floral and faunal remains inform about the subsistence system of a community; these kinds of assemblages represent pooled data derived from a variable number of individuals over variable amounts of time and include materials collected for a variety of uses (e.g., raw materials, competition suppression, and dietary consumption). In contrast, diet is best addressed through chemical analysis of skeletal remains from individuals.

This distinction between subsistence and diet is important because, in simple societies, the individual organism is the unit of selection (Dunnell 1989, 1995; Dunnell and Wenke 1979). Thus, community-scale data may be epiphenomenal;

that is, they may be explained as effects of processes operating at a lower scale. The distribution of diet within and between communities provides crucial information concerning the units of change (scale of individuals, lineages, communities, or populations). For example, did dietary change occur allopatrically (i.e., some individuals changed their diet, were favored by selection, and thereby replaced members of the population who did not change their diet) or sympatrically (i.e., all individuals changed their diet, were equally favored by selection, and thus, change happened across the entire population)?

That an organism's diet is functional, i.e., it measurably affects reproductive fitness, is clearly documented (Frisch 1975, 1977; Keys et al. 1950; Pebley et al. 1985; Stein and Susser 1975). Indeed, maternal reproductive performance is one criterion used by many practitioners of animal husbandry to evaluate the adequacy of experimental diets (McLester 1949). Both nutritional deprivation (undernutrition) and specific nutritional deficiencies or toxicities have documented ramifications for reproduction.

There may be a stylistic (adaptively neutral) component to diet, as well. However, such components are likely minor contributors to the overall diet and will be highly context dependent. Different brands of cola provide a contemporary example of a stylistic component of the diet. These varieties generally have the same cost and nutrition value; the temporal and spatial distributions of such alternative, functionally equivalent resources as components of the diet are probably governed by stochastic processes. Our current level of resolution is probably insufficient to identify the stylistic components of prehistoric diets.

## ESTABLISHING PREHISTORIC DIETARY VARIATION

The chemical composition of skeletal tissues provides a direct, yet complex, measure of individual dietary content (e.g., Ambrose and Norr 1993; DeNiro and Epstein 1978, 1981; Hare et al. 1991; Lambert and Weydert-Homeyer 1993; Price et al. 1985). Stable carbon isotope analysis of archaeological human bone provides crucial evidence regarding the dietary commitment to maize by Late Woodland (400–1000 A.D.) and Late Prehistoric (1000–1650 A.D.) populations in the Eastern Woodlands. Trace element concentrations (e.g., strontium, barium, zinc, manganese) may provide dietary information complementary to the stable carbon isotopes. These two sources of dietary information reflect different biochemical sources, metabolic processes, and susceptibilities to post-depositional alteration. Hence, they provide different kinds of information about diet and pose different kinds of problems for archaeological analyses.

### Stable Carbon Isotopes

The stable carbon isotope ratios[1] of terrestrial plants reflect the biochemical pathway of atmospheric carbon dioxide ($CO_2$) in photosynthesis. In the Eastern Woodlands, where the native vegetation is strongly skewed toward plants that utilize the $C_3$ (Calvin-Benson) photosynthetic pathway, the $\delta^{13}C$ values of most plants range from $-35$ to $-20$ $^o/_{oo}$ (Deines 1980; O'Leary 1981, 1988; Smith and Epstein 1971). Only a few plants in the region (e.g., *Amaranthus, Atriplex,* and some species of Gramineae) are known to use the $C_4$ (Hatch-Slack) photosynthetic mode, with $\delta^{13}C$ values ranging from $-16$ to $-7$ $^o/_{oo}$ (Deines 1980; O'Leary 1981, 1988; Smith and Epstein 1971). Since animal consumers reflect the isotopic composition of the plants they consume with some fractionation (DeNiro and Epstein 1978; Vogel 1978), $\delta^{13}C$ values of the local fauna generally range from $-20$ to $-23$ $^o/_{oo}$ (Bender et al. 1991; Boutton et al. 1991; Conard 1988; Katzenberg 1989). Fauna in a $C_4$ dominated environment have higher $\delta^{13}C$ values, up to about $-7$ $^o/_{oo}$ (Vogel 1978).

Maize, an introduced plant of tropical origin, uses the $C_4$ photosynthetic pathway; this makes it a rare resource in the area, easily distinguished isotopically from most native floral resources. Certainly, the few other $C_4$ resources in the area could potentially have contributed to the isotopic diet of prehistoric populations. However, most of the other floral resources suggested from archaeobotanical evidence to have been consumed in significant amounts (goosefoot, maygrass, erect knotweed, beans, squash, sunflower, and mast) have been analyzed and they have been identified as $C_3$ plants (Buikstra et al. 1988; Smith and Epstein 1971). In the Ohio Valley, then, stable carbon isotopes reflect the degree to which the diet of an individual is focused on maize.

Both the mineral and organic phases of bone contain carbon. Experiments with rats have demonstrated that the organic phase, dominated by the protein collagen, primarily reflects the protein component of the diet, while the carbonate fraction of the mineral phase better reflects the whole diet (Ambrose and Norr 1993; Tieszen and Fagre 1993). Archaeologists working in the Eastern Woodlands have relied on the isotopic composition of the organic fraction[2] for dietary studies, because researchers believe it is better preserved. Even so, the protein fraction of archaeological bones may have experienced post-depositional changes (see "Data Quality" below), and thus, the extract that archaeologists obtain is not strictly the protein collagen. For example, the extract may lack some amino acids or contain some extraneous noncollagenous materials. To reflect this, I refer to the extract as "collagen" (cf., Ambrose 1990). As a consequence of both pre-mortem and postmortem fractionation processes, the diet-tissue relationship is not a simple one in archaeological skeletal materials. While dietary differences between individuals are identifiable in "collagen," attempts to reconstruct dietary composition quantitatively (i.e., calculate the percent contribution of maize to the diet) are not warranted.

## Trace Elements

Because the concentrations of trace elements vary among different classes of plants and animals, archaeologists have looked to their concentrations in human bones as a reflection of the consumption of particular kinds of foods. For example, strontium is known to be discriminated against increasingly as one moves up the food chain from plants to herbivores to omnivores to carnivores (Sillen and Kavanagh 1982). Archaeologists have used this empirical observation to argue that people with relatively higher strontium concentrations consumed primarily plant products, while those with relatively lower strontium concentrations ingested more meat (e.g., Brown 1974; Schoeninger 1979). Following the same logical structure, other trace elements (e.g., barium, zinc, iron, copper, manganese, and vanadium) have also been used to reconstruct various aspects of prehistoric diet using different categories of resources (e.g., Beck 1985; Hatch and Geidel 1983; Katzenberg 1984; Lambert et al. 1984).

Arguing that those earlier efforts were overly simplistic, more recent contributions (e.g., Burton 1996; Ezzo 1994; Lambert and Weydert-Homeyer 1993) have emphasized the complex nature of elemental consumption and metabolism. For example, Ezzo noted that strontium and barium are the only trace elements for which physiological models exist that relate concentrations in bone with dietary intake. While other elements may also be dietary indicators, this has not been established conclusively; controlled feeding studies (e.g., Lambert and Weydert-Homeyer 1993) and better models of trace element metabolism are both crucial steps that are currently underway. Even for those trace elements known to be dietary indicators, the successful use of trace element concentrations for dietary analyses presumes that the elemental composition of archaeological human bone has not been significantly altered by post-depositional processes (e.g., Greenlee 1996; Price et al. 1992; Radosevich 1993).

## Previous Dietary Research in the Ohio Valley

To date, the middle and upper Ohio River valley has been the subject of considerable research aimed at documenting prehistoric diets through bone chemistry analysis (Figures 7.1 and 7.2). Below, I briefly review the results of those efforts.

### Stable Carbon Isotope Analyses

The first stable carbon isotope research conducted on archaeological human bone samples from the middle and upper Ohio River valley was conducted by van der Merwe and Vogel (1978). As one of the first applications of isotope chemistry to address questions about prehistoric diet, it demonstrated significant differences in maize consumption between populations of the Late Prehistoric and earlier periods (Figure 7.2). Specifically, Archaic and Woodland populations did not consume isotopically measurable amounts of maize in their diets, while diets of individuals from contexts postdating 1000 A.D. were apparently dominated by maize.

Bender et al. (1981) expanded upon that previous work, emphasizing skeletal materials from Middle Woodland Hopewell contexts in Wisconsin, Illinois, and Ohio. Until that time, many archaeologists believed that the cultural elaborations characteristic of Hopewell could only have been possible with a maize-based agri-

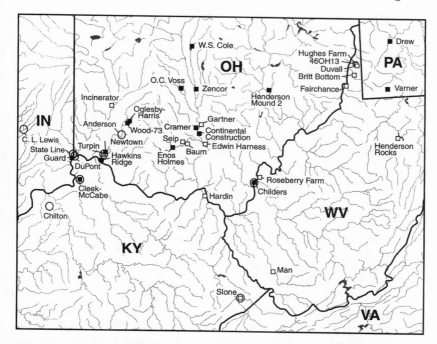

**Figure 7.1. Map of the middle and upper Ohio River valley, showing the locations of previously acquired (□) (Bender et al. 1981; Brashler and Reed 1991; Broida 1983; Conard 1988; Farrow 1986; Greenlee 1990; Schurr and Schoeninger 1995; van der Merwe and Vogel 1978) and newly acquired (■) stable carbon isotope data. The gray-filled symbol indicates a locale with both previously and newly acquired isotope data. The locations of previously acquired trace element data (○)(Greenlee 1996; Price 1985; Schneider 1986) are shown as well.**

cultural system. They showed conclusively that, even though maize occurred spo-radically in the archaeobotanical record of the Middle Woodland period, it was not an important component of the diets of the Hopewell populations studied.

Stable carbon isotopic studies since these two groundbreaking papers have concentrated on establishing the relative degree to which various Late Prehistoric groups in the region were committed to maize as a dietary staple. Although sometimes hampered by small sample size and/or relatively uneven coverage, these studies nevertheless demonstrate a high commitment to maize (Figure 7.2) with significant temporal and environmental variation. High levels of commit-ment to that nutritionally inadequate crop had a positive impact on the reproduc-tive success of those populations, even if it involved negative "health" consequences (Buikstra 1992; Cassidy 1984; Perzigian et al. 1984).

In sum, previously acquired stable carbon isotope evidence from the Ohio Valley (Figure 7.2) supports the notion that, while maize was present in many areas of the Eastern Woodlands since at least 200 A.D. (Chapman and Crites

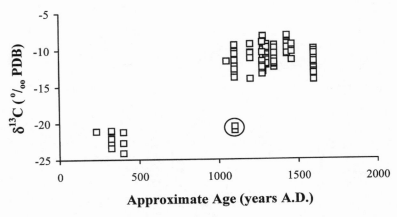

Figure 7.2. Plot showing previously acquired stable carbon isotope ratios δ13C (⁰/₀₀ PDB) versus approximate age. See Figure 7.1 caption for references. The circled values are suggested by Schurr and Schoeninger to be associated with earlier occupations at Baum and Gartner.

1987; Riley et al. 1994), it did not play a major dietary role until the Late Prehistoric period (cf., Ambrose 1987; Bender et al. 1981; Buikstra 1992). This is not a new observation. Indeed, it is frequently implied that all evidence agrees—maize was not of much dietary significance until after 1000 A.D. Of particular interest is the dearth of isotopic information from the Late Woodland period. There is a gap in the evidence that encompasses the appearance of maize-based agricultural subsistence systems in the middle and upper Ohio River valley. Thus, we know little about how the documented dietary change happened, and even less about its role in roughly concurrent settlement changes.

### Trace Element Analyses

Trace element analysis has played only a minor role in documenting prehistoric diet in the Ohio Valley. Indeed, I am aware of only two cases where trace element concentrations in archaeological skeletal materials from the region have been used in studies of prehistoric diet (Figure 7.1). The first example involves skeletal materials from DuPont, a Late Archaic deposit in southwestern Ohio (Price 1985). That analysis documented high concentrations of strontium in human remains relative to both herbivores (white-tailed deer) from that site and to Late Archaic populations from other locales. These high concentrations were argued to reflect consumption of freshwater mollusks (the meat of which may contain high levels of strontium [Schoeninger and Peebles 1981]) and high environmental background levels of strontium (Price 1985).

The second case involves the elemental analysis of tooth enamel from several Ohio locales, including the Late Prehistoric occupations at Turpin, State Line, and Anderson in southwestern Ohio (Schneider 1986). Quantitative data for the thirteen elements analyzed were not presented, but Schneider (1986) did conclude that there were significant differences in the elemental composition of tooth enamel among the different populations and that these differences were related to the frequencies of carious lesions in those populations. Differences in the elemental composition of tooth enamel among populations were ascribed to both environmental and dietary variation.

Neither of these trace element studies provides illumination on dietary change through time in the Ohio Valley, nor do they inform on the relationship between diet and village settlement. While trace element analysis is a potentially valuable tool in documenting prehistoric diets in the Ohio Valley, its successful application will require great care to ensure that post-depositional processes have not altered the relevant bones' chemical compositions and to warrant that appropriate conclusions are drawn.

## THE CURRENT RESEARCH

The reasons for the documented dietary change and its potential role in village settlement cannot be addressed until variation in the timing, tempo, and distribution of diet throughout the Late Woodland and Late Prehistoric periods is determined. Fortunately, relevant skeletal assemblages are curated in museum collections and many have been made available for this research. To date, I have obtained samples of roughly 350 individuals from 75 deposits; temporally, this sample spans the Late Woodland and Late Prehistoric periods and spatially, it covers, albeit somewhat unevenly, the middle and upper Ohio River valley.

### Sampling

Because this research requires the documentation of dietary variation associated with different settlement options both through time and across different environments, sample sizes larger than those typically used by archaeologists are required to ensure that the range of dietary variation is represented. The geographic scope of the study allows comparisons between a variety of environmental settings through time that would not be possible within, for example, a single river valley. At the same time, more communities represented by greater numbers of individuals are needed to provide information about intracommunity dietary variation.

Biases in archaeological research in this region toward large sites, particularly those with mounds, and the "invisible" nature of small settlements and particular burial practices to many kinds of archaeological surveys, combine to make the available sample of Late Woodland materials comparatively small. Late Prehistoric skeletal collections available for this analysis are both larger and more numerous; sample selection emphasized considerations of temporal and environmental context, preservation condition, and availability of other complementary data.

Criteria for bone sample selections for analysis included: 1. that the burial context be undisturbed and clearly documented; 2. that the bone be in reasonable condition and in sufficient quantity to provide for replicate measurements; 3. that individuals be adults to avoid potential variation associated with age-based metabolic or dietary differences (Conard 1988; Katzenberg 1993; Schwarcz et al. 1985); 4. that cortical bone, particularly long bone shafts, be used in order to reduce diagenetic effects (Grupe 1988; Lambert et al. 1982); and 5. that samples with "preservatives" be avoided whenever possible, even though it has been demonstrated that some of these potential contaminants may be reliably removed (Moore et al. 1989).

In this research, I determine stable carbon isotope ratios for independently extracted replicate "collagen" samples from all available individuals in those skeletal collections comprised of less than ten adults. In cases where the replicate measurements differ by more than 0.25 $^o/_{oo}$ (roughly twice the analytic error), a third replicate is extracted and measured. For collections with greater than ten individuals, I use an incremental sampling strategy and analyze additional individuals until no new information is gained; i.e., new data do not significantly change the mean and standard deviation for that community.

Following a brief discussion of sample quality below, I present the results of stable carbon isotope analyses of 103 individuals from 19 Late Woodland- and early Late Prehistoric-aged deposits (Table 7.2, Figure 7.1). I use these data to demonstrate the value of this research design in addressing questions of dietary change and nucleated sedentary settlement.

## Data Quality

The structure and chemistry of bone virtually ensures that it will interact with most post-depositional environments, potentially disrupting the direct relationship between dietary content and the composition of skeletal tissues. Bone's microstructure, in conjunction with its canaliculated histomorphological macrostructure, creates a huge surface area (10 meters$^2$/gram [Hedges and van Klinken 1992]) that provides significant opportunity for ionic adsorption onto and exchange with the mineral hydroxyapatite and subsequent deterioration of the collagen fibrils. The specific chemical reactions that occur are highly variable, being determined by factors such as pH, moisture conditions, temperature, microbiology, and the geochemistry of the local environment. Thus, before patterns in archaeological human bone chemistry can be assumed to reflect dietary variation, one must evaluate the potential influence of diagenesis. Prior to isotopic analysis, I evaluate the chemical integrity of my samples in the following ways:

### *"Collagen" Yield*

Modern bone is roughly 25% collagen by weight. The amount of "collagen" extracted from archaeological bones will vary depending upon the nature of post-depositional processes. There appears to be an empirical threshold of about 2%

**Table 7.2**
**List of Skeletal Collections, Number of Adult Individuals for Which Stable Carbon Isotope Data Are Presented in This Paper, and Approximate Age of the Relevant Occupations**

| Skeletal Collection | # of Individuals | Approximate Age[a] |
|---|---|---|
| Henderson Mound 2 | 2 | LW |
| Zencor | 14 | LW |
| Continental Construction | 1 | LW |
| Hawkins Ridge | 2 | LW |
| Varner | 4 | LW |
| Childers | 5 | LW |
| W.S. Cole | 2 | LW |
| Turpin (Stone Mound) | 16 | LW |
| Cleek-McCabe Mound | 2 | LW |
| Wood-73 | 1 | eLP |
| Newtown Firehouse | 4 | eLP |
| Cramer | 3 | eLP |
| Enos Holmes Mound | 8 | eLP |
| O.C. Voss Mound | 6 | eLP |
| Oglesby-Harris | 1 | eLP |
| Guard | 15 | eLP |
| Drew | 1 | eLP |
| Turpin (Earthen Mound) | 9 | eLP |
| Turpin (Pattern) | 7 | eLP |

[a] LW = Late Woodland (400–1000 AD)
eLP = Early Late Prehistoric (1000–1250 AD)

(milligram extract/milligram dry bone); when "collagen" yields are 1–2% or less, other indicators of extract quality often, but not always, indicate that the extracts are not reliable measures of prehistoric diet (Ambrose 1990; DeNiro and Weiner 1988).

The "collagen" yields for the two independent replicate extractions from 102 of the 103 individuals considered here[3] are both positively and significantly related ($r = .907$; $F = 462.57$; $p = 0.000$). The average "collagen" yield for all extracts ± 1 standard deviation was 6.851 ± 3.191%. Five measurements (both replicates for two individuals and a single replicate for one individual) were below the 2% threshold and warrant particular attention with respect to other indicators of sample quality. The "collagen" yields for the rest of these samples are above the empirical threshold and other measures of sample quality should confirm that they are largely collagen.

### Carbon and Nitrogen Composition

By weight, modern collagen is approximately 45% carbon and 15% nitrogen, with atomic ratios of carbon to nitrogen ranging from 2.9–3.6. These characteristics serve as useful criteria in establishing the integrity of "collagen" extracts. Variation may be due to the loss of collagen components, the preservation of non-collagenous proteins (Masters 1987), or the inclusion of exogeneous contaminants (DeNiro 1985; DeNiro and Weiner 1988; Stafford et al. 1988; Tuross et al. 1988). "Collagen" samples that have elemental C/N ratios (DeNiro 1985; DeNiro et al 1985; DeNiro and Weiner 1988) or carbon and nitrogen concentrations (Ambrose 1990; Ambrose and Norr 1992; Greenlee 1990) outside the range of modern collagen often have significantly altered isotopic compositions.

Elemental carbon and nitrogen concentrations, obtained using a CHN microanalyzer are plotted against C/N ratios for 43 "collagen" samples in Figure 7.3a. Of these, only one sample has a C/N ratio outside the established 2.9–3.6 range, and its carbon and nitrogen concentrations are significantly outside the range of the rest of the samples. Figure 7.3b plots these data against average "collagen" yield. "Collagen" quality as reflected by carbon and nitrogen composition does not appear to vary systematically with sample yield. When the sample with the aberrant C/N ratio is excluded from further consideration, the compositions of all of the remaining samples are consistent with expectations from modern collagen. I note further that, for the 60 samples lacking microanalytically acquired carbon and nitrogen concentrations, carbon concentrations were obtained manometrically during $CO_2$ purification prior to isotopic analysis; they were all within the range of the microanalyzed samples, indicating that they, too, are probably primarily collagen.

### Amino Acid Analysis

Collagen has a distinct amino acid composition (Woodhead-Galloway 1980). As the protein in archaeological bones deteriorates, it becomes fragmented and "leaches" away. Some residues will be preferentially retained because of charge interactions with the mineral phase and exogenous amino acids may become incorporated into the organic mass. Noncollagenous proteins, which have amino acid compositions different from collagen, may come to dominate the protein fraction as collagen is removed. Systematic changes in the relative concentration of amino acids in "collagen" as it degrades have been identified; consequently, amino acid analysis of "collagen" extracts is a valuable tool for evaluating sample quality (Hare 1980; Masters 1987; Schoeninger et al. 1989). Figure 7.4 shows the amino acid composition of 19 "collagen" samples in comparison to modern collagen. While there is slight variation in the amino acid composition of these "collagen" samples, neither systematic degradation nor dominance by noncollagenous proteins are indicated.

### Summary

According to criteria for evaluating the integrity of biological isotopic signals, the potential impact of post-depositional alterations on these bones is slight. The

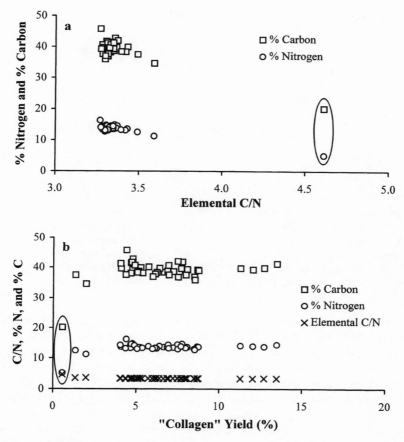

**Figure 7.3. a) Nitrogen (○) and carbon (□) concentrations (weight %) are plotted against C/N ratios for 43 "collagen" samples; b) nitrogen (○) and carbon (□) concentrations (weight %) and C/N ratios (✖) plotted against "collagen" yield (mean of two replicates). All samples but one (circled) have C/N ratios that fall within the 2.9–3.6 range of well-preserved "collagen."**

"collagen" appears to be relatively well-preserved and should provide accurate dietary information.

## Some Preliminary Results

Figure 7.5 presents the results of stable carbon isotope analyses of the sample of 102 individuals that were evaluated above and were found to have qualities consistent with modern collagen. The isotope ratios of individuals from Late Woodland-aged "nonmaize" contexts such as Henderson Mound, Newtown Firehouse, and Zencor show little intracommunity variation, particularly when

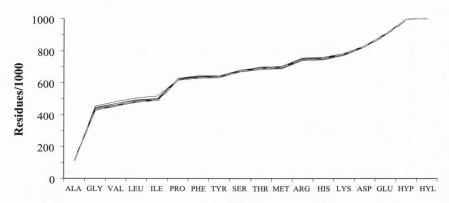

**Figure 7.4. Amino acid composition of 19 "collagen" samples (thin black lines) compared to the composition of modern human bone collagen (broken gray line). ALA, alanine; ARG, arginine; ASP, aspartic acid; GLU, glutamic acid; GLY, glycine; HIS, histidine; HYL, hydroxylysine; HYP, hydroxyproline; ILE, isoleucine; LEU, leucine; LYS, lysine; MET, methionine; PHE, phenylalanine; PRO, proline; SER, serine; THR, threonine; TYR, tyrosine; VAL, valine.**

compared to previously reported $\delta^{13}C$ values of Middle Woodland deposits (Figure 7.2). As it now stands, I cannot determine whether the previously reported Middle Woodland data truly reflect greater intracommunity dietary variation or whether they reflect some other factor (e.g., variation in preservation, extract quality, or sample measurement). Given such low variance within the "nonmaize" populations documented here, indicating that all individuals sampled within those communities were eating essentially the same isotopic diet, slight intercommunity differences may be more significant than traditionally assumed. Thus, even though the terrestrial vegetation is strongly $C_3$, variation in the local isotopic background may be discernible in bone "collagen" $\delta^{13}C$ values.

The implicit prevailing picture of dietary change associated with the appearance of maize farming is one of gradual, i.e., sympatric, change. That position holds that all members of the population ate essentially the same diet and all gradually increased their levels of maize consumption through time. Instead, the distribution of isotope values presented here suggests that an allopatric model might provide a better account of dietary change, i.e., some individuals changed their diets, experienced increased reproductive fitness, and replaced those who did not change their diets. I point to three pieces of evidence for this:

First, if sympatric change was involved, one might anticipate finding individuals with isotope values midway between the two extremes reflecting those individuals lacking maize in their diets and those highly dependent upon it. In this large sample that spans the relevant time period, *no* individuals were found with $\delta^{13}C$ values in the range between −19.04 and −13.44 $^o/_{oo}$. Second, Figure 7.5 also shows that there is considerable intercommunity variation in diet between occu-

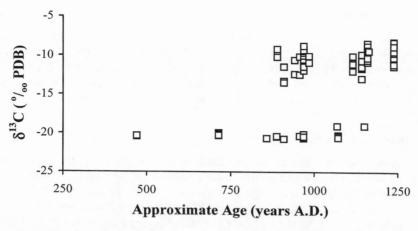

**Figure 7.5. Newly acquired stable carbon isotope ratios δ13C (º/ₒₒ PDB) versus approximate age. Plotted are 102 individuals from 19 deposits.**

pations of roughly the same age. Clearly, not all Ohio Valley communities were involved in the same subsistence systems during the Late Woodland and early Late Prehistoric time periods. Some individuals, who were not reliant on maize, continued to live in the region for a considerable time after maize farming was established.

Finally, the skeletal assemblages from some deposits (e.g., Turpin Stone Mound, Childers, and Cramer) are not consistent with the notion of a sympatric change in diet. Each of these assemblages contains individuals with radically different δ13C values. Maize is not a significant component of the diet for some individuals, while other individuals were highly committed to maize in their diets. It should be noted here that this distribution of δ13C values documented thus far does not correspond to sex or age at death of the individuals, nor is there evidence for unusual burial treatment that might indicate the presence of foreigners. This observation, of course, hinges on the assumption that the individuals within each of the three assemblages are contemporaries (see "Temporal Assessment" below).

How does this pattern of dietary change fit with our understanding of settlement change? I make two observations. First, the stable carbon isotope record is consistent with arguments that the initial appearance of nucleated sedentary settlements in the Ohio Valley was not tied to maize farming (Dunnell and Greenlee 1999; Wymer 1993). Second, the isotope record is consonant with the notion that maize farming was a factor in the later reappearance of sedentary villages in the early Late Prehistoric period (Cowan 1988; Fuller 1981). To further evaluate the role of dietary change in the settlement record of the region, however, requires the introduction of additional data beyond the scope of this chapter.

## FUTURE DIRECTIONS

Before the occurrence of nucleated sedentary villages can be explained, other kinds of data will need to be collected and integrated with the accumulating dietary evidence. Some of those data (e.g., from botanical and faunal remains, settlement location, and settlement structure) may be obtained from the published literature. Below, I briefly outline other issues that must be addressed.

### Temporal Assessment

Documenting changes in diet and settlement through time requires the construction of a sensitive chronology. Burial populations are typically assumed by archaeologists to be the same age as other, more frequently dated materials (e.g., wood charcoal) in associated deposits. Although this is not unreasonable in isolated, single-use mortuary contexts, the assumption is problematic for many settlements, because they have experienced multiple occupations. It is rarely certain to which occupation particular burials should be assigned. Additional difficulties result from the separation of domestic and mortuary activities that occurred during Ohio Valley prehistory. Burials may be temporally unrelated to domestic materials occurring at the same locale. To resolve this problem, dates should be obtained directly from the skeletal remains analyzed chemically. I have acquired radiocarbon dates on skeletal materials from seven of the deposits considered here. Of those seven cases, dates on human bone were in agreement with dates on associated wood charcoal for two locales; dates on bone were earlier than other estimates for two locales; and dates on bone were later than other estimates for three locales. Thus, the relationship between the age of settlement-related debris and skeletal remains varies. Clearly, this is an issue worthy of more attention.

### Demographic Structure

Analysis of DNA extracted from hard tissues, teeth in particular, may allow archaeologists to establish clearly the reproductive success of lineages. In the absence of DNA or skeletal nonmetric/metric traits to demonstrate the degree of relatedness between individuals, determining reproductive fitness in archaeological skeletal populations is a difficult proposition. The relative fitness associated with different settlement and dietary combinations will be reflected in the demographic structure and trajectories of the populations considered. Addressing the demographic structure of prehistoric groups requires inferences about trends in fertility, mortality, and evidence for generalized physiological stress ("health" indicators) on the basis of cross-sectional data from potentially biased mortuary populations. As recent papers indicate, this is not without problems (Cohen 1994; Goodman 1993; Wood and Milner 1994; Wood et al. 1992). Settlement counts, settlement areas, and roofed areas may be useful as a source of information about ordinal scale changes in relative population size and density (e.g., Ramenofsky 1987).

## Isotopic Analysis of Individual Amino Acids

The reliable detection of slight dietary differences through time and/or across environments might be aided by the isolation and isotopic analysis of individual amino acids. The isotopic signals obtained from individual amino acids in both modern and fossil animal bone collagen appear to record consistent patterns (Hare et al. 1991; Tuross et al. 1988; van Klinken 1991). In general, the isotope ratios of essential (must be nutritionally acquired) amino acids are more similar to those of the source protein than nonessential (can be synthesized by the body) amino acids. Thus, the isolation and analysis of individual, particularly essential, amino acids may provide increased dietary specificity beyond that of the bulk collagen extract. Isotopic analyses of individual amino acids on a sample of the individuals with bulk "collagen" data will be used to obtain more detailed dietary information.

This portion of the research design places demands on our background knowledge of diet-tissue relationships that are currently unmet. Pigs, unlike the small laboratory animals (e.g., mice, rats, chickens, and mink) and large free-ranging herbivores (e.g., deer and kudus) typically used in such research, have digestive tracts physiologically and anatomically similar to people. They are omnivores, too, and, as such, they have nutritional requirements like our own. Thus, pigs provide an excellent nutritional model for humans (e.g., Benevenga 1986; Fleming and Arce 1986; Reeds and Odle 1996) and they are the focus of the following controlled feeding study.

Twenty pigs were raised in a controlled environment at the Swine Research and Teaching Facility (in conjunction with ongoing research by Dr. John Froseth of Washington State University, Pullman, Wash.). They were randomly divided into four feed groups of five pigs each; each group was fed a nutritionally adequate feed that differed from the others in its isotopic composition. Once the pigs reached reproductive maturity, they were slaughtered and bone samples were collected for analysis, along with feed and water samples.

Analysis of the pig bones will allow detailed understanding of isotope fractionation between diet and skeletal tissues in a relevant nutritional surrogate. These data will add to our pool of knowledge about individual variation in digestion and metabolism for animals raised on constant diets. Controlled feeding studies, though, will not resolve the problem of equifinality, i.e., that many different diets may result in similar chemical signatures in bone. Therefore, appropriate use of these data does not attempt to reconstruct diet quantitatively based on isotopic signatures, but rather documents intracommunity variation in dietary patterns.

### Trace Element Analysis

As mentioned earlier, trace element analysis has great potential to contribute dietary data complementary to the isotope analysis. There are two substantial difficulties that must be overcome, however. First, there is the issue raised by Ezzo (1994) that we do not have sufficient understanding of trace element metabolism to use elements other than strontium or barium in dietary studies. Experimental feeding studies can help to guide efforts in building models that relate diet, metabolism, and tissue composition. The diets fed to the pigs in this research differed elementally as well as isotopically. Thus, I can examine the relationship between diet and skeletal tissues in terms of trace element metabolism.

The second issue involves the potential effects of post-depositional alterations on concentrations of trace elements in archaeological human skeletal materials from the region. Previously, I examined bone microstructure and chemical composition for bones from five locales (C.L. Lewis, Chilton, Childers, Cleek-McCabe, and Slone) of varying age and post-depositional context in the middle Ohio Valley (Figure 7.1; Greenlee 1996). Using backscattered electron images, like that in Figure 7.6, I documented the common occurrence of destructive foci,

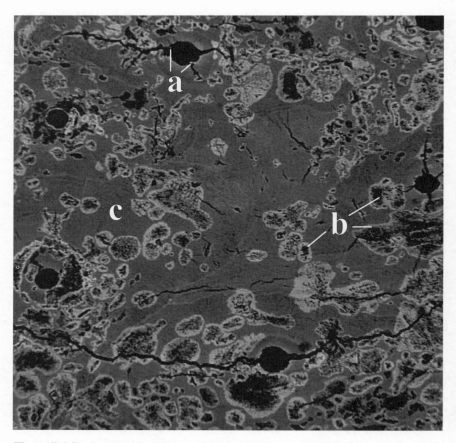

**Figure 7.6. Backscattered electron micrograph of an undecalcified transverse section of an archaeological bone illustrating the presence of a) contaminating particles, b) damage by soil microorganisms, and c) structurally intact bone.**

which are rounded, irregular blobs with hypermineralized borders that result from mineral dissolution associated with microorganismic activities and subsequent remineralization (e.g., Garland 1989; Hackett 1981; Hanson and Buikstra 1987). Even in poorly preserved bones, though, there are often pockets of structurally intact tissue (Figure 7.6).

X-ray maps and wavelength-dispersive spectrometry showed that some elements (e.g., Mn, Fe) are often highly concentrated in the recrystallized hydroxyapatite that marks the destructive foci, indicating that those areas are both chemically and structurally altered (Greenlee 1996). The structurally intact areas of bone, although compositionally less varied than the obviously altered areas, still evidenced post-depositional chemical alterations. A pilot study to test the efficacy of acetic acid washes in removing post-depositional chemical alterations is underway; preliminary results indicate that such pretreatments do not completely remove at least some kinds of post-depositional contamination found in these samples (Greenlee, unpublished data). These observations reflect only a very small sample, however, and additional work is necessary before any conclusions can be reached regarding the applicability of trace element analysis to this research problem.

## SIGNIFICANCE

I have outlined the necessary components of a research design constructed to document dietary change associated with the appearance and distribution of nucleated sedentary settlements in the middle and upper Ohio River Valley. I noted that nucleated sedentary settlements represent one settlement option that may arise for several reasons and that the cause(s) of settlement change may be established by examining several parameters, including settlement size and location, subsistence structure and content, and diet. Here, I emphasized the chemical characterization of human bone as a source of direct information about individual diet. When integrated with traditional sources of archaeological information, these data will provide critical information about the relationship between subsistence, settlement, diet, and the environment, thus shedding new light on an old problem—explaining the record of nucleated village settlement in the Eastern Woodlands. From a broader perspective, the more we know about the relationship between these critical parameters, the better prepared we will be to develop effective policies regarding such issues as population growth, natural resource use, and environmental quality that will determine the future of our species.

## ACKNOWLEDGMENTS

First, I thank R. C. Dunnell for his insightful guidance as this research project developed and I acknowledge M. J. O'Brien, R. D. Leonard, and the editors for helpful comments on earlier versions of this chapter. Of course, I accept full responsibility for any errors or omissions in this work. I also thank the staff of the

University of Washington Quaternary Isotope Laboratory, particularly M. Stuiver, P. J. Reimer, and T. L. Saling, for their assistance with collection of the stable carbon isotope data presented here. L. and N. Ericsson of AAA Laboratories generously assisted with the amino acid analyses. I gratefully acknowledge the cooperation of several institutions that provided skeletal specimens for the isotope analysis: the Carnegie Museum of Natural History, the Cincinnati Museum of Natural History, the Cleveland Museum of Natural History, the Glenn A. Black Laboratory of Archaeology at Indiana University, the Museum of Anthropology at the University of Kentucky, the Ohio Historical Society, and the U.S. Army Corps of Engineers, Huntington District. C. W. Cowan and P. S. Sciulli were especially helpful in identifying relevant skeletal populations. A portion of this research was supported by a National Science Foundation Graduate Fellowship and the chemical analyses were funded by NSF Dissertation Improvement Grant SBR-9310137, awarded to R. C. Dunnell for D. M. Greenlee. Finally, thanks to J. L. and G. T. Libby for helping in so many ways.

## NOTES

1. Stable carbon isotope ratios are expressed as delta ($\delta$) values in parts per thousand ($^o/_{oo}$) relative to the isotopic composition of a standard and are calculated as follows:

$$\delta^{13}C = \frac{\frac{^{13}C}{^{12}C}\text{sample} - \frac{^{13}C}{^{12}C}\text{standard}}{\frac{^{13}C}{^{12}C}\text{standard}} \times 1000$$

The standard, known as PDB, is a marine carbonate (belemnite) from the Peedee Formation of South Carolina; by convention, PDB has a $\delta^{13}C$ value of 0 $^o/_{oo}$ (Craig 1957). Because most materials have lower concentrations of $^{13}C$ than PDB, their $\delta^{13}C$ values are negative.

2. Some (e.g., Ambrose and Norr 1993; Hart 1999) have suggested that, because it incorporates $^{13}C$ from the entire diet and not just the protein fraction, the isotopic composition of the carbonate fraction of bone mineral might provide a more sensitive record of low-level maize consumption than that provided by "collagen." Where the two data sets have been compared in samples from the Eastern Woodlands (e.g., Schober and Ambrose 1995; Katzenberg and Harrison1999), the isotopic signals from carbonate have not indicated patterns of maize consumption different from those documented by collagen.

3. A malfunctioning electronic balance resulted in only a single yield measurement for one individual.

## REFERENCES CITED

Ahler, S. R.
  1987   Middle-Late Woodland Occupation at the Hansen Site, Greenup County, Kentucky. In *Current Archaeological Research in Kentucky,* Volume One, edited by D. Pollack, pp. 44–77. The Kentucky Heritage Council, Frankfort.
Ambrose, S. H.
  1987   Chemical and Isotopic Techniques of Diet Reconstruction in Eastern North America. In *Emergent Horticultural Economies of the Eastern Woodlands,* edited by W. F. Keegan, pp. 87–107. Center for Archaeological Investigations Occasional Paper No. 7. Southern Illinois University, Carbondale.
  1990   Preparation and Characterization of Bone and Tooth Collagen for Isotopic Analysis. *Journal of Archaeological Science* 17:431–451.
Ambrose, S. H., and L. Norr
  1992   On Stable Isotopic Data and Prehistoric Subsistence in the Soconusco Region. *Current Anthropology* 33:401–404.
  1993   Experimental Evidence for the Relationship of the Carbon Isotope Ratios of Whole Diet and Dietary Protein to Those of Bone Collagen and Carbonate. In *Prehistoric Human Bone: Archaeology at the Molecular Level,* edited by J. B. Lambert and G. Grupe, pp. 1–37. Springer Verlag, Berlin.
Bar-Yosef, O., and A. Belfer-Cohen
  1991   From Sedentary Hunter-Gatherers to Territorial Farmers in the Levant. In *Between Bands and States,* edited by S. A. Gregg, pp. 181–202. Center for Archaeological Investigations Occasional Paper No. 9. Southern Illinois University, Carbondale
Beardsley, R. K., P. Holder, A. D. Krieger, B. J. Meggers, J. B. Rinaldo, and P. Kutsche
  1955   Functional and Evolutionary Implications of Community Patterning. In *Seminars in Archaeology: 1955,* edited by R. Wauchope, pp. 129–157. Memoirs of the Society for American Archaeology, Number 11.
Beck, L. A.
  1985   Bivariate Analysis of Trace Elements in Bone. *Journal of Human Evolution* 14:493–502.
Bender, M. M., D. A. Baerreis, and R. L. Steventon
  1981   Further Light on Carbon Isotopes and Hopewell Agriculture. *American Antiquity* 46:346–353.
Benevenga, N. J.
  1986   Amino Acid Metabolism in Swine: Applicability to Normal and Altered Amino Acid Metabolism in Humans. In *Swine in Biomedical Research,* Volume 2, edited by M. E. Tumbleson, pp. 1017–1030. Plenum Press, New York.
Binford, L. R.
  1980   Willow Smoke and Dogs' Tails: Hunter-Gatherer Settlement Systems and Archaeological Site Formation. *American Antiquity* 45:4–20.
  1983   *In Pursuit of the Past: Decoding the Archaeological Record.* Thames and Hudson, New York.
Boutton, T. W., M. J. Lynott, and M. P. Bumsted
  1991   Stable Carbon Isotopes and the Study of Prehistoric Human Diet. *Critical Reviews in Food Science and Nutrition* 30:373–385.

Brashler, J. G., and D. M. Reed
    1991    Health and Status on the Eastern Periphery of Fort Ancient. *West Virginia Archeologist* 42:36–41.

Breitburg, E.
    1992    Vertebrate Faunal Remains. In *Fort Ancient Cultural Dynamics in the Middle Ohio Valley,* edited by A. G. Henderson, pp. 209–241. Monographs in World Archaeology, No. 8. Prehistory Press, Madison.

Broida, M.
    1983    *Maize in Kentucky Fort Ancient Diets: An Analysis of Carbon Isotope Ratios in Human Bone.* M. A. thesis, Department of Anthropology, University of Kentucky, Lexington.

Brose, D. S.
    1982    The Archaeological Investigation of a Fort Ancient Community Near Ohio Brush Creek, Adams County, Ohio. *Kirtlandia* 34:1–69.

Brown, A. B.
    1974    Bone Strontium as a Dietary Indicator in Human Skeletal Populations. *Contributions to Geology* 13:47–48.

Buikstra, J. E.
    1992    Diet and Disease in Late Prehistory. In *Disease and Demography in the Americas,* edited by J. W. Verano and D. H. Ubelaker, pp. 87–101. Smithsonian Institution, Washington, D.C.

Buikstra, J. E., W. Autry, E. Breitburg, L. Eisenberg, and N. van der Merwe
    1988    Diet and Health in the Nashville Basin: Human Adaptation and Maize Agriculture in Middle Tennessee. In *Diet and Subsistence: Current Archaeological Perspectives,* edited by B. V. Kennedy and G. M. LeMoine, pp. 243–259. Proceedings of the Nineteenth Annual Conference of the Archaeological Association of the University of Calgary. University of Calgary, Calgary.

Burton, J. H.
    1996    Trace Elements in Bone as Paleodietary Indicators. In *Archaeological Chemistry: Organic, Inorganic, and Biochemical Analysis,* edited by M. V. Orna, pp. 327–333. ACS Symposium Series 625. American Chemical Society, Washington, D.C.

Carskadden, J., and J. Morton
    1989    An Unusual Intrusive Mound Pipe from Dresden, Ohio. *Ohio Archaeologist* 39:4–7.

Cashdan, E.
    1992    Spatial Organization and Habitat Use. In *Evolutionary Ecology and Human Behavior,* edited by E. A. Smith and B. Winterhalder, pp. 237–266. Aldine de Gruyter, New York.

Cassidy, C. M.
    1984    Skeletal Evidence for Prehistoric Subsistence Adaptation in the Central Ohio River Valley. In *Paleopathology at the Origins of Agriculture,* edited by M. N. Cohen and G. J. Armelagos, pp. 307–341. Academic Press, Orlando.

Chapman, J., and G. D. Crites
    1987    Evidence for Early Maize (Zea mays) from the Ice House Bottom Site, Tennessee. *American Antiquity* 52:352–354.

Cleland, C. E.
    1976    The Focal-diffuse Model: An Evolutionary Perspective on the Prehistoric Cultural Adaptations of the Eastern United States. *Mid-Continental Journal of Archaeology* 1:59–78.

Cohen, M. N.

    1994   The Osteological Paradox Reconsidered. *Current Anthropology* 35:629–631.

Conard, A. R.

    1988   Analysis in Dietary Reconstruction. In *A History of 17 Years of Excavation and Reconstruction—a Chronicle of 12th Century Human Values and the Built Environment,* Volume One, edited by J. M. Heilman, M. C. Lileas, and C. A. Turnbow, pp. 112–156. Dayton Museum of Natural History, Dayton.

Cowan, C. W.

    1979   Excavations at the Haystack Rockshelters, Powell County, Kentucky. *Mid-Continental Journal of Archaeology* 4:3–33.

    1988   From Pithouse to Longhouse, from Community to Chaos: Late Prehistoric and Proto-historic Developments in the Middle Ohio Valley. Paper presented at the Midwest Archaeological Conference, Champaign-Urbana.

Craig, H.

    1957   Isotopic Standards for Carbon and Oxygen and Correction Factors for Mass-spectrometric Analysis of Carbon Dioxide. *Geochimica et Cosmochimica Acta* 12:133–149.

Dancey, W. S.

    1992   Village Origins in Central Ohio: The Results and Implications of Recent Middle and Late Woodland Research. In *Cultural Variability in Context: Woodland Settlements of the Mid-Ohio Valley,* edited by M. F. Seeman, pp. 24–29. MCJA Special Paper No. 7. Kent State University, Kent.

Deines, P.

    1980   The Isotopic Composition of Reduced Organic Carbon. In *Handbook of Environmental Isotope Geochemistry,* Volume One, edited by P. Fritz and J. C. Fontes, pp. 329–406. Elsevier, Amsterdam.

DeNiro, M. J.

    1985   Postmortem Preservation and Alteration of *in vivo* Bone Collagen Isotope Ratios in Relation to Palaeodietary Reconstruction. *Nature* 317:806–809.

DeNiro, M. J., and S. Epstein

    1978   Influence of Diet on the Distribution of Carbon Isotopes in Animals. *Geochimica et Cosmochimica Acta* 42:495–506.

    1981   Influence of Diet on the Distribution of Nitrogen Isotopes in Animals. *Geochimica et Cosmochimica Acta* 45:341–351.

DeNiro, M. J., M. J. Schoeninger, and C. A. Hastorf

    1985   Effect of Heating on the Stable Carbon and Nitrogen Isotope Ratios of Bone Collagen. *Journal of Archaeological Science* 12:1–7.

DeNiro, M. J., and S. Weiner

    1988   Chemical, Enzymatic and Spectroscopic Characterization of "Collagen" and Other Organic Fractions from Prehistoric Bones. *Geochimica et Cosmochimica Acta* 52:2197–2206.

Dunnell, R. C.

    1989   Aspects of the Application of Evolutionary Theory in Archaeology. In *Archaeological Thought in America,* edited by C. C. Lamberg-Karlovsky, pp. 35–49. Cambridge University, New York.

    1995   What Is It That Actually Evolves? In *Evolutionary Archaeology: Methodological Issues,* edited by P. A. Teltser, pp. 33–50. University of Arizona, Tucson.

    1998   Comment On: Cheating at Musical Chairs: Territoriality and Sedentism in an Evolutionary Context, by M. Rosenberg. *Current Anthropology* 39:667–668.

Dunnell, R. C., and D. M. Greenlee
    1999   Late Woodland Period "Waste" Reduction in the Ohio River Valley. *Journal of Anthropological Archaeology* 18:376–395.
Dunnell, R. C., and R. J. Wenke
    1979   An Evolutionary Model of the Development of Complex Society. Paper presented at the Annual Meeting of the American Association for the Advancement of Science, San Francisco.
Essenpreis, P. S.
    1978   Fort Ancient Settlement: Differential Response at a Mississippian-Late Woodland Interface. In *Mississippian Settlement Patterns,* edited by B. D. Smith, pp. 141–167. Academic Press, New York.
Ezzo, J. A.
    1994   Putting the "Chemistry" Back into Archaeological Bone Chemistry Analysis: Modeling Potential Paleodietary Indicators. *Journal of Anthropological Archaeology* 13:1–34.
Farrow, D. C.
    1986   A Study of Monongahela Subsistence Patterns Based on Mass Spectrometric Analysis. *Mid-Continental Journal of Archaeology* 11:153–179.
Fleming, S. E., and D. Arce
    1986   Using the Pig to Study Digestion and Fermentation in the Gut. In *Swine in Biomedical Research,* Volume 1, edited by M. E. Tumbleson, pp. 123–134. Plenum Press, New York.
Ford, R. I.
    1974   Northeastern Archaeology: Past and Future Directions. *Annual Review of Anthropology* 3:385–413.
Frisch, R. E.
    1975   Demographic Implications of the Biological Determinants of Female Fecundity. *Social Biology* 22:17–22.
    1977   Critical Weights, a Critical Body Composition, Menarche, and the Maintenance of Menstrual Cycles. In *Biosocial Interrelations in Population Adaptation,* edited by E. S. Watts, F. E. Johnston, and G. W. Lasker, pp. 319–352. Mouton, The Hague.
Fuller, J. W.
    1981   *Developmental Change in Prehistoric Community Patterns: The Development of Nucleated Village Communities in Northern West Virginia.* Ph.D. dissertation, Department of Anthropology, University of Washington, Seattle.
Garland, A. N.
    1989   Microscopical Analysis of Fossil Bone. *Applied Geochemistry* 4:215–229.
Graybill, J. R.
    1981   The Eastern Periphery of Fort Ancient (A.D. 1050–1650): A Diachronic Approach to Settlement Variability. Ph.D. dissertation, Department of Anthropology, University of Washington, Seattle.
Greenlee, D. M.
    1990   *Environmental and Temporal Variability in δ¹³C Values in Late Prehistoric Subsistence Systems in the Upper Ohio Valley.* Paper presented for the M.A., Department of Anthropology, University of Washington, Seattle.
    1996   An Electron Microprobe Evaluation of Diagenetic Alteration in Archaeological Bone. In *Archaeological Chemistry: Organic, Inorganic, and Biochemical Analysis,*

edited by M. V. Orna, pp. 334–354. ACS Symposium Series 625. American Chemical Society, Washington, D.C.

2000 Changes in Vertebrate Faunal Exploitation with the Appearance of Maize Farming in the Ohio Valley. In *Explanations of Change: Case Studies in Evolutionary Archaeology,* edited by R. C. Dunnell and R. D. Leonard. (Manuscript in review.)

Griffin, J. B.

1967 Eastern North American Archaeology: A Summary. *Science* 156:175–191.

Grupe, G.

1988 Impact of the Choice of Bone Samples on Trace Element Data in Excavated Human Skeletons. *Journal of Archaeological Science* 15:123–129.

Hackett, C. J.

1981 Microscopical Focal Destruction (Tunnels) in Exhumed Human Bones. *Medicine, Science, and the Law* 21:243–265.

Hanson, D., and J. E. Buikstra

1987 Histomorphological Alteration in Buried Human Bone from the Lower Illinois Valley: Implications for Paleodietary Research. *Journal of Archaeological Science* 14:549–563.

Hare, P. E.

1980 Organic Geochemistry of Bone and its Relation to the Survival of Bone in the Natural Environment. In *Fossils in the Making: Vertebrate Taphonomy and Paleoecology,* edited by A. K. Behrensmeyer and A. P. Hill, pp. 208–219. University of Chicago Press, Chicago.

Hare, P. E., M. L. Fogel, T. W. Stafford, Jr., A. D. Mitchell, and T. C. Hoering

1991 The Isotopic Composition of Carbon and Nitrogen in Individual Amino Acids Isolated from Modern and Fossil Proteins. *Journal of Archaeological Science* 18:277–292.

Hart, J. P.

1993 Monongahela Subsistence-settlement Change: The Late Prehistoric Period in the Lower Upper Ohio River Valley. *Journal of World Prehistory* 7:71–120.

1995 Storage and Monongahela Subsistence-settlement Change. *Archaeology of Eastern North America* 23:41–56.

1999 Maize Agriculture Evolution in the Eastern Woodlands of North America: A Darwinian Perspective. *Journal of Archaeological Method and Theory* 6:137–180.

Hatch, J. W., and R. A. Geidel

1983 Tracing Status and Diet in Prehistoric Tennessee. *Archaeology* 36:56–59.

Hedges, R. E. M., and G. J. van Klinken

1992 A Review of Current Approaches in the Pretreatment of Bone for Radiocarbon Dating by AMS. *Radiocarbon* 34:279–291.

Heffley, S.

1981 The Relationship between Northern Athapaskan Settlement Patterns and Resource Distribution: An Application of Horn's Model. In *Hunter-Gatherer Foraging Strategies: Ethnographic and Archeological Analyses*, edited by B. Winterhalder and E. A. Smith, pp. 126–147. University of Chicago Press, Chicago.

Henderson, A. G. (editor)

1992 *Fort Ancient Cultural Dynamics in the Middle Ohio Valley*. Monographs in World Archaeology, No. 8. Prehistory Press, Madison.

Jochim, M. A.
  1981   *Strategies for Survival: Cultural Behavior in an Ecological Context.* Academic Press, New York.
Jones, J.
  1978   A Preliminary Report on a Puzzling Single-component Woodland Site in Southwestern Ohio. *Ohio Archaeologist* 28:17–20.
  1979   Clark Site Ware: Southwestern Ohio Pottery Related to Central Indiana Late Woodland. *Ohio Archaeologist* 29:20–24.
Katzenberg, M. A.
  1984   *Chemical Analysis of Prehistoric Human Bone from Five Temporally Distinct Populations in Southern Ontario.* National Museum of Man Mercury Series, Paper No. 129. Archaeological Survey of Canada.
  1989   Stable Isotope Analysis of Archaeological Faunal Remains from Southern Ontario. *Journal of Archaeological Science* 16:319–329.
  1993   Age Differences and Population Variation in Stable Isotope Values from Ontario, Canada. In *Prehistoric Human Bone: Archaeology at the Molecular Level,* edited by J. B. Lambert and G. Grupe, pp. 39–62. Springer Verlag, Berlin.
Katzenberg, M. A., and R. Harrison
  1999   Further Evidence for the Adoption of Maize in Southern Ontario Using Stable Carbon Isotopes in Bone Carbonate. Paper presented at the 64th Annual Meeting of the Society for American Archaeology, Chicago.
Kelly, R. L.
  1992   Mobility/Sedentism: Concepts, Archaeological Measures, and Effects. *Annual Review of Anthropology* 21:43–66.
Kent, S.
  1986   The Influence of Sedentism and Aggregation on Porotic Hyperostosis and Anaemia: A Case Study. *Man* 21:605–636.
Keys, A., J. Brozek, A. Henschel, O. Mickelsen, and H. L. Taylor
  1950   *The Biology of Human Starvation,* Volume One. University of Minnesota, Minneapolis.
Lambert, J. B., S. V. Simpson, C. B. Szpunar, and J. E. Buikstra
  1984   Ancient Human Diet from Inorganic Analysis of Bone. *Accounts of Chemical Research* 17:298–305.
Lambert, J. B., S. M. Vlasak, A. C. Thometz, and J. E. Buikstra
  1982   A Comparative Study of the Chemical Analysis of Ribs and Femurs in Woodland Populations. *American Journal of Physical Anthropology* 59:289–294.
Lambert, J. B., and J. M. Weydert-Homeyer
  1993   The Fundamental Relationship between Ancient Diet and the Inorganic Constituents of Bone as Derived from Feeding Experiments. *Archaeometry* 35:279–294.
Lee, R. B.
  1972a The Intensification of Social Life among the !Kung Bushmen. In *Population Growth: Anthropological Implications,* edited by B. Spooner, pp. 343–350. MIT Press, Cambridge, Massachusetts.
  1972b Population Growth and the Beginnings of Sedentary Life among the !Kung Bushmen. In *Population Growth: Anthropological Implications*, edited by B. Spooner, pp. 329–342. MIT Press, Cambridge, Massachusetts.

Lipo, C. P., M. E. Madsen, R. C. Dunnell, and T. Hunt
  1997   Population Structure, Cultural Transmission, and Frequency Seriation. *Journal of Anthropological Archaeology* 16:301–333.
Masters, P. M.
  1987   Preferential Preservation of Noncollagenous Protein during Bone Diagenesis: Implications for Chronometric and Stable Isotopic Measurements. *Geochimica et Cosmochimica Acta* 51:3209–3214.
McLester, J. S.
  1949   *Nutrition and Diet in Health and Disease.* 5th ed. W. B. Saunders, Philadelphia.
Morton, J.
  1984   Toward a Late Woodland Taxonomy for the Central Muskingum Valley. *Ohio Archaeologist* 34:41–47.
Nass, J. P., Jr.
  1995   An Examination of Social, Economic, and Political Organization at the Throckmorton Site, a Monongahela Community in Greene County, Pennsylvania. *Archaeology of Eastern North America* 23:81–93.
Oetelaar, G. A.
  1990   Faunal Analysis. In *Childers and Woods: Two Late Woodland Sites in the Upper Ohio Valley, Mason County, West Virginia,* edited by M. J. Shott, pp. 617–690. Program for Cultural Resource Assessment Archaeological Report 200. University of Kentucky, Lexington.
O'Leary, M. H.
  1981   Carbon Isotope Fractionation in Plants. *Phytochemistry* 20:553–567.
  1988   Carbon Isotopes in Photosynthesis. *BioScience* 38:328–336.
Ormerod, D. E.
  1983   *White Rocks: A Woodland Rockshelter in Monroe County, Ohio.* Research Papers in Archaeology, Number 4. Kent State University, Kent.
Pebley, A., S. Huffman, A. Chowdhury, and P. Stupp
  1985   Intrauterine Mortality and Maternal Nutritional Status in Rural Bangladesh. *Population Studies* 39:425–440.
Perzigian, A. J., P. A. Tench, and D. J. Braun
  1984   Prehistoric Health in the Ohio River Valley. In *Paleopathology at the Origins of Agriculture,* edited by M. N. Cohen and G. J. Armelagos, pp. 347–366. Academic Press, Orlando.
Price, T. D.
  1985   Late Archaic Subsistence in the Midwestern United States. *Journal of Human Evolution* 14:449–459.
Price, T. D., J. Blitz, J. Burton, and J. A. Ezzo
  1992   Diagenesis in Prehistoric Bone: Problems and Solutions. *Journal of Archaeological Science* 19:513–529.
Price, T. D., M. Connor, and J. D. Parsen
  1985   Bone Chemistry and the Reconstruction of Diet: Strontium Discrimination in White-tailed Deer. *Journal of Archaeological Science* 12:419–422.
Prufer, O. H.
  1967   Chesser Cave: A Late Woodland Phase in Southeastern Ohio. In *Studies in Ohio Archaeology,* edited by O. H. Prufer and D. H. McKenzie, pp. 1–62. Western Reserve University, Cleveland.

1981   *Raven Rocks: A Specialized Late Woodland Rockshelter Occupation in Belmont County, Ohio.* Research Papers in Archaeology, Number 1. Kent State University, Kent.

Prufer, O. H., and D. H. McKenzie
1966   Peters Cave: Two Woodland Occupations in Ross County, Ohio. *The Ohio Journal of Science* 66:233–253.

Radosevich, S. C.
1993   The Six Deadly Sins of Trace Element Analysis: A Case of Wishful Thinking in Science. In *Investigations of Ancient Human Tissue: Chemical Analyses in Anthropology,* edited by M. K. Sandford, pp. 269–332. Gordon and Breach, Langhorne, Pennsylvania.

Rafferty, J. E.
1985   The Archaeological Record on Sedentariness: Recognition, Development, and Implications. In *Advances in Archaeological Method and Theory,* edited by M. B. Schiffer, pp. 113–156. Academic Press, New York.

Railey, J. A.
1984   *The Pyles Site (15MS28): A Newtown Village in Mason County, Kentucky.* Occasional Paper 1, William S. Webb Archaeological Society, Lexington.

Ramenofsky, A. F.
1987   *Vectors of Death: The Archaeology of European Contact.* University of New Mexico Press, Albuquerque.

Reeds, P., and J. Odle
1996   Pigs as Models for Nutrient Functional Interaction. In *Advances in Swine in Biomedical Research,* Volume 2, edited by M. E. Tumbleson and L. B. Schook, pp. 709–711. Plenum Press, New York.

Rice, G. E.
1975   *A Systematic Explanation of a Change in Mogollon Settlement Patterns.* Ph.D. dissertation, Department of Anthropology, University of Washington, Seattle.

Rosenberg, M.
1998   Cheating at Musical Chairs: Territoriality and Sedentism in an Evolutionary Context. *Current Anthropology* 39:653–681.

Rossen, J.
1992   Botanical Remains. In *Fort Ancient Cultural Dynamics in the Middle Ohio Valley,* edited by A. G. Henderson, pp. 189–208. Monographs in World Archaeology, No. 8. Prehistory Press, Madison, Wisconsin.

Schneider, K. N.
1986   Dental Caries, Enamel Composition, and Subsistence among Prehistoric Amerindians of Ohio. *American Journal of Physical Anthropology* 71:95–102

Schober, T. M., and S. H. Ambrose
1995   Reevaluation of Maize Introduction in West-Central Illinois: The Evidence of Bone Carbonate and Collagen. Paper presented at the 60th Annual Meeting of the Society for American Archaeology, Minneapolis, Minnesota.

Schoeninger, M. J.
1979   Diet and Status at Chalcatzingo: Some Empirical and Technical Aspects of Strontium Analysis. *American Journal of Physical Anthropology* 51:295–310.

Schoeninger, M. J., K. M. Moore, M. L. Murray, and J. D. Kingston
1989   Detection of Bone Preservation in Archaeological and Fossil Samples. *Applied Geochemistry* 4:281–292.

Schurr, M. R., and M. J. Schoeninger
1995 Associations Between Agricultural Intensification and Social Complexity: An Example from the Prehistoric Ohio Valley. *Journal of Anthropological Research* 14:315–339.
Schwarcz, H. P., J. Melbye, M. A. Katzenberg, and M. Knyf
1985 Stable Isotopes in Human Skeletons of Southern Ontario: Reconstructing Palaeodiet. *Journal of Archaeological Science* 12:187–206.
Seeman, M. F.
1980 A Taxonomic Review of Southern Ohio Late Woodland. Paper presented at the Midwest Archaeological Conference, Chicago.
1992 The Bow and Arrow, the Intrusive Mound Complex, and a Late Woodland Jack's Reef Horizon in the Mid-Ohio Valley. In *Cultural Variability in Context: Woodland Settlements of the Mid-Ohio Valley,* edited by M. F. Seeman, pp. 41–51. MCJA Special Paper No. 7. Kent State University, Kent.
Shott, M. J.
1990 *Childers and Woods: Two Late Woodland Sites in the Upper Ohio Valley, Mason County, West Virginia.* Program for Cultural Resource Assessment Archaeological Report 200. University of Kentucky, Lexington.
Sillen, A., and M. Kavanagh
1982 Strontium and Paleodietary Research: A Review. *Yearbook of Physical Anthropology* 25:67–90.
Smith, B. D.
1992 *Rivers of Change: Essays on Early Agriculture in Eastern North America.* Smithsonian Institution, Washington, D.C.
Smith, B. N., and S. Epstein
1971 Two Categories of $^{13}C/^{12}C$ Ratios for Higher Plants. *Plant Physiology* 47:380–384.
Smyth, M. P.
1989 Domestic Storage Behavior in Mesoamerica: An Ethnoarchaeological Approach. In *Archaeological Method and Theory,* Volume 1, edited by M. B. Schiffer, pp. 89–138. University of Arizona Press, Tucson.
Stafford, T. W., Jr., K. Brendel, and R. C. Duhamel
1988 Radiocarbon, $^{13}C$ and $^{15}N$ Analysis of Fossil Bone: Removal of Humates with XAD-2 Resin. *Geochimica et Cosmochimica Acta* 52:2257–2267.
Stein, Z., and M. Susser
1975 Fertility, Fecundity, Famine: Food Rations in the Dutch Famine 1944/5 Have a Causal Relation to Fertility, and Probably Fecundity. *Human Biology* 47:131–154.
Testart, A.
1982 The Significance of Food Storage among Hunter-Gatherers: Residence Patterns, Population Densities, and Social Inequities. *Current Anthropology* 25:523–537.
Tieszen, L. L., and T. Fagre
1993 Effect of Diet Quality and Composition on the Isotopic Composition of Respiratory $CO_2$, Bone Collagen, Bioapatite, and Soft Tissues. In *Prehistoric Human Bone: Archaeology at the Molecular Level,* edited by J. B. Lambert and G. Grupe, pp. 121–155. Springer Verlag, Berlin.
Trigger, B. G.
1968 The Determinants of Settlement Patterns. In *Settlement Archaeology,* edited by K. C. Chang, pp. 53–78. National Press Books, Palo Alto.

Turnbow, C. A., C. E. Jobe, and N. O'Malley
    1983    Archaeological Excavations of the Goolman, Devary, and Stone Sites in Clark County, Kentucky. Program for Cultural Resource Assessment Archaeological Report 78. University of Kentucky, Lexington.
Tuross, N., M. L. Fogel, and P. E. Hare
    1988    Variability in the Preservation of the Isotopic Composition of Collagen from Fossil Bone. *Geochimica et Cosmochimica Acta* 52:929–935.
van der Merwe, N. J., and J. C. Vogel
    1978    ¹³C Content of Human Collagen as a Measure of Prehistoric Diet in Woodland North America. *Nature* 276:815–816.
van Klinken, G. J.
    1991    *Dating and Dietary Reconstruction by Isotopic Analysis of Amino Acids in Fossil Bone Collagen—with Special Reference to the Caribbean.* Uitgaven Natuurwetenschappelijke Studiekring voor het Caraïbisch Gebied, Amsterdam.
Vogel, J. C.
    1978    Isotopic Assessment of the Dietary Habits of Ungulates. *South African Journal of Science* 74:298–301.
Wagner, G. E.
    1983    Fort Ancient Subsistence: The Botanical Record. *West Virginia Archeologist* 35:27–39.
    1987    *Uses of Plants by the Fort Ancient Indians.* Ph.D. dissertation, Department of Anthropology, Washington University, St. Louis.
Watson, P. J.
    1989    Early Plant Cultivation in the Eastern Woodlands of North America. In *Foraging and Farming: The Evolution of Plant Exploitation,* edited by D. R. Harris and G. C. Hillman, pp. 555–571. One World Archaeology Series, No. 13. Unwin Hyman, London.
Whitlam, R. G.
    1981    *Settlement-subsistence System Type Occurrence and Change in Coastal Environments: A Global Archaeological Perspective.* Ph.D. dissertation, Department of Anthropology, University of Washington, Seattle.
Wood, J. W., and G. R. Milner
    1994    Reply To: The Osteological Paradox Reconsidered, by M. N. Cohen. *Current Anthropology* 35:631–637.
Wood, J. W., G. R. Milner, H. C. Harpending, and K. M. Weiss
    1992    The Osteological Paradox: Problems of Inferring Prehistoric Health from Skeletal Samples. *Current Anthropology* 33:343–370.
Woodhead-Galloway, J.
    1980    *Collagen: The Anatomy of a Protein.* The Institute of Biology's Studies in Biology, No. 117. Edward Arnold, London.
Wymer, D. A.
    1992    Trends and Disparities: The Woodland Paleoethnobotanical Record of the Mid-Ohio Valley. In *Cultural Variability in Context: Woodland Settlements of the Mid-Ohio Valley,* edited by M. F. Seeman, pp. 65–76. MCJA Special Paper No. 7. Kent State University, Kent.
    1993    Cultural Change and Subsistence: The Middle and Late Woodland Transition in the Mid-Ohio Valley. In *Foraging and Farming in the Eastern Woodlands,* edited by C. M. Scarry, pp. 138–156. University Press of Florida, Gainesville.

# 8

# Resource Intensification and Late Holocene Human Impacts on Pacific Coast Bird Populations: Evidence from the Emeryville Shellmound Avifauna

## Jack M. Broughton

## INTRODUCTION

Anthropologists and conservation biologists have commonly assumed that the distributions and abundances of vertebrate resources recorded during the early historic period in North America reflected a "pristine" condition. This view follows from the perception that Native American population densities and technological capabilities were simply too low to deplete or extirpate vertebrate populations, or, alternatively, that native peoples were "children of nature" and the original conservationists (Alvard 1993, 1994; Kay 1994). In fact, these perceptions underlie modern wildlife management policies and practices. For example, because pre-Columbian environments are routinely viewed as "primordial wilderness" (Hewes 1973:150), restoring ecosystems to their "original condition" simply requires the elimination of European influences; this is the principle behind "hands-off" or "natural regulation" management (Kay 1994).

This traditional view has, however, been recently challenged on theoretical as well as empirical grounds in several contexts in western North America (e.g., Broughton 1994a, 1994b, 1995, 1997; Hildebrandt and Jones 1992; Jones and Hildebrandt 1995; Kay 1994). And since aboriginal human population densities were extremely high in prehistoric California (Cook 1976), it is not surprising that late Holocene California has been the focus of many of these recent challenges.

In the California setting, recent evidence for human impacts on prehistoric faunas has emerged from analyses of vertebrate remains from late Holocene archaeological sites. These analyses have documented steadily declining abundances of *large-sized* prey species from environmentally distinct regions throughout the state (see Broughton 1994a, 1994b, 1995, 1999; Grayson 1991; Hildebrandt and Jones 1992; Jones and Hildebrandt 1995). Most of these analyses have been conducted in the context of evaluating ecologically oriented models of subsistence change, and all have concluded that the documented declines in the archaeological abundances of large prey are a function of expanding prehistoric forager densities and game depletion.

The ecological models that underlie these analyses suggest that late prehistoric subsistence adaptations in California were characterized by a focus on low-return resources and that significant decreases in foraging efficiency occurred during the late Holocene (Basgall 1987; Beaton 1991; Bettinger 1991; Cohen 1981). As human population densities increased steadily during the late Holocene, some argue, the per capita and/or absolute abundances of such high-return resources as large-bodied terrestrial herbivores decreased. As a result, diets expanded to include higher frequencies of such smaller, lower-return resources as molluscs, smaller fishes, and acorns. These hypothetical models suggest the occurrence of *resource intensification*, classically defined as a process by which the total productivity per areal unit of land is increased at the expense of overall declines in return rates or foraging efficiency (Boserup 1965; Earle 1980). Insofar as declining per capita efficiencies in resource extraction implies decreases in average fitness among individuals in these populations, the widening of diet breadths can be seen to predict changes in other aspects of local human behavior and morphology. These range from higher levels of morbidity and mortality and smaller body size and stature, to changes in technology reflecting increasing investments in the processing of (as opposed to the search for) resources (see Hawkes and O'Connell 1992; Broughton and O'Connell 1999).

While recent analyses of archaeological vertebrate faunas from California have documented that late Holocene human populations of this region appear to have had substantial impacts on both terrestrial and marine fish and mammal populations, ultimately driving dramatic declines in foraging efficiency, evidence for harvest pressure on waterfowl and seabird populations in these settings has yet to be provided. Indeed, outside of oceanic island settings (see Steadman 1995 and references therein), there are as yet no well-described cases documenting that prehistoric foragers ever had substantial impacts on any avian population worldwide.

Through the integration of models drawn from evolutionary ecology and demography, I derive testable hypotheses that pertain to the nature of avian prey choice under conditions of expanding forager densities and declining foraging return rates. I propose that declining efficiencies in bird exploitation should be signaled by 1. decreasing abundances of large-sized prey types among sets of taxa occurring in the same local resource patches; and/or 2. increasing abundances of species that inhabit resource patches located far from a particular site locality. Additionally, harvest pressure on exploited avian populations should be indicated by declines in the mean age of individuals in a population. Analyses of the taxonomic composition and age structure of seabird and waterfowl materials from deeply stratified and well-dated late Holocene residential village sites, such as the Emeryville Shellmound of the San Francisco Bay, will thus allow fine-scale evaluations of the long-term dynamics of avian exploitation by populations of prehistoric human foragers. This research will have far-reaching implications not only for the management of resources and ecosystems currently threatened by human-caused habitat alteration, but for models involving the nature and causes of change in the behavior of prehistoric hunter-gatherers as well.

## ARCHAEOLOGICAL VERTEBRATE MEASURES OF FORAGING EFFICIENCY AND HARVEST PRESSURE

### Taxonomic Composition and Foraging Efficiency

Resource intensification models posited for California predict declines in foraging efficiency during the late Holocene. Efficiency refers to the overall net rate of return associated with a particular strategy of resource exploitation. Therefore, measuring foraging efficiency from archaeological faunas minimally requires consideration of the relative abundances of prey types with distinct differences in energetic returns. The prey and patch models of optimal foraging theory provide a framework for assessing the relative costs and benefits of exploiting different prey resources and patch types (see Stephens and Krebs 1986 and references therein) and, ultimately, the derivation of archaeological vertebrate measures of foraging efficiency.

The *fine-grained prey model*, or simply the prey model, was designed to predict prey selection by predators foraging within more or less homogeneous resource patches. The model assumes that foragers are designed by natural selection to maximize the long-term net rate of energy capture and that prey are encountered sequentially and taken one at a time. Initially, the various prey types potentially exploited by a predator are ranked according to their profitability. The model predicts that the most profitable or highest-ranked prey will be taken whenever they are encountered, while prey of lower rank may or may not be selected, depending on the abundance of the highest-ranked prey. Prey ranks are defined as a ratio of the net value gained by acquiring a prey item, on the one hand, to the time costs of pursuing and processing the prey once it has been encountered, on the other. Prey ranks are, thus, established independent of encounter rates of prey taxa. Prey selection, however, *is* fully dependent on the encounter rates of prey. As the encounter rates of higher-ranked prey decrease, prey are added to the diet sequentially in order of decreasing rank (see Stephens and Krebs 1986:17–24). From this, it follows that the relative frequency with which high- and low-ranked prey are selected within a given resource patch can provide an index of foraging or predation efficiency. Other things being equal (see below), a diet dominated by high-ranked prey indicates a higher energetic return per unit foraging time relative to a diet dominated by low-ranked prey.

However, for the relative abundances of differently ranked prey to be a measure of foraging efficiency, the stringent assumptions of the prey model must be met. The *fine-grained search* assumption is particularly important in this context. This assumption stipulates that all prey types must be sought simultaneously, and randomly encountered, within a more or less homogenous resource patch. This assumption is critical because it allows search, travel, and transport time to be detached from specific prey types and assigned to the set of resources as a whole. Thus, it is possible to predict that prey types will be added to or dropped from the optimal diet strictly as a function of their post-encounter return rates (Smith 1991:206; see also Cannon in press).

The fine-grained search assumption may seem to be particularly unrealistic for hunter-gatherers: Are all resources in the diet ever searched for simultaneously in the fine-grained manner required by the prey model? Clearly they are not. This issue, as Smith (1991:207) notes, has led to two mistakes. First, many researchers, and virtually all archaeologists, have completely ignored this assumption in testing implications of the prey model. Unfortunately, such an approach can easily lead to fallacious conclusions. Second, some researchers have found the limitations posed by this assumption insurmountable, suggesting the prey model cannot be applied when prey are distributed heterogeneously in a given environment (e.g., Belovsky 1987).

Smith (1991:207) reasons correctly that both approaches are inappropriate and provides a general strategy for applying the prey model among foragers utilizing a patchy environment:

the most useful approach is to define the foraging decision hierarchically, applying the fine-grained prey model only *within each patch* (where patches are defined so as to have fine-grained encounter patterns). And in cases in which foraging techniques and capabilities differ even within a patch, the model must be applied anew to each *hunt type*.

Applications of the prey model to archaeological settings would, thus, require that subsets of resources be assigned to discrete patches or *hunt types*. In practice, this will require separate analyses for prey types that occupied distinct habitat types and/or were likely pursued and captured with different methods and technologies. Addressing changes in the relative frequencies of prey resources that occurred in *different* hunt types or patches falls under the purview of patch-use models discussed below.

To the extent that an approximation of fine-grained search is met for prey resources handled singly with broadly similar methods, and taken within the same habitat type directly adjacent to a site locality, the relative abundances of high-and low-ranked prey types selected from such habitats can be a valid measure of foraging efficiency. Prey rank estimates are, thus, an important first step toward measuring foraging efficiency in archaeological faunas.

Prey ranks can be established empirically through actual measurement of pursuit and processing times and returns in actual tests of foraging models. However, animal ecologists often rely on proxy measures of prey rank when actual return rates cannot be measured. The most common proxy measure of prey rank is the *body size* of prey items (see Broughton 1994a, 1994b; 1995, 1997; Broughton and Grayson 1993). Figure 8.1 illustrates the hypothetical relationships between the critical variables that affect prey rank (following Bayham 1982; Griffiths 1975). Figure 8.1a depicts the energetic *value* of an organism as more or less directly proportional to its weight. In conjunction with the energy value of an item, consideration must also be given to absolute *costs* as a function of prey body size. Foraging theorists have proposed that pursuit and processing costs are at a minimum for certain intermediate body sizes, with increases incurred at the small and large end of the size spectrum (Figure 8.1b). In other words, there are upper and lower limits on the sizes of prey that a given predator species can efficiently capture and process for consumption: Extremely large and small prey require higher absolute pursuit and processing costs per item. The difference between the energy gain and cost curves represents the net energy gain per individual prey item (Figure 8.1c). The shape of this hypothetical curve is particularly important, for it specifies the relative overall energetic returns of a prey item as function of body size; consequently, it may serve as an indication of prey rank. As depicted in Figure 8.1c, for a large size range of prey species, the order of prey rank is the same as the order of prey size: large prey are high-ranked, while small prey are low-ranked.

While this simplified relationship between prey body size and prey profitability is strictly hypothetical, the basic relationship has strong support from empirical research on a diverse array of predatory species, including people (e.g., Alvard 1993; Bird 1996; Hill et al., 1987; Simms 1987; Smith 1991). At least among the size range of vertebrate species that occurred during the late Holocene in western North America, the larger the animal, the higher the post-encounter return rate (Broughton 1999).

While the extant data show that prey body mass and return rates are positively correlated, suggesting that prey size is probably the most important variable influencing profitability, some variation in return rates exists beyond that contained in body weight differences. That is, prey of the same body weight, whether from the same or different species, can potentially yield variable post-encounter return rates. This may be due to variation in either the handling costs or the energetic values of prey types. Variation in fat content, for example, has been shown to be especially critical in affecting differences in return rates for similarly sized prey items

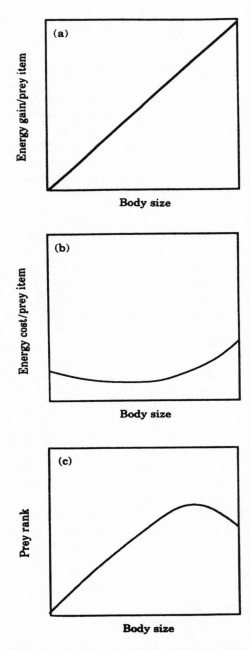

Figure 8.1. The hypothetical relationship between a) prey body size and energy gain; b) prey body size and energy cost; and c) prey body size and prey rank (see text for explanation; adapted from Griffiths 1975; Bayham 1982).

(see Hill et al. 1987; Kelly 1995; Smith 1991; see also Speth 1990; Speth and Spielmann 1983 for the nutritional importance of fat). Similarly, intra-annual variation in the flight or defense mechanisms of single prey species has been shown to affect substantial differences in their return rates across seasons. For instance, the handling times for Canada Geese *(Branta canadensis)* decline significantly during the summer molt when these birds temporarily become flightless (Smith 1991). As a result, the post-encounter returns for Canada Geese are substantially higher during the summer molt period than at other times of the year.

Handling costs for different prey types may also be differentially affected by changes in capture technologies. The introduction of netting or harpoon technologies, for example, might reduce handling times associated with the capture of specific aquatic and/or avian prey types (see Kelly 1995:80 for additional examples).

In sum, while body size is probably the best context-independent measure of prey rank available to archaeologists, this "rule of thumb" should be viewed with some caution. Indeed, in any particular setting, factors such as fat content and/or other peculiarities in the defense mechanisms of particular taxa can be examined and the body size-return rate generalization adjusted accordingly. Similarly, changes in archaeological tool assemblages can be monitored to evaluate changes in handling costs of specific prey resources.

Since the prey model predicts that the highest-ranked taxa should be attacked whenever they are encountered, large-sized prey species should be the most susceptible to population declines due to human foraging activities, other things being equal. A reduction in the densities and/or capturability of prey resources within patches is known as *resource depression* (Charnov et al. 1976; see also Cannon in press). This phenomenon is due to direct harvesting of prey, to increased wariness of the prey species due to the continued presence of predators, and/or to local movements of prey species out of areas densely inhabited by predators. Resource depression is especially pronounced where dense, expanding predator populations forage from a central base (Charnov et al. 1976). The depression of prey within resource patches directly adjacent to a residential base has implications for changes in patch-use strategies in the wider environment surrounding a locality.

Charnov's (1976) patch-use model, the *marginal value theorem*, addresses the decision of how long predators should forage in different resource patches within their range. The key prediction derived from this model is that a forager should depart a depleting patch when the return rate drops to the average return rate for all of the patches in the habitat as a whole. It follows that the depression of resource patches adjacent to a site locality should drive an increasing use of distant, less-depleted patches. Indeed, this phenomenon has been empirically documented in several ethnographic settings (Hames 1989; Hames and Vickers 1982; Vickers 1980, 1988).

Considered together, the prey and patch models suggest that the depression of high-ranked prey within local resource patches should lead to the selection of more abundant but lower-ranked prey species in those patches and/or increased foraging effort in less-depleted patches located farther away from the central place. Both options entail substantial declines in foraging efficiency.[1]

### Harvest Rates and Age Composition

Again, resource intensification models predict declines in foraging efficiency during the late Holocene of California due to absolute and/or per capita reductions in the encounter rates of high-ranked prey types. If increasing human harvest rates caused absolute reductions in the densities of particular prey types, the exploited populations represented archaeologically should exhibit demographic indications of harvest pressure. Specifically, the harvest rates of vertebrate populations are systematically reflected in the age composition of individuals in a population. An increase in the harvest rate of a population typically causes reductions in the mean and maximum ages of individuals. With increased harvest rates, individual animals are captured well before reaching their full growth potential so that overall longevity is decreased. This, in turn, decreases intraspecific competition for resources and increases overall recruitment of young individuals into a population. Reductions in the mean and maximum ages of individuals in vertebrate populations as a result of increasing harvest rates have been documented empirically for a number of modern species including seabirds (e.g., Coulson et al. 1982; Duncan 1978). Hence, harvest pressure on prehistoric bird populations should be reflected in declines in the mean age of adult birds within archaeological samples.

The effects of increasing harvest rates on the population densities and age composition of different bird taxa should also vary according to certain life history parameters of the species involved. Specifically, *K-selected* species, those that produce smaller numbers of offspring, exhibit slower growth rates, a delayed onset of sexual maturity, and longer lifespans should be most susceptible to harvest pressure and the demographic effects of that pressure. By contrast, *r-selected* species, those that produce larger numbers of young, exhibit faster growth rates and attain reproductive maturity at a younger age, should be less susceptible to overharvesting and declines in mean age (see MacArthur and Wilson 1967:149).

Finally, the susceptibility of species to population declines due to harvest pressure should also vary according to their residence times within the predator's range. For example, prey species that migrate out of the predator's foraging range seasonally to breed would be less susceptible to depression than resident prey types (see Charnov et al. 1976:251).

### Paleoclimatic Variables

The models outlined above focus on human-induced declines in foraging efficiency and the archaeological measures of those declines. Other factors can, of course, cause changes in the natural abundances of vertebrate populations and ultimately declines in the efficiency of animal exploitation. In particular, abiotic or climatic factors can, through their effects on habitat structure, ultimately reduce the natural abundance and, hence, the encounter rates of prey taxa. Consequently, paleoenvironmental records are required to monitor potential climatically based effects on the encounter rates of specific avian taxa and foraging dynamics.

## Summary

In sum, declining efficiencies in bird exploitation should be indicated by 1. decreasing abundances of large-sized species among a set of prey types that inhabit the same local resource patches; and/or 2. steadily increasing abundances of taxa that occur in resource patches located at distances far from the site locality. In addition, increasing harvest rates or harvest pressure on exploited avian populations should be signaled by declines in the mean age of individuals represented in archaeological samples, and human foraging activities should be most detrimental to resident species with *K-selected* life history characteristics. A background record of environmental change is critical to assess the potential effects of climatically driven environmental change on prey encounter rates and resource selection.

## TESTING THE MODEL: THE EMERYVILLE SHELLMOUND

Since the focus of this research is on testing hypotheses concerning *diachronic* patterns in avian resource use during the late Holocene of northern California, a collection of archaeological avifaunal materials must be assembled from contexts that meet several specific criteria. First, since my primary predictions deal with temporal variation in avian foraging dynamics, and prey choice should be influenced by spatial variation in prey encounter rates that could confound temporal trends, it is advantageous to hold space constant. Hence, collections derived from a single site or set of sites at a single point on the landscape are ideal. The site must also represent substantial time depth and exhibit clear physical stratigraphy. In addition, the site must have been excavated by those natural strata and the vertebrate materials provenienced by those strata. Finally, the site must provide a rich collection of avifaunal remains. The Emeryville Shellmound (CA-ALA-309) of the San Francisco Bay meets these criteria and this research will focus on the enormous avifaunal collections from that site.

The Emeryville Shellmound is a deeply stratified, well-dated deposit that was once located on the east shore of San Francisco Bay, California, before it was destroyed in the early 20th century (Figure 8.2). The site was situated in a complex mosaic of terrestrial and aquatic habitat types, including open estuary, tidal mudflats, freshwater marsh, salt marsh, oak woodland, grassland, and redwood-fir forest.

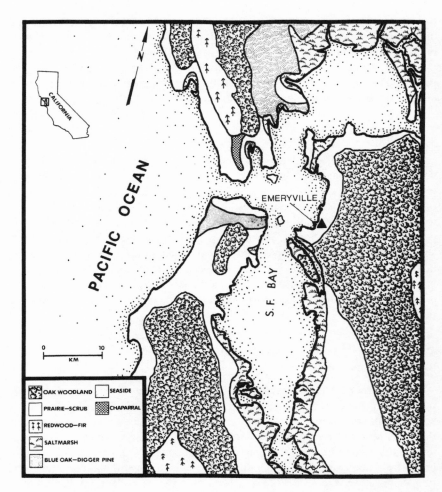

**Figure 8.2. Map of the San Francisco Bay area indicating location of the Emeryville Shellmound and historic period vegetation (vegetation redrawn from Küchler 1977).**

## History of Excavations

Prior to its destruction in 1924, the Emeryville Shellmound was the site of three separate archaeological excavations. Max Uhle and John C. Merriam of the University of California, Berkeley, conducted the initial excavation of Emeryville in 1902. Uhle and Merriam excavated a lateral section on the west slope of the mound and a tunnel that extended into its center. In this work, they excavated over 200 cubic meters of midden and removed the sediments "stratum by stratum." In all, 10 distinct strata were encountered and all of the artifacts, including a large sample of vertebrate remains, were collected and provenienced by these strata (Uhle 1907). The vertebrate materials as well as the other artifacts were collected with sieves of an unspecified mesh size (Schenck 1926:167; Uhle 1907:20). The nature of the vertebrate faunal collection is, however, consistent with moderate- to large-mesh (e.g., 1/4″ to 1/3″) screening (Broughton 1995).

In the spring of 1906, Nels C. Nelson led the second excavation at Emeryville; Nelson stratigraphically excavated a 6′ × 6′ unit in the east side of the mound. Nelson identified 11 natural strata in this work and collected and provenienced all of the artifacts, including vertebrate remains, by these natural strata (Broughton 1996; Nelson 1906).

The Emeryville Shellmound was leveled in 1924 to allow the construction of a paint factory. However, after the mound had been reduced to the level of the surrounding plain, W. E. Schenck excavated three 50′ × 6′ trenches in the base of the deposit near the center of the mound. These trenches, excavated in 1′ arbitrary levels to a depth of nearly 10′, produced a sizable faunal collection (Schenck 1926).

## Chronology

Fourteen radiocarbon assays have been provided for bone and charcoal specimens recovered from various strata throughout the Emeryville deposit. Figure 8.3 shows a profile of the Uhle/Merriam excavation with the radiocarbon dates indicated in stratigraphic context. The dates range from 2620 ± 70 B.P. at the basal contact between midden and the alluvial clay upon which the mound sits, to 950 ± 50 B.P. for stratum 2. For the Nelson strata, the dates range from 2370 ± 70 B.P.. for stratum 11, to 720 ± 60 B.P.. for stratum 3. There are no inconsistencies in the stratigraphic ordering of the dates from either the Uhle/Merriam or Nelson excavations; within each excavation, the oldest dates are from the lowest strata, while the youngest dates are from the highest strata.

A single radiocarbon date was obtained near the top (the 1′–2′ level) of one of Schenck's trenches, while six dates were obtained for the base of the mound. Together, these dates serve to bracket the deposition of the Schenck trench sediments between 2600 and 1970 B.P. This time interval incorporates the period of the deposition for the basal four strata (stratum 10 through 7) from Uhle's excavation. Accordingly, I will aggregate the 1′-level samples from Schenck's three trenches into a total of four temporal-analytic units.

The ten Uhle strata, the three radiocarbon-dated Nelson strata[2], and the four Schenck trench levels together yield a total of 17 independent temporal-analytic units. I refer to these units collectively as the Emeryville "strata" below. These strata will allow a fairly fine-grained ordinal-scale analysis of change in the efficiency of bird exploitation and evidence for harvest pressure on local bird populations at a single point on northern California's late Holocene landscape between ca. 2600 and 700 B.P.[3]

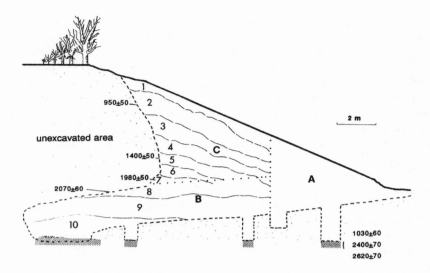

**Figure 8.3. Profile of the Uhle/Merriam excavation showing radiocarbon dates placed into stratigraphic context (map redrawn from Uhle 1907: Plate 4).**

## THE EMERYVILLE SHELLMOUND MAMMAL AND FISH FAUNAS: EVIDENCE FOR DECLINING EFFICIENCIES AND HARVEST PRESSURE

My identification and analysis of some 18,000 fish and mammal specimens from the Emeryville Shellmound provide evidence for dramatic human-induced impacts on local populations of large-sized taxa, such as sturgeon (*Acipenser* spp.), tule elk (*Cervus elaphus*), and black-tailed deer (*Odocoileus hemionus*), across the occupational history of this site (Broughton 1995, 1997). To provide a broader context within which to understand patterns in the avifaunal data, I provide a brief summary of the results from the analyses of these other vertebrate classes.

Among the fishes, the abundance of sturgeon, by far the largest fish taxon represented in the Emeryville collection, declined significantly relative to the other smaller fishes from the oldest to the youngest strata (Figure 8.4; $r_s = -.49$, $P =.05$).[4] In addition, the mean age of the exploited sturgeon, as measured by dentary widths, also declined significantly across the history of mound occupation (Figure 8.5; $r_s = -.762$, $P < .05$). These changes are not correlated with late Holocene variation in estuarine salinity (Ingram et al. 1996), the most influential variable that currently limits the density of sturgeon in the central San Francisco Bay. The decrease in the relative abundance of sturgeon provides evidence for a significant decline in the efficiency of fish exploitation through time at Emeryville. The decreasing mean age supports the hypothesis that the decline in sturgeon abundances was due to an increasing harvest rate of this fish resource by the inhabitants of Emeryville, as well as other human groups occupying the San Francisco Bay margin.

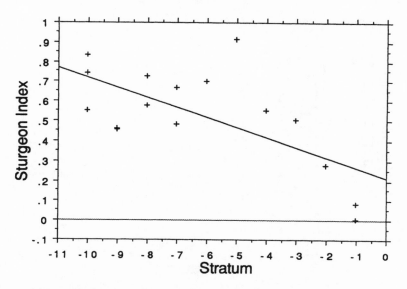

Figure 8.4. The distribution of sturgeon index ($\Sigma$NISP sturgeon/$\Sigma$NISP identified fishes) across the Emeryville strata.

Similar conclusions were reached from analyses of the mammal materials from this site. Among terrestrial mammals, for example, black-tailed deer and tule elk dominate the earliest strata, but decline relative to smaller mammals, namely small terrestrial carnivores (e.g., coyote, *Canis latrans;* raccoon, *Procyon lotor;* and striped skunk, *Mephitis mephitis*) across the initial 600 years of human occupation (Figure 8.6). While tule elk frequencies remain low throughout the remaining occupation of the mound, perhaps reflecting the limited available grassland habitat for elk in the region, deer numbers steadily increase in relative frequency throughout the remaining millennia of mound occupation. In my earlier work, I hypothesized that this resurgence in deer abundances reflected continuing depression of local resource patches and an ever-increasing use of distant, less-depleted deer patches in the oak woodland hinterlands of the Bay area. This hypothesis was strongly supported by changes in artiodactyl skeletal part frequencies across the Emeryville strata (Broughton 1999).

Recent theoretical and ethnoarchaeological research (Barlow and Metcalfe 1996; Binford 1978; Metcalfe and Barlow 1992; O'Connell et al. 1990) have made one point clear with respect to the economics of large mammal carcass transport: Transport costs determine the degree to which low-utility body parts are returned from kill sites to base camps, and transport distance is the single most important component of transport costs. It follows that if the resurgence in artiodactyl abundances documented across the upper strata at Emeryville is reflecting an ever-increasing use of distant, less-depleted deer patches, it should be associated with increasing relative frequencies of high-utility body parts. My analysis showed that after taphonomic biases in skeletal part representation were

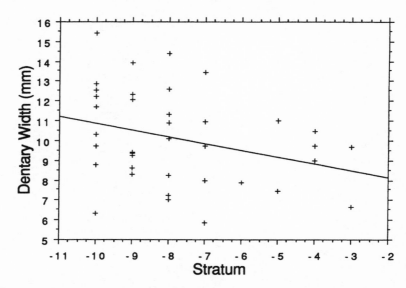

**Figure 8.5. Dentary widths by stratum for the Emeryville sturgeon. (A least-squares regression line shows the direction of the trend.)**

isolated and removed[5], the mean Food Utility Index (see Metcalfe and Jones 1987) of the represented anatomical parts increased significantly across the upper six strata of the Emeryville Shellmound (mean utility versus stratum $r_s$ = .96, $P$ < .02; see Broughton 1995:213–219). The skeletal part frequency data from the Emeryville artiodactyls, thus, strongly supports the local depression and distant patch use hypothesis. Many other aspects of the Emeryville mammal record—from change in the age structure of artiodactyls and marine mammals to cut-mark and bone fragmentation patterns—strongly support this hypothesis as well (Broughton 1999).

In sum, analyses of both the mammal and fish faunas from Emeryville provide support for the hypothesis that expanding forager densities depressed local vertebrate populations, ultimately driving declines in vertebrate foraging efficiencies. Is evidence of human impacts on prehistoric bird populations of San Francisco Bay indicated by patterns in the Emeryville Shellmound avifauna?

### THE EMERYVILLE SHELLMOUND AVIFAUNA: EXPECTATIONS AND PRELIMINARY RESULTS

In her 1929 study of the Emeryville avifauna, Hildegarde Howard published what remains one of the premier paleontologically oriented analyses of avifaunal materials from a North American archaeological site (Howard 1929). In that work, Howard identified 4,155 bird specimens from a total of about 15,000 bird remains recovered from the Emeryville Shellmound. Howard, however, did not

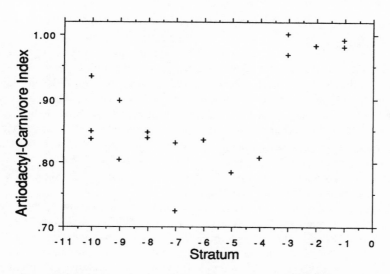

**Figure 8.6. The distribution of the artiodactyl-carnivore index ($\Sigma$NISP artiodactyls/$\Sigma$ NISP [artiodactyls + small carnivores]) across the Emeryville strata.**

provide stratigraphic information for those identifications. From her unpublished laboratory catalog, on file with the vertebrate faunal collection at the Phoebe Hearst Museum of Anthropology, University of California, Berkeley, I was able to place 2,302 of her identifications into stratigraphic context (Broughton 1995:121–123). A preliminary analysis of this sample of identified bird specimens from Emeryville hints that local bird populations may have suffered substantial impacts from late Holocene human foragers in this estuarine setting. Ducks and geese (Anatidae) and cormorants *(Phalacrocorax)* comprise 83.5% of the 2,302 identified bird specimens from the provenienced Emeryville avian assemblage, and I focus this preliminary analysis of the intensification of bird exploitation on these taxonomic groups.

Three species of cormorant were identified by Howard in the Emeryville Shellmound avifauna: Double-crested Cormorant *(Phalacrocorax auritis)*, Brandt's Cormorant *(P. penicillatus)*, and Pelagic Cormorant *(P. pelagicus)*. Of the 491 identified cormorant specimens, Howard could securely identify 159 to species. Of this latter sample, 119, or 74.8%, were Double-crested Cormorant. To judge from the degree of bone ossification of the cormorant material, almost half (46.4%) of the specimens represented at Emeryville were fledgling-aged birds, indicating the exploitation of local breeding colonies (Howard 1929).

Adult Double-crested Cormorants range in weight from 1.75 to 2.75 kilograms. Brandt's and Pelagic Cormorants are slightly smaller, weighing between 1.4 and 2.6, and 1.4 and 2.4 kilograms, respectively (Johnsgard 1993:173, 202, 292).

All of these species are year-round residents of the San Francisco Bay area, and breed in colonies on islands, or virtually inaccessible rocky cliff faces on the mainland coast. The nearest historically recorded colony to Emeryville was at Seal Rocks near the Golden Gate; exploiting cormorants on this island would require a 34-kilometer round-trip journey by water from Emeryville (Grinnell and Wythe 1927:47). The nearest island that may have supported cormorant nesting colonies in the past is Treasure Island, located 9 kilometers west of Emeryville.

Cormorant colonies are well known for their sensitivity to disturbance and vandalized or disturbed sites are routinely abandoned (e.g., Boekelheide et al. 1990:165–166). As a group, these cormorants begin to breed at about the age of three years, usually produce clutches of three to four eggs between April and June, and fledge two chicks per nest (Boekelheide et al 1990; Johnsgard 1993:202). Cormorants are piscivorous and use their excellent diving abilities to capture fish prey (Ainley et al. 1990:105–107).

In sum, the life history characteristics of cormorants are similar to the typical *K-selected* reproductive strategies of most seabirds. This adaptation includes relatively small clutches, slow growth rates, delayed sexual maturity, and long lifespans. Cormorants appear to be "geared" to maintain slow population turnover rates, and are unlikely to quickly rebound from intensive human exploitation (cf., Johnsgard 1993:125–126).

Howard identified 1,431 anatid specimens from the Emeryville strata. Most of those identifications were, however, only made to the family level. Only 78 specimens were identified to the genus or species level. The anatids are highly variable in size, from as large as 11 kilograms for Canada goose *(Branta canadensis)*, to as small as 0.5 kilograms for teals *(Anas* spp.) (Palmer 1976:199, 488).

The anatid species that Howard identified in the Emeryville assemblage occur in the San Francisco Bay area only as winter visitants. These birds migrate to northern latitudes or the interior of the continent during spring to breed, where they produce relatively large broods of precocious chicks (geese 3–7 chicks; ducks 5–12). This characterizes the seasonal distribution of most of the anatid species, including all of the geese that occur in the San Francisco Bay area. In fact, of the 33 anatid species whose ranges include San Francisco Bay, only five duck species of the genus *Anas* are year-round residents here (Grinnell and Wythe 1927).

Diet is highly variable among the different species of anatids. Many anatid species routinely forage in terrestrial settings. In fact, all of the identified geese, including White-fronted Goose *(Anser albifrons)*, Snow Goose *(Chen caerulescens)*, Ross's Goose *(Chen rossii)*, and Canada Goose are largely terrestrial vegetarians that prefer to forage in grassland or marshland settings. These species are generally quite gregarious, forming large impressive flocks, sometimes containing over 5,000 individuals in these settings (Palmer 1976).

According to ethnographic and ethnohistoric accounts, aboriginal foragers of this region used a wide variety of methods to capture waterfowl and seabirds, including the bow and arrow, bolas consisting of two pieces of bone or stone tied to each end of a string, snares or nooses hung by cords above the water's surface or within tule marshes, and nets used in association with stuffed skin decoys.

Cormorant rookeries on offshore islands were reached by small watercraft (tule balsas) (Beechey 1831:75; Johnson 1978:364; Levy 1978:491; Wallace 1978:450). Both watercraft and netting technologies were well established in the San Francisco Bay area well before the occupation of Emeryville (Broughton 1994b; Follet 1975; Howard 1929; Wallace and Lathrap 1975).

If expanding human forager densities drove declining foraging efficiencies across the occupational history of Emeryville, several predictions follow involving changes in the taxonomic composition and age structure of the Emeryville avian materials. First, since the different anatid species occur within the same resource patches, they should have been part of the same hunt type. And since the anatids share similar life history and antipredator adaptations, but differ substantially in body mass, declining efficiencies in anatid foraging should be signaled by declining abundances of geese relative to ducks across the history of mound occupation. In addition, since geese are larger in size than cormorants and occur in high densities in grassland and marshland settings close at hand to Emeryville, the abundances of geese relative to cormorants should also decline across the history of site occupation. That is, the relative abundances of cormorants in the Emeryville strata should signal the depression of *local* resource patches and the relative frequency that *distant* patches were exploited.

Cormorants should also be much more susceptible to absolute declines due to human harvest pressure than the anatids, since they are year-round residents of the Bay area, their breeding colonies can be directly exploited and disturbed, and they exhibit more *K-selected* life history strategies. Hence, if overall foraging returns declined enough to drive the intensive foraging of distant island-nesting cormorants, such exploitation may be relatively short-lived. Finally, if the resident populations of cormorants were depressed or extirpated from the region, indications of harvest pressure should be indicated by declines in the average age of the exploited cormorants from the Emeryville strata.

None of these predictions can be fully addressed with the very limited data now available. Because virtually all of the anatids were identified only to the family level, it is not possible to address the first two predictions at all. The present data do allow a cursory glance at the third prediction, that local cormorant populations could not sustain intensive long-term exploitation of breeding colonies.

The cormorant index:

$$\Sigma\text{NISP Cormorants}/\Sigma(\text{NISP Cormorants + Anatids})$$

summarizes the relative abundances of cormorants and anatids in the Emeryville Shellmound faunal assemblage, where NISP refers to the numbers of identified specimens per taxon. Figure 8.7 shows the relationship between the cormorant index and time as represented by selected Emeryville strata. Again, identified avian samples were lacking for many strata, hence it is not possible to reach any firm conclusions from these data. However, the data do suggest an increase in the exploitation of cormorants relative to ducks and geese across the lower four strata

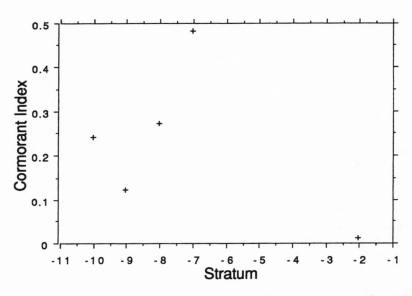

Figure 8.7. The distribution of the cormorant index ($\Sigma$NISP cormorants/$\Sigma$NISP [cormorants + anatids]) across selected Emeryville strata.

(i.e., 10 through 7). It is also intriguing that by stratum 2, the cormorant index has dropped to less than .01. Did declining foraging efficiencies drive a steadily increasing use of distant cormorant patches? And did this ultimately cause the extirpation of breeding populations of cormorants in San Francisco Bay? Addressing these and other questions requires a fine-scale analysis of the Emeryville Shellmound avifaunal collection.

## DATA REQUIREMENTS

### Taxonomic Composition

Identifications of the Emeryville Shellmound avian specimens are required to test the predictions concerning changes in taxonomic composition across the history of site occupation. These data will allow the calculation of taxonomic ratios, such as the cormorant index, that incorporate the abundances of differently ranked resources that occur in distinctive resource patches. These indices can then be plotted across the Emeryville strata to reveal temporal patterns in the energetics of avian prey choice and patch use.

### Age Determination

The prediction concerning changes in age structure as a function of harvest pressure requires that estimates of the age of death be determined for the

Emeryville cormorant material. However, despite several little-known or otherwise unsuccessful attempts (Koubek and Hrabe 1984; Nelson and Bookhout 1980; Schaaf 1979; Stone and Morris 1981; van Soest and van Utrecht 1971), no well-documented, osteologically based methods for determining the age of adult birds have been fully developed. Hence, ornithologists, avian paleontologists, and archaeologists have been limited to assigning osteological bird remains to two broad age classes: subadults and adults. Finer-scale age assessments are required to measure harvest pressure and other demographic variables from archaeological avian faunas.

Fortunately, a recently described method of age determination for adult birds, based on analyses of annual rings registered in the circumferential lamellae of long bones, has produced very promising results. Specifically, Klomp and Furness (1992) use a sample of 12 known-aged birds of four species (Great Skua, *Catharacta skua*; Redshank, *Tringa totanus*; Northern Fulmar, *Fulmaris glacialis*; and European Shag, *Phalacrocorax aristotelis*) to demonstrate that the number of endosteal lamellae revealed in transverse thin sections of the tibiotarsus corresponded tightly with age in years. Reading photographs of 1-millimeter thick, polished thin sections, taken through a transmitted light microscope at 100x, naive observers correctly determined the age of the birds within one year for specimens less than 12 years, and within two years for birds older than 12 years. The age of the single known-aged cormorant in the sample, the European Shag, was correctly determined *to the year* by each of the six observers.

In addition to demonstrating the annual nature of endosteal ring formation among small samples of individuals representing four bird species, Klomp and Furness (1992) also documented the *presence* of endosteal rings among individuals of three other species. Previous investigators have also documented the presence of rings in the circumferential lamellae in either the periosteum or endosteum in a number of different skeletal elements from ten other species of bird (Koubek and Hrabe 1984; Nelson and Bookhout 1980; Schaaf 1979; Stone and Morris 1981; van Soest and van Utrecht 1971). Seasonal climatic changes, dietary shifts, and reproductive cycles have been proposed as possible factors resulting in the layered growth of avian bone, but further research is required to determine the precise biological basis of this phenomenon (Klomp and Furness 1992:134).

Applying this technique to archaeological specimens requires well-preserved incremental structures of avian long bone samples. And while the histological structures of bone, such as endosteal lamellae, are routinely preserved in archaeological and paleontological contexts, including fossilized specimens (e.g., Grupe and Garland 1993; Reid 1981; de Ricqles 1986, 1993; Stout 1992), bone microstructure can be damaged or obscured by mechanical abrasion or diagenetic processes, such as fungal or bacterial invasion (see Hanson and Buikstra 1987).

Based on chemical and structural analyses of seven samples of mammal bone distributed across the Emeryville strata, the structural preservation of bone at this site appears to be excellent. Specifically, after demineralization, all but one of the specimens retained original bone color and structure and provided high collagen yields (Broughton 1995:89–90). Hence, analyses of bone microstructure for age determination from the Emeryville osteological samples should provide fruitful results.

Prior to applying this age-determination technique to the Emeryville cormorant materials, it is necessary to establish experimentally the precise nature of the periodicity of ring formation in the circumferential lamellae of these birds. To this end, I will analyze a large sample (n = 54) of modern, known-aged Double-crested Cormorants to conduct these analyses.[6] With this sample, I will follow the protocol described by Klomp and Furness (1992) to verify the accuracy and precision of this technique for this species.

Finally, I have been granted permission by the Phoebe Hearst Museum, University of California, where the Emeryville materials are presently curated, to remove partial thin sections from 340 samples of cormorant long bones for the age determination analyses. This sample will allow an average of 20 specimens to be aged from each of the 17 temporal-analytic units of the site. Mean cormorant ages can then be determined for each Emeryville strata to evaluate diachronic patterns of harvest pressure on this resource.

### Paleoenvironmental Data

In addition to human harvest pressure, environmental change can affect the densities, encounter rates, and ultimately the spectrum of avian prey choice options available to the prehistoric foragers that occupied particular localities on the landscape. Since the winter visitant anatid resources of San Francisco Bay are derived from multiple breeding populations from localities distributed across the continent, monitoring long-term environmentally based changes in the densities of these migrant populations is not feasible. However, regional late Holocene paleoenvironmental records will allow an assessment of environmentally based changes in the densities of the resident cormorant populations in this region.

Research on cormorant breeding colonies of the Farallon Islands, located 45 kilometers east of the Golden Gate, has indicated that interannual fluctuations in ocean water temperature influence the feeding ecology and, ultimately, the regional population densities of Pelagic, Brandt's, and Double-crested Cormorants. Specifically, during years with elevated sea surface temperatures associated with the El Nino Southern Oscillation (ENSO), the fish populations upon which cormorants feed are profoundly disrupted, foraging efficiencies decline, as does the number of pairs attempting to breed and the average number of chicks fledged per pair. As a result, Farallon cormorant populations during and immediately subsequent to ENSO years are substantially depressed (Ainley and Boekelheide 1990). Similar population declines among cormorant populations have been associated with warm-water years along the coasts of both South America and South Africa (Boekelheide et al. 1990; Crawford and Shelton 1978; Jordan 1967).

While cormorant populations gradually rebound from these short-term population declines associated with episodic, warm-water years, prolonged periods of elevated sea temperature in the past, on the scale of hundreds or thousands of years, might have produced significant long-term declines in cormorant populations or even local extirpation events. Evaluating the effect of ocean paleotemperature variation on the densities of San Francisco Bay cormorant populations and human exploitation of these resources requires fine-scale records of late Holocene fluctuations in ocean temperature in this region.

Several Holocene records of surface sea temperature have been provided for the California coast (e.g., Jones and Kennett 1999; Kennett and Ingram 1995; Pisias 1979). These records are based on a variety of paleoclimatic proxies derived from radiocarbon-dated ocean basin sediment cores. These proxies include $\delta^{18}O$ values from planktonic and benthic foraminifers, relative abundance changes of cold- and warm-water foraminifer and rodiolarian taxa, the morphology of foraminifer shell coils, and the degree of preservation of laminated ocean basin sediments. Variations in Holocene ocean temperature derived from these different proxies have provided internally consistent results and will allow a precise evaluation of correlation between late Holocene changes in eastern Pacific sea temperatures and the relative abundances of cormorants represented at the Emeryville Shellmound.

## SIGNIFICANCE

Resource intensification models predict declines in foraging efficiency during the late Holocene of California due to expanding forager densities and declining encounter rates with certain especially profitable vertebrate resources. In many settings, it has been suggested that the declining encounter rate with high-ranked prey types was the result of depletion caused by human foraging activities. Through the integration of models drawn from evolutionary ecology and demography, I have deduced archaeological measures of foraging efficiency and harvest pressure that involve the taxonomic composition and age structure of the bird remains recovered from the famous, but long-since destroyed Emeryville Shellmound. The application of these measures in a fine-scale test of resource intensification models will have strong implications for 1. our knowledge of the specifics concerning the emergence of complex hunter-gatherers in late prehistoric California; 2. the causes of change in prehistoric hunter-gatherer behavior in general; as well as for 3. the long-term management of Pacific Coast bird populations currently threatened by human-caused habitat alteration.

Insofar as widening diet breadths imply lower average fitness within local populations, documenting declines in foraging efficiency entail predictions for variation in many other aspects of human behavior and morphology during the late Holocene of California. Such features include, but are not limited to, technological changes associated with intensive processing of lower-ranked resources, increasing disease loads and declines in body size and stature, greater attention to resource defense with the development of more tightly circumscribed territories, and higher levels of interpersonal violence (Broughton and O'Connell 1999). Insofar as strong gradients develop in local resource densities and abundances as a consequence of the overall declines in foraging returns, opportunities would increasingly emerge for the growth of disparities in wealth and the exaggeration of social hierarchies.

Finally, informed ecosystem management clearly cannot be accomplished without detailed knowledge of the factors that structured pre-Columbian and historic period environments. Analyses of archaeological vertebrate faunas can provide a central avenue for attaining this knowledge and an objective means of evaluating the impact that people had on prehistoric environments. For many regions of the world, this knowledge resides untapped in museum collections that were derived from archaeological excavations conducted over the last century. Archaeology is in a unique position to contribute to modern management policies that will ultimately determine the nature of our planet's future environments.

## ACKNOWLEDGMENTS

I thank D. K. Grayson and R. D. Leonard for helpful comments on drafts of this chapter.

## NOTES

1. Transport models developed by Metcalfe and Barlow (Barlow and Metcalfe 1996; Metcalfe and Barlow 1992), for instance, indicate that even modest increases in round-trip travel times to resource patches for central place foragers rapidly diminish the return rates of resource types exploited in those patches.

2. The Nelson excavation yielded a comparatively small sample of vertebrate specimens aside from the basal stratum 11. For this reason and because only two of the upper 10 strata were radiocarbon dated, I selected only the three dated strata (strata 3, 5, and 11) for the following analyses.

3. Given the coarse-grained recovery methods discussed above, there is undoubtedly a systematic recovery bias against the recovery of very small-sized vertebrate specimens. However, this bias should be internally consistent throughout the various strata of the deposit. Moreover, the bird taxa of primary interest here are of such substantial sizes that such a bias should be negligible.

4. Stratum 10 is at the base of the deposit; stratum 1 is at the top of the mound. The multiple points per stratum in Figure 8.4 and several figures to follow represent temporally equivalent stratigraphic units from the three different excavations conducted at three different horizontal locations of the mound.

5. Eight of the 17 strata exhibited positive Spearmann's rank order correlations between relative skeletal abundances and deer bone density values (from Lyman 1984). Fortunately, the positive correlations were concentrated (7 of the 8) in the lower strata of the deposit, so do not affect interpretations of skeletal part frequencies across the period of the artiodactyl resurgence in the upper strata of the deposit (Broughton 1995).

6. The known-aged cormorants are curated at the Museum of Zoology, University of Michigan, and have been made available for these analyses.

## REFERENCES CITED

Ainley, D. G. and R. J. Boekelheide
  1990   *Seabirds of the Farallon Islands*. Stanford University Press, Palo Alto.
Ainley, D. G., C. S. Strong, T. M. Penniman, and R. J. Boekelheide
  1990   The Feeding Ecology of Fallon Seabirds. In *Seabirds of the Farallon Islands*, edited by D. G. Ainley and R. J. Boekelheide, pp. 51–127. Stanford University Press, Palo Alto.
Alvard, M. S.
  1993   A Test of the Ecologically Noble Savage Hypothesis: Interspecific Prey Choice by Neotropical Hunters. *Human Ecology* 21:355–387.
  1994   Conservation by Native Peoples: Prey Choice in a Depleted Habitat. *Human Nature* 5:127–154.
Barlow, K. R., and D. Metcalfe
  1996   Plant Utility Indices: Two Great Basin Examples. *Journal of Archaeological Science* 23:351–371.
Basgall, M. E.
  1987   Resource Intensification among Hunter-Gatherers: Acorn Economies in Prehistoric California. *Research in Economic Anthropology* 9:21–52.
Bayham, F. E.
  1982   A Diachronic Analysis of Prehistoric Animal Exploitation at Ventana Cave. Unpublished Ph.D. dissertation, Department of Anthropology, Arizona State University, Tempe.
Beaton, J. M.
  1991   Extensification and Intensification in Central California Prehistory. *Antiquity* 65:947–951.
Beechy, F. W.
  1831   *Narrative of a Voyage to the Pacific and Bering's Strait* 2. Henry Colburn and Richard Bentley, London.
Belovsky, G. E.
  1987   Hunter-Gatherer Foraging: A Linear Programming Approach. *Journal of Anthropological Archaeology* 6:29–76.
Bettinger, R. L.
  1991   *Hunter-Gatherers: Archaeological and Evolutionary Theory*. Plenum Press, New York.
Binford, L.
  1978   *Nunamiut Ethnoarchaeology*. Academic Press, New York.
Bird, D. W.
  1996   *Intertidal Foraging Strategies among the Meriam of the Torres Strait Islands, Australia: An Evolutionary Ecological Approach to the Ethnoarchaeology of Tropical Marine Subsistence*. Unpublished Ph.D. dissertation, University of California, Davis.
Boekelheide, R. J., D. G. Ainley, S. H. Morrell, and T. J. Lewis
  1990   Brandt's Cormorant. In *Seabirds of the Farallon Islands*, edited by D. G. Ainley and R. J. Boekelheide, pp. 163–194. Stanford University Press, Palo Alto.
Boserup, E.
  1965   *Conditions of Agricultural Growth: The Economics of Agrarian Change under Population Pressure*. Aldine, Chicago.

Broughton, J. M.
1994a Late Holocene Resource Intensification in the Sacramento Valley, California: The Vertebrate Evidence. *Journal of Archaeological Science* 21:501–514.
1994b Declines in Mammalian Foraging Efficiency during the Late Holocene, San Francisco Bay, California. *Journal of Anthropological Archaeology* 13:371–401.
1995 *Resource Depression and Intensification during the Late Holocene, San Francisco Bay: Evidence from the Emeryville Shellmound Vertebrate Fauna*. Ph.D. dissertation, University of Washington. University Microfilms, Ann Arbor.
1997 Widening diet breadth, declining foraging efficiency, and prehistoric harvest pressure: ichthyofaural evidence from the Emeryville Shellmound, California. *Antiquity* 71:845–862.
1999 Resource Depression and Intensification during the Late Holocene, San Francisco Bay: Evidence from the Emeryville Shellmound Vertebrate Fauna. *University of California Anthropological Records* 32.
Broughton, J. M. (Editor)
1996 *Excavation of the Emeryville Shellmound, 1906: Nels C. Nelson's Final Report*. Contributions of the University of California Archaeological Research Facility 54. University of California, Berkeley.
Broughton, J. M., and D. K. Grayson
1993 Diet Breadth, Adaptive Change and the White Mountains Faunas. *Journal of Archaeological Science* 20:331–336.
Broughton, J. M., and J. F. O'Connell
1999 On Evolutionary Ecology, Selectionist Archaeology, and Behavioral Archaeology. *American Antiquity* 64:153–165.
Cannon, M. D.
In press Zooarchaeological Relative Abundance and Resource Depression: A Consideration of Theoretical Models and Statistical Methods. *Journal of Anthropological Archaeology*.
Charnov, E. L.
1976 Optimal Foraging: The Marginal Value Theorem. *Theoretical Population Biology* 9:129–136.
Charnov, E. L., G. H. Orians, and K. Hyatt
1976 Ecological Implications of Resource Depression. *American Naturalist* 110:247–259.
Cohen, M. N.
1981 Pacific Coast Foragers: Affluent or Overcrowded? In *Affluent Foragers: Pacific Coasts East and West*, Volume 9, edited by S. Koyama and D. H. Thomas, pp. 275–295. Senri Ethnological Studies.
Cook, S. F.
1976 *The Population of the California Indians 1796–1970*. University of California Press, Berkeley.
Coulson, J. C., N. Duncan, and C. S. Thomas
1982 Changes in the Breeding Biology of the Herring Gull (*Larus argentatus*) Induced by Reduction in the Size and Density of the Colony. *Journal of Animal Ecology* 51:739–756.
Crawford, R. J. M., and P. A. Shelton
1978 Pelagic Fish and Seabird Interrelationships Off the Coast of Southwest and South Africa. *Biological Conservation* 14:85–109.

Duncan, N.
   1978   The Effects of Culling Herring Gulls (*Larus argentatus*) on Recruitment and Population Dynamics. *Journal of Applied Ecology* 15:697–713.
Earle, T. K.
   1980   A Model of Subsistence Change. In *Modeling Change in Prehistoric Subsistence Economies*, edited by T. Earle and A. Christenson, pp. 1–30. Academic Press, New York.
Follet, W. I.
   1975   Appendix B: Fish Remains from the West Berkeley Shellmound (Ca-Ala-307), Alameda County, California. In *West Berkeley (Ca-Ala-307): A Culturally Stratified Shellmound on the East Shore of San Francisco Bay*, Volume 29, edited by W. J. Wallace and D. W. Lathrap, pp. 71–98. Contributions of the University of California Archaeological Research Facility, Berkeley.
Grayson, D. K.
   1991   Alpine Faunas from the White Mountains California: Adaptive Change in the Late Prehistoric Great Basin. *Journal of Archaeological Science* 18:483–506.
Griffiths, D.
   1975   Prey Availability and the Food of Predators. *Ecology* 56:1209–1214.
Grinnell, J., and M. W. Wythe
   1927   Directory of the Bird Life of the San Francisco Bay Region. *Cooper Ornithological Club Pacific Coast Avifauna* 27.
Grupe, G., and A. N. Garland
   1993   *Histology of Ancient Human Bone: Methods and Diagnosis.* Springer-Verlag, Heidelberg.
Hames, R. B.
   1989   Time, Efficiency, and Fitness in the Amazonian Food Quest. *Research in Economic Anthropology* 11:43–85.
Hames, R. B., and W. T. Vickers
   1982   Optimal Foraging Theory as a Model to Explain Variability in Amazonian Hunting. *American Ethnologist* 9:358–378.
Hanson, D. B., and J. E. Buikstra
   1987   Histomorphological Alteration in Buried Human Bone from the Lower Illinois Valley: Implications for Paleodietary Research. *Journal of Archaeological Science* 14:549–563.
Hawkes, K., and J. F. O'Connell
   1992   On Optimal Foraging Models and Subsistence Transitions. *Current Anthropology* 33:63–219.
Hewes, G. W.
   1973   Indian Fisheries Productivity in Pre-Contact Times in the Pacific Salmon Area. *Northwest Anthropological Research Notes* 7:133–155.
Hildebrandt, W. R., and T. L. Jones
   1992   Evolution of Marine Mammal Hunting: A View from the California and Oregon Coasts. *Journal of Anthropological Archaeology* 11:360–401.
Hill, K. H., K. Kaplan, and A. M. Hurtado
   1987   Foraging Decisions among the Ache Hunter-Gatherers: New Data and Implications for Optimal Foraging Theory. *Ethology and Sociobiology* 8:1–36.

Howard, H.
  1929   The Avifauna of the Emeryville Shellmound. *University of California Publications in Zoology* 32:302–389.
Ingram, B. L., J. C. Ingle, and M. E. Conrad
  1996   Stable Isotope Record of Late Holocene Paleosalinity and Paleodischarge in San Francisco Bay, California. *Earth and Planetary Science Letters* 141:237–247.
Johnsgard, P. A.
  1993   *Cormorants, Darters, and Pelicans of the World*. Smithsonian Institution Press, Washington, D.C.
Johnson, J. J.
  1978   Yana. In *Handbook of North American Indians, California, Volume 8*, edited by R. F. Heizer, pp. 361–369. Smithsonian Institution Press, Washington, D.C.
Jones, T. L., and W. R. Hildebrandt
  1995   Reasserting a Prehistoric Tragedy of the Commons: Reply to Lyman. *Journal of Anthropological Archaeology* 14:78–98.
Jones, T. L., and D. J. Kennett
  1999   Late Holocene Sea Temperatures along the Central California Coast. *Quaternary Research* 51:74–82.
Jordan, R.
  1967   The Predation of Guano Birds on the Peruvian Anchovy (*Engraulis ringens* Jenyns). *California Cooperative Fish Investigation, Report* 11:105–109.
Kay, C.
  1994   Aboriginal Overkill: The Role of Native Americans in Structuring Western Ecosystems. *Human Nature* 5:359–398.
Kelly, R. L.
  1995   *The Foraging Spectrum: Diversity in Hunter-Gatherer Lifeways*. Smithsonian Institution Press, Washington, D.C.
Kennett, J. P., and B. L. Ingram
  1995   A 20,000-year Record of Ocean Circulation and Climate Change from the Santa Barbara Basin. *Nature* 377:510–514.
Klomp, N. I., and R. W. Furness
  1992   A Technique Which May Allow Accurate Determination of the Age of Adult Birds. *Ibis* 134:245–249.
Koubek, P., and V. Hrabe
  1984   Estimating the Age of Male *Phasianus colchicus* by Bone Histology and Spur Length. *Folia Zoologica* 33:303–313.
Küchler, A.V.
  1977   *Map of the Natural Vegetation of California*. University of Kansas, Lawrence.
Levy, R.
  1978   Costanoan. In *Handbook of North American Indians, California, Volume 8*, edited by R. F. Heizer, pp. 485–495. Smithsonian Institution Press, Washington, D.C.
Lyman, R. L.
  1984   Bone Density and Differential Survivorship of Fossil Classes. *Journal of Anthropological Archaeology* 3:259–299.
MacArthur, R. H., and E. O. Wilson
  1967   *The Theory of Island Biogeography*. Monographs in Population Biology. Princeton University Press, Princeton.

Metcalfe, D., and K. R. Barlow
   1992   A Model for Exploring the Optimal Trade-Off Between Field Processing and Transport. *American Anthropologist* 94:340–356.
Metcalfe, D., and K. T. Jones
   1987   A Reconsideration of Animal Body-part Utility Indices. *American Antiquity* 53:486–504.
Nelson, N. C.
   1906   Excavation of the Emeryville Shellmound, Being a Partial Report of Exploration for the Department of Anthropology During the Year 1906. Vol. 248. Archaeological Research Facility Manuscript, University of California, Berkeley.
Nelson, R. C., and T. A. Bookhout
   1980   Counts of Periosteal Layers Invalid for Aging Canada Geese. *Journal of Wildlife Management* 44:518–521.
O'Connell, F., K. Hawkes, and N. Blurton Jones
   1990   Re-analysis of Large Mammal Body Transport Among the Hadza. *Journal of Archaeological Science* 17:301–316.
Palmer, R. S.
   1976   *Handbook of North American Birds, Volume 2, Waterfowl*. Yale University Press, New Haven.
Pisias, N. G.
   1979   Model for Paleoceanographic Reconstructions of the California Current during the Last 8000 Years. *Quaternary Research* 11:373–386.
Reid, R. E.
   1981   Lamellar-zonal Bone with Zones of Annuli in the Pelvis of a Sauropod Dinosaur. *Nature* 292:49–51.
Ricqles, A. de
   1986   On the Usefulness and Prospects of Bone Histology for Vertebrate Paleontology. *Paleopathology Association News* 5:16.
   1993   Some Remarks on Paleohistology from a Compartive Evolutionary Point of View. In *Histology of Ancient Human Bone: Methods and Diagnosis*, edited by G. Grupe and A. N. Garland, pp. 37–77. Springer-Verlag, Heidelberg.
Schaaf, L. E.
   1979   *Age Determination of Mallard Ducks* Anas platyrhynchos *by Layers in Periosteal Zone*. M.S., Eastern Kentucky University, Richmond.
Schenk, W. E.
   1926   The Emeryville Shellmound Final Report. *University of California Publications in American Archaeology and Ethnology* 23:150–282.
Simms, S. R.
   1987   Behavioral Ecology and Hunter-Gatherer Foraging: An Example from the Great Basin. *BAR International Series* 381:1–157.
Smith, E. A.
   1991   *Inujjuamiut Foraging Strategies: Evolutionary Ecology of an Arctic Hunting Economy*. Aldine De Gruyter, New York.
Speth, J. D.
   1990   Seasonality, Resource Stress, and Food Sharing in So-called "Egalitarian" Foraging Societies. *Journal of Anthropological Archaeology* 9:148–88.

Speth, J. D., and K. A. Spielmann
   1983   Energy Source, Protein Metabolism, and Hunter-Gatherer Subsistence Strategies. *Journal of Anthropological Archaeology* 2:1–31.
Steadman, D. W.
   1995   Prehistoric Extinctions of Pacific Island Birds: Biodiversity Meets Zooarchaeology. *Science* 267:1123–1130.
Stephens, D. W., and J. R. Krebs
   1986   *Foraging Theory*. Princeton University Press, Princeton.
Stone, W. B., and K. Morris
   1981   Aging Male Ring-neck Pheasants by Bone Histology. *New York Fish and Game Journal* 28:223–229.
Stout, S. D.
   1992   Methods of Determining Age at Death Using Bone Microstructure. In *Skeletal Biology of Past Peoples: Research Methods*, edited by S. R. Saunders and A. Katzenberg, pp. 21–36. Wiley-Liss, New York.
Uhle, M.
   1907   The Emeryville Shellmound. *University of California Publications in American Archaeology and Ethnology* 7:1–106.
van Soest, R. W. M., and W. L. van Utrecht
   1971   The Layered Structure of Bones of Birds as a Possible Indication of Age. *Bijdragen tot De Dierkunde* 41:61–66.
Vickers, W. T.
   1980   An Analysis of Amazonian Hunting Yields as a Function of Settlement Age. In *Working Papers on South American Indians, Volume 2*, edited by R. B Hames, pp. 7–29. Bennington College Press, Bennington.
   1988   Game Depletion Hypothesis of Amazonian Adaptation: Data from a Native Community. *Science* 239:1521–1522.
Wallace, W. J.
   1978   Southern Valley Yokuts. In *Handbook of North American Indians, California, Volume 8*, edited by R. F. Heizer, pp. 448–461. Smithsonian Institution Press, Washington, D.C.
Wallace, W. J., and D. W. Lathrap
   1975   *West Berkeley (CA-ALA-307): A Culturally Stratified Shellmound on the East Shore of San Francisco Bay*. Contributions of the University of California Archaeological Research Facility 29, University of California, Berkeley.

# 9

# Evolutionary Bet-Hedging and the Hopewell Cultural Climax

## Mark E. Madsen

**INTRODUCTION**

Since 1772, when missionaries David Zeisberger and David Jones noted mounds in the Muskingum and Scioto River valleys of Ohio (Anonymous 1775; Zeisberger 1910), the earthworks and mounds of the Hopewell mortuary complex have been a constant source of interest and contention among professionals and the public alike. Archaeologists have devoted a huge amount of archaeological effort to the excavation and description of these earthworks, mounds, and their contents. Attributes of burial features have been used to define separate cultural groups, to provide support for chronologies of the prehistoric East, and to support theories explaining the progress of pre-Columbian peoples toward complex society (Ford and Willey 1941; Griffin 1948, 1952; Morgan 1952; Willey 1966).

Throughout the long history of Hopewell scholarship, explanation of the spectacular earthworks, burial mounds, and their contents has often been descriptive or based on unexamined notions of cultural progress (e.g., Ford and Willey 1941; Griffin 1952). Most archaeological researchers of the first half of this century have focused on the problems of chronology and culture history. Making sense of culture-historical sequences was mostly ad hoc and based either on anthropological notions or simple common sense. Within the last forty years, however, the problems of chronology have waned in importance relative to explanatory issues. Consequently, the major issue in contemporary Hopewell scholarship is the explanation of burial ceremonialism, its origin and demise, and the existence within burial contexts of nonlocal materials hailing from hundreds or thousands of miles away. In fact, at least three major groups of explanations exist for the Hopewellian "cultural climax." The earliest accounts were descriptive, followed by the cultural-evolutionary "surplus" and "leisure-time" model, and more recently, ecological-functionalist models. As scientifically defensible explanatory accounts of Hopewell cultural elaboration, these models vary considerably in quality. None are independently sustainable as a scientific theory for the evolution of cultural elaboration.

The purpose of this chapter is to envision a testable, theoretical, and thus explanatory framework for Hopewellian cultural elaboration. I do not claim to provide an empirical test of the hypotheses we can derive from an evolutionary account of elaboration; given our current understanding of the problem and the quality of archaeological data from the region such a goal remains elusive. The present work, however, with other recent advances (Madsen et al. 1999), provides a necessary first step in generating a scientific framework for explaining the evolution of cultural elaboration.

## OHIO HOPEWELL

Mills (1906, 1907) defined Ohio Hopewell as the result of excavations at the Baum Village and Edwin Harness mounds. These localities had produced materials that contrasted with the burial remains Mills defined as Adena (Mills 1902). Hopewell is considered a Woodland cultural unit with the presence of mound burial and ceramics (Griffin 1952, 1958). Distinctive features include the construction of geometric earthworks enclosing both conical and loaf-shaped mounds, and the appearance of imported obsidian in raw and finished form within burial contexts (Greenman 1932; Griffin 1965, 1966; Prufer 1964; Shetrone 1920; Shetrone and Greenman 1931; Squier and Davis 1848). In common with the Adena burial complex, Hopewell sites often contain imported mica, marine shell, galena, extra-local cherts, and native copper (Prufer 1964; Webb and Snow 1945). To acquire raw materials, Ohio Hopewell groups engaged in trade with other populations throughout the Eastern Woodlands, including those represented by the Havana and Crab Orchard phases in Illinois, Copena in Tennessee, and Marksville and Crystal River in the South (Griffin 1967; Seeman 1979a; Streuver and Houart 1972).

Though the chronological relationship of Hopewell to other cultural units in the East was initially unclear (Griffin 1948), the current consensus is that Ohio Hopewell spanned the period between 200 B.C. and 500 A.D. (Dancey and Pacheco 1997; contra Griffin 1993). Within this general characterization, however, lurks considerable local variability in chronology and assemblage content. Many artifact classes associated with burials have distributions restricted to only a portion of the total temporal and spatial range of Ohio Hopewell (Greber 1991; Prufer 1964; Seeman 1977, 1979a; contra Streuver and Houart 1972). Seeman

(1977, 1979a) showed that finished goods constructed of imported raw materials had local, or at most regional, distributions, while raw materials flowing out of Ohio had supraregional distributions. As Greber (1991) notes, the emerging picture of Hopewellian regional organization appears to be one of localized groups that are similar to others in a region, but distinguished by particular suites of styles and artifact classes.

The relationship of burial elaboration and exchange to subsistence and the social organization of Hopewell populations is poorly understood. Early archaeologists, interested almost entirely in retrieval of spectacular artifacts for museum display, defined Ohio Hopewell entirely from burial contexts (Mills 1906, 1907; Shetrone 1920). Because the definition of Hopewell was focused exclusively on burials, recognition of domestic sites as belonging to the same cultural unit was virtually precluded. Moorehead (1892), for example, may have known the location of the Murphy site, later shown by Dancey (1991) to represent a Hopewell domestic settlement. Moorehead, along with Shetrone, Mills, and other workers of the time, was primarily interested in monumental architecture and spectacular artifacts and did not recognize the site as significant. Efforts to reconcile what Mills and others had described and a more representative picture of the archaeological record did not begin until the middle of this century, when Griffin and others began to examine the chronological and cultural relationships of Hopewell, Adena, and other cultural units in the Eastern Woodlands.

## EXPLANATIONS FOR HOPEWELLIAN BURIAL ELABORATION

The earliest accounts for Hopewellian elaboration are descriptive, and consist entirely of labeling the phenomenon a "florescence" of cultural creativity and art (Ford and Willey 1941). Such "explanations" lack any notion of process, and thus fail to integrate theory in a scientific context. Alternatives to a simple descriptive mode come from two approaches: cultural evolution and ecological functionalism (e.g., Caldwell 1958; Griffin 1967; Hall 1973; Seeman 1979b; Willey 1966). There are two general means of evaluating competing explanations: the sufficiency of such explanations on a philosophical (or "meta-theoretical") level, and the utility of an explanation in accounting for the existing data in at least gross detail. Using the criteria outlined by Lewontin (1974), Dunnell (1980) has critically examined cultural evolution and functionalism. His argument is not repeated here; it is sufficient to say that neither framework is suitable for explaining historical phenomena in a scientific context. In this chapter, my evaluation of existing explanations is based on their empirical efficacy in accounting for existing data.

Until recently, few data on domestic sites existed with which to evaluate competing explanations. In the absence of data, archaeologists simply assumed that Hopewell settlements were nucleated villages, and that Woodland populations were dependent upon maize agriculture for subsistence (Converse 1993; Griffin

1952, 1967, 1983, 1993; Morgan 1952; Prufer 1964, 1965; Seeman 1979b). Such assumptions rely on flawed notions of "cultural levels" from nineteenth century unilinear cultural evolution (see Dunnell 1980).

The traditional picture of Hopewellian domestic life is almost entirely incorrect, as careful fieldwork and analysis over the last thirty years has shown. Studies of nonmound sites have revealed that Hopewellian settlements were not nucleated villages, and Hopewellian populations were not dependent on maize agriculture (e.g., Bender et al. 1981; Buikstra 1992; Greenlee 1991, this volume; Gremillion 1996; Riley and Walz 1992; contra Willey 1966; Wymer 1992, 1997). Based on work conducted in the Scioto River Valley, Prufer (1965) proposed that settlement was dispersed around ceremonial centers in a series of small dwellings or "hamlets." Survey and excavation throughout the middle and upper Ohio Valley region lends strong support to Prufer's hypothesis (Aument 1997; Blank 1965; Church 1997; Dancey 1991; Fuller 1981; Genheimer 1984, 1997; Greenlee this volume; Kozarek 1997; Pacheco 1988-89, 1993a, 1993b; Phagan 1977; Prufer 1965, 1975; Shane 1971), although some scholars maintain that Hopewell populations lived in nucleated villages (e.g., Converse 1993; Griffin 1993).

The cultural-evolutionary explanation for Hopewellian elaboration is based on the notion that agricultural surpluses, leisure time, or both, are responsible for the ability of Hopewellian populations to achieve complex cultural elaboration (Griffin 1952; Morgan 1952; Prufer 1964; Willey 1966). Elaboration, culture evolutionists argue, requires individuals to attain freedom from the burdens of basic subsistence (Boas 1940; Childe 1936; Steward 1949). Therefore, cultural elaboration will occur wherever and whenever surpluses or leisure time are sufficient to allow significant investment in nonsubsistence activities (Boas 1940; Braidwood 1973). Such ideas rely heavily on the nineteenth-century notion of cultural "progress" through a series of upward-trending stages. Though deeply rooted in anthropological tradition and thought, the cultural-evolutionary explanation is not dynamically sufficient, because it lacks any mechanism for progressive change (Harris 1959; Polanyi 1957). Progressive change is simply expected as a fundamental part of how societies work.

We can also examine the general fit of the cultural-evolutionary explanation against existing evidence. In general, the hypothesis fails to offer an explanation of why some agricultural societies display high levels of investment in elaboration (e.g., the late Mississippian of the American South), but others do not (e.g., Monongahela or Fort Ancient). In addition, the cultural-evolutionary linkage between elaboration and agriculture does not fit the evidence for Hopewell. Virtually every study of macrobotanical and bone chemistry evidence has led to the conclusion that Hopewellian populations ate a generalized diet, without reliance on maize or other major crops, and thus, had no agricultural "surpluses" to fuel elaboration (Bender et al. 1981; Buikstra 1992; Greenlee 1991, this volume; Gremillion 1996; Riley and Walz 1992; Wymer 1992, 1997). The Hopewellian diet is an extension of Caldwell's (1958) "Primary Forest

Efficiency," instead of the deep reliance on maize seen in later populations. Despite empirical and logical problems with the explanation, archaeologists have not abandoned cultural evolution. Smith (1992) and Yarnell (1993), for example, attempt to substitute species of the Eastern Agricultural Complex for maize in a combined ecological/cultural-evolutionary account of Hopewell.

Ecological explanations for Hopewellian elaboration tend to emphasize the economic benefits that structured social interaction and trade would confer on the participating populations. Proponents of the ecological explanations argue that in particular Hopewell exchange functions as "insurance" or "buffering" against shortfalls in an economy based on wild plant and animal resources whose availability and productivity fluctuate over time (Braun 1985, 1988; Ford 1979; Seeman 1979b). Hall (1973), for example, suggests that the Hopewellian burial attributes, shared across a wide area, are epiphenomena of a primary exchange network based on the economic exchange of food and other critical goods. Among ecological explanations, Seeman (1979b) is unique in seeking to firmly link burial ceremonialism with economic exchange. Seeman proposes that redistribution of subsistence surpluses takes place within a group by a chief or ceremonial official in conjunction with seasonal burial rituals. Although Seeman held the contemporary belief that Hopewellian groups were maize-based agriculturists, there is nothing in his model requiring an agricultural subsistence base. Ford (1979) presents a similar argument to Seeman's, that differs only in the view that the Hopewellian diet was composed of wild plant and animal foods obtained in a foraging economy.

As examples of ecological explanations, arguments from Hall and Seeman are merely restatements of the well-known buffering effect that exchange can have on local carrying capacity. Nevertheless, purely ecological explanations fall prey to confusion between causation and function, or put another way, between proximate and ultimate causation (Mayr 1982; Rindos 1989). Seeman (1979b) himself warns that understanding how a particular behavior might function is no guide to knowing why it developed. Thus, purely functionalist or ecological explanations for Hopewell elaboration are insufficient explanations for historical phenomena in a scientific context.

Nevertheless, studies like Seeman's (1979b) and Hall's (1973) that explore the functions of elaboration have made a good start toward isolating potential proximate causes for the prevalence of elaboration in Hopewell groups. Despite some progress from cultural-evolutionary accounts, explaining why cultural elaboration existed when and where it did remains incomplete with respect to dynamic and empirical sufficiency. Since it is ecologically feasible that exchange may have been beneficial in buffering Woodland populations from the worst effects of an unpredictable environment, we must ask how such a system could have developed and persisted, especially considering the enormous costs of building large earthworks, burial complexes, and of conducting long-distance exchange or acquisition of raw materials. In particular, we lack a temporal framework that links proximate causation, of the type studied by ecological theorists, into a testable narrative of ultimate causation. Consequently, in order to translate our question about Hopewell elaboration into a testable hypothesis, we need a theory of cultural elaboration that is truly evolutionary.

## EVOLUTION AND ARCHAEOLOGY

Because people are a product of biological evolution, an increasing number of anthropologists are turning to Darwinian theory to explain the evolution of culture and social behavior. Darwinian evolution combines unique historical events and general ecological and physical processes into a theory accounting for change in populations of individuals that reproduce with fidelity. Change in Darwinian theory is selectionist, not transformational (Mayr 1959). Darwinian evolution has two distinct components: 1. the generation and transmission of variation; and 2. the sorting of variation through interaction of individuals and the environment.

To say that change is selectionist, however, does not mean that natural selection is the only, or even the chief mechanism by which evolution occurs. Instead, an evolutionary perspective on change simply means that populations evolve through differential perpetuation of traits over time, as the result of processes that alter the representation of those traits within a reproducing group of individuals. Natural selection is only one such process. Biases in mate selection give rise to sexual selection (e.g., Darwin 1871; Grant 1986), and the exigencies of the landscape and environment often give rise to isolating factors and other sampling effects (Dobzhansky 1937; Lack 1947; Mayr 1942, 1963).

To understand how evolutionary theory may be applicable not just to genetic change, but to human societies, we must recall that selection and other sorting processes operate on the entire phenotype, not on specific traits (Mayr 1969; Lewontin 1970; Sober 1984). Natural selection is nothing more than the population-level consequences of individuals differing in their chances of survival and reproduction, due to a myriad of phenotypic traits. Despite the fact that the most common definition of evolution is change in gene frequencies over time, genetic inheritance is not the only mechanism for transmission of variation between individuals. Both in humans and in other species, nongenetic transmission of information, via language, imitation, and direct teaching, is an important component of the behavioral portion of the phenotype (e.g., Bonner 1980; Caro and Hauser 1992; Jenkins 1978; Lindaur 1960; Marler and Tamura 1964; Woolfenden and Fitzpatrick 1978). There is growing recognition that "cultural" transmission is the dominant method by which behavior is inherited within humans, and an important mechanism in many vertebrate species (Bonner 1980; Boyd and Richerson 1985; Cavalli-Sforza and Feldman 1981). Consequently, the phenotypes of humans and many other animals are constructed from both culturally transmitted and genetically coded variation. If a suite of culturally transmitted rules results in phenotypes with different abilities to survive and reproduce, selection will result in the evolution of the frequencies of both culturally and genetically transmitted traits.

Several problems loom in any effort to apply an evolutionary perspective to archaeological phenomena. First among these is the issue of demonstrating the relationship between behavioral traits, manifested in classes of artifacts, and heritable variation in information or rules. Evolutionary biologists have long recognized that the phenotype is produced by the interaction of heredity and the environment during development. Schmalhausen (1949) introduced the term "norm of reaction" to denote the range of possible phenotypes a single genotype may express across different environments. In addition to ontogenetic differences produced by development interacting with the environment, the norm of reaction is increased through the evolution of traits whose expression in the phenotype is facultative or plastic (West-Eberhard 1989). Behavior, even more so than morphology, is suited to phenotypic plasticity and facultative expression. Thus, when studying the evolution of phenotypic traits such as behaviors or artifactual remains, we must understand whether the trait reflects a directly heritable rule or datum, or whether it is part of a complex of traits that represent the facultative "norm of response" of a single heritable variant. Understanding this relationship is difficult enough when dealing with living populations; in archaeological cases, the relationship between heritable variation and phenotype presents a significant challenge.

Consequently, the first challenge we face is one of defining the units of evolution in an archaeological case. Following Hull's (1980) terminology, two sorts of units are required in order to create a dynamically and empirically sufficient explanation within an evolutionary framework. The units within which inheritance is measured are called "replicators." In the biological literature, "replicator" is often taken to be synonymous with "gene," but replicators need not be genetic (Sterelny et al. 1996). Replicators are any unit of information that is heritable with fidelity, whether the mechanism of inheritance is genetic or cultural. The units within which interaction with the environment creates differential persistence of replicators are called "interactors." Phenotypes are thus classes of interactors that share the same visible characteristics. Defining replicators and interactors in empirical situations is not easy, and the effort has just begun within archaeology (Dunnell 1995; Madsen and Lipo 1993).

Further complicating our efforts to apply evolutionary models to archaeological phenomena are the formation processes of the archaeological record. The archaeological record is a composite of portions of many interactors averaged over spans of time that are often substantial. Because evolutionary models are typically written in terms of equations that relate the frequencies of replicators or phenotypes to environmental parameters, a translation step is necessary before such models can be made empirically sufficient for archaeological use. We must determine, by derivation or simulation, the dynamics of our models over time and space and the appropriate algorithms for aggregating and sampling the parameters of the model. Our model must be dynamically sufficient to produce expectations suitable for comparison with assemblages that are the results of deposition by multiple phenotypes over spans of time longer than the individual transmission event.

Given the complexities of applying evolutionary explanations to archaeological phenomena, we must face the fact that many archaeological data are simply not adequate for use in testing evolutionary hypotheses. Evolutionary theory, fundamentally, is a theory concerning the consequences of individual variation and its interaction with environments (Mayr 1959; Lewontin 1977). Existing practice in archaeology tends to generate modal or "averaged" descriptions of subsistence, settlement, and behavior. A description of the variation that is inevitably present in any group of individuals is reduced, by inclination or methodological constraint, or both, to "strategies" practiced by whole groups. And archaeological data are largely generated and described in terms of modal tendencies for phases, locales, or other artificial groupings. Consequently, use of existing data from earlier excavations and surveys alone to evaluate the veracity of an evolutionary explanation for some portion of the archaeological record will be difficult, if not impossible. We cannot, however, understand the evolution of Hopewellian elaboration using only newly acquired data; many of the burial sites and earthworks, as well as areas of likely domestic occupation, are gone or were excavated using an earlier, incompatible set of methods and techniques. We must, therefore, achieve a synthesis of both new and extant data. Ideally, we can generate new data to form a quantitative framework and thus assess the quality and limitations of previously gathered data.

## Rethinking Hopewell: Dunnell's Explanation for the Evolution of Elaboration

Elaborate burial ceremonialism and acquisition of nonlocal materials are common features of the Late Archaic and Woodland records in the Eastern United States, though not ubiquitous. The need to explain the spatial and temporal distribution of cultural elaboration within an historical, evolutionary framework led Dunnell (1989, 1999) to formulate an explanation based on the consequences of two observations. First, elaboration is not obligatory for survival, nor is it present in all times and places in eastern North American prehistory. The history of burial ceremonialism and exchange is one that differs from one population to another. Second, burial ceremonialism and acquisition of exotic materials from long distances involves significant expenditures of energy, energy then unavailable for subsistence and reproduction. From the standpoint of maximizing one's reproductive success, or foraging efficiency, energy invested in burial ceremonialism is counterproductive. Because the energy does not have immediate fitness-enhancing consequences, Dunnell referred to such phenomena as "waste."

Dunnell's (1989, 1999) explanatory sketch ties these two observations together through the invocation of an evolutionary "bet-hedging" argument (Madsen et al. 1999). The general outlines of Dunnell's argument may be summarized as follows. All vertebrates expend energy not directly connected to subsistence and reproduction, with the result that real reproductive rates are always lower than the potential maximum. In terms of an energy budget, some energy is diverted from survival and reproduction. Most organisms store at least some energy for later use; other energy not stored is used for a myriad of purposes, many of which may not increase fitness. Use of a portion of the energy budget for activities other than survival and reproduction, therefore, necessarily lowers fecundity (Dunnell 1989; Madsen et al. 1999; Seger and Brockmann 1987). Because such uses of energy are not obligatory, these behaviors create a potential reserve of energy and resources usable for survival and reproduction during difficult times. Furthermore, because energy allocation is an individual behavior that is transmissible and inherently plastic, variation would certainly exist upon which selection could act to fix "waste" behavior under the right environmental circumstances. The significant question is not whether selection *can* act to promote suboptimal allocation of the energy budget toward reproduction, but whether selection *has* acted in a specific population in this manner, and what factors in the selective environment led to the fixation of the trait.

Burial ceremonialism and long-distance acquisition of raw materials are evolutionary "bet-hedging" in that they yield fitter populations in a changing environment despite losses of potential individual fitness. It is important to note that there is nothing special about burial ceremonialism or long-distance trade or acquisition; any behavior that accomplished the same effect could have been fixed within populations, and may have been. The phenotypic traits that represent bet-hedging in the Hopewell and other Woodland groups are merely the result of the contingent history of a group of lineages in the East, among which burial ceremonialism was included as transmitted phenotypic variability.

Burial ceremonialism can be traced, in the eastern half of North America, to two separate lineages. Elaboration in burial appears in the Maritime Archaic of southern Canada (e.g., Tuck 1984), and in the Archaic and Woodland of the eastern United States (e.g., Caldwell 1958; Cunningham 1948; Dragoo 1963; Webb and Snow 1945). Burial ceremonialism in the Eastern Archaic first appears along the dry western margins of the deciduous forest zone, where mast-producing species occur in low densities compared to forests further east or south (Buikstra 1981; Chapman 1975; Charles and Buikstra 1983). In the Midwest, burial elaboration appears first in the cultural forms known as Glacial Kame and Red Ocher, at the northern edge of the *Quercus-Carya* forest zone, where oaks and hickory environments give way to the beech and elm-dominated forest of the Lake Forest zone (Cunningham 1948; Griffin 1948; Railey 1990; Ritzenthaler 1957).

The cultural-evolutionary "surplus" explanation for these features fails, at this largest scale, to account for the history of burial ceremonialism. Burial elaboration does not originate in the most productive mid-continental environments and spread outward from there. Rather, it begins on the margins, in the zones where the productivity of the oak- and hickory-dominated forest is giving way to sparser ecosystems. Along the western edge of the deciduous forest zone, and along the northern ecotone of the Lake Forest Zone, temporal variation in mast productivity is large compared to the forests east and south. A deductive consequence of the "bet-hedging" model is that the fixation of bet-hedging behaviors would be earliest in variable and less productive environments, particularly those in which the major component of variation in food productivity is temporal rather than spatial (see Dunnell 1999; Dunnell and Greenlee 1999; Hamilton 1999).

These expectations of Dunnell's explanatory sketch fit the general outlines of eastern North American prehistory. Using the model to account for the specifics of history in a particular region, however, is another matter entirely. The explanatory sketch is still cast in very general terms, suggesting, but not directly referring to the variation in phenotypes we must measure to arrive at an empirically sufficient explanation. Consequently, we must recast our view of the question again, this time from general evolutionary terms to a firmer quantitative understanding of the bet-hedging model (see Madsen et al. 1999).

## Models of Selection in Fluctuating Environments

Biologists have long argued that suboptimal reproductive levels are frequently selected for by strong temporal variation in the environment, as are other forms of evolutionary "bet-hedging" (Boyce and Perrins 1987; Charnov and Krebs 1974; Gillespie 1977, 1991; Lack 1968; Seger and Brockmann 1987; Slatkin 1974). Simple models of selection are unable to generate this result, however. The simplest measure of fitness is the reproductive success of individuals having a particular phenotype (or genotype), totaled over individual lifetimes (Endler 1986). Evolution is, however, a probabilistic rather than deterministic phenomenon. More fit individuals are those which have, on average, more offspring *that survive to reproductive age*. The phrase "on average" is needed in this statement because of the obvious presence in natural populations of stochastic environmental and developmental factors that can cause individuals with identical cultural and genetic endowments to have different numbers of offspring and differing chances of survival. When heritable variants result in phenotypically plastic traits, yet another source of variation is added to the equation linking heritable variation and fitness. Thus, when summarizing the fitness of individuals having a particular phenotype, we are obligated to measure both the average reproductive success and the variance surrounding the mean.

As Dempster (1955) and Gillespie (1977, 1991) show, when stochastic elements are introduced into simple models of selection, something unexpected happens: phenotypes with higher average numbers of offspring do not necessarily increase in frequency over the long term. The actual outcome is highly dependent on whether the fitness of phenotypes experiences temporal fluctuations on the time scales that reproduction (i.e., transmission) occurs. When the stochastic element in individual reproductive success is caused by temporal fluctuations in fitness, the best measure of overall fitness is the geometric mean of offspring number, averaged over time (Dempster 1955; Gillespie 1977). Under a variety of circumstances, increases in the variance of fitness *decrease* the mean fitness of a phenotype. Thus, selection may act in a fluctuating environment to favor any behavior or trait that reduces the variance in offspring survival, since reducing the variance will increase the geometric mean fitness of the phenotype in question (Gillespie 1977).

An interesting corollary to Gillespie's (1977) incorporation of a stochastic element to fitness within a fluctuating environment is the fact that selection will favor variance-reducing phenotypes even at the expense of absolute reproductive success. When variance in fitness is zero, the geometric mean and arithmetic mean of reproductive success are equal, but when variance is positive, the geometric mean of reproductive success will always be less than the arithmetic mean. Seger and Brockmann (1987) explore the ramifications of this fact in their review of evolutionary "bet-hedging" phenomena, describing many examples of selection reducing variance in individual fitness (over the set of encountered environments) at some cost to *expected* fitness.

By way of example, Boyce and Perrins (1987) evaluated three possible explanations for suboptimal reproductive efforts among a well-studied population of Great Tits (*Parus major*), including the bet-hedging hypothesis. The population in question averages 8.53 eggs per clutch, whereas in good years, some individuals may lay clutches of 10–12 eggs. Using data gathered on 4,489 clutches of birds over 24 years, Boyce and Perrins demonstrate that mortality is greater among birds with a larger clutch size than those laying a smaller clutch during years that are poor for survival of young. Moreover, this effect reduces the mean and increases the variance in fitness for individuals laying larger clutch sizes, yielding higher geometric mean fitness for the phenotypes laying smaller clutches. The bet-hedging phenomenon is not isolated to birds or even to animals; investigators have found similar effects in bud dormancy rates within herbaceous plants (Nilsson et al. 1996), and germination timing in annual and perennial plants (Bulmer 1984, 1985; Cohen 1966).

Despite the success of bet-hedging models in nonhuman cases, the very simplest models do not offer us much confidence that the bet-hedging argument is applicable to evolution with cultural transmission. The hallmark of cultural transmission is the fact that reproduction does not proceed in "generations." To model the effects of continuous transmission of traits with continual replication episodes not concentrated at a single point in the life cycle, Seger and Brockmann's (1987:194) haploid temporal model with overlapping generations and iteroparity is an excellent starting point. In their model, overlapping generations are created by allowing a proportion ($s$) of the current time period's transmitting individuals to survive and continue to replicate during the next interval. Thus, each time period's population is composed of a relatively large number of individuals that have replicated previously, and a smaller number of "new" individuals ($1$-$s$). When using this model for culturally transmitted variability, the variable $s$ represents the fact that individuals may experience few, or many fluctuations in environment during their lifetimes, during the time in which they are passing on their phenotypic traits to others. If we consider a population with two traits A and B, with the fitness of A scaled to that of B, the recurrence equation for each interval is:

$$p_t + 1 = p_t \left[ s + (1-s)W_t \, / \, V_t \right]$$

where $W_t$ is the relative fitness of A in generation $t$,
and $V_t$ is the population mean fitness $1 + p_t(W_t - 1)$.          (Equation 1)

When $s = 0$, individuals each experience only one kind of environment during their lifetimes, and this model reduces to the simple mean fitness models discussed previously. As $s$ increases, however, temporal variation in the environment is averaged across an individual's lifetime. Over time, selection tends to favor a weighted sum of the geometric mean population and individual fitnesses, according to Seger and Brockmann (1987). If one simplifies the model to a situation with "good" and "bad" periods in roughly equal proportions, the mean frequency of phenotype A is the frequency that maximizes:

$$f(p) = s\sqrt{V_g(p)V_b(p)} + (1-s)\left[p\sqrt{W_g W_b} + (1-p)\right]$$          (Equation 2)

where $V_i(p)$ are the population mean fitnesses in good and bad periods (Equation 1), and $W_i$ are the individual fitnesses in good and bad periods.

When individuals experience few episodes of environmental fluctuation between "good" and "bad" states, the population's average composition will tend to emphasize individual geometric mean fitness. As $s$ increases and individuals experience more fluctuations (either because they live longer or fluctuations occur at a higher frequency), more weight is given to the first term in the equation, which tends to emphasize the population geometric mean fitness. Seger and Brockmann (1987) go on to show that the size of the advantage gained by bet-hedging phenotypes declines as $s$ increases, although the effect is still weakly present when $s$ is large. In particular, *population* geometric mean fitness may often be maximized where there is phenotypic variation and only some individuals exhibit the bet-hedging phenotype. Thus, we would expect that bet-hedging behaviors be would most easily favored in environments with unpredictable fluctuations in the fitness of individuals, but where fluctuations tend to be long and the recurrence interval infrequent during the lifetime of individuals.

During the past few years, there has been a great increase in interest in models of selection in fluctuating environments (Gillespie 1991; Yoshimura and Clark 1991). Of particular interest are attempts to apply theories of selection in fluctuating environments to game theory models used in the optimality analysis of behavior. Haccou and Iwasa (1995) note that temporal variation of the environment and stochasticity of strategies are frequently neglected in optimality modeling, possibly because stochastic strategies and environmental fluctuations do not maximize the expected long-term success of individuals, a key assumption of game theoretic approaches (Maynard Smith 1982). Haccou and Iwasa (1995) point out, however, that it is the long-term success of the *phenotype* and, thus, the heritable variation that is important in evolutionary processes, not the success of individuals per se. McNamara (1997) has extended Haccou and Iwasa's stochastic optimality model yet further by examining the fitness of offspring number strategies in structured populations within a fluctuating environment. Development of bet-hedging theory has yielded important predictions already, such as Haccou and Iwasa's (1995) observation that there is a minimum threshold of environmental stochasticity required before the geometric mean fitness effects noted earlier will manifest themselves.

## DERIVING ARCHAEOLOGICAL EXPECTATIONS FOR THE BET-HEDGING MODEL

The model presented above is clearly plausible, yet relatively simple with respect to the real world. It is dichotomized to "good" and "bad" periods, rather than having a continuous function for the quality of the environment at a particular point in time. The real world is also characterized by variation in space as well as time, which greatly increases the complexity of the equations. With the contributions of works such as Gillespie and McNamara, however, the theory has enough dynamic sufficiency to begin the process of explaining many real situations.

### Simulation as a Means of Enhancing Empirical Sufficiency

Archaeological use of the bet-hedging theory, however, requires that we face the translation step noted above to generate an empirically sufficient explanation. With living organisms, reproductive success, as well as energy budgets, can be measured. In the archaeological case, none of the relevant variables may be directly measured. Instead, we must extend the theory to predict the quantitative effects of selection within a fluctuating environment on the aggregated record of phenotypes. Given the mathematical complexity of the selection models under discussion (e.g., McNamara 1997), translating the bet-hedging explanation into archaeological units by direct derivation seems unlikely.

Instead, a more direct approach to the problem is to implement the relatively simple model described by Equations 1 and 2, within the context of an agent-based simulation system. Several systems exist that fully support evolutionary simulations, including Swarm and the "Sugarscape" model of Epstein and Axtell (1996). Within such a model, individuals ("agents") with a distribution of metabolisms and abilities to reproduce themselves and transmit simple cultural traits may be placed in environments that fluctuate in productivity. To examine the empirical behavior of Equations 1 and 2 with respect to their ability to select for bet-hedging behaviors in various environments, individuals are given a range of simple reproductive behaviors and the necessity of satisfying the metabolisms for themselves and their offspring (until mature) through extraction of resources from the environment. By allowing the environment to fluctuate both in space and time, it should be possible to examine systematically the effects of the frequency and amplitude of environmental unpredictability on the fitness of various reproductive behaviors and uses of the energy budget. My colleagues and I have constructed a model that incorporates these dimensions (Madsen et al. 1999), and others have examined the model's expectations and fit with real world cases (e.g., Aranyosi 1999; Dunnell and Greenlee 1999; Hamilton 1999; Kornbacher 1999; Sterling 1999).

Once our simulation model approximates the theory from which it is derived, the model can be extended to allow us to examine the effects of sampling on various temporal and spatial scales, such that we can express the bet-hedging theory in terms that are concordant with archaeological units. We have seen success in this regard (Madsen et al. 1999). Simulation is thus a tool for increasing the empirical sufficiency of theory, or a means of exploring complex mathematics and its implications for different observational units.

## Expectations and Data Requirements

Our simulation modeling, while simple, tells us a great deal about the relationship between "wasteful" behavior, environmental uncertainty, mobility, and the distribution of wasteful phenotypes across a population (Madsen et al. 1999). The model, its expectations of the real world, and data requirements for research will fit cases worldwide, as recent publications have illustrated (e.g., Aranyosi 1999; Dunnell and Greenlee 1999; Hamilton 1999; Kornbacher 1999; Sterling 1999). Although it is premature to "test" the bet-hedging explanation against the Hopewell record given the complexities of empirical sufficiency, we can at least outline the classes of data that will be required.

### Environmental Uncertainty

Our simulations confirmed the significance of environmental uncertainty in the evolution of cultural elaboration. Marked unpredictability or uncertainty is indeed capable of selection for "wasteful" phenotypes, where these agents tended to have higher geometric mean fitness than their nonwasteful counterparts.

Measuring palaeoenvironmental variation with respect to archaeological data is a demanding aspect of research, but one that has recently seen significant advances (e.g., Broughton, this volume; Greenlee, this volume; Kornbacher 1999). New high-resolution climatic studies that provide proxy measures of variation in rainfall, temperature, other factors affecting productivity, as well as documentation of catastrophic events are critical adjuncts to testing bet-hedging hypothesis.

### Subsistence, Mobility, and Scale of Social Integration

Many of the data requirements for testing the bet-hedging explanation stem from the fact that burial ceremonialism and exchange are group phenomena in Hopewell. Communities are structured as a series of small domestic localities (Dancey 1991), with a number of domestic localities apparently participating in the construction of local or regional earthworks and burial mounds. Thus, data concerning the phenotypes of individuals from any single community will be found in several locations, including domestic sites and burial mounds. The first class of data required to test a bet-hedging explanation, therefore, will be information on the subdivision of populations into communities obtained by mapping relative interaction frequencies using functional and stylistic artifact classes across numerous controlled surface collections, and careful dating (Fuller 1981; Lipo et al. 1997; Madsen 1997).

The second important class of data required for tests of the bet-hedging explanation concerns the spatial-temporal organization of subsistence in Hopewell populations. And in this regard, mobility and migration are linked to settlement systems and subsistence. As we point out, mobility and migration act as a form of income averaging, particularly where critical resources are spatially stable (Madsen et al. 1999:272–3). Our simulation runs showed that agents with greater mobility evolved lower levels of "waste" than those more restricted in their movement in search of resources. Thus, data on the positioning (and scale) of communities across microenvironments bear directly on the magnitude of temporal variability in fitness each population might have experienced. On a coarse scale, one would expect that communities composed of domestic sites spread across multiple microenvironments would suffer less variability in mean environmental quality, since the effects of temporal variability would be partially mitigated by uncorrelated cycles of productivity in the different niches. In contrast, communities that are located in a single microenvironment, and concomitantly enjoy less mobility, would likely experience greater temporal variability in fitness. Such communities should exhibit the artifactual correlates of bet-hedging earlier and in higher magnitude than communities spread across microenvironments.

Data on the participation of domestic sites in the group burial ceremonialism and exchange are also needed, in order to link together evidence on demographics and environment obtained from settlement studies with the phenotypes we posit as leading to higher long-term success. While much of the artifactual evidence for burial ceremonialism and participation in exchange is aggregated in community-created deposits at mound and earthwork sites, some of the same artifact classes also occur in domestic sites (Dancey 1991; Dancey and Pacheco 1997). With large samples from surface collections at domestic sites, it should be possible to measure at least relative differences in elaboration-related artifact classes between domestic locales.

### Demographic Structure

Our work has also shown that selection for "waste" can be linked to the average age distribution of the agent-based simulated populations. In each run, we recorded age at death for each individual, providing testable predictions for archaeological skeletal populations. Simulations with higher frequencies of "waste" tended to have roughly equal ratios of adults to juveniles within the population and in death assemblages. But in less "wasteful" populations, we found higher juvenile mortality, and higher ratios of juveniles to adults in the living population. The archaeological consequences of this observation is for age-at-death statistics from skeletal populations to be relatively right-skewed, reflecting longer life expectancy overall (Madsen et al. 1999; Sterling 1999). We should thus expect differences in age-at-death distributions for "wasteful" and "non-wasteful" populations.

### Phenotypic Success

Finally, in order to test a bet-hedging explanation, data on the actual success of different phenotypes is required. Our simulations showed that "wasteful" and "nonwasteful" phenotypes could co-exist in a stable polymorphism. We found that the *mean* value of "wastefulness" was frequently unaffected by selection, but that markedly unpredictable environments exhibited strongly right-skewed distributions—or skewed in the direction of having more "wasteful" phenotypes (Madsen et al. 1999:273; Figure 8). This kind of distributional evidence for "waste" is significant for archaeology, given the difficulty of measuring "wasteful" behavior in individuals.

While we cannot measure the behavior or fitness of individuals directly from archaeological remains, there are several sources of archaeological evidence that inform on *rates* of survival and reproductive success. The first is the size of communities measured through time, measured as the number of domestic sites and the rate of increase of new domestic occupations within a community. A second measure is the duration of domestic sites, since phenotypes with the highest mean fitness should persist longer in the record than those with lower fitness.

## CONCLUSIONS

We do not yet have an answer as to whether Dunnell's (1989, 1999) "waste" explanation, as a representative of evolutionary bet-hedging models, adequately accounts for the evolution of cultural elaboration in the forested eastern United States during the Woodland period. Nevertheless, our examination has allowed us to rephrase the generic question of explaining burial ceremonialism as a hypothesis that the evolution of elaboration may be a manifestation of a more general evolutionary phenomenon (Madsen et al. 1999). This phenomenon, often called "evolutionary bet-hedging" in the biological literature, is widespread in situations where the fitness of phenotypes fluctuates in a temporally variable environment.

One of the chief benefits of re-expressing the explanation in increasingly quantitative terms is that we sharpen our ability to make "predictions" from the theory and derive new research questions, as recent research has already shown (see Aranyosi 1999; Dunnell and Greenlee 1999; Hamilton 1999; Kornbacher 1999; Madsen et al. 1999; Sterling 1999). For example, the model raises the question of the spectacular degree to which bet-hedging appears to be fixed within Hopewell populations in the form of monumental architecture and lavish burial ceremonialism. Why would selection continue to favor greater investment in bet-hedging? In quantitative terms, we are asking whether there exists, throughout the Hopewell period, any evolutionarily stable level of investment in bet-hedging behavior. Is the balance between temporal variability and population growth rates really that tenuous? An alternative is that selection for bet-hedging reaches a dynamic equilibrium at some intermediate degree of investment. However, since communities that practice bet-hedging in the form of burial ceremonialism tend to persist and are residentially stable, burial and earthwork sites over time tend to accrete larger numbers of burials and evidence for exotic raw materials. The spectacular nature of the contemporary Hopewell record is, in this view, a consequence of archaeological formation processes in addition to bet-hedging. Yet another alternative is that the particular behaviors linked with bet-hedging in the Hopewell record are pleiotropic and are under selection from different directions. If burial ceremonialism also functions as part of the economic system in the ways that Seeman (1979b), Ford (1979), and Hall (1973) envisioned, some of the behaviors and artifacts associated with cultural elaboration may be under selection from multiple directions, leading to strong pressure for increasing levels of energy investment.

Considerable work remains before a plausible test can be built for the bet-hedging model, let alone the additional research questions the model generates. The process of refining questions and specifying theoretical models has its own rewards, however, independent of the knowledge we hope to gain about the past. In general, we can hope to gain two distinct kinds of products from any archaeological study conducted within a scientific context. The first, of course, is testable and cumulative knowledge concerning the past. The second product is theoretical explanations, such as the bet-hedging model discussed in this chapter, along with guidelines about the classes of phenomena to which they apply. As theoretical models are used to generate knowledge about the past, they become more valuable as scientific theories in their own right, capable of use anywhere and anytime the phenomena of interest meet the requirements for explanation by that model. My contribution here is an attempt to create a product of the second kind (bet-hedging for continuous transmission) as an explanation for situations in which burial and other forms of elaboration covary with unpredictable environments, including, but not limited to, the Hopewell.

## ACKNOWLEDGMENTS

I wish to thank, in particular, the two individuals who are ultimately responsible for this chapter: R. C. Dunnell, without whom we'd not have started down this particular path, and C.P. Lipo, with whom, for nearly a decade, I've argued, discussed, modeled, and written about the challenge of using evolutionary theory to ask archaeological questions. T. L. Hunt offered special help in revising and editing this work. My colleagues K. Kornbacher, K. Wilhelmsen, S. Sterling, F. Hamilton, and T. Hunt have also read drafts, sketches, and versions of this chapter and offered good suggestions. I can only hope these are reflected in the final product. P. Fitzpatrick assisted immeasurably by editing and helping me express myself in written form. Portions of this work were done during the author's tenure as a National Science Foundation Graduate Research Fellow.

## NOTE

This is the first essay in Mayr's collection of essays, translated from the German.

## REFERENCES CITED

Anonymous
   1775   A Plan of an Old Fort and Intrenchment in the Shawnese Country, Taken on Horseback, by Computation Only. *Royal American Magazine for January, 1775* pp. 29–30.
Aranyosi, E. F.
   1999   Wasteful Advertising and Variance Reduction: Darwinian Models for the Sigificance on Nonutilitarian Architecture. *Journal of Anthropological Archaeology* 18(3):356–375.
Aument, B. W.
   1997   Ohio Middle Woodland Intracommunity Settlement Variability: A Case Study from the Licking Valley. In *Ohio Hopewell Community Organization*, edited by W. S. Dancey and P. J. Pacheco, pp. 41–84. Kent State University Press, Kent.
Bender, M. M., D. A. Baerreis, and R. A. Steventon
   1981   Further Light on Carbon Isotopes and Hopewell Agriculture. *American Antiquity* 46:346–353.
Blank, J. E.
   1965   The Brown's Bottom Site, Ross County, Ohio. *Ohio Archaeologist* 15:16–21.
Boas, F.
   1940   *Race, Language, and Culture*. Macmillan, New York.
Bonner, J. T.
   1980   *The Evolution of Culture in Animals*. Princeton University Press, Princeton.
Boyce, M. S., and C. M. Perrins
   1987   Optimizing Great Tit Clutch Size in a Fluctuating Environment. *Ecology* 68:142–153.
Boyd, R., and P. J. Richerson
   1985   *Culture and the Evolutionary Process*. University of Chicago Press, Chicago.
Braidwood, R.
   1973   The Early Village in Southwestern Asia. *Journal of Near Eastern Studies* 31:34–39.
Braun, D. P.
   1985   Midwestern Hopewellian Exchange and Supralocal Interaction. In *Peer-Polity Interactions in Prehistory*, edited by C. Renfrew and J. S. Cherry, pp. 117–126. Cambridge University Press, Cambridge.
   1988   The Social and Technological Roots of "Late Woodland." In *Interpretations of Culture Change in the Eastern Woodlands during the Late Woodland Period*, edited by R. W. Yerkes, pp. 17–38. Ohio State University Occasional Papers in

Anthropology. Department of Anthropology, The Ohio State University, Columbus, Ohio.

Buikstra, J. E.
1981 Mortuary Practices, Paleodemography, and Paleopathology: A Case Study from the Koster Site (Illinois). In *The Archaeology of Death*, edited by R. Chapman, I. Kinnes, and K. Randsborg, pp. 123–132. Cambridge University Press, Cambridge.
1992 Diet and Disease in Late Prehistory. In *Disease and Demography in Late Prehistory*, edited by J. W. Verano and D. H. Ubelaker, pp. 87–102. Smithsonian Institution Press, Washington, D.C.

Bulmer, M. G.
1984 Delayed Germination of Seeds: Cohen's Model Revisited. *Theoretical Population Biology* 26:367–377.
1985 Selection for Iteroparity in a Variable Environment. *American Naturalist* 126:63–71.

Caldwell, J. R.
1958 *Trend and Tradition in the Prehistory of the Eastern United States*. American Anthropological Association, Memoir No. 88.

Caro, T. M., and M. D. Hauser
1992 Is There Teaching in Nonhuman Animals? *Quarterly Review of Biology* 67:151–174.

Cavalli-Sforza, L. L., and M. W. Feldman
1981 *Cultural Transmission and Evolution: A Quantitative Approach*. Princeton University Press, Princeton.

Chapman, C. H.
1975 *The Archaeology of Missouri I*. University of Missouri Press, Columbia.

Charles, D. K., and J. E. Buikstra
1983 Archaic Mortuary Sites in the Central Mississippi Drainage: Distribution, Structure, and Behavioral Implications. In *Archaic Hunters and Gatherers in the American Midwest*, edited by J. L. Phillips and J. A. Brown, pp. 117–145. Academic Press, New York.

Charnov, E. L., and J. R. Krebs
1974 On Clutch Size and Fitness. *Ibis* 116:217–219.

Childe, V.G.
1936 *Man Makes Himself*. Watts, London.

Church, F.
1997 Beyond the Scioto Valley: Middle Woodland Occupation in the Salt Creek Drainage. In *Ohio Hopewell Community Organization*, edited by W. S. Dancey and P. J. Pacheco, pp.331–360. Kent State University Press, Kent.

Cohen, D.
1966 Optimizing Reproduction in a Randomly Varying Environment. *Journal of Theoretical Biology* 12:110–129.

Converse, R. N.
1993 The Troyer Site: A Hopewellian Habitation Site, and a Secular View of Ohio Hopewell Villages. *Ohio Archaeologist* 43:4–12.

Cunningham, W. M.
1948 *A Study of the Glacial Kame Culture in Michigan, Ohio, and Indiana*. Occasional Contributions from the Museum of Anthropology of the University of Michigan, No. 12, Ann Arbor.

Dancey, W. S.
  1991   A Middle Woodland Settlement in Central Ohio: A Preliminary Report on the Murphy Site (33Li212). *Pennsylvania Archaeologist* 61:37–72.
Dancey, W. S., and P. J. Pacheco
  1997   The Ohio Hopewell Settlement Pattern Problem in Historical Perspective. In *Ohio Hopewell Community Organization*, edited by W. S. Dancey and P. J. Pacheco, pp. 3–40. Kent State University Press, Kent.
Darwin, C.
  1871   *The Descent of Man and Selection in Relation to Sex.* John Murray, London.
Dempster, E. R.
  1955   Maintenance of Genetic Heterogeneity. *Cold Spring Harbor Symposia on Quantitative Biology* 20:25–32.
Dobzhansky, T.
  1937   *Genetics and the Origin of Species.* Columbia University Press, New York.
Dragoo, D. W.
  1963   *Mounds for The Dead.* Annals of the Carnegie Museum. Carnegie Museum, Pittsburgh.
Dunnell, R. C.
  1980   Evolutionary Theory and Archaeology. *Advances in Archaeological Method and Theory* 3:35–99.
  1989   Aspects of the Application of Evolutionary Theory in Archaeology. In *Archaeological Thought in America*, edited by C. C. Lamberg-Karlovsky, pp. 35–99. Cambridge University Press, Cambridge.
  1992   Archaeology and Evolutionary Science. In *Quandaries and Quests: Visions of Archaeology's Future*, edited by L. Wandsnider, pp. 209–224. Center for Archaeological Investigations, Occasional Paper No. 20. Southern Illinois University Press, Carbondale.
  1995   What Is It That Actually Evolves? In *Evolutionary Archaeology: Methodological Issues*, edited by P. A. Teltser, pp. 33–50. University of Arizona Press, Tucson.
  1999   The Concept of Waste in Evolutionary Archaeology. *Journal of Anthropological Archaeology* 18(3):243–250.
Dunnell, R. C., and D. M. Greenlee
  1999   Late Woodland Period "Waste" Reduction in the Ohio River Valley. *Journal of Anthropological Archaeology* 18(3):376–395.
Endler, J.
  1986   *Natural Selection in the Wild.* Princeton University Press, Princeton.
Epstein, J. M., and R. Axtell
  1996   *Growing Artificial Societies: Social Science from the Bottom Up.* Brookings Institute Press/MIT Press, Cambridge, Massachusetts.
Ford, J. A., and G. R. Willey
  1941   An Interpretation of the Prehistory of the Eastern United States. *American Anthropologist* 43:325–363.
Ford, R. I.
  1979   Gathering and Gardening: Trends and Consequences of Hopewell Subsistence Strategies. In *Hopewell Archaeology: The Chillicothe Conference*, edited by D. S. Brose and N. Greber, pp. 234–238. Kent State University Press, Kent.

Fuller, J. W.
   1981   *Developmental Change in Prehistoric Community Patters: The Development of Nucleated Village Communities in Northern West Virginia.* Unpublished Ph.D. dissertation, Department of Anthropology, University of Washington, Seattle.
Genheimer, R. A.
   1984   *A Systematic Examination of Middle Woodland Settlements in Warren County, Ohio.* Report submitted to Ohio Historic Preservation Office, Columbus, Ohio,
   1997   Stubbs Cluster: Hopewellian Site Dynamics at a Forgotten Little Miami River Valley Settlement. In *Ohio Hopewell Community Organization*, edited by W. S. Dancey and P. J. Pacheco, pp. 283–310. Kent State University Press, Kent.
Gillespie, J. H.
   1977   Natural Selection for Variances in Offspring Numbers: A New Evolutionary Principle. *American Naturalist* 111:1010–1014.
   1991   *The Causes of Molecular Evolution.* Oxford University Press, New York.
Grant, P. R.
   1986   *The Ecology and Evolution of Darwin's Finches.* Princeton University Press, Princeton.
Greber, N. B.
   1991   A Study of Continuity and Contrast between Central Scioto Adena and Hopewell Sites. *West Virginia Archaeologist* 43(1&2):1–26.
Greenlee, D. M.
   1991   Patterns in Late Prehistoric Subsistence through Mass Spectrometric Analysis. Paper presented at the 56th Annual Meeting of the Society for American Archaeology, New Orleans, Louisiana.
Greenman, E. F.
   1932   Excavation of the Coon Mound and an Analysis of the Adena Culture. *Ohio Archaeological and Historical Quarterly* 41:366–532.
Gremillion, K. J.
   1996   Early Agricultural Diet in Eastern North America: Evidence from Two Kentucky Rockshelters. *American Antiquity* 61(3):520–536.
Griffin, J. B.
   1948   *An Interpretation of the Glacial Kame Culture.* Occasional Contributions from the Museum of Anthropology of the University of Michigan, No. 12, Ann Arbor.
   1952   Culture Periods in Eastern United States Archeology. In *The Archeology of Eastern North America*, edited by J. B. Griffin. University of Chicago Press, Chicago.
   1958   *The Chronological Position of the Hopewellian Culture in the Eastern United States.* Anthropological Papers No. 12. Museum of Anthropology, University of Michigan, Ann Arbor.
   1965   Hopewell and the Dark Black Glass. *Michigan Archaeologist* 11:115–155.
   1966   A Non-Neolithic Copper Industry in North America. *XXXVI Congreso Internacional de Americanistas* 1:281–285.
   1967   Eastern North America Archaeology: A Summary. *Science* 156:175–191.
   1983   The Midlands. In *Ancient North Americans*, edited by J. D. Jennings, pp. 243–302. W. H. Freeman and Co., New York.
   1993   *Major Hopewell Sites without People and Minor Hopewell Sites without Goodies.* Chillicothe, Ohio.

Haccou, P., and Y. Iwasa
    1995    Optimal Mixed Strategies in Stochastic Environments. *Theoretical Population Biology* 47:212–243.
Hall, R. L.
    1973    An Interpretation of the Two-Climax Model of Illinois Prehistory. Paper presented at the 9th International Congress of Anthropological and Ethnological Sciences, Chicago.
Hamilton, F. E.
    1999    Southeastern Archaic Mounds: Examples of Elaboration in a Temporally Fluctuating Environment? *Journal of Anthropological Archaeology* 18(3):344–355.
Harris, M.
    1959    The Economy Has No Surplus. *American Anthropologist* 61:185–199.
Hull, D.
    1980    Individuality and Selection. *Annual Review of Ecology and Systematics* 11:311–332.
Jenkins, P. F.
    1978    Cultural Transmission of Song Patterns and Dialect Development in a Free-living Bird Population. *Animal Behavior* 25:50–78.
Kornbacher, K. D.
    1999    Cultural Elaboration in Prehistoric Coastal Peru: An Example of Evolution in a Temporally Variable Environment. *Journal of Anthropological Archaeology* 18(3):282–318.
Kozarek, S. E.
    1997    Determining Sedentism in the Archaeological Record. In *Ohio Hopewell Community Organization*, edited by W. S. Dancey and P. J. Pacheco, pp. 131–152. Kent State University Press, Kent.
Lack, D.
    1947    *Darwin's Finches*. Cambridge University Press, Cambridge.
    1968    *Ecological Adaptations for Breeding in Birds*. Methuen, London.
Lewontin, R. C.
    1970    The Units of Selection. *Annual Review of Ecology and Systematics* 1:1–18.
    1974    *The Genetic Basis of Evolutionary Change*. Columbia University Press, New York.
    1977    Sociobiology—A Caricature of Darwinism. In *Proceedings of the 1976 Biennial Meeting of the Philosophy of Science Association (Vol. 2)*, edited by F. Suppe and P. D. Asquith, pp. 22–31.
Lindaur, M.
    1960    Time-compensated Sun Orientation in Bees. *Cold Spring Harbor Symposia in Quantitative Biology* 25:371–377.
Lipo, C. P., M. E. Madsen, R. C. Dunnell, and T. Hunt
    1997    Population Structure, Cultural Transmission, and Frequency Seriation. *Journal of Anthropological Archaeology* 16:301–333.
Madsen, M. E.
    1997    Problems and Solutions in the Study of Dispersed Communities. In *Ohio Hopewell Community Patterns*, edited by W. S. Dancey and P. J. Pacheco, pp. 85–104. Kent State University Press, Kent.

Madsen, M. E., and C. P. Lipo
1993 Units of Evolution in a Darwinian Approach to Anthropology: Unit Requirements and Implications for the Subdisciplines. Paper presented at the Annual Meeting of the American Anthropological Association, Washington D.C.
Madsen, M., C. Lipo, and M. Cannon
1999 Fitness and Reproductive Trade-Offs in Uncertain Environments: Explaining the Evolution of Cultural Elaboration. *Journal of Anthropological Archaeology* 18(3):251–281.
Marler, P., and M. Tamura
1964 Culturally Transmitted Patterns of Vocal Behavior in Sparrows. *Science* 146:1483–1486.
Maynard Smith, J.
1982 *Evolution and the Theory of Games.* Oxford University Press, Oxford.
Mayr, E.
1942 *Systematics and the Origin of Species.* Dover Publications, New York.
1959 Typological and Population Thinking. In *Evolution and Anthropology: A Centennial Appraisal*, edited by B. J. Meggers, pp. 409–412. Anthropological Society of Washington, Washington, D.C.
1963 *Animal Species and Evolution.* Harvard University Press, Cambridge, Massachusetts.
1969 *Principles of Systematic Zoology.* McGraw Hill, New York.
1982 *The Growth of Biological Thought.* Belknap Press, Harvard, Cambridge, Massachusetts.
McNamara, J. M.
1997 Optimal Life Histories for Structured Populations in Fluctuating Environments. *Theoretical Population Biology* 51:94–108.
Mills, W. C.
1902 Excavations of the Adena Mound. *Ohio State Archaeological and Historical Quarterly* 10:451–479.
1906 Baum Prehistoric Village. *Ohio State Archaeological and Historical Quarterly* 15:45–136.
1907 Explorations of the Edwin Harness Mound. *Ohio State Archaeological and Historical Quarterly* 16:113–193.
Moorehead, W. K.
1892 *Primitive Man in Ohio.* G. P. Putnam's Sons, New York.
Morgan, R. G.
1952 Outline of Cultures in the Ohio Region. In *Archeology of Eastern North America*, edited by J. B. Griffin, pp. 83–98. University of Chicago Press, Chicago.
Nilsson, P., J. Tuomi, and M. Astrom
1996 Bud Dormancy as a Bet-hedging Strategy. *American Naturalist* 147:269–281.
Pacheco, P. J.
1988–89 Ohio Middle Woodland Settlement Variability in the Upper Licking River Drainage. *Journal of the Steward Anthropological Society* 18:87–117.
1993a *Ohio Hopewell Settlement Patterns: An Application of the Vacant Center Model to Middle Woodland Period Intracommunity Settlement.* Ph.D. dissertation, Department of Anthropology, The Ohio State University, Columbus.

1993b Ohio Hopewell Regional Community and Settlement Patterns. Paper presented at "A View from the Core: A Conference Synthesizing Ohio Hopewell Archaeology," Ohio Archaeological Council, November 19, 1993, Chillicothe, Ohio.

Phagan, C. J.
1977 *Intensive Archaeological Survey of the S.R. 315 Wastewater Treatment Facility Location Known as the DECCO-1 Site (33-DI-28).* Progress Report to the Board of County Commissioners, Delaware County, Ohio,

Polanyi, K.
1957 *Trade and Market in the Early Empires: Economics in History and Theory.* Free Press, Glencoe, Illinois.

Prufer, O. H.
1964 The Hopewell Complex of Ohio. In *Hopewellian Studies*, edited by J. Caldwell and R. Hall, pp. 35–48. Illinois State Museum Scientific Papers, Volume 22.
1965 *The McGraw Site: A Study in Hopewellian Dynamics.* Cleveland Museum of Natural History, Scientific Publications 4(1), Cleveland, Ohio.
1975 The Scioto Valley Archaeological Survey. In *Studies in Ohio Archaeology*, edited by O. H. Prufer and D. McKenzie, pp. 267–328. Kent State University Press, Kent.

Railey, J. A.
1990 Woodland Period. In *The Archaeology of Kentucky: Past Accomplishments and Future Directions*, edited by D. Pollack, pp. 247–374. Kentucky Heritage Council State Historic Preservation Comprehensive Plan Report No. 1.

Riley, T. J., and G. Walz
1992 AMS Dating of Maize from the Middle Woodland Holding Site (11MS118) in the American Bottom of Illinois. Paper presented at the 49th Annual Meeting of the Southeastern Archaeological Conference, Little Rock, Arkansas.

Rindos, D.
1989 Undirected Variation and the Darwinian Explanation of Cultural Change. In *Archaeological Method and Theory*, edited by M. B. Schiffer, pp. 1–44. University of Arizona Press, Tucson.

Ritzenthaler, R. E.
1957 The Old Copper Culture of Wisconsin. *Wisconsin Archaeologist* 38:183–332.

Schmalhausen, I. I.
1949 *Factors of Evolution: The Theory of Stabilizing Selection.* Blakiston, Philadelphia.

Seeman, M. F.
1977 *The Hopewell Interaction Sphere: The Evidence for Inter-Regional Trade and Structural Complexity.* Unpublished Ph.D. dissertation, Department of Anthropology, Indiana University, Bloomington.
1979a *The Hopewellian Interaction Sphere: the Evidence for Inter-Regional Trade and Structural Complexity.* Prehistory Research Series, Vol. V, No. 2. Indiana Historical Society, Bloomington.
1979b Feasting with the Dead: Ohio Hopewell Charnel House Ritual as a Context for Redistribution. In *Hopewell Archaeology: The Chillicothe Conference*, edited by D. Brose and N. Greber, pp. 39–46. Kent State University Press, Kent.

Seger, J., and H. J. Brockmann
1987 What is Bet-Hedging? In *Oxford Surveys in Evolutionary Biology*, edited by P. H. Harvey and L. Partridge, pp. 182–211. Oxford University Press, Oxford.

Shane, O. C. I.
   1971   The Scioto Hopewell. In *Adena: The Seeking of an Identity*, edited by B. K. Swartz, pp. 142–145. Ball State University Press, Muncie.
Shetrone, H. C.
   1920   The Culture Problem in Ohio Archaeology. *American Anthropologist* 22:144–172.
Shetrone, H. C., and E. F. Greenman
   1931   Explorations of the Seip Group of Prehistoric Earthworks. *Ohio State Archaeological and Historical Quarterly* 40:343–509.
Slatkin, M.
   1974   Hedging One's Evolutionary Bets. *Nature* 250:704–705.
Smith, B. D.
   1992   Hopewellian Farmers of Eastern United States. In *Rivers of Change: Essays on Early Agriculture in Eastern North America*, edited by B. D. Smith, pp. 201–248. Smithsonian Institution Press, Washington, D.C.
Sober, E.
   1984   *The Nature of Selection: Evolutionary Theory in Philosophical Focus*. The MIT Press, Cambridge, Massachusetts.
Squier, E. G., and E. H. Davis
   1848   *Ancient Monuments of the Mississippi Valley*. Smithsonian Contributions to Knowledge, Vol. 1. Smithsonian Institution, Washington, D.C.
Sterelny, K., K. C. Smith, and M. Dickison
   1996   The Extended Replicator. *Biology and Philosophy* 11:377–403.
Sterling, S.
   1999   Mortality Profiles as Indicators of Slowed Reproductive Rates: Evidence from Ancient Egypt. *Journal of Anthropological Archaeology* 18(3):319–343.
Steward, J.
   1949   Cultural Causality and Law: A Trial Formulation of the Development of Early Civilizations. *American Anthropologist* 51:1–27.
Streuver, S., and G. L. Houart
   1972   An Analysis of the Hopewell Interaction Sphere. In *Social Exchange and Interaction*, edited by E. N. Wilmsen, pp. 47–79. Museum of Anthropology, University of Michigan, Anthropological Papers 46, Ann Arbor.
Tuck, J. A.
   1984   *Maritime Provinces Prehistory*. National Museum of Canada, Ottawa.
Webb, W. S., and C. E. Snow
   1945   *The Adena People*. University of Kentucky Reports in Anthropology and Archaeology, Vol. 6. University of Kentucky, Lexington.
West-Eberhard, M. J.
   1989   Phenotypic Plasticity and the Origins of Diversity. *Annual Review of Ecology and Systematics* 20:249–278.
Willey, G. R.
   1966   *An Introduction to American Archaeology, Volume I*. Prentice-Hall, Englewood Cliffs.
Woolfenden, G. E., and J. W. Fitzpatrick
   1978   The Inheritance of Territory in Group-breeding Birds. *BioScience* 28:104–108.

Wymer, D. A.
  1992   Trends and Disparities: The Woodland Paleoethnobotanical Record of the Mid-Ohio Valley. In *Cultural Variability in Context: Woodland Settlements of the Mid-Ohio Valley*, edited by M. F. Seeman, pp. 65–76. MCJA Special Paper No. 7, Kent State University Press, Kent.
  1997   Paleoethnobotany in the Licking River Valley, Ohio: Implications for Understanding Ohio Hopewell. In *Ohio Hopewell Community Organization*, edited by W. S. Dancey and P. J. Pacheco, pp. 153–174, Kent State University Press, Kent.
Yarnell, R. A.
  1993   The Importance of Native Crops during the Late Archaic and Woodland Periods. In *Foraging and Farming in the Eastern Woodlands*, edited by C. M. Scarry, pp. 13–26. University Press of Florida, Gainesville.
Yoshimura, J., and C. W. Clark
  1991   Individual Adaptations in Stochastic Environments. *Evolutionary Ecology* 5:173–192.
Zeisberger, D.
  1910   David Zeisberger's History of North American Indians. *Ohio Archaeological and Historical Publications* 19:30–31.

# Index

Allen, M. S., 79, 87
American Archaeology
  North American archaeology; impor-
    tance of projectile points, 97
  and scientific evolutionary paradigm,
    99
Ancient Egypt
  and cultural evolution paradigms,
    152–53
  functional differentiation, 147
Ancient Egypt's ceramic traditions,
  145–46
  Archaic period pottery, 151
  artifact types construction/chronology,
    157–58. *See also* unit construc-
    tion
  centralization questions for Old
    Kingdom production, 147
  Late Predynastic pottery, 149–51, 150f
  and modern technological research
    tools; inductively coupled plasma
    (ICP) mass spectometry, 157
  Old Kingdom pottery, 152
  research on Meidum bowl, 147
    data sources, 165–66
    empirical consequences, 166–67
    hypothesis, 149
    network mapping goal, 148, 156,

    167–68
    rim morphology classification/sty-
      listic attributes based seriation,
      162–63
    variants, 148–49, 148f, 149t, 157
    *standardization* as key to scientific
      study, 147, 154
    unit construction; functional attributes,
      158–59
Anthropology
  British social and archaeology, 5
  and Darwinian theory, 284
  and scientific archaeology, 2
Archaeological record, 126
  subsistence vs. diet distinction, 223–24
Archaeology, cultural historical foundations, 4
Artifacts
  analysis
    distributional, 28
    engineering, 28, 75
    pleiotropic, 29, 56, 74
  and assumptions of progress, 146
  diffusion vs. trade, 156–57
  functional labels assigned by analogy,
    24, 153, 180–81
  and human phenotype, 27–28
  hybrid classifications, 200, 201t

# About the Contributors

JACK M. BROUGHTON is Associate Professor in the Department of Anthropology at the University of Utah. His research interests include evolutionary ecology, zoo-archaeology, and biogeography, particularly in western North America. He has published on diet breadth, foraging efficiency, and on resource depression and intensification during the late Holocene from evidence from the Emeryville site on the San Francisco Bay.

DIANA M. GREENLEE is a doctoral candidate in the Department of Anthropology at the University of Washington. She has done extensive research on stable carbon isotope analysis of human bone to establish dietary variation and the effects on settlement in Late Woodland and Late Prehistoric populations of eastern North America. She has published on changes in environmental carrying capacity that came with maize and the reduction of cultural elaboration ("waste") in the Late Woodland period of eastern North America.

TERRY L. HUNT is Associate Professor and Graduate Chair in the Department of Anthropology at the University of Hawai`i. His research interests include evolutionary archaeology, historical ecology, and biogeography. He has conducted field research throughout Oceania, including work in Hawai`i, Fiji, Samoa, and Papua New Guinea. He is commencing a field research program on Rapa Nui (Easter Island) to evaluate dimensions of prehistoric cultural elaboration in a remote, variable environment. He has published on prehistoric environmental and landscape change (*Historical Ecology in the Pacific Islands*) and on human diversity and prehistory in the Pacific.

KIMBERLY D. KORNBACHER is a doctoral candidate in the Department of Anthropology at the University of Washington. Her research interests focus on prehistoric ground stone tool engineering and function, for northern South American assemblages in particular. She has worked extensively on the prehistory of the Pacific Northwest and has published on cultural elaboration in the temporally variable environment of prehistoric coastal Peru.

CARL P. LIPO is a Systems Architect at Internap Network Services. He also serves as an affiliate faculty member in the Department of Anthropology at the University of Hawaii. His research interests include evolutionary archaeology with a focus on cultural transmission, multilevel selection, and the origins of complex social systems. He has published on frequency seriation, cultural transmission, and population structure; on fitness and reproductive tradeoffs in uncertain environments to explain the evolution of cultural elaboration or "waste"; on neutrality and style, and on cultural transmission and the spatial patterning of populations.

MARK E. MADSEN is the Director of Core Software and Systems Development for Internap Network Services. His research interests include cultural transmission, the evolution of complex social organization, and cultural elaboration. He has published on community patterning in Hopewell populations (*Ohio Hopewell: Community Organization*); neutrality and style (*Style and Function*); on frequency seriation, cultural transmission, and population, and on fitness and reproductive tradeoffs in uncertain environments to explain the evolution of cultural elaboration or "waste."

MICHAEL T. PFEFFER is a doctoral candidate in the Department of Anthropology at the University of Washington and Vice President of Persis Corporation. He has done extensive research on marine environments, underwater archaeology, and ancient marine procurement strategies, including analysis of the associated artifacts for Hawai`i and other islands of the Pacific. He has published on the temporal distribution of octopus lures, and fishhooks in Hawaiian prehistory (*Style and Function*).

SARAH L. STERLING is a doctoral candidate in the Department of Anthropology at the University of Washington. She has conducted several field seasons in the Nile River Valley of Egypt. Her research addresses ceramics, production specialization, and complex societies. She has published on ancient mortality profiles and slowed reproductive rates and their potential links to the evolution of cultural elaboration in the Nile River Valley.

KRIS H. WILHELMSEN is a doctoral candidate in the Department of Anthropology at the University of Washington and the Manager of Technical Writing at Internap Network Services. His interests include the evolution of hunting technology and temporal changes in projectile points in the eastern woodlands of North America. He has published on lithic technologies in the Pacific Northwest (*Deciphering a Shell Midden*).